Teaching Social Studies in the Elementary and Middle Schools

Teaching Social Studies in the Elementary and Middle Schools

**William W. Joyce and
Janet E. Alleman-Brooks**
Michigan State University

HOLT, RINEHART AND WINSTON
New York   Chicago   San Francisco
Dallas   Montreal   Toronto

Cover photograph: Courtesy Kenneth Karp

Acknowledgment is made to the following for permission to include their photographs in the book.

pp. 5, 19, 34, 66, 87, 132, 156, 166, 190: Courtesy Michael Musci, elementary guidance counselor, Okemos Public Schools, Michigan

pp. 28, 72, 139, 337, 370: Courtesy Holt, Rinehart and Winston Photo Library; Russell Dian, photographer.

pp. 80, 312: Courtesy National Education Association; Carl Purcell, photographer.

pp. 182, 227, 244, 278, 296, 326: Courtesy of Tom Brooks, DeWitt, Michigan

pp. 262, 346: Courtesy Sheral Vuillemot, teacher, Swartz Creek Schools, Swartz Creek, Michigan

p. 359: Courtesy of William W. Joyce, Michigan State University, East Lansing, Michigan

p. 364: Courtesy of Robert Venners, Jackson Public Schools, Jackson, Michigan

Library of Congress Cataloging in Publication Data

Joyce, William W.
　Teaching social studies in the elementary and middle schools.

Includes index.
1. Social sciences—Study and teaching (Elementary)
2. Social sciences—Study and teaching (Secondary)
3. Middle schools. I. Alleman-Brooks, Janet.
II. Title.
LB1584.J69　　　372.8'3'044　　　78–10691
ISBN 0–03–045046–2

DEDICATION

We dedicate this book to the two most important persons in our lives, our spouses: Mary Bosser Joyce and Tom Brooks. Without their constant inspiration and understanding, we could not have written this book.

PREFACE

Written for beginning and experienced teachers and for curriculum specialists at the elementary level (grades K–8), this textbook is intended to be used in pre- and in-service instruction and in curriculum development in the social studies. Our basic premise is that the primary reason for teaching the social studies is to help children and youth become knowledgeable, adaptive humans, capable of functioning competently within the range of roles that they aspire to perform throughout their productive lives. Emphasized throughout the text are lifelong roles of citizen, family member, occupation, avocation, and personal efficacy. Our second premise is that pupils can grasp the significance of these roles and apply them to their daily lives if the roles are taught through appropriate, timely themes. For illustrative purposes, we propose ten organizing themes: consumerism, ecology, energy, government and politics, human equality, the human life cycle, intercultural relations, our legal system, media, and morality.

Organization

The textbook consists of two interrelated parts. The first part, *Elements of the Social Studies*, focuses on the major decisions confronting a teacher of the social studies. The second part, *Exemplars in Methodology*, deals intensively with the methods and materials used in teaching the social studies.

The first part consists of seven chapters, each of which blends theory with practice, while exploring your role as a social studies teacher from a variety of perspectives. Chapter 1 presents the assumptions of the text, explains our conception of the lifelong roles and organizing themes, and explores current and emerging trends in social studies curricula. Chapter 2 analyzes elements of six representative social studies programs, and then compares them with our conception of the lifelong roles and organizing themes. It also presents a series of proven procedures for selecting and evaluating social studies instructional material. Chapter 3 applies current theory and research in the psychology of learning and child growth and development to the teaching of social studies. Stressed are three modes of instruction: expository teaching, guided discussion, and inquiry. Chapter 4 explores the instructional capabilities of dramatic play, role play, and simulation, and demonstrates procedures for selecting, creating, and using these types of media. Chapter 5 deals intensively with the teaching of basic skills which have immediate, compelling significance for the social studies: critical thinking and problem solving, communication (reading, writing, listening, and speaking), map and globe reading, and group work and social skills. Chapter 6 analyzes the philosophical rationales and instructional capabilities of two of the most widely used approaches to the teaching of value processes: values clarification and moral education. Chapter 7, the last chapter in this part, explores approaches to formative and summative evaluation, and presents techniques for designing a wide range of measures for assessing the skills, knowledge, attitudes, and values acquired by your pupils.

At the conclusion of each chapter in Part 1 is a subsection entitled "Cross-

References to Teaching Modules." This section demonstrates how various ideas presented in the chapter can be translated into teaching modules presented in Part 2 of the book.

The second part attaches even greater emphasis to the methodology, the how-to-do-it of social studies teaching. There are three components in this part. Section A demonstrates how you can design and use a teaching module, a carefully organized and integrated series of combination lesson plans—teaching units designed expressly for teaching the five lifelong roles and the ten organizing themes. Sections B and C present a series of illustrative teaching modules centering on the lifelong roles and organizing themes, respectively. To each module we have appended annotations to enable the teacher to adjust instruction to the needs of slow learning and gifted pupils. Following each module is a section entitled "Classroom Results," which reports the results of actual classroom tryouts of the module. These reports reveal the instructional capabilities of modules, when used in classrooms, and show how the modules might be modified to accommodate the differing needs and abilities of pupils. Illustrative modules in these chapters center on a wide range of compelling topics, including sexism, agism, globalism, racism, ethnocentrism, and futuristics.

Other Features

Our book contains additional distinguishing features which we hope will facilitate its use by beginning and experienced teachers. We have made a special effort to insure that the book:

1. demonstrates how our conceptions of the lifelong roles and organizing themes can revitalize the social studies, as typically taught in our nation's classrooms

2. emphasizes techniques of teaching reading, writing, speaking, listening, geography, and thinking skills

3. presents penetrating appraisals of recently published social studies programs and teaching materials

4. stresses the teaching of such compelling topics as energy, ecology, sexism, racism, agism, consumerism, advertising, print and electronic media, attitudes and values, morality, globalism, and changing life styles

5. critically analyzes the use of values clarification and moral education strategies in the classroom

6. shows clearly and concisely how teachers can design, teach, and evaluate successful lessons

7. applies theory and research on child growth and development, and on the psychology of learning to social studies instruction and to curriculum development

8. explores procedures for selecting, designing, and using dramatic play activities, role plays, simulations, and case studies

9. describes the use of preliminary, formative, and summative evaluation procedures, and explores techniques for designing and using objective and essay tests, observing pupil behavior, and assessing pupil attitudes

10. includes a wide variety of illustrative teaching modules, each of which contains annotations showing how the modules can be adapted to the needs of slow learning and gifted pupils, and are cross-referenced with each chapter in the text

11. recognizes the growing demand for stressing "the basics" in social studies classes.

The "Classroom Results" which follow each teaching module in Part 2 were submitted by preservice and by experienced teachers with a broad range of background and experience in Kindergarten through 8th grade. These teachers utilized the modules in a variety of settings including public and nonpublic schools located in rural and urban areas. Children in these schools represented a variety of socieconomic and ethnic backgrounds. Teachers used the modules with "normal" children as well as with mainstreamed and gifted pupils. While the data continue to be gathered, we invite you to review the existing results, to acquire clues that will be of assistance to you as you plan for using the teaching modules in your classroom.

Many individuals contributed their talents to the preparation of this textbook. We are especially grateful to our undergraduate and graduate students at Michigan State University, and to the reviewers for their candid, inspired criticism and support; to Loren Procton and Dick Owen of Holt, Rinehart and Winston and to our former Holt editor, Louise Waller, for applying their professional expertise to the editing and publication of the text; to our secretaries, Ruth Bratt, Julie Baglien, Carol Duguay, and Kim Smythe, who competently typed the textual materials that were tried out in our classes. Finally, we owe a special debt of gratitude to Jim Snoddy, former Chairperson of the Department of Elementary and Special Education at Michigan State University, for his constant encouragement, and for providing the resources which enabled our manuscript to be tested in our classes, and to Ruth Stark, for her competent, sensitive orchestration of the production of this book, and for her uncanny ability to enhance the communicative qualities of our manuscript.

William W. Joyce
Janet E. Alleman-Brooks

CONTENTS

SECTION C **THE ORGANIZING THEMES: EXEMPLARS FOR TEACHING**   **317**

ELEMENTS OF THE SOCIAL STUDIES

This part centers on the basic arenas of decision-making confronting elementary social studies teachers. The opening chapter presents our philosophical rationale for this textbook, and explores its implications for the elementary social studies curriculum. Of major importance is our advocacy of five lifelong roles and ten organizing themes as viable organizing elements of the curriculum. Chapter 2 centers on the process of selecting and evaluating basal social studies programs. Elements of six representative programs are described, then critiqued in terms of their relevance for the lifelong roles and organizing themes. Chapter 3 applies the professional literature in the psychology of learning and child growth and development to the teaching of elementary social studies. Stressed are three modes of instruction: expository teaching, guided discovery, and inquiry. The central theme of Chapter 4 is that social studies instruction will have limited meaning for children unless it involves them in activities that have meaning for their daily lives. To this end, three activities are stressed: dramatic play, role play, and simulation. Chapter 5 centers on the teaching of skills which have immediate significance for the social studies: critical thinking and problem solving, communication skills, map reading skills, and group work skills (often referred to as social skills). Teaching about values is the central theme of Chapter 6, which analyzes the philosophical rationale and instructional capabilities of the two most widely used approaches: values clarification and moral education. Chapter 7, the concluding chapter in this part, focuses on the use of formative and summative approaches to evaluating social studies learning.

Following each chapter is a subsection labeled *Cross-References to Teaching Modules.* This component shows how ideas presented in each of these chapters can be translated into teaching plans presented in Part 2 of the book.

ELEMENTARY SOCIAL STUDIES AND THE HUMAN CONDITION

GOALS

1. Perceive the fundamental importance of teaching social studies in grades K–8.
2. Evaluate the philosophical assumptions underlying this book and the authors' definition of the social studies.
3. Assess the authors' definition of the lifelong roles and organizing themes, and compare this conception with current and emerging trends in the field of elementary social studies.
4. Become aware of the scope and sequence of conventional K–8 social studies programs, their rationale, and their relevance to the authors' conception of the lifelong roles and organizing themes.

During man's tenure on this planet, he has yet to conquer the perennial scourge of famine, war, death, and pestilence. The energy crisis now confronting the nations of the world is intensifying global tensions by widening the gap between the wealthy, well-fed nations and the impoverished, starving nations. Indeed, it may be that unless the earth's energy resources and food supply are redistributed equitably, the "have not" nations may of necessity be compelled to wage a relentless war of survival against the "have" nations. And, looming on the horizon is the ever-present danger of thermonuclear, genetic, or germ warfare. If unleashed, these terrible weapons of destruction could easily obliterate *Homo sapiens* from the face of the earth.

These grim realities impose awesome demands upon our schools in general and upon the social studies in particular. No longer can educators lull themselves into believing that the safe, comfortable topics studied in the past will enhance the child's ability to cope with relentless, often cataclysmic, change. What is needed is a penetrating reappraisal of the social studies as taught in American schools. Such an undertaking should yield a sound, defensible rationale based on our current knowledge regarding: (a) realities confronting children today and in the foreseeable future; (b) child growth and development; (c) cognitive and affective learning of children; and (d) methods of planning, implementing, and evaluating instruction.

While this book was in preparation we initiated such a reappraisal. Our search for a rationale for teaching social studies in the elementary grades led us to the professional literature; into elementary classrooms; to conversations with teachers, supervisors, publishers of student materials; to state departments of education; and to various professional organizations, including the National Council for the Social Studies, the Social Science Education Consortium, the Association for Supervision and Curriculum Development, the Association for Childhood Education International, and others. Our travels took us to schools in the United States; to U.S. Armed Forces Dependents Schools in England, Japan, Okinawa, and the Philippines; and to local schools in Italy, Great Britain, the U.S.S.R., Guatemala, and Mexico.

ASSUMPTIONS

Our search for a rationale for teaching elementary social studies yielded a series of assumptions from which we worked in developing this book. They are cited in the following list:

1. Since the purpose of the social studies is to prepare children to act wisely and selflessly in the world of today and the future, this subject should command a key, pivotal position in the school program.
2. The thrust of the social studies should be toward improving the human condition—the quality of life afforded mankind by prevailing physical, social, economic, and political conditions.
3. The content of the social studies should center on those critical problems which impede human progress and prevent people from attaining their lifelong aspirations.
4. Since pupils, teachers, and parents are inextricably involved in the learning process, social studies programs should be designed with a view toward involving all three types of participants in the instructional program.
5. Since each child learns in his own unique way, teachers should use a wide variety of teaching methods and materials consistent with the varied learning styles of pupils.
6. Since the learning process is continuous, teachers should therefore base their teaching of the social studies on children's experiences both in and out of school.
7. The social studies bear a strong affinity to other school subjects; therefore it is illogical and unrealistic to divorce the social studies from other areas of the elementary curriculum.
8. A basic question facing social studies educators is *not* "Should we teach values?" but "*How* should we teach values?" Neglecting values constitutes a denial of the basic reasons why the social studies are taught.
9. In order for social studies instruction to prove meaningful to pupils, teachers should begin with those concerns and problems confronted by children and youth.
10. Content for the social studies should be drawn from our knowledge about: (a) the world of children and youth; (b) the social science disciplines; and (c) the lives of people past, present, and future.

These basic assumptions were gleaned from our experiences as students of the social studies and, in turn, led us to what we believe is a sound, compelling rationale for teaching the social studies in the elementary grades. Simply stated, our rationale is this: *The primary purpose of teaching social studies in the elementary grades is to help children and youth to become active, knowledgeable, adaptive human beings, capable of functioning within the range of the lifelong roles they aspire to, and capable of improving the quality of the human condition.* Granted, this rationale may depart from that espoused by some of our colleagues, particularly those who would ascribe to the social studies a more limited role. But we believe that since our domestic and world problems have reached crisis proportions, and since each of us is directly and immediately affected by decisions made in Peking, Moscow, or Washington, the time has come for social studies teachers and their pupils to focus their attention on ways of improving world circumstances. We believe that our continuing existence on this planet warrants this emphasis. Indeed, we suspect that any attempt to blunt or redirect this emphasis would be regarded by you, the reader, as a blatant denial of our obligations as responsible social studies educators.

LIFELONG ROLES

Our rationale for teaching social studies, as stated above, embraces the idea of lifelong roles. We use this term in reference to a series of roles that Americans typically occupy during most of their productive lives, including: (a) citizenship; (b) family membership; (c) occupation; (d) avocation; and (e) personal efficacy.

Preserving our delicate ecosystem should be a vital element in elementary social studies classes.

Citizenship. Most U.S. children and adults are citizens of their local community, state, nation, and world. Our legal system conveys to citizens certain rights and freedoms, but incumbent upon them are certain responsibilities and obligations. As children participate in the citizenship role, they should grow in their knowledge of this reciprocal relationship.

Family Membership. Most children are born into some form of family structure and occupy various positions of responsibility within it throughout their lives. As is the case with citizenship, the role of family membership is based on a series of reciprocal relationships involving shared responsibility within the family structure.

Occupation. Consider for a moment the last time you were introduced to a stranger. Early in your conversation, it is likely that you exchanged information regarding your respective occupations. This happened primarily because we tend to rely on one's occupation as a means of classifying, identifying with, and seeking information about a person. Although the occupational role is not directly ascribable to our children and youth, it becomes, nonetheless, a significant, viable area of study by virtue of its basic importance in their daily lives.

Avocation. Admittedly, one's leisure pursuits may or may not be as powerful a conversational ice-breaker as one's occupation. But in view of the increased leisure time now available to our population as a consequence of the trend toward voluntary earlier retirement, longer life expectancy, and shortened work week, the avocational role will continue to grow in importance. This role has far-reaching implications for childhood. Among these is the idea that children need to become competent consumers of leisure time; they need to learn how to derive happy, satisfying, productive experiences from it.

Personal Efficacy. All of us have certain needs, wants, and aspirations. All of us set for ourselves goals and standards of attainment, however realistic or unrealistic these may be. To a great extent these are influenced by others, particularly those whom we admire and desire to emulate, and/or who have authority over us. The process by which we seek to attain these goals or standards of achievement constitutes the life role of personal efficacy. Basic to this role is the need to understand ourselves, what we want to become, our aspirations and those of others, and to perceive how our quest for self-fulfillment impinges on and is affected by others.

Bear in mind that we are not suggesting even for a moment that these are the only life roles that Americans perform. To be sure, we aspire to and accept various roles by virtue of our membership in religious, social, or political groups, or because of our commitment to a particular cause. Also, we assume the role of leader or follower as a result of particular situations we confront in our daily lives. Some of these roles are short-lived and transitory; others are of greater intensity and permanence. However, these are not lifelong in scope; nor can they be generalized to the entire American population. In our opinion, the five roles listed and described above should, if used as organizers of social studies content, enable teachers to make the social studies meaningful and useful to students in the elementary and middle grades.

ORGANIZING THEMES

Now that we have defined these lifelong roles that we believe should be the foundation of a social studies program geared to children's needs of today and tomorrow, how can they be translated into instruction? To facilitate this process we propose a series of organizing themes illustrative of the basic problems affecting mankind. If explored in elementary social studies classes, these themes will enable pupils to embark on meaningful study of their lifelong roles. These themes, listed alphabetically, are:

Consumerism
Ecology
Energy
Government and Politics
Human Equality
Human Life Cycle
Intercultural Relations
Our Legal System
Media
Morality

How do these themes relate to the five lifelong roles? Our answer is *extensively* and *intensively*—extensively because the themes enable us to explore one or more dimensions of each of the life roles, and intensively because they enable us to identify significant problems affecting the personal lives of children and youth, and to generalize these problems and their solutions to the larger society of which they are a part.

How extensive and intensive is this relationship between our lifelong roles and organizing themes? We believe that the answer can be found by asking a second, more basic question: *To what extent do pupils' knowledge of these themes enable them to begin acquiring proficiency in the lifelong roles?* If we apply this question to the relationship between one of the ten themes, let us say, consumerism, and the lifelong role of, for example, citizen, the question literally becomes: To what extent do pupils' knowledge of consumerism enable them to acquire proficiency in performing the life role of citizen?

By examining each of these themes individually you will observe that some appear to bear a stronger affinity to the lifelong role of citizen than others. For example, a good citizen will: (a) exercise his rights and responsibilities as a *consumer;* (b) strive to conserve *energy* resources while preserving our delicate ecosystem; (c) become knowledgeable about the *governmental and political* structure of his nation; and (d) work toward promoting *human equality* in his relations with others. Few of us would deny that a series of relationships exist between these themes and the lifelong role of *citizen.*

But how do *intercultural relations, human life cycle, our legal system, media,* and *morality* relate to the role of citizen? That we reside in a multiethnic, pluralistic nation and in a multinational, global society suggests that a good citizen—a citizen of the U.S. and a citizen of the world—will learn to balance his own and his nation's social, economic, and political interests with those of other persons and other nations. Accordingly, it is this dual citizenship that gives credence to the relationship between intercultural relations and the lifelong role of citizen.

The theme, *human life cycle,* might intersect with the role of citizen in the sense that one's regard for the sanctity of human life must be reconciled with the global problem of overpopulation. The task of recognizing that the right to life of the individual must be viewed in terms of the survival of mankind strengthens the relationship between life and death and citizenship.

That *our legal system* and the role of citizen are inextricably interrelated is self-evident. Unfortunately, the law is often perceived by children and youth as a formidable array of inflexible controls devised and imposed by an inflexible, faceless society. They need to learn that if society is to hold its members account-able for their actions, it becomes axiomatic that all citizens must become aware of the laws they are obliged to obey, the rationales underlying these laws, available avenues of redress, and implications for their behavior.

To what extent do the *media* impinge on the life role of citizen? We submit that they do, to the extent that they provide a person with ever-changing percep-tions of the role that government plays in his/her life. Not only do the media inform our citizenry of decisions made by governmental leaders, they afford citizens an opportunity to assess these decisions, and ultimately hold the decision-makers accountable for their actions.

The theme, *morality,* bears still a different relationship to the lifelong role of *citizen.* If there is any fundamental moral precept that has tended to guide the destiny of our nation and that of the Western world, it is a belief in the dignity and worth of the individual. We suggest that since this precept is an integral part of our nation's heritage, it provides a frame of reference with which one can judge the behavior of government leaders. In this sense morality contributes to the lifelong role of citizen.

PUPILS' CONCERNS

Thus far our discussion of lifelong roles and organizing themes has been rather general—perhaps too general for your needs. Also, this discussion has not cen-tered directly on the focal point of the teaching–learning process—*the kids in your classroom.*

Below we attempt to show in a specific manner how, by organizing instruc-tion around our ten basic themes, you can facilitate your pupils' ability to acquire proficiency in the lifelong roles. To help you visualize this process, we have listed for each theme examples of pupils' concerns that we have encountered in elementary classrooms. Of course, you would not pursue all of the themes when studying each of the lifelong roles at any given time. But even the most cursory, top-of-the-head inspection of the interface between the roles and themes will suggest that at various times during a child's formal and informal education, each of the organizing themes will intersect with each of the lifelong roles. Tables 1–1 to 1–5 show how this process operates with regard to the lifelong roles of citizenship, family membership, occupation, avocation, and personal efficacy.

THE SOCIAL STUDIES CURRICULUM

In the previous discussion we described the five lifelong roles and ten organizing themes. Is our conception clear to you? Is it realistic? Can it be successfully implemented in the elementary classroom? Will it add meaning and purpose to your social studies teaching? We will attempt to respond in two ways: first, by exploring in greater depth the nature and function of the lifelong roles and organizing themes, and then by considering how this conception compares with current and emerging trends in the social studies curriculum.

Nature and Function

As we mentioned earlier, citizenship, family membership, occupation, avocation, and personal efficacy constitute most of the basic roles that Americans occupy for most of their productive lives. These roles: (a) are consistent with the major purpose for teaching elementary social studies, i.e., to teach pupils to act wisely and selflessly in human affairs, past and present; (b) encompass in- and out-of-school learning experiences; viewed from this perspective, the roles tend to stress the *totality* of human experience; (c) should be taught in school primarily from the perspective of the social sciences, and secondarily from the perspective of the humanities and the natural and physical sciences; (d) are inextricably linked with the other school subjects; (e) deal directly and intensively with the everyday world of children and youth.

The organizing themes occupy a central, pivotal role in this conception, for they help us to translate the lifelong roles into reality, as perceived by pupils. Since the themes focus on immediate, compelling questions, concerns, and problems affecting man's continuing existence on this planet, they serve as the focal points of lessons which, when taught, will enable pupils to begin grappling with issues and problems affecting themselves and their contemporaries, and most important to become directly involved in their resolution.

If there is any inherent weakness in the social studies as taught in the majority of our classrooms, it is the inability of teachers to make this school subject meaningful and practical to students. Unless students see the social studies as a valuable, worthwhile subject from which they derive tangible benefits and unless it makes a *difference* in their lives, we fear that they may regard the social studies as little more than a mere academic hurdle confronting them in their schooling. Once again, we believe that the ten organizing themes, when taught within the context of the student's daily life, can make the social studies a valuable, meaningful school subject, one that helps pupils to learn to act wisely and selflessly in human affairs.

TABLE 1–1   CITIZENSHIP: INTERFACE BETWEEN LIFELONG ROLE OF CITIZENSHIP, ORGANIZING THEMES, AND PUPILS' CONCERNS.

Consumerism	Ecology and Energy	Government and Politics	Human Equality	Inter-Cultural Relations	Our Legal System	Human Life Cycle	Media	Morality
We traded our big car in for a little car, because it's cheaper to run. Why don't more people do this?	This Saturday we're going to clean up the neighborhood. Want to help?	Carlos is too bossy. Would he make a good president of our fifth grade?	Why are there so few lady doctors and dentists?	Why does our government sell wheat to the Russians and not to the poor nations?	That man is driving too fast. Why don't the cops arrest him?	Why do people have to be buried in cemeteries?	I couldn't watch "Charlie's Angels" on TV because the President was giving a speech. Is that fair?	Brad has never been caught shoplifting. How does he get away with it?
Why are they building that solar house next door? It sure looks weird!	My dad put a holding tank in our boat. Why didn't you put one in yours?	My uncle says that politics are dirty. What does that mean?	Why are most of our government leaders white men? What was the Civil Rights Movement?	Our social studies textbook says that the U.S.-Canada border is the longest fortified border in the world. What does that mean?	Why do we have laws against lighting firecrackers?	What is a birth certificate? Do I have one?	Why do the newspapers print stories about the government on the front page and the baseball scores on the back pages?	Yesterday I reported Fred to the police for stealing Jimmy's bike. Will Fred try to get even with me?
My mother just purchased a toaster. It doesn't work. She's unable to get service for it. My father says, "Forget it. Go to another store and get another one." Shouldn't she take action against the store or maybe write a letter to "Open Forum" warning others of her problem?	We didn't use our airconditioner this summer because it was too expensive to operate. Will we have to make other sacrifices to save energy?				Is there a law that says I have to say the "pledge of allegiance" at school?	My grandfather is 65 years old and lives in a nursing home. He doesn't pay any taxes. Should he vote in public elections?	I really think police are rough, power-hungry people. My friend asked, "Do you think TV shows have influenced your attitude toward these people?"	I saw a purple van pull up at Laurie's house. Somebody ran to the porch and grabbed a lawn chair and ran back to the van with it. Should I have called the police?
					We have a new car. Why isn't it OK for my dad to race it on the open highway?			

TABLE 1–2   FAMILY MEMBERSHIP: INTERFACE BETWEEN LIFELONG ROLE OF FAMILY MEMBERSHIP, ORGANIZING THEMES, AND PUPILS' CONCERNS.

Consumerism	Ecology and Energy	Government and Politics	Human Equality	Inter-Cultural Relations	Our Legal System	Human Life Cycle	Media	Morality
Mom says our family won't buy any more junk food because it's got empty calories and too many artificial ingredients. Is she right? We bought a color TV and the dealer won't fix it for free because he says the warranty expired. Can he do that?	Why don't we turn up the heat in the house? I'm freezing to death! We're trying to conserve water by not watering our lawn. Why isn't everyone doing this?	My dad says he controls the money in our family because he earns all of it. Is your dad the same way? All the kids in our family have to do certain jobs or they lose privileges. Does that make sense to you? Do you think the "family man" image helps a public official get elected?	Why does my older sister get the new clothes, while I get the hand-me-downs? The bank won't lend my mother any money because she's divorced. Is that fair?	Lisa is celebrating her First Communion. Do Jews have them? Do you know why females and not males cover their faces in the Arab countries?	The city wants to build a drain through our backyard. Do we have to let them do this? Mom and Dad hired a lawyer to draw up their wills. Why did they do this? Do you think the government should pass laws about family size?	Why will our family be buried in a cemetery? Doesn't that waste a lot of valuable land? Why does my baby brother cry so much? It's driving me nuts! Bobby says he likes living with his grandparents. What are the advantages and disadvantages?	Why do they make so few good movies for families to see? All the families on TV are rich, live in fancy houses, and are good-looking. Why don't they show average people like us? My dad won't wax the floor. He says it's a woman's job. I don't agree, but why don't you ever see a male on TV scrubbing the floor?	My sister is pregnant and is not married. Will they let her in the hospital when the baby is born? My dad cheats on his income tax, but he hits me when he catches me lying. Is that being fair? How come Donna's mother doesn't live at home with the family anymore?

TABLE 1–3   OCCUPATION: INTERFACE BETWEEN LIFELONG ROLE OF OCCUPATION, ORGANIZING THEMES, AND PUPILS' CONCERNS.

Consumerism	Ecology and Energy	Government and Politics	Human Equality	Inter-Cultural Relations	Our Legal System	Human Life Cycle	Media	Morality
How can I decide which college I want to attend?	My father works at Oldsmobile. He can't smoke there because the foreman says that's harmful. (They are trying to purify the air.) Is that really a form of pollution?	Are there government regulations about the amount of money I make at Dairy Queen?	Why do the counselors advise girls to be nurses and not doctors, teachers and not administrators?	My friend Jim is black. He says my boss wouldn't hire him. The reason he gave was lack of photography skills. Jim was voted the outstanding student in our school.	Why are lawyers called "ambulance chasers"?	Why did my dad change careers at 40?	Why do women always wash clothes on TV?	My grandmother is very ill. She's in a coma and hooked up to all sorts of machines. She'll never get better. Should Dr. L turn off the machines?
My mother is a nurse. I want to go into medicine. I think I want to be a doctor or a dentist. How can I decide?	The government says the company will have to shut down unless they will find ways to control the smoke. That will be very expensive. What should they do?	I'm only 14 and I work at Jim's Service Station. My aunt says that's against government regulations. I don't understand.	My dad is a beautician. My friends tease me a lot about this. Is that fair?	My mom says that most Chinese are in either the restaurant or laundry business. Is this true?	Do judges have to be lawyers first?	My grandfather was forced to retire from his job. He says that was unfair. Do you think he's right?	On TV you often see people waxing floors and smiling. I can't believe that's a fun job. Why do they do that?	My cousin says her doctor is very willing to perform abortions. In fact, I think that's her area of specialization. Is that an acceptable thing to do?
I got an infection a week after I had a tooth pulled. My physician says it was connected with the dental care I had. Should my mother file a complaint against the dentist?		My mother and dad work. I overheard a conversation the other day about taxes. My mother said that half of their income goes back to pay the federal government. Does the government steal the money? What's going on anyway?	I want to be a pilot, but I'm a girl. I've been sending for information about this. All the pictures are of men. Couldn't I be a good pilot?		My mom says that Nixon and the others in the Watergate scandal were lawyers. Does that mean that most lawyers are crooks?	My mother says the career I'll pursue when I grow up probably hasn't been developed yet. What is she talking about anyway?	Recently there has been lots of advertising about military careers. The commercials always make military life look really appealing. Is it really that great?	I read in the paper the other evening that there is an increasing number of prostitutes. Why?

major topics taught in grades K–8. This summary is based on our analysis of courses of study, curriculum guides, basal programs, and the professional literature.

Kindergarten.   Few social studies topics are specified at this level. Teachers are encouraged to design their own programs. Most commonly studied topics center on social learning experiences and on home, family, school, and other elements of the local environment. Some effort is made to introduce cross-cultural comparisons involving comparisons of lifestyles in the U.S. and elsewhere in the world. Examples of topics taught in kindergarten:

Discovering Myself
Why We Have Rules
Working Together
Belonging to a Family
Children in Other Lands
The Globe
People Who Help Us
Health and Safety
National Holidays

Grade One.   This level is an extension of kindergarten, with social learning, family, and school studied a bit more intensively than in the previous grade. A few of the newer programs provide children with initial exposure to such ideas as role, nuclear and extended family, specialization, division of labor, occupation, energy, ecology, fairness, cooperation, honesty, and work. Cross-cultural comparisons are dealt with a bit more intensively than in kindergarten. Such geographic skills as the cardinal directions, place location, and pictorial map symbols are introduced. Examples of topics taught in grade one:

Exploring Our Five Senses
Personal Responsibilities at Home and at School
Producers and Consumers
Needs of Families
Making Maps of My Surroundings
I Grow and Change
Toys Used in Other Cultures
National Holidays
Using Our Spare Time Wisely

Grade Two.   The world beyond the immediate family and school assumes greater importance. Basic elements of the neighborhood and local environment are stressed. These include transportation, communication, local services, local history, division of labor, food distribution, energy needs, ecological problems, and changes in neighborhoods. Cross-cultural comparisons are stressed, with specific attention focused on similarities and differences in the food, clothing, shelter, vocations, and avocations of Americans and people in other lands. Examples of topics taught in grade two:

How Our Neighborhood Has Changed
People in Other Lands
Where We Get Our Electricity, Water, and Gas
Protecting Our Environment
Where Our Food Comes From
Transportation and Communication
Urban and Rural Living

Grade Three.   The concept of community comes into sharp focus at this level. Many programs stress urban communities in the U.S. and abroad, the role of business and industry in the growth and decline of communities, how communities are governed, and how they provide for basic wants and needs of people. History assumes greater importance than in earlier grades. Many programs contain units on pioneers and native Americans, which stress such values as resourcefulness, bravery, and hard work. Examples of topics taught in grade three:

What Makes a City
Changes in Cities
Family of Early New England
American and Foreign Cities
Understanding Myself and Others
Why We Have Laws
How Our Natural Environment Affects Us
Interdependence between People
The Role of Mass Media in Our Lives

Grade Four.   In many schools the pupil's own state is stressed during at least a part of the school year. Typically this involves a study of the geography, history, and government of the state. World regional geography is another strong emphasis at this grade level. Increasingly this topic is studied more in terms of the social and cultural features of the earth and less in terms of its physical features. In this regard environmental problems are stressed. In some areas, United States regional geography and history are taught. Examples of topics taught in grade four:

People Who Built Our State
Our State's History
Living in Different Regions
Our Mobile Population
Feeding the World's Hungry
Emerging African Nations
Conserving the World's Resources
The Sun Belt
Japan: a New World Power

Grade Five.   With few exceptions the United States is the focal point of fifth-grade social studies programs, most of which stress the historical antecedents, geography, and growth and development of our nation. Although most social studies programs at this level deal exclusively with the United States, the scope of

The study of the students' home state can be an exciting, worthwhile adventure.

some programs has been expanded to stress the United States, while according Canada, Latin America, and other nations incidental treatment. Increasingly there is a trend toward emphasizing historical, geographical, economic, and political concepts, the contributions of minority groups, and scientific, technological, and cultural advancements. Traditionally most programs tended to overemphasize U.S. history through 1900; increasingly they are beginning to give more attention to significant developments since World War II, and to relate these developments to the contemporary scene. Examples of topics taught in grade five:

> Building a New Nation
> The American Mosaic
> A California Gold-Mining Camp
> Westward Ho!
> The Immigrants
> Discovering Our Heritages
> The Roaring '20s
> Our American Neighbors
> The Search for Human Rights
> The U.S.: Defender of Freedom

Grade Six. Typically the social studies program consists of the study of either the Western or the Eastern Hemisphere nations—and never the twain shall meet! In many schools where the Western Hemisphere is studied in sixth grade, the Eastern Hemisphere is reserved for the seventh grade, or vice-versa. A few schools continue to study Western civilization from primarily an historical perspective, but this is on the decline. A perennial problem confronting teachers at this level is the vast array of topics associated with the Eastern or Western Hemispheres, and with Western civilization. Curriculum guides and courses of study produced at the local level reflect a tendency to teach in depth a limited number of key topics from an historical–geographical point of view, to generalize these to other nations, and then to relate these topics to contemporary social, political, and economic problems. Examples of topics taught in grade six:

Western Hemisphere
The Maritime Provinces
The Trail of the Conquistadores
The Organization of American States
Brazil: The Slumbering Giant
Revolutions in Latin America
The St. Lawrence Seaway
The Central American Nations
Our Old World Beginnings

Eastern Hemisphere
Ancient Greece and Rome
The Middle Ages
The Renaissance
The U.S.S.R.
Problems of Newly Emerged Nations
Western Europe
The Middle East
North Africa
Sub-Saharan Africa
India
China
The Mediterranean World

Grade Seven. As we have already indicated, traditionally the content of seventh-grade programs has been based to a great extent on the content of sixth-grade programs, and vice-versa. Increasingly school districts have abandoned broad, panoramic studies of the Eastern and Western Hemispheres, owing to the inability of teachers and students to cope with the morass of subject matter. In recent years seventh-grade social studies programs have begun to stress world cultures, world geography, nations, or groups of nations, the home state (when not studied in grade four), or on United States history (as background for U.S. history in grade eight). Examples of topics taught in grade seven:

Old World Backgrounds
Latin America
Canada
Africa
Globalism

Preserving the Environment
Land, Resources, and Energy
The Home State
Asia
Social Change

Grade Eight. The United States—particularly its history—has been, is, and will continue to be the major content emphasis in the vast majority of our schools. This phenomenon can be largely ascribed to state requirements which are not likely to change, at least in the foreseeable future. Although U.S. history predominates at this level, the Constitution, U.S. geography, and federal, state, and local government are also taught. Other content emphases include the use of social science concepts for in-depth study of selected topics, increased attention to the role of minorities in the history of our nation, and interrelationships between local, state, and national governments. One recent trend that is growing in significance is for programs at this level to relate the study of the U.S. to the daily lives of pupils. Examples of topics taught in grade eight:

Exploration and Discovery
Independence from England
Forging a New Government
Westward Expansion
The Rise of Cities
An Industrial Giant Is Born
Our Nation Divided
A World Power Emerges
Human Rights
Relations with Other Nations
The United States in the Next Century
Your Responsibilities as a Citizen

Can our conception of the lifelong roles and organizing themes be applied to existing social studies programs, most of which follow the expanding horizons sequence? Consider Figure 1–1, which shows how these elements might fit together. Note, for example, that the lifelong role of citizenship might be developed initially in the primary grades through the study of school, neighborhood, and local communities, and later in the upper grades through the study of the pupil's home state, the United States, and various nations and civilizations, past and present, of the Eastern and Western Hemispheres. The remaining lifelong roles can also be taught through this progression of topics. At this point, we suggest that you consult Section B, p. 237 which contains a series of illustrative lessons (referred to as modules) centering on the five lifelong roles. Similarly, the ten organizing themes can be taught as a part of existing programs, as illustrated in Section C, p. 317. For teachers' evaluations of the instructional capabilities of the lifelong roles and organizing themes, consult the "Classroom Results" heading after each module in Sections B and C.

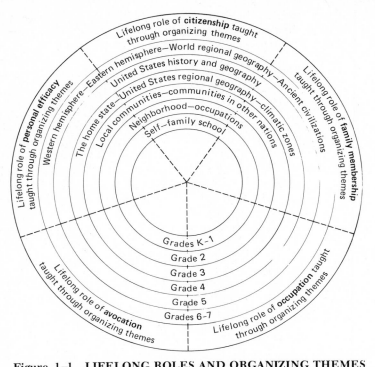

Figure 1-1   LIFELONG ROLES AND ORGANIZING THEMES
APPLIED TO WIDENING HORIZONS

Emerging Trends

As you consider how our conception of lifelong roles and organizing themes relates to the social studies curriculum in your school, we urge you to consider carefully some significant changes in content emphasis that are beginning to occur in the schools. These changes are highlighted below.

1. The "back-to-the-basics" movement appears to be generating a new awareness of the fundamental importance of *applied* citizenship, family membership, and personal efficacy; these topics are beginning to acquire a K–8 focus. Also, this movement attaches great importance to the teaching of communicative skills—particularly those involving reading, writing, arithmetic, and map reading.

2. The schools are placing greater emphasis than ever before on combating racism, sexism, and ethnic and sex-role stereotyping. Moreover, ageism or age-role stereotyping are beginning to appear in the curriculum. These developments should enhance the viability of the themes of human relations, intercultural relations, and morality.

3. Despite the horrendous financial problems plaguing the schools, many teachers are encouraged to investigate options to the regular program—particularly options that take into account the out-of-school experiences of children and youth. Increasingly we are observing units on consumerism, advertising, careers, birth and death, television,

law-related studies, human values, and interpersonal relations. In many states teachers' organizations, civic groups, and business and industry are actively promoting these emphases—a trend which underscores the importance of our organizing themes.

4. It appears that there is a new brand of morality that is affecting our schools. This morality, accelerated by the horrors of Viet Nam, and by the Watergate debacle, and articulated through religious revivalism, stresses a return to such basic values as moderation, respect for authority, honesty, loyalty, perseverance, simpler lifestyles, the work ethic, and the Golden Rule. If our assumptions are correct, the theme of morality is likely to become a viable component of the social studies.

5. Increasingly social studies programs stress the unitary nature of our planet and the complex network of interdependencies in our world. This trend toward teaching global thinking is a prominent element in several recently published social studies programs, and is consistent with our organizing themes, particularly human equality and intercultural relations.

6. Finally, energy and ecology are likely to become pervasive, dominant themes in social studies programs, if only because educators acknowledge that all of us are directly and personally affected by the stark realities of the growing energy and ecological crises confronting us. Energy management and environmental conservation, coupled with the urgent need to adapt to less energy-intensive lifestyles, will of necessity become high priority matters in our social studies programs. Our conception of lifelong roles and organizing themes reflects this need.

Admittedly, all five lifelong roles cannot be translated into all ten organizing themes and taught simultaneously at each grade level. All we ask is that you keep an open mind to the instructional possibilities of these elements, decide for yourself which of them are most suitable for your pupils, and then determine how you will teach them. The balance of this book is designed to help you reach and implement these decisions.

SUMMARY

The primary purpose for teaching the social studies in the elementary grades is to help children and youth to become active, knowledgeable, adaptive humans, capable of functioning within the range of lifelong roles that they encounter throughout their lives, and capable of improving the human condition. This proposition is based on our assumptions regarding the fundamental importance of the social studies, content emphases, pupil-teacher-parent involvement, children's learning, other school subjects, values instruction, and sources of social studies content.

In our opinion, the five lifelong roles and ten organizing themes can serve as effective vehicles for planning and implementing instruction. The lifelong roles include citizenship, family membership, occupation, avocation, and personal efficacy. The organizing themes include consumerism, ecology, energy, government and politics, human equality, the human life cycle, intercultural relations, our legal system, media, and morality. We hope that this conception can help you to make more effective use of your present social studies program; and can aid you and your colleagues in designing a new one.

Our examination of current and emerging trends regarding the content of elementary social studies programs demonstrates that the widening horizons approach predominates in American schools, and that our conception of lifelong roles and organizing themes is consistent with this approach. Indeed, it appears that many of the emerging trends lend even greater credence to our conception!

CROSS-REFERENCES TO TEACHING MODULES

The instructional capabilities of the five lifelong roles are illustrated in the following teaching modules which appear later in this book in Part II under the subsection, "The Lifelong Roles: Exemplars for Teaching."

Citizenship: "First-Hand Experiences in Citizenship" (Part 2, p. 239). This teaching module, designed for pupils in the middle elementary grades (roughly grades 4 to 6), focuses on the rights and responsibilities of pupils, and presents ideas about rules, laws, fairness, and justice. The module stresses citizenship in terms understandable to pupils, and it can provide initial exposure to the organizing theme, our legal system. Content for this teaching module was drawn from the fields of political science and history.

Family Membership: "What Is a Family?" (Part 2, p. 259). Designed for children in the lower elementary grades (roughly grades K–3), this teaching module centers on the structure, composition, function, and needs of families, and the rights and responsibilities of family members. The organizing themes, the human life cycle, human equality, and morality could be easily developed through the study of this module, whose content was drawn primarily from sociology.

Occupation: "Occupations and Human Equaltiy" (Part 2, p. 282). Teachers of the upper elementary grades (roughly grades 5 to 8 or 6 to 8) should find this teaching module useful in exposing their pupils to the range of career opportunities that exist in the local community, to the changing occupational roles becoming available to males and females, and to the insidious effects of sexism in the world of work. This module can have special meaning for boys and girls when taught through the organizing theme, human equality. Content for the module was drawn from the fields of economics and sociology.

Avocation: "The Community as a Resource for Physical Fitness" (Part 2, p. 295). Used with upper elementary pupils, this teaching module enables teachers to correlate physical education and the social studies, and teaches pupils to make productive use of their leisure time by participating in physical fitness activities commonly found in the community. The human life cycle is an organizing theme which could serve as a point of departure for extending this module. The field of geography contributes content for this module, as it stresses surveying and mapping those natural and man-made features of the community which can be used to promote physical fitness.

Personal Efficacy: "All of Us Are Unique Individuals" (Part 2, p. 304). This teaching module, designed for lower elementary pupils, advocates the use of music, art, and oral language activities in teaching children about themselves—their unique characteristics, needs, problems, and aspirations. The organizing themes of human equality, intercultural relations, and morality could be developed and extended through this module, the content of which is derived primarily from social psychology and sociology.

BIBLIOGRAPHY

Each of the methods textbooks cited below advocates a different philosophical rationale for the teaching of social studies in grades K–9. We urge you to compare their rationales with the one that we presented in this chapter.

Banks, James A. *Teaching Strategies for the Social Studies* (2d ed.). Reading, Mass.: Addison-Wesley, 1977.

Dunfee, Maxine. *Social Studies for the Real World*. Columbus: Merrill, 1978.

Ellis, Arthur K. *Teaching and Learning Elementary Social Studies*. Boston: Allyn and Bacon, 1977.

Gross, Richard, et al. *Social Studies for Our Times*. New York: Wiley, 1978.

Jarolimek, John. *Social Studies in Elementary Education* (5th ed.). New York: Macmillan, 1977.

Lee, John R. *Teaching Social Studies in the Elementary School*. New York: Free Press, 1974.

Martorella, Peter H. *Elementary Social Studies as a Learning System*. New York: Harper & Row, 1976.

Massialas, Byron G. and Joseph B. Hurst. *Social Studies in a New Era: The Elementary School as a Laboratory*. New York: Longmans, 1978.

Ryan, Frank L. *Exemplars for the New Social Studies*. Englewood Cliffs, N.J.: Prentice-Hall, 1971.

Seif, Elliot. *Teaching Significant Social Studies in the Elementary School*. Skokie, Ill.: Rand McNally, 1977.

Welton, David A. and John T. Mallan. *Children and Their World: Teaching Elementary Social Studies*. Skokie, Ill.: Rand McNally, 1976.

After you have compared these texts' rationales, you may wish to examine the views expressed in two recent National Council for the Social Studies publications, cited below:

Barr, Robert D., James L. Barth, and S. Samuel Shermis. *Defining the Social Studies*. Bulletin No. 51. Washington, D.C.: National Council for the Social Studies, 1977.

Shaver, James P. (ed.). *Building Rationales for Citizenship Education*. Bulletin No. 52. Washington, D.C.: National Council for the Social Studies, 1977.

PROGRAMS, TEXTBOOKS, AND MULTIMEDIA KITS

GOALS

1. Recognize the importance of using good judgment in the selection and use of instructional materials designed for use in social studies classes.
2. Become aware of the strengths and weaknesses of commercially produced basal social studies programs.
3. Understand the instructional capabilities of three types of basal programs: textbook-centered, multimedia, and combination textbook–multimedia.
4. Comprehend why the process of evaluation and selection of social studies programs should be conducted in an organized, systematic manner.
5. Evaluate and select basal social studies programs and related instructional materials consistent with the perceived needs, abilities, and interests of pupils.

Several years ago we attempted to take a foreign educator on an abbreviated tour of the instructional materials exhibit at the annual meeting of the National Council for the Social Studies. As we slowly moved from one exhibit to the next, it became increasingly apparent that our "quickie" tour was not to be. Our guest was so captivated by the bewildering array of materials that he wanted to savor the experience as long as he could. There was so much to read, to hear, to touch. As he departed from the exhibit area several hours later, he remarked (partly in jest), "You Americans must find it quite easy to teach social studies; there are so many wonderful materials available."

Admittedly, publishers are producing a dazzling cornucopia of attractive, stimulating, imaginative materials. Despite this, we are not as competent social studies teachers as we would like to be. Too many of us have failed to learn how to select and use these materials properly. Too often we deceive ourselves into believing that merely because we happen to be attracted to a given textbook series or multimedia kit of materials, they will prove to be of value in the classroom. Gathering dust in classrooms around the country are numerous unused materials, many of recent vintage. Often these materials are not in use because teachers have found them to be inadequate for their needs. Perhaps they are too difficult to read or their conceptual level is too high. Perhaps they impose unreasonable demands on the time or energy (or patience?) of students and teachers. Perhaps they are lacking in relevance for the experiential backgrounds of students. Whatever the reasons, we cannot afford such self-deception. Our school budgets can ill afford it either.

Accordingly, the purpose of this chapter is quite simple: to help you to become competent in selecting and using various instructional materials designed for classroom use. With this goal in mind, we have organized this chapter into two sections. The first section describes the various types of basal social studies textbooks and multimedia kits currently in use in our schools, and shows how they interface with our conception of the lifelong roles and organizing themes. The second section presents a series of techniques for evaluating the instructional capabilities of these materials.

BASAL PROGRAMS

Essentially there are three types of basal social studies programs: (a) textbook-centered; (b) multimedia; and (c) combination textbook–multimedia. The textbook-centered program, by far the most widely used social studies program, is based solely on the textbook. Although most publishers of these programs market such supplementary aids as recordings, filmstrips, or workbooks, these are advertised and sold as adjuncts to the textbook. The multimedia program consists of a variety of multisensory learning aids, usually sold as a series of self-contained kits. Among these are recordings, filmstrips, workbooks, models, construction materials, photographs, study prints, learning games, transparencies, maps, trade books, and artifacts. The combination textbook–multimedia program contains a textbook or resource book that is less complete than a typical textbook and a media kit that is usually not as extensive as those kits found in the multimedia program.

These types of programs have several common characteristics. Typically they:

1. Represent a multimillion dollar investment by the publisher
2. Are under development several years before they are released for sale to schools
3. Are produced by teams of authors (mostly college professors and teachers) and editors
4. Reflect a philosophical rationale and conceptual scheme that is believed to be consistent with prevailing and emerging views of the social studies (This is invariably interpreted by publishers as "Give teachers what we think they need.")
5. Are organized according to scope (the topics, generalizations, or concepts to be taught at specific grade levels) and sequence (the order in which these topics, generalizations, or concepts are taught) reflecting the expanding horizons approach described in Chapter 1
6. Are written at a higher reading level than the grade level at which they are designated to be used
7. Are designed with the so-called "average" student in mind
8. Tend to avoid conflict and controversy by concentrating on "safe" topics
9. Accord varying degrees of emphasis to skill development (particularly inquiry, map and globe skills, and reading, writing, listening, and speaking skills) and such emerging areas of concern as energy, conservation, ecological problems, etc.)

10. Give little recognition to other school subjects—as if to create the impression that the user of the program teaches only the social studies

11. Vary in their coverage of performance objectives and evaluation of learning.

If this is an accurate description of the commercially developed social studies programs used in the majority of our classrooms below the high school level, it becomes axiomatic that, despite the imaginative, well-intentioned efforts of authors and publishers, each program is bound to have certain inherent limitations. First, few programs are capable of meeting the diverse needs of children of varying abilities and of varying socioeconomic backgrounds; few are designed with a view toward individualizing instruction. Second, those programs that rely heavily on the printed word are bound to create learning problems for the poor reader and/or for the child who has been moved or "mainstreamed" from a special education classroom into a "regular" classroom. Third, since the publication of commercially produced social studies programs is a profit-making venture, publishers are not likely to risk endangering sales by producing materials that deal

Despite their limitations, textbooks continue to be the most widely used teaching device in elementary social studies classes.

with topics that may be perceived by schools as controversial. Even today most social studies programs do not deal directly with such potentially explosive topics as morality, poverty, racism, sexism, consumer rights, inherent injustices of our legal system, excesses of government and business, or the blatant flag-waving pro-American brand of ethnocentrism that has long been endemic to textbooks dealing with the United States.

These inherent deficiencies suggest that no commercially produced social studies program should ever be regarded as the total social studies curriculum for a school. Indeed, publishers constantly remind us that no matter how complete a given social studies program may appear to be, no matter how many multisensory learning aids it contains, it cannot possibly work equally well in all classrooms. Thus it becomes the ultimate responsibility of teachers to adapt whatever program they are using to the needs and learning styles of students. This will involve deleting inappropriate units and materials, adding supplementary materials, or creating homemade units, teaching aids, and evaluative instruments.

The previous discussion was not intended to dissuade you from using commercially produced basal programs. Quite the contrary. They have been and will continue to be the primary vehicle for social studies instruction. A few of the better basal programs possess most of these characteristics:

1. They present a well-organized, carefully sequenced body of knowledge that is worthy of study.
2. They enhance the ability of pupils to read, interpret, and use data gleaned from the printed word as well as from maps, graphs, charts, pictures, and other realia.
3. They provide teachers—especially inexperienced ones—with competent guidance in the selection of content, in the planning and teaching of lessons, and in the assessment of learning.
4. They present students with reasonably accurate portrayals of the social realities of their world.
5. They are written by competent author-scholars, most of whom are former teachers, who are knowledgeable about social studies subject matter and the psychology of learning, and who are genuinely concerned about the effectiveness of their materials.
6. They are colorful, eye-catching, well-illustrated, and seem to do an effective job of motivating students.

If all or perhaps most of the basal programs possessed these characteristics and did not have the deficiencies described earlier, we could end this chapter at this point. But since this is decidedly not the case, we feel compelled to take you on an excursion through a representative sampling of basal programs.

Illustrative Programs, Grades K–6

At the beginning of this chapter we noted the three types of basal social studies programs—textbook-centered, multimedia, and combination textbook–multimedia. There are nearly thirty of these programs in use. Below are the publishers and titles of most of the programs that are widely used throughout the country.

Textbook-Centered
Addison-Wesley, *People: Cultures, Times, Places*
Addison-Wesley, *The Taba Social Studies Program*
Allyn and Bacon, *Concepts and Inquiry*
Field, *Field's Social Studies Program*
Follett, *Exploring Our World*
Follett, *The World of Mankind*
Ginn, *Ginn Social Studies Series*
Harcourt Brace Jovanovich, *The Social Sciences: Concepts and Values*
Harper & Row, *Our Family of Man*
Houghton Mifflin, *Windows on Our World*
Laidlaw, *Understanding the Social Sciences Program*
McGraw-Hill, *McGraw-Hill Elementary Social Studies Program*
Macmillan, *Social Studies: Focus on Active Learning*
Noble, *Man and His World*
Rand McNally, *Social Studies through Inquiry*
Scott, Foresman, *Investigating Man's World*
Silver Burdett, *Contemporary Social Science Curriculum*
Silver Burdett, *Silver Burdett Social Science*

Multimedia
Selective Educational Equipment, *Family of Man*
Curriculum Development Associates, *Man: A Course of Study*

Textbook–Multimedia
Holt, Rinehart and Winston, *Holt Databank System*
Science Research Associates, *Our Working World*

To illustrate the variety of these programs, we will describe distinctive features of six representative programs. We will begin with four K–6 programs: *Windows on Our World* and the *McGraw-Hill Elementary Social Studies Program* (both are textbook-centered), *Family of Man* (multimedia), and *Holt Databank System* (textbook–multimedia); we will conclude with components of a K–7 program, *Exploring Our World,* and a K–8 program, *The Social Sciences: Concepts and Values* (both of which are textbook-centered programs).

Textbook-Centered Programs

Since 1975 two major publishers, McGraw-Hill and Houghton Mifflin, have entered the elementary social studies textbook market. Although the basic topics stressed in both basal programs resemble those of their competitors, both programs have certain distinguishing characteristics which appear to render them more teachable than other programs. The McGraw-Hill program contains these features:

1. The textbooks, written in a personalized, conversational tone, and with carefully controlled vocabulary, seek to establish a dialogue between their authors and the

reader. Although the vocabulary and concepts are carefully controlled, the textual material is surprisingly stimulating to kids.

2. The teachers' editions contain measurable objectives for each lesson, chapter, and unit, daily evaluation techniques, and alternative teaching plans. Bound in the back of the teachers' editions are tear-out sheets (designed to be duplicated for distribution to pupils), containing an impressive array of activities, and a log for use by teachers in tracking the progress of individual students.

3. For kindergartners there are consumable materials, including activity sheets and a student reaction chart, which enables children to keep daily records of their feelings and assists them in the development of self-awareness.

4. For kindergartners and first graders there are picture packets, consisting of illustrated cards which promote self-awareness, self-realization, and awareness of cultural traditions.

5. Activity booklets providing opportunities to practice skills and process information are available for grades 2–6.

6. Posters containing enlargements of maps and illustrations of key social studies concepts are provided for children in grades 2–6.

7. A testing program modeled after the national standardized tests measures attainment of chapter and unit objectives.

8. Case studies are used extensively at each level.

Learning about People, the second-grade textbook in the McGraw-Hill program, illustrates some of this program's distinguishing features. The pupil textbook is divided into four units, described below.

"What Do People Do?"—develops such concepts as *behavior, trust,* and *habit;* stresses individual and group behavior, emotions, friendship, ways of studying behavior (gathering and recording facts, making guesses, collecting facts, checking guesses); and formation of personal habits.

"How Do We Learn?"—develops such concepts as *learned* and *instinctive behavior, modeling,* and *reward;* stresses what children learn, how they learn (modeling and copying); where learning occurs; appropriate behavior, rewarded and unrewarded behavior; individual learning, instinctive learning, and learning through others.

"How Do We Communicate?"—develops such concepts as *message, communication, medium* (of communication), *map,* and *advertising;* stresses the processes of verbal and nonverbal communication, how dogs, cats, and birds communicate; mediums of communication (maps, music, art, traffic light, ice cream cones, arrow, etc.); types of advertising (sky writing, TV commercials, and cereal boxes).

"How Do We Make Decisions?"—develops such concepts as *decision-making, choice,* and *result;* stresses the role of wants, needs, choices in decision-making, making personal decisions; predicting results, role of prior knowledge, feelings, how we and others are affected by decisions, and dynamics of group decision-making.

The central concepts of this book are introduced and developed in a manner designed to facilitate learning by second graders. Also, the authors introduce time—past, present, and future—as a personal dimension of the life space of the reader. Throughout the book are short, easily read, and highly meaningful case studies about children with similar interests and concerns as the young reader. Clearly, this textbook provides children with satisfying, challenging experiences in the study of human behavior.

Windows on Our World also belongs to the new generation of textbook-centered basal social studies programs. This program centers on one question that children frequently ask, "Who am I?"; it explores this question in terms of four dimensions of human identity: children's understandings of themselves as individuals, as members of groups, as human beings, and as inhabitants of the earth. Philosophically this focus is extremely different from that of the traditional programs, which typically view the social studies as a vehicle for transmitting the cultural heritage of the past, or for teaching children about the methods and findings of the social science disciplines. An examination of the components of this program reveals additional differences:

1. There is a strong global emphasis throughout the program.
2. Energy and ecology and their implications for the lifestyles of pupils is a recurring theme in the program.
3. Consistently emphasized are map and globe skills. These are carefully interrelated with textual material.
4. The textbooks are replete with full-color photographs, drawings, paintings, and other illustrations, calculated not only to stimulate interest, but also to complement the textual material.
5. For kindergarten pupils there are colorful, well-illustrated activity sheets. These are to be combined with "hands-on" activities in cutting, pasting, and drawing, and are designed to develop manipulative skills.
6. The teachers' annotated editions are very comprehensive. Identified for each lesson are goals, skills, appropriate textual material, new vocabulary terms, instructional methodology, and provisions for meeting individual differences.
7. The reading level of this program is carefully controlled.
8. Inquiry skills are stressed throughout the program.
9. Various optional materials are available, including a testing program, student workbooks, activity cards, and for kindergartners, a media kit containing filmstrips and overhead visuals.

The United States, the fifth-level (or roughly the fifth grade) book in this program contains several distinguishing features. The pupil textbook is divided into eight units:

1. The United States: People and Places
2. The United States: Our Natural Environment
3. Culture in the United States
4. The United States in the Global Community
5. The Beginnings of the United States
6. The United States Grows and Changes
7. The Modern United States
8. The United States in Today's World

This textbook is much different from competing texts at the fifth-grade level.

The first four units (roughly the initial 177 pages) provide students with an exceptionally meaningful account of social, economic, and political aspects of the contemporary United States. Note that Unit 4, "The United States in the Global Community," seeks to promote global mindedness in pupils. Units 5 through 7 present a compressed chronological account of the origins and development of the United States, while the concluding unit, "The United States in Today's World," presents a view of contemporary life in Canada and Mexico, and then shifts to an account of U.S. history since 1900.

Windows on Our World is an unusual social studies program, one that could easily become the progenitor of social studies programs of the next decade. Admittedly, one may criticize this program for its tendency to accord uneven coverage to inquiry and reading–language arts skills, and to deemphasize United States history and other conventional topics. But we are convinced that its highly defensible philosophical foundations, strong global emphasis, and excellent pupil and teacher material offset such criticisms.

Multimedia Programs

Family of Man possesses several qualities that clearly set it apart from most basal programs. First, it is one of the few multimedia programs, and contains a greater variety of media than any of the other programs. Second, it is one of the few existing elementary social studies programs whose genesis dates back to a federally funded curriculum project of the 1960s. (*Family of Man* is a spin-off of the University of Minnesota Curriculum Development Project, directed by Edith West.) Finally, as you will discover below, the content of this program departs significantly from that of other programs. The basic units in *Family of Man* are:

Level I (Grades 1–2 or 1–3)
Hopi Indian Family
Japanese Family
Ashanti Family of Ghana

Level II (Grades 2–3 or 2–4)
Early New England Family
Kibbutz Family in Israel
Russian Family in Moscow

Level III (Grades 3–4 or 3–5)
Contrasting Communities in the United States
The People of Paris
Early California Gold Mining Camp

Level IV (Grades 4–6 or 4–7)
Our Own Community—Economic Aspects
Village in India
Economic Life in the People's Republic of China

The purpose of *Family of Man* is to teach children to become nation-minded and world-minded. Through a series of family and community studies (detailed above), this program attempts to develop an understanding of human behavior. To this end, inquiry, geography, and data-gathering skills and concepts are stressed.

"The Ashanti Family of Ghana," one of the initial units developed for *Family of Man*, typifies the unusual qualities of this program. Centering on the study of contrasting lifestyles within a newly independent nation, this unit provides primary-grade students with keen insights into elements of Ashanti culture, family structure, roles, the marketplace, and the effects of environment on culture. When used with other Level I and II kits, the Ashanti kit helps children to recognize cultural diversity, the uniqueness of culture and cultural universals, and to apply this knowledge to their own culture.

Included in this unit are these components: many different types of media, including five authentic, hand-made Ashanti artifacts (Akuba doll, gold weight, kente cloth, oware board, and stool), magnetic compasses, an Ashanti newspaper, a package of cocoa beans, filmstrips on the physical and cultural features of the Ashanti environment, study prints on Ashanti lifestyles, an audiotape cassette of Ashanti music and children's folktales, printed originals for making student hand-outs and overhead transparencies of outline maps, floor plans of an Ashanti compound, a set of books and booklets dealing with life in Ghana, an atlas for children, and various children's stories. In addition, there is a comprehensive teacher's resource guide including a background paper on the Ashanti family,

Using appropriate instructional materials is an essential component of the teaching-learning process.

behavioral objectives, general goals, content outline, teaching suggestions, and a detailed list of classroom activities. Also included is a paper which presents the rationale and overview of the total program. The materials for each unit in *Family of Man* are boxed in a durable (albeit awkward to carry) classroom display case, which can be used for storage and for transfer from one classroom to another.

Clearly, this is an unusual social studies program. We suspect that it could easily become the prototype of future basal programs, owing to its abundance of multisensory learning aids and its imaginative, carefully presented teaching suggestions. Unfortunately several factors discourage publishers from producing multimedia programs. One problem is cost: It is more expensive to produce kits of multisensory materials than conventional textbooks. Another is the uncertainty of the market. We must bear in mind that teachers appear to be devoting less time—particularly in the primary grades—to the social studies, a circumstance undoubtedly attributable in large part to the back-to-basics movement described in Chapter 1. Finally, we suspect that teachers tend to be more comfortable with textbooks, perhaps because they have grown accustomed to using them over the years. Collectively these realities do not augur well for the short-range future of multimedia kits.

Another reality which has militated against the acceptance of some social studies programs is controversy. *Man: A Course of Study*, another multimedia program, is a case in point.

Conceived by the eminent psychologist, Jerome S. Bruner, funded by massive grants from the National Science Foundation, and produced by Educational Development Corporation, *Man: A Course of Study* (hereafter referred to as *Man*) has been the object of continuing controversy among educators, politicians, and parents. Through the study of salmon, herring gulls, baboons, chimpanzees, and Netsilik Eskimos, pupils (usually fifth and sixth graders) contrast human with animal behavior in an effort to discern man's continuity with his animal forebears. Life cycle, parenthood, learned and instinctive behavior, and social organization are among the concepts which provide a framework for the animal units, which compose the first half of the program. A year in the life of a Netsilik family of the 1920s is the focal point of the second half of *Man*. Stressed are five great humanizing forces: tool making, language, social organization, management of man's prolonged childhood, and man's desire to explain his world.

One of the major bones of contention among its critics is *Man's* inclusion of such potentially explosive topics as evolution, wife swapping and trial marriage, life and death, religion, cannibalism, reproduction, communal living, the occult, infanticide, and senilicide. Although these topics are presented in an explicit, incidental, and intellectually honest manner, many critics regard their mere presence in the program as offensive and inappropriate for fifth and sixth graders. Strong objections have also have been raised concerning *Man's* advocacy of modes of inquiry and values explorations which depart significantly from those found in conventional social studies programs. That *Man* encourages pupils to become open, inquiring, independent thinkers, and fails to stress "getting the right answer" as the goal of learning, is regarded by some critics as heretical. Finally, some critics reject the program because it displaces the study of United States history in the fifth grade.

Unfortunately there is insufficient space here to weigh the pros and cons of the controversy over *Man*. Despite the many virtues of this program (for example, it contains an amazing array of multisensory teaching aids, including a series of outstanding films as well as simulation games, songs, stories, plays, etc.), its unconventional format, its unconventional conception of the teaching process, and particularly its inclusion of controversial topics have contributed to its gradual demise. The fact that *Man: A Course of Study* dared to be different has proven to be its downfall.

Textbook–Multimedia Program

Some publishers claim that they market combination textbook–multimedia social studies programs for the elementary grades. Typically they will produce a textbook series and then eventually, especially if it appears potentially profitable, will offer prospective purchasers a collection of such teaching aids as filmstrips, audiotape cassettes, study prints, posters, and the like. These aids are useful additions to textbooks, for they serve to reinforce or extend major themes or concepts previously introduced in the parent text. But since they are intended to supplement or augment the textbook, and are limited in scope, they cannot be accurately described as multimedia programs.

The *Holt Databank System* offers more, for its publisher has made a concerted effort to give the elementary teacher the best of both worlds: a comprehensive collection of teaching aids and a textbook. Originally published in 1972 and substantially revised in 1976, this basal program is a multimedia information storage-retrieval system, containing for each grade level: (a) a media kit, or "Databank," consisting of a wide variety of multisensory teaching aids; (b) a textbook designed to focus student attention on topics under study; and (c) an extensive teacher's guide which contains a comprehensive, detailed series of lesson plans. By design, all three components are so closely interrelated and interdependent that they do indeed constitute a system.

The *Holt Databank System* is designed for kindergarten through grade six, and is organized according to conventional themes:

Level K: Inquiring about Myself
Level 1: Inquiring about People
Level 2: Inquiring about Communities
Level 3: Inquiring about Cities
Level 4: Inquiring about Cultures
Level 5: Inquiring about American History
Level 6: Inquiring about Technology

These themes tend to resemble closely the themes of many of the traditional textbook-centered programs. The only apparent exceptions tend to occur at levels 4 and 6: Typically in grade four the state and/or regional geography is stressed, and in grade six the Western or Eastern Hemispheres are stressed.

But don't allow this list of themes to deceive you! Although the themes of *Databank* may resemble those of other programs, the *subject matter* used in developing these themes is unique. The third level of this program, "Inquiring about Cities," illustrates many of its unique characteristics. At this level the program is divided into eight units:

"City Life"—a kaleidoscopic view of the human and physical features of cities

"Were These Cities?"—case studies of the sites of three ancient cities in Guatemala, Rhodesia, and Pakistan

"Where on Earth"—order and pattern of the location and growth of cities, with emphasis on Timbuktu, Cairo, Denver, Chicago, and New York

"Cities from Inside Out"—central business districts and concepts of population and density

"Where are the Edges?"—relationships between cities and their hinterlands, megalopolis, and physical geography of selected U.S. cities

"Tin Lizzie"—economic concepts developed via study of origins and development of the automobile industry

"River and Cloud"—quality of a city's environment explored through three topics: water resources, city air, and weather

"City Planning"—how to plan cities of the future

A second unique characteristic of *Databank* is that for each level there is a variety of media. Below are examples of media used in "Inquiring about Cities":

"Data Packs"—pictures of city art, Mayan wall paintings, photographs of artifacts, 1897 Sears, Roebuck catalogue

"Audiotape Cassettes"—actual sounds of a modern city, music about cities, Mayan stories and poems, African folktales

"Data Masters"—survey forms, maps of cities and air routes, games, materials for building simulated cars, stories about old cars

"Filmstrips"—of ancient Tikal, city planning, mapping exercises, concept of megalopolis, water cycle, effects of tides, collecting and interpreting facts

"Data Cards"—maps, charts, diagrams, and pictures of elements of various cities

"Data Foldouts"—a Mississippi River puzzle regarding the location of cities, a story of the Connecticut River, and "Castle Gaillard," an evaluation tool

"Simulations and Games"—building a spool engine, assembly line, and city planning

"Data Comix"—comic books centering on home design and construction, and on neighborhood planning

Another unique component of *Databank* is the books. For use at the kindergarten level there are six different books designed to be read aloud to children.

For grades one through six there are textbooks which are carefully articulated with the total system. Although colorful and abundantly illustrated, the textbook is intended to be used as a vehicle for isolating and focusing certain problems under study. Since this textbook is essentially a source of information for pupils, it lacks the comprehensiveness of coverage characteristic of conventional textbooks. It would be exceedingly difficult for a teacher to use this book if its corresponding Databank kit was unavailable. Conversely, it would be equally difficult to use the Databank kit without the textbook. Nevertheless, some school districts are attempting to use it in this way.

A final feature of this basal program is the teacher's guide. If there is any comparable publication in existence, we have yet to see it. This is by far the most comprehensive teacher's guide that we have ever seen. Not only does it explain precisely how the *Holt Databank System* is to be used, it also: (a) specifies unit-by-unit and lesson-by-lesson behavioral objectives; (b) presents activities that seek to develop basic social studies, reading, and language arts skills; (c) supplies worthwhile background material for teachers; and (d) contains comprehensive, carefully sequenced, day-by-day lesson plans.

At this writing Holt has produced a testing program designed to measure subject matter, knowledge, skill development, and affective learnings. This program, intended for use in grades three through six, is sold separately from the *Databank System*.

Illustrative Materials, Grades 7–8

There are no social studies programs published for grades 7 and 8. Most of the instructional materials produced for these levels are a part of entire programs spanning grades K–7 or K–8; some are discrete publications which exist apart from conventional programs. Indeed, a few publishers produce separate materials for grade 7 and for grade 8. Despite these differences, instructional materials at these levels have one common characteristic: They consist of textbooks plus supplementary materials.

Most of the textbooks sold at these levels tend to stress for grade 7 the Western Hemisphere (excepting the U.S., which is taught with regularity in the fifth grade), and to a lesser extent, the Eastern Hemisphere, and for grade 8, the U.S. Only a few textbooks at these levels deviate from this pattern.

With very few exceptions these textbooks were originally published in the late 1960s or the early 1970s, and were subsequently revised. Two textbooks which illustrate the basic differences in emphasis in grades 7 and 8 are *Latin America and Canada*, published by Follett, and sold as a part of their *Exploring Our World Series* (grades 1–7) and *Sources of Identity*, published by Harcourt Brace Jovanovich, and sold as a part of their *Concepts and Values* program (grades K–8).

Latin America and Canada, a grade 6–7 textbook published by Follett, has several noteworthy features:

1. More than any other text at these levels, this book stresses the development of skills

used in reading social studies material, map and globe work, thinking, communicating, and conducting research.

2. Extensive use is made of original source materials, including contemporary eyewitness accounts and such historical documents as old maps, letters, charts, diaries, and essays.

3. Abundantly illustrated, the textbook is replete with a wide variety of visuals, including cartoons, diagrams, time lines, picture stories, cross-sectioned maps, full-color photographs, and paintings. For example, Riviera's paintings and Orozco's murals are effective devices for teaching students about the emotionalism prevalent during the nineteenth-century revolutions in Mexico.

4. With few exceptions, the reading level of this book is at grades 6 and 7, as indicated by the Dale-Chall formula.

5. Included with the text are various supplementary aids, including a pupil workbook, unit tests (for diagnostic and evaluation purposes), a student atlas, and an activity book designed to reteach the fundamentals of map and globe skills.

6. A recurring feature of this text is the case-study approach, which presents pupils with basic information about a given topic and encourages them to form generalizations, draw inferences, and test predictions and hypotheses.

7. The teacher's guide is relatively nondirective, yet contains helpful suggestions for teachers, activities expressly designated for low-achieving, average, and above-average pupils, numerous annotations, and succinct background notes on topics under study, metric conversion tables, references, and the like.

This textbook (and the others in the Follett program) might be labeled as "conventional" or "basic." Built around such traditional chapter topics as "The First Americans," "Mexico," "Central America," "Canada's Past," and "Ontario and Quebec," *Latin America and Canada* employs a conventional, expository format. Although inquiry and valuing skills are presented, they are subordinate to geographic skills and to those reading and language arts skills having relevance for the social studies. If you are searching for a traditional basic text, one that is very teachable, easily supplemented, and requires a minimum of teacher in-service training, is replete with excellent visual aids and buttressed by a useful, easy-to-follow teacher's guide, *Latin America and Canada* may be the book for you. And, since the other texts in Follett's *Exploring Our World* program possess these qualities, you may find the entire series to your liking.

Sources of Identity is the seventh-level (roughly corresponding to the seventh grade) textbook of a K–8 social studies program, *The Social Sciences: Concepts and Values*, published by Harcourt Brace Jovanovich. This textbook is significantly different than Follett's *Latin America and Canada*—and nearly every other text at this level—in several respects. First, it is organized around a series of social science concepts that are observable in the pupil's daily world. Second, the concepts are carefully developed from simple to complex, to encourage pupils to acquire them cumulatively. Third, the narrative portion of the textbook heavily stresses the research findings, the theories, and the methods used by psychologists, sociologists, anthropologists, political scientists, geographers, and economists. Finally, the text is well articulated and in combination with the other texts in the Harcourt program, facilitates the reinforcement and extension of concepts introduced and developed in lower-level books. These characteristics appear to be common to the entire Harcourt program.

Following is a summary of the units presented in *Sources of Identity* and *Latin America and Canada*, the two seventh-grade texts under discussion.

Contents of *Sources of Identity* (Harcourt)

You as an Individual
Chapter 1.   Patterns of Necessity
Chapter 2.   Patterns of Experience
Focus on the Concept
Focus on the Psychologist

Individuals as Group Members
Chapter 1.   Patterns of Behavior
Chapter 2.   Patterns of Interaction
Focus on the Concept
Focus on the Psychologist

Individuals as Policy Makers
Chapter 1.   Patterns of Decision
Chapter 2.   Patterns of Influence
Focus on the Concept
Focus on the Political Scientist

Individuals in Their Environments
Chapter 1.   Patterns of Habitat
Chapter 2.   Patterns of Balance
Focus on the Concept
Focus on the Geographer

Individuals as Producers
Chapter 1.   Patterns of Technology
Chapter 2.   Patterns of Choice
Focus on the Concept
Focus on the Geographer

Following each unit are two special features. The first, "Focus on the Concept," presents additional information about the central concepts in the unit; this new material enables students to recognize generalizations with which they have been working, and to apply them to new evidence. The second, "Focus on the Social Scientist," is a brief biographical sketch centering on the work of a particular social scientist; it helps students to understand how the material that they have been studying applies to problems of the real world. You will note that the Follett text contains a similar feature.

Contents of *Latin America and Canada* (Follett)

Unit 1.   Our World and Its People
Unit 2.   The First Americans
              The Archaeologist

Unit 3.   Conquest and Colonial Days
Unit 4.   Wars for Independence
          The Historian
Unit 5.   Mexico
          The Political Scientist
Unit 6.   Central America
          The Geographer
Unit 7.   The West Indies

Exploring Regions of South America
Unit 8.   Venezuela, Colombia, and Ecuador
Unit 9.   Peru, Bolivia, and Chile
Unit 10.   Argentina, Uruguay, and Paraguay
           The Sociologist
Unit 11.   Brazil and the Guianas
           The Economist

Exploring Regions of Canada
Unit 12.   Canada's Past
Unit 13.   The Atlantic Provinces
Unit 14.   Quebec and Ontario
Unit 15.   The Prairie Provinces, British Columbia,
           and the Northlands

Clearly these texts are organized very differently. Those of you who are more comfortable with a familiar, traditional method of organization may find the topical approach of *Latin America and Canada* more to your liking. If you prefer a conceptually organized text, one that is heavily based on the social sciences, and which departs significantly from traditional textbooks, *Sources of Identity* may be more to your liking.

Sources of Identity has several exceptional qualities worthy of your consideration:

1. The visuals in this text—particularly the full-color photographs—are outstanding. Indeed they are far better than those in most textbooks published at this level.
2. The textbook makes a concerted effort to relate the concepts under study to the daily experiences of pupils.
3. Presented at the conclusion of each section are four types of pupil exercises, each of which is intended to be done in a different instructional setting: one for the individual pupil to pursue as review, reinforcement, and evaluation, one for group work, one for review of key vocabulary terms, and one for individuals or groups to pursue outside of school.
4. At the conclusion of each chapter are two exercises: one helps students to relate and apply concepts under study, the other helps students to apply the major ideas of chapters to actual problematic situations.
5. Accompanying the text is a workbook, containing a wide variety of stimulating, worthwhile activities. Among these are constructing a personal coat of arms, completing unfinished cartoons, reconstructing a family tree, writing laws, and preparing an environmental impact report.

Clearly *Sources of Identity* is a well-organized, well-written program, one that can make learning social studies a meaningful, exciting experience for pupils. Admittedly, it is likely that teachers who have weak backgrounds in the social sciences and/or who are unfamiliar with concept-based instruction will require in-service instruction in order to use this text effectively. Also, some "back-to-basics" proponents may find that the text does not provide enough instruction in geography skills. But these potential criticisms aside, *Sources of Inquiry* and the other textbooks in this series are singularly successful in using the social science disciplines as a basis for the social studies.

Lifelong Roles and Organizing Themes

You will recall that in the previous chapter we advanced the thesis that the primary purpose for teaching social studies in the elementary grades is to help children and youth to become active, knowledgeable, adaptive humans, capable of functioning within the range of lifelong roles that they aspire to attain, and capable of improving the quality of the human condition. We proposed five lifelong roles of citizenship, family membership, occupation, avocation, and personal efficacy that in our opinion should be the foundation elements of a social studies program. Further, we proposed the ten organizing themes, consumerism, ecology, energy, government and politics, human equality, the human life cycle, intercultural relations, our legal system, media, and morality, which will enable us to teach the lifelong roles in a meaningful way.

To what extent do commercially produced, basal social studies programs fit in with the conception of the lifelong roles and organizing themes? Our analysis of the six representative programs described earlier in this section yielded the results described below.

Elements of all five of the lifelong roles are present (in varying degree) in all six of the programs. One role, avocation, is accorded limited, perhaps even incidental treatment by many programs. Two programs, the *McGraw-Hill Elementary Social Studies Program* and *Windows on Our World* (Houghton Mifflin), accord elements of the five lifelong roles the most intensive and extensive treatment, while *Family of Man* (Selective Educational Equipment) and *Exploring Our World* (Follett) accorded these roles the least consistent coverage.

The ten organizing themes are treated evenly in some programs and unevenly in others. Table 2–1 provides a program-by-program breakdown of this coverage.

An inspection of this chart reveals that a majority of the ten organizing themes are covered in the six programs. Three programs, *McGraw-Hill*, *The Social Sciences: Concepts and Values*, and *Windows on Our World* include all ten themes, while two programs, *Exploring Our World*, and *Family of Man*, include at least half of the themes. Two themes, consumerism and morality, are not covered in three of the six programs.

The programs do not accord all of these themes consistent coverage throughout grades K–6 or K–8. Moreover, some of the programs provide the themes

TABLE 2–1   ELEMENTS OF ORGANIZING THEMES IN REPRESENTATIVE SOCIAL STUDIES PROGRAMS

Program	Consumerism	Ecology	Energy	Government and Politics	Human Equality	Intercultural Relations	Our Legal System	Life Cycle	Media	Morality
Exploring Our World (1977)		X	X	X	X	X			X	
Family of Man (1976)				X	X	X		X	X	
Holt Databank System (1976)		X	X	X	X	X	X	X	X	
McGraw-Hill Elementary Social Studies Program (1979)	X	X	X	X	X	X	X	X	X	X
The Social Sciences: Concepts and Values (1977)	X	X		X	X	X	X	X	X	X
Windows on Our World (1976)	X	X	X	X	X	X	X	X	X	X

consistently more coverage in their teachers' guides and pupil workbooks than in the textbooks or media kits or vice-versa. In those programs where the pupil and teacher materials are carefully articulated, this is unlikely to happen, but our examination of the six programs demonstrates that these components are better articulated in some programs than in others.

Despite the inherent limitations in our analysis of the six programs, our inability to predict how these programs are actually used in the classroom, and the basic differences in the programs, we believe that our conception of the lifelong roles and organizing themes appears to be consistent with the assumptions and content of the six representative programs. Accordingly, we conclude that our conception is a valid point of departure for assisting teachers with their instructional and curriculum development responsibilities.

EVALUATING BASAL PROGRAMS

One of the most demanding tasks confronting a teacher is that of evaluating basal social studies programs. The sheer number and variety of these programs present many formidable challenges to even the most dedicated, experienced teacher. Moreover, the task of establishing criteria for use in evaluating programs, applying these criteria, and deciding on the program that is best suited to the needs and abilities of students is at best a difficult, often frustrating task.

Traditionally, the task of evaluating and selecting a social studies program was performed by school administrators. But with the advent of professional negotiations and aggressive teachers' unions, this responsibility shifted to teachers, who felt that since they, not the administrators, actually used the social studies program in their classes, they were best qualified to decide which program they wanted to use.

Most likely, many of you will be asked, during your first few years of teaching, to participate in the selection of a new basal social studies program, or at least to help in the selection of various types of instructional materials. The experienced teachers have probably already participated in such an undertaking. If the old-timers already possess the skills needed to select an appropriate basal program, the remainder of this section may not interest them. But if you found this to be a confusing, complex task for which you were not qualified, we hope that this section will help you to become a competent evaluator the next time the need arises.

Who Should Select the Program?

Before turning to the procedures involved in the evaluation of basal programs, we feel obliged to respond to a basic question often asked by our undergraduate and graduate students: Is it best for the individual teacher, the faculty of the school, or the entire school district to select a basal social studies program? Although we are ardent supporters of academic freedom, we do not believe that it makes any sense for a given teacher to select his or her own basal program, because it simply is not practical to have a multiplicity of programs in one school. It may be argued persuasively that a sensible solution would be for the faculty of a given elementary school to select their own program; however, most business managers of large school districts do not allow this practice because of the logistical problems involved. But we tend to uphold our longstanding conviction that the teachers in a school are best qualified to determine whether the needs of their students can best be served by a program that they have selected expressly for them. Indeed, we believe that this practice makes far greater sense than allowing the individual teacher to select the program, or selecting one program for an entire school district.

Unfortunately, too few administrators share our philosophy. But worse still, too few teachers' unions are willing to expend the time and energy needed to negotiate such an arrangement, since salaries, fringe benefits, working conditions, class size, school calendars, and other more tangible benefits continue to dominate their thinking. Thus we must acknowledge with regret that the majority of our school districts—large and small—are inclined to adopt one or more basal programs for the entire system. Until teachers (like yourselves, we hope) are willing to bargain for the right to select a basal program for their own school, this practice will continue.

Procedures for Evaluating Programs

Our experiences as consultants to school districts have demonstrated that there are several basic procedures, which if followed, should enable you and your colleagues to do an effective job of evaluating and selecting basal social studies programs for your school or school district. These procedures involve establishing a social studies committee, putting the committee to work in evaluating basal programs, and piloting new programs.

Establishing a Committee

The initial procedure of establishing a committee is a crucial one, for the individuals who serve on this committee will be expected to shoulder a great deal of responsibility. Not only are they charged with the responsibility of evaluating and selecting the basal program, but also they should be capable of defending the program to their colleagues and to the administration of their school district. Although the primary impetus for selecting a new basal program tends to be initiated by teachers who are dissatisfied with the existing program, typically these concerns are communicated to the superintendent or to another high-level administrator—often the director of instruction or social studies coordinator (or someone serving in a similar capacity), who assumes initial responsibility for initiating curriculum change in the social studies. Accordingly, the following suggestions are directed toward the administrator, as well as the teacher, from whom administrators tend to seek advice about curricular changes—especially those that involve considerable expenditures of funds and significant alterations in the curriculum.

Who serves on the committee? How is it structured? For how long do members serve? What are they to do? These are the basic questions that need to be answered as quickly as possible. Instead of arbitrarily assigning staff members to this committee (and incurring the risk of acquiring a few disinterested, perhaps even antagonistic members), it is better to solicit volunteers who are genuinely interested in the field of social studies. Try to structure the committee to insure that it provides for representation by grade level, type of school, and length of teaching experience. If specialists in reading, language arts, the fine arts, special education, guidance, multicultural education, and media do not volunteer to serve on the committee, encourage them to serve. These specialists have unique perspectives and competencies which, if used by the committee, can add an extremely significant dimension to the committee's work.

Once the committee has been assembled, secure from its members a commitment to serve a one-year term, as it will take that long to evaluate and pilot basal social studies programs. Simultaneously, secure from the superintendent or director of instruction the following commitments: (a) that committee members will not be assigned to curriculum development work in other areas during their tenure on the social studies committee; (b) that facilities as well as secretarial assistance will be provided for the committee's work; and (c) that teachers who serve on the committee will be released from their classroom responsibilities one day each month for the duration of the project. Admittedly, these commitments may be difficult to obtain, but since the task of evaluating and selecting basal social studies programs is a difficult, time-consuming undertaking (one that cannot be performed by tired teachers at the end of the school day or on weekends), and since the purchase of basal programs constitutes a significant investment of school funds, it is best to utilize whatever human, physical, and financial resources are needed.

As soon as possible, copies of basal programs should be obtained from publishers and stored in a central location accessible to committee members. Publishers are pleased to provide school districts with copies of their materials, but bear in mind that it may take more time than you would imagine—sometimes several months—to obtain copies of some programs. Whenever possible, publishers' representatives should be invited to give presentations before your social studies committee and to demonstrate their programs in classrooms.

Putting the Committee To Work

Once several sample copies of each of the basal programs have been secured, the first step is to select those programs that in the committee's collective opinion appear to be best suited to the interests and needs of pupils and most consistent with the social studies curriculum of the school or school district. This is an important step, because ultimately the program or programs that are adopted will be chosen from this group of finalists. In the event that all of the program materials have not arrived when the committee is ready to make these selections, it is a good idea to proceed with the initial selections, and then consider the remaining programs when they arrive. Below are criteria that your committee may find useful in selecting programs to be evaluated:

1. Does the content depict the real world of today?
2. Is the content factually accurate and unbiased?
3. Can pupils learn from the instructional components—*i.e.*, are reading materials, photos, pictures, charts, maps, etc. within their level of comprehension?
4. Are concepts presented in such a way that the typical pupil can understand them?
5. Does the content promote intercultural understanding?
6. Is the content personalized? Does it stimulate pupils to raise questions about themselves and their interactions with others?
7. Does the program provide pupils with a wide range of multisensory learning experiences?
8. Does the program relate social studies skills and concepts to other school subjects, to out-of-school learning experiences?
9. Does the program consciously promote the development of such basic skills as reading, writing, listening, speaking, map and globe reading, problem solving and critical thinking, and values analysis?
10. Are the objectives for lessons and units stated in clear, unambiguous terms?
11. Does the program provide the teacher with a variety of ways to evaluate student achievement?
12. Does the teacher's guide include a variety of approaches that can be adjusted to the needs of slow-learning, gifted, and culturally different pupils?
13. Are the goals of the program consistent with the goals of the school or school district?

As soon as you have selected those programs to be evaluated, the next step is to evaluate them. To assist you in this process, we present below an instrument that we have used with many school districts. We warn you, however, that this instrument is incomplete to the extent that it contains only *suggested* criteria for evaluating basal programs. Obviously, the type of program under evaluation, the type of student likely to use the program, and the biases of the user of the instrument will vary. Accordingly, we have made the instrument as flexible as possible to accommodate these differences.

Since the instrument is designed to be used in evaluating grade level components of a total program, it is a good idea to ask two or three committee members to independently evaluate the same component. Once they have completed their evaluations, they can be compared, with a view toward areas of agreement and disagreement. Obviously there will be differences of opinion among committee members who evaluate the same textbook or media package, but before proceeding further, these disagreements will need to be resolved.

Readability Estimates

A major reason why pupils do not achieve well in social studies is that the reading material is too difficult for them. Over the years researchers have found that the readability of these materials—especially textbooks—tends to be higher (often two or more grades higher) than the grade level at which they are used. You will recall that in the previous section we noted that the readability of several textbook-centered programs has been controlled in accordance with one or more readability estimates (or formulae, as many reading specialists prefer to call it). Do not let this delude you into believing that this gives you an iron-clad guarantee that your pupils will be able to understand the ideas presented in the program. *Readability estimates do not test concepts;* instead, they merely attempt to measure such quantifiable factors as word length, sentence length, number of syllables, pronouns, affixes, prepositional phrases, difficult words occurring in vocabulary lists, and the prevalence of simple and complex sentences. Accordingly, there is no readability estimate that measures the density of facts, the number and type of illustrations, the purpose of the reading material, the interest it evokes from the reader, the concept load, the way in which material is organized and presented, and the interrelatedness of ideas.[1]

Despite these limitations, readability estimates do have value. Used with care, they can enable your social studies committee to obtain a quick measure of the difficulty of the printed material in a basal program. Of the thirty-odd readability estimates that have been constructed over the past fifty years, there is one that we prefer because it is easy to administer and can be used with confidence: the *Fry Readability Graph.* This instrument is presented in Figure 2–1.

Unlike many other readability estimates, the *Fry Readability Graph* can be applied to primary-grade through college materials, is fairly simple, gives quick results, and can be used for a variety of purposes. Not only does it yield an estimate of the difficulty of the reading material in a basal social studies program, it can help you to identify difficult words and sentences in a book, and to identify appropriate supplementary materials for your students. There are very few instruments that can be effectively used with grade 1–8 reading material. One effective instrument for primary-grade materials is the *Spache Readability Formula.*[2] Three instruments that work well with material above grade three are *SMOG Grading*[3] (named after the author's London birthplace), the *CLOZE Procedure,*[4] and the *Dale-Chall Readability Formula.*[5] A discussion of the use of these estimates appears in Chapter 5.

There are several procedures that, if followed, will enable you to use our instrument as effectively as possible. We suggest that you follow these procedures in sequential order.

---

[1] Barbara Jacoby, *Readability,* mimeographed bulletin (Mason, Mich.: Ingham Intermediate School District, undated), pp. 2–4.

[2] George Spache, "A New Readability Formula for Primary-Grade Reading Materials," *Elementary School Journal 53* (March 1953), pp. 410–413.

[3] G. Harry McLaughlin, "SMOG Grading—A New Readability Formula," *Journal of Reading 12* (May 1969), pp. 639–646.

[4] John R. Bormuth, "Readability: A New Approach," *Reading Research Quarterly, 1* (Spring 1966), pp. 79–132; W. L. Taylor, "CLOZE Procedure: A New Tool for Measuring Readability," *The Journalism Quarterly 30* (Fall 1953), pp. 415–433.

[5] Jeanne Chall and Edgar Dale, "A Formula for Predicting Readability," *Educational Research Bulletin 27* (January 1948), pp. 11–20.

Average number of syllables per 100 words

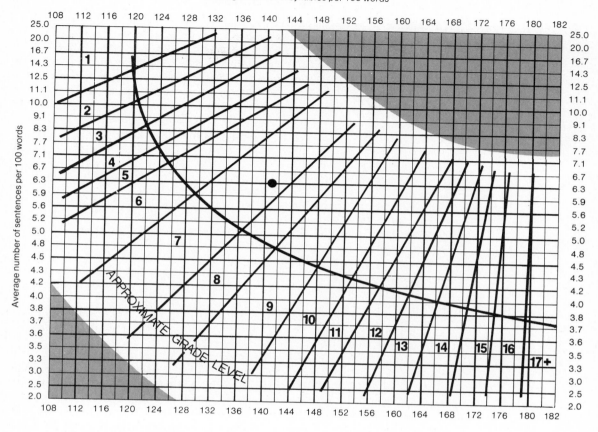

DIRECTIONS: Randomly select 3 one hundred word passages from a book or an article. Plot average number of syllables and average number of sentences per 100 words on graph to determine the grade level of the material. Choose more passages per book if great variability is observed and conclude that the book has uneven readability. Few books will fall in gray area but when they do grade level scores are invalid.

Count proper nouns, numerals and initializations as words. Count a syllable for each symbol. For example, "1945" is 1 word and 4 syllables and "IRA" is 1 word and 3 syllables.

EXAMPLE:

	SYLLABLES	SENTENCES
1st Hundred Words	124	6.6
2nd Hundred Words	141	5.5
3rd Hundred Words	158	6.8
AVERAGE	141	6.3

READABILITY 7th GRADE (see dot plotted on graph)

Figure 2–1 GRAPH FOR ESTIMATING READABILITY—EXTENDED.[6]

[6]Edward Fry, "Fry's Readability Graph: Clarifications, Validity, and Extension to Level 17," *Journal of Reading 21* (December 1977), pp. 242–252. Reproduced by permission of Edward Fry, Rutgers University Reading Center, New Brunswick, N.J. 08904.

1. Before using the instrument, read it *carefully*, to insure that you get a basic idea of its contents and function.

2. Examine *each criterion* listed in the instrument. If your committee disagrees with any criteria, delete them, and add those that are best suited to your purposes.

3. Ask the committee to establish a *common weighting scale* for the instrument. We suggest using a scale of 1 to 3 or 1 to 5, to simplify the computations that you will need to make. For illustrative purposes we will use a 1 to 5 scale for the criteria.

4. Ask the committee to assign *to each criterion* a *common weighting*, one which reflects its relative importance. Mark these common weightings in the spaces provided throughout the instrument. For example, it is likely that your committee will assign a lower weighting to Criterion A, *Physical Features*, than to Criterion C, *Basis for Student Decision-Making*, because the former criterion would be regarded as more important than the latter.

5. Ask the committee to establish a *common rating scale* and mark it in the space provided at the beginning of the instrument. A rating scale of 1 to 3 or 1 to 5 should be sufficient. For illustrative purposes, we will use a 1 to 5 scale for the ratings.

6. Assign teams of 2 to 3 committee members to evaluate grade-level components of the program. As these teams examine the program material (each member working independently), members should append their numerical ratings and comments to the appropriate places in the instrument.

7. As the individual team members mark their ratings and comments on the instrument, they should compute the *weighted score* that the material receives for each criterion. This involves multiplying the weighting times the rating. For Criterion A, *Physical Features*, we multiplied *3* (weighting) times *4* (rating), which yields a weighted score of *12* points. Then sum these weighted scores and record them in the space labeled *Overall Evaluation*. Do this for the Student Material and for the Teacher's Guide.

8. To determine the *maximum* number of points for the Student Material and for the Teacher's Guide, multiply the weighting that your committee gave to the program material for each criterion times the maximum possible rating, and then sum these products. Thus, for Criterion A, *Physical Features*, we multiplied *3* (weighting) times *5* (rating), which yields a theoretical maximum score of *15*. Repeat this procedure for the remaining criteria under Student Material and sum the products. The same procedure is to be followed in calculating the theoretical maximum score for the Teacher's Guide.

9. The final step is to compare the *results* of your evaluations within programs and between programs. When doing this you may find that, for example, the primary-grade components of a given program score relatively higher than the upper-grade components of the same program. If this happens, your committee may wish to consider adopting one program for the primary grades, another for grades 4 to 6, and a third for grades 7 to 8. We do not, however, advocate adopting grade-level components of different programs at different levels (for example, adopting *Databank* for kindergarten, *Family of Man* for grade one, *McGraw-Hill* for grade two, etc.). Such a decision would make it extremely difficult, if not impossible, to articulate your social studies instruction between grade levels.

Piloting the Programs

This, the final stage in the process of evaluating and selecting basal programs, is often ignored by social studies committees. Too often they feel that the results of their evaluations of social studies programs provide them with a sound, defensible basis for adopting a program. We tend to disagree, largely because of our conviction that teachers and their pupils are bound to see programs differently. No teacher, operating independently or as a member of a committee, can ever predict with certainty that a highly rated program will fulfill pupil expectations in the classroom. It is precisely for this reason that once your committee has identified the best programs, they should make arrangements for these to be tried out in classrooms over an extended period of time. Below are some suggestions that may help you to do this.

1. Arrange for each program to be tried out in three or four different schools, in classes taught by teachers of varying experience.
2. Keep careful records of pupils' reactions to the program materials.
3. Arrange for social studies committee members to periodically visit these pilot classes, and to confer with their teachers outside of class.

INSTRUMENT FOR ASSESSING COMPONENTS OF BASAL SOCIAL STUDIES PROGRAMS

Evaluator: _____ Date: _____

Author(s): _____ Copyright(s): _____

Title: _____

Approximate Grade Level(s): _____ Publisher: _____

Weighting Scale: $\dfrac{1}{\text{minimum}}$ _____ $\dfrac{3}{\text{maximum}}$

Rating Scale: $\dfrac{1}{\text{minimum}}$ _____ $\dfrac{5}{\text{maximum}}$

1. STUDENT MATERIAL

Criterion	Weighting	Rating	Weighted Score	Maximum Score
A. *Physical Features*	_____	× _____	= _____	_____

Eye-catching? Stimulates curiosity? Physically attractive? Seductive? Cite specific examples. Comments?

B. *Organization*	_____	× _____	= _____	_____

Conceptual? Topical? Chronological? Combination of these? Others? How effective is method of organization used? Cite specific examples. Comments?

C. *Basis for Student Decision Making* _____ × _____ = _____   _____
Open-ended questions? Identification of alternatives? Presentation of evidence? Student encouraged to be independent inquirer? Cite specific examples. Comments?

D. *Inclusion of Learning Aids* _____ × _____ = _____   _____
Maps? Charts? Graphs? Diagrams? Photographs? Pictures? Time Lines? Creative Dramatics? Role plays? Simulations? Cartoons? Filmstrips? Audio cassettes? Puppets? Artifacts? Mock trials? Other aids? Are any conspicuously absent? Cite examples of aids. Comments?

E. *Skill Development* _____ × _____ = _____   _____
Reading? Writing? Listening? Speaking? Maps and Globes? Time and chronology? Problem solving and critical thinking? Valuing? Are these skills taught purposefully? Incidentally? How effectively are they taught? Cite specific examples. Are any conspicuously absent? Comments?

F. *Relationship with Learner* _____ × _____ = _____   _____
Relates knowledge relevant to learner's personal experiences? Author(s) and learner are co-inquirers? Designed for students of varying ability (provisions for slow learners? gifted? handicapped?)? Dialogue between author(s) and learner? Cite specific examples. Comments?

G. *Treatment of Socially Significant Issues and* _____ × _____ = _____   _____
Problems
War and peace, militarism, law and justice, freedom, racism, agism, ethnocentricism, provincialism, urbanization, poverty, overpopulation, political alienation, energy and ecological problems, moral problems, sexism, apathy, etc.? Cite specific examples. Which of these issues and problems are included? How honestly are they treated? Are any conspicuously absent? Comments?

H. *Treatment of Minorities* _____ × _____ = _____   _____
Reflects pluralistic, multiethnic nature of our society, past and present? Accurate? Acknowledges legitimacy of variety of lifestyles? Presents critical issues? Present-day problems realistically presented? Criteria for presenting heroes? Moral stand on issues? Encourages positive self-image? Deals with controversy? Controversial issues dealt with in an honest, straight-forward manner? Cite specific examples. Which minorities are covered? How honestly are they covered? Are any conspicuously absent? Comments?

I. *Difficulty* _____ × _____ = _____   _____
Are major concepts presented and developed with a view toward maximizing their understanding? Would a student encumbered by reading disabilities be at a serious disadvantage? Cite specific examples. Readability? Cite formula(ae) used. Comments?

J. *Absence of Bias* _____ × _____ = _____   _____
By omission? By commission? Because of poor scholarship? Cite specific examples of biased and unbiased material. Comments?

K. *Overall Evaluation* _____ × _____ = _____   _____
I rate this student material as (encircle one):
               Excellent   Good   Fair   Poor
(Before writing any comments here, carefully review the preceding criteria, your weightings and ratings, and your written comments.)

II. TEACHER'S GUIDE

A. *Interrelated with Student Materials*   _____ × _____ = _____   _____
To what extent does the guide directly relate to specific sections of the student material? Does the guide focus on specific concepts and/or generalizations presented in the student material? Cite specific examples. *Comments?*

B. *Objectives*   _____ × _____ = _____   _____
Included? Behavioral? Attainable? Attainment can be evaluated? Cite specific examples of objectives presented. Comments?

C. *Sample Lessons*   _____ × _____ = _____   _____
Do lessons offer imaginative, viable, alternative strategies for teaching? Are lessons spelled out in specific terms? Cite specific examples from lessons. Comments?

D. *References*   _____ × _____ = _____   _____
Quality? Variety? Currency? Availability? If you used this book, would you attempt to locate and use these references? Comments?

E. *Evaluation*   _____ × _____ = _____   _____
Discussion questions? Observation? Check lists? Diaries and/or logs? Tests? Sociometric devices? Other evaluative strategies? How effective are existing evaluative strategies? Are any conspicuously absent? Cite specific examples. Comments?

F. *Overall Evaluation*   _____ × _____ = _____   _____
I rate this teacher's guide as (encircle one):

      Excellent   Good   Fair   Poor

(Before responding to this final section of the instrument, review the preceding criteria, your weightings and ratings, and your comments.)

---

4. Beware of the novelty effect of the new programs that are being used on a pilot basis. Initially, children may respond quite favorably to the newness or uniqueness of the program materials and instructional procedures, but as the novelty wears off, their enthusiasm may diminish. To minimize this phenomenon, pilot the programs over an extended period of time—ideally during the period from early January to the conclusion of the school year.

5. As the programs are being piloted, invite representatives of their publishers to consult with the teachers who are using their materials and to teach demonstration lessons in the experimental classes.

When the tryouts of the programs have ended, your committee should be prepared to present to the school administration those programs that they recommend for adoption in specific schools or throughout the school district. At this point approximately one year will have passed since the committee was convened. If the committee has functioned effectively and can defend its recommendations on the basis of its evaluations and classroom tryouts of program materials, it will have accomplished its intended purpose.

SUMMARY

There would be less need to create social studies programs for teachers if they had the resources, the time, and the inclination to do it themselves. But since this rarely happens, commercially produced basal social studies programs fulfill a vital need. There are three types of basal programs: (a) textbook-centered; (b) multimedia; and (c) combination textbook–multimedia. The textbook-centered program, by far the most widely used of the three, consists of a textbook and a few supplementary learning aids. The multimedia program is a series of self-contained kits containing a wide variety of multisensory learning aids. The combination textbook–multimedia program contains textbooks and a multimedia kit. These two components are generally far less comprehensive than corresponding components of a textbook-centered or a multimedia program.

Despite the imaginative, well-intentioned efforts of publishers to produce comprehensive, teachable programs, all programs have certain inherent limitations. None of them enable a teacher to truly individualize instruction, since they are developed with the "average" student in mind. Few respond to the unique needs of slow learners, poor readers, or culturally different pupils. Few deal directly with controversial topics that have immediate relevance for the lives of children. None of them provide for the needs of children who have been mainstreamed from special education classes into regular classrooms. These limitations suggest that no basal social studies program should ever be regarded as the total social studies curriculum for a school or school district. Accordingly, you will need to adjust your basal program to the unique needs, learning styles, and interests of your pupils, and to supplement the program as the need arises.

To what extent do basal social studies programs fit with our conception of the five lifelong roles introduced in the preceding chapter? Our analysis of representative programs demonstrates that all of the lifelong roles are covered in these programs, but with avocation receiving limited, often incidental coverage. On the other hand, of the ten organizing themes, seven receive extensive coverage, and three (consumerism, life cycle, and morality), receive incidental coverage.

The sheer number and variety of basal social studies programs make it exceedingly difficult for teachers to select appropriate programs for their pupils. But there are procedures of demonstrated effectiveness which can facilitate this process. These include establishing a social studies committee, putting the committee to work in evaluating basal programs, and piloting selected programs in classrooms. At the conclusion of this process—usually a year after it was initiated—the social studies committee should be capable of submitting to the administration of the school district informed, defensible recommendations regarding the purchase of basal social studies programs.

CROSS-REFERENCES TO TEACHING MODULES

This chapter suggested that several representative elementary social studies programs included topics that were consistent with our ten organizing themes (see p. 317). Among those teaching modules presented in Part 2 which can add a significant dimension to existing social studies programs are "Exploring Human Needs," and "Why We Need Rules."

Intercultural Relations: "Exploring Human Needs" (Part 2, p. 362). This teaching module, created for use in the upper grades (roughly 5 to 8 or 6 to 8), explores the concepts of culture, needs, and technology, and encourages pupils to explore the lifestyles of people different from themselves. Throughout the module, pupils are encouraged to keep an open mind to various forms of culturally patterned behavior and to view behavior within its geographical and cultural contexts. Geography and anthropology are the two major social sciences that are stressed in this module.

Our Legal System: "Why We Need Rules" (Part 2, p. 368). Teachers of the lower grades (approximately K–3) will find that this teaching module affords their pupils opportunities to learn through direct experience that their actions are governed by various informal and formal social controls that are made to protect their health and safety, and to help them to work and play harmoniously. Once children begin to comprehend these controls, their rationale, and their implications for human behavior, they should begin to see that rules and laws are not only desirable but necessary elements of society. Political science and sociology are the sources of content for this module.

BIBLIOGRAPHY

Capron, Barbara J. and Charles Mitsakos. *Successful Models and Materials for Elementary Social Studies.* Mimeographed paper. Boulder, Colo.: Social Science Education Consortium, 1977.
> A timely, practical publication which will help you to integrate new topics into your social studies curriculum.

Ellis, Arthur K. *Teaching and Learning Elementary Social Studies.* Boston: Allyn and Bacon, 1977.
> Chapter 14 of this text presents the author's curriculum analysis system and describes several exemplary social studies materials; pages 151–167 contain reprints of position papers on the *Man* controversy.

Joyce, William W. (ed.). "Man: A Course of Study." *Social Education* 38 (May 1974), pp. 441–457.
> This collection of articles by John G. Herlihy, V. Robert Agostino and George S. Morrison, Gene Vert and Donald MacFadyen, and Thomas D. Inkpen recounts the experiences of schools where *Man* was taught in their social studies curriculum.

Morrissett, Irving. "Curriculum Information Network." *Social Education:* "Third Report: Ratings of Social Studies Materials," 39 (February 1975), pp. 96–99; "Fifth Report: Ratings of 21 Social Studies Materials," 39 (November-December 1975), pp. 510–513; and "Sixth Report: Preferred Approaches to the Teaching of Social Studies," 41 (March 1977), pp. 206–209.
> A unique series of periodical surveys of teacher preferences and practices regarding

the social studies curriculum. These and subsequent C.I.N. reports will enable you
to keep informed about the ever-changing social studies curriculum.

Social Science Education Consortium. *Social Studies Curriculum Materials Data Book*.
Boulder, Colo.: S.S.E.C. Updated annually.

The only source of its kind in the United States, the *Data Book* contains over 450
analyses of social studies materials. This is an absolute "must" for all school districts.
Order from the S.S.E.C., 855 Broadway, Boulder, Colorado 80302.

Welton, David A. and John T. Mallan. *Children and Their World: Teaching Elementary
Social Studies*. Skokie, Ill.: Rand McNally, 1976.

Chapter 13 of this text contains a fine account of the do's and don'ts of selecting and
using instructional resources.

MODES OF INSTRUCTION

GOALS

1. Identify the strengths and weaknesses of each mode of instruction and determine how these can be most useful in the individual classroom.
2. Learn how to facilitate guided discussion in the classroom.
3. Learn to apply the findings of child development and psychology of learning to social studies instruction.
4. Gain greater insight into the research concerning modes of instruction and be challenged to read the studies identified and others concerned with similar issues.

In this chapter we will explore three modes of teaching and learning. The first mode has been labeled expository. This mode tends to focus on the teacher and it is characterized by little interaction between the teacher and the student. Its main purpose tends to be the transmission of knowledge.

We have called the second mode of teaching and learning guided discussion. Much more teacher-pupil interaction occurs and questioning strategies are of utmost consideration for those utilizing this method.

The final mode that we will explore has been labeled inquiry. Other authors have called it discovery learning, the research approach, or the problem method. All of these terms refer to the ways in which teachers involve students in active roles to process information using various sources, in an attempt to acquire facts, concepts, and generalizations.

The authors will attempt to describe these modes of teaching and learning and supply the reader with ideas for using these methods. Sections A, B, and C will provide numerous examples of how these forms of teaching and learning can be implemented into social studies lessons.

EXPOSITORY

A common form of teaching and learning in schools today could be labeled the expository or discourse mode. Expository teaching tends to focus on the teacher. The purpose of teaching as perceived by the individual who uses this form is the transmission of knowledge. Generally it follows the read–recite–lecture–test format. Usually a specific text serves as the major resource for the pupils. Films and other media are occasionally used for variety. The information that the students receive is in the form of a finished product. Examples of this type of learning include the history of a place, the geography of a country, or the cultural background of a people. The emphasis is on one-directional verbal communication.

Among the advocates of this approach has been Jacques Barzun. In 1945 he wrote *Teacher in America* in which he suggests that teaching is communication, imparting of knowledge, and its ideal aim is to have two minds share one thought. In his view, teaching, when done properly, can rise to the level of intellectual drama where emotion and intellect are fused into one. In his book, he describes the teacher as "performing dramatically" in lectures, discussions, and tutorials. He states that lectures alone are not sufficient to teach but that the increased interaction in tutorials and discussions is needed as a supplement.[1]

Another advocate of the expository method is David Ausubel. He has developed a model known as the "Advance Organizer" which is especially suited to written verbal material and used for conveying the discipline of knowledge.[2] For example, before students read descriptive studies of communities from different cultures, the lesson or unit task might be preceded by a major idea from anthropology such as "Every society, however primitive, has a certain set of beliefs, customs, and values." The hierarchical power of the major anthropological concepts is used to organize the pertinent material. These concepts can be used as organizers for the study of historical periods and places. The organizer can be a statement, descriptive paragraph, a question, a demonstration, or even a film.[3]

According to Ausubel each lesson should be preceded by the presentation to the learner of an advance organizer. The organizer is thus an idea that can provide the learner with the conceptual framework on which the student can "handle" new material.

The advance organizer model is summarized below.

ADVANCE ORGANIZER MODEL[4]

	Phase I	Phase II
Syntax:	Presentation of organizer.	Presentation of verbal material to be learned.
Principles of Reaction:	Teacher is seen as presenter. No consistent principles characterize the model.	
Social System:	High Structure. Teacher defines roles and controls norms. Learner roles carefully defined.	
Support System:	Development of organizer and system for presenting it is crucial. Material, however, must be organized so it *pertains* to the organizer.	

[1]Jacques Barzum, *Teacher in America* (Boston: Little, Brown, 1945), Ch. 3.
[2]David P. Ausubel, *The Psychology of Meaningful Verbal Learning* (New York: Grune & Stratton, 1963).
[3]Bruce Joyce and Marsha Weil, *Models of Teaching* (Englewood Cliffs, N.J.: Prentice-Hall, 1972), p. 174.
[4]Joyce and Weil, p. 179.

While Ausubel stresses the expository or didactic presentation, Joyce and Weil indicate that advance organizers are not purely expository in an interactive situation. Children often break into an interesting topic with their questions. Thus the material being organized takes the form of a dialogue.[5]

GUIDED DISCUSSION

The dialogue, which often includes more than two individuals, is referred to as guided discussion. This is a widely adopted form practiced in many elementary school classrooms. It is often used in situations in which teachers feel that students are not intellectually mature enough to handle the lecture or expository approach. Usually the teacher asks students to read the assignment and the class period is spent in discussing the written material. Too often it is a verbal "rehash." In addition the teacher will explain, clarify, and add factual details or additional information.

In a recent article entitled "Ten Discoveries about Basic Learning," it is reported that research indicates that the teacher who discusses the content of a section of the textbook before asking the student to read it gets better results educationally than the teacher who requires the reading before the class discussion. Research suggests it is essential that the teacher identify with the students the objectives and concepts of the lesson so that they can concentrate on the important things. It also gives the student an active part in the learning.[6]

A vital aspect of the guided discussion that needs careful consideration is the questioning strategy that is used. Since effective questioning and questioning strategies are integral parts of good teaching and learning, teachers need to plan questions carefully. We highly recommend that you get a copy of Hunkins' text entitled *Questioning Strategies and Techniques*.[7] It can serve as an outstanding guide for helping you formulate effective questioning strategies.

In planning your discussion sessions, you might refer to Bloom's taxonomy in which he establishes six levels, namely: knowledge, comprehension, application, analysis, synthesis, and evaluation.[8] While there is disagreement concerning the distinguishing characteristics among the levels in actuality, perhaps these levels can be helpful for centering or focusing the discussion and for expanding it.

Robert F. Biehler in his text *Psychology Applied to Teaching* describes Bloom's taxonomy by identifying a question for each descriptive level. The following examples may serve as guides:

[5]Joyce and Weil, p. 175.

[6]Raymond English, "Ten Discoveries about Basic Learning," *Social Education*, Vol. 41, No. 2 (February 1977), p. 106.

[7]Francis P. Hunkins, *Questioning Strategies and Techniques* (Boston: Allyn and Bacon, 1972).

[8]Benjamin S. Bloom and David R. Krathwohl, *Taxonomy of Educational Objectives: Classification of Educational Goals; Handbook I, Cognitive Domain* (New York: McKay, 1956).

> 1. Knowledge: Can students recall information?
> 2. Comprehension: Can students explain ideas?
> 3. Application: Can students use ideas?
> 4. Analysis: Do students see relationships?
> 5. Synthesis: Can students combine ideas?
> 6. Evaluation: Can students make judgments?[9]

As the teacher, you need to plan ahead to make sure you have formulated questions that stretch the mind and go beyond knowledge level. If the students have been studying consumerism, for example, it is perfectly legitimate to begin with such questions as "What is consumerism?" At this point, the teacher's role is to seek information. Usually there's a right or a wrong answer. From recall level, the teacher can move to explaining or comprehension. An example would be "Why is it important to do comparative shopping when you need to buy cereal?" From explaining ideas the discussion can move to using ideas. The teacher might ask, "From your observations and analysis yesterday of cereals in the large supermarket, do you think the same pattern can be seen at the neighborhood store? Why? Why not?" After expanding that consideration, the discussion moves to such questions as: "Do you think the same pattern in prices will exist for soups within the large supermarket?" "Between the supermarket and neighborhood store?" The level of discussion can be further expanded and the mind "stretched" if the teacher continues to encourage divergence and asks questions that combine ideas. "Can you think of what could be done to abolish price discrepancies between stores?" Finally, students can begin to evaluate their findings and begin to make some judgments. An evaluation question might be "How do you feel about Consumer Protection?"

Another three-stage classification that might be useful in formulating questions includes literal understanding, interpretive thinking, and evaluative/creative thinking. The chart on the following page might be helpful as you begin to plan a discussion.

These categories are intended to serve as examples to assist you in analyzing and developing your own system(s). We would suggest that if you find yourself asking lots of low-level convergent questions or asking only literal questions, for example, that you write out your questions for a few sessions or invite a student teacher, principal, or another adult to analyze your questions according to a predetermined hierarchy.

Hilda Taba pointed out in her book, *Teachers' Handbook for Elementary Social Studies*, that teachers and students rarely give much thought to the questions they pose or the sequence of the questions. While she did not identify cognitive stages she ranked them as, "What?" "Why?" and "What does this mean?" These questions were tied into three cognitive tasks: Cognitive Task I:

---

[9]Robert F. Biehler, *Psychology Applied to Teaching*, 2d ed. Copyright © 1974 by Houghton Mifflin Company, p. 382.

LEVELS OF QUESTIONS TO DEVELOP

Literal—Rote, recall, or recognition
    Key words used:
           What. . .
           How many. . .
           Did. . .
           Is. . .
           Can you recall. . .
           Can you name. . .
           Did you recognize. . .
           What did you observe. . .
Interpretive—Analysis or interaction of given or remembered data
    Key words used:
           Why. . .
           Would you. . .
           Explain. . .
           Relate. . .
           Compare. . .
           Perceive. . .
Evaluative/Creative—Deal with matters of judgment, attitude, and value
    Key words used:
           Infer. . .
           Originate. . .
           Hypothesize. . .
           Predict. . .
           What ways might. . .
           Do you agree. . .
           In your opinion. . .
           Judge. . .
           Think. . .
           Order. . .
           What ways could. . .
           What ways can. . .
           What if. . .
           How did you feel when. . .
           Do you regard. . .

Concept Formation; Cognitive Task II: Interpretation of Data; and Cognitive Task III: Application of Principles.[10]

    These three cognitive tasks make up the process of inductive thinking as Taba described it. Each task represents a stage in the inductive process. The first task (concept formation) involves: (a) identifying and enumerating the items of data

---

[10]Hilda Taba, *Teachers' Handbook for Elementary Social Studies* (Reading, Mass.: Addison-Wesley, 1967), p. 109.

which are relevant to the problem; (b) grouping those items according to some basis of similarity; and (c) developing categories and labels for the groups.[11]

An example of this strategy or task can be drawn from the Taba Curriculum. One second grade unit attempts to develop the idea that the supermarket needs a place, equipment, goods, and services.[12] As a means of opening the unit, the children are faced with the hypothetical situation of Mr. Smith wanting to open a supermarket. "What will he need?" The student responses are all recorded. After the list has been completed, the students will be asked, "Which items appear to go together?" The purpose of this task or strategy is to induce students to expand the conceptual system and to enable them to process information.[13]

The second task deals with interpreting, inferring, and generalizing. The three main points are: (a) differentiating among the characteristics of the data; (b) explaining items that have been identified; and (c) making inferences. If the students were able to label the lists "goods" and "services" they will then begin to differentiate between them and arrive at some reasons for their responses. Students will begin to go beyond what is given, or make some inferences. They might infer, for example, that the stock boy needs goods in order to keep his job or that the supermarket manager supplies goods and services to the people in the community.[14]

The third cognitive task is concerned with the application of principles to explain new phenomena, or predicting consequences from conditions which have been established.[15] If, for example, in Phase II, the students learned that the supermarket provides both goods and services the students might predict that the stock boy would get fired if he stopped putting goods on the shelves or that if the grocery were to run out of goods, he also would not be able to provide services.

Taba's three cognitive tasks in the inductive model are presented below:

CONCEPT FORMATION[16]

Overt Activity	Covert Mental Operations	Eliciting Questions
1. Enumeration and listening	Differentiation	What did you see? Hear? Note?
2. Grouping	Identifying common properties, abstracting	What belongs together? On what criterion?
3. Labeling, categorizing	Determining the hierarchical order of items, super- and subordination	How would you call these groups? What belongs to what?

[11]Joyce and Weil, pp. 124-125.
[12]Taba, p. 52.
[13]Taba, p. 92.
[14]Taba, p. 101.
[15]Taba, p. 109.
[16]Taba, p. 92.

INTERPRETATION OF DATA[17]

Overt Activity	Covert Mental Operations	Eliciting Questions
1. Identifying points	Differentiating	What did you notice? See? Find?
2. Explaining items of identified information	Relating points to each other Determining cause and effect relationships	Why did so and so happen?
3. Making inferences	Going beyond what is given Finding implications, extrapolating	What does this mean? What picture does it create in your mind? What would you conclude?

APPLICATION OF PRINCIPLES[18]

Overt Activities	Covert Mental Operations	Eliciting Questions
1. Predicting consequences, explaining unfamiliar phenomena, hypothesizing	Analyzing the nature of the problem or situation, retrieving relevant knowledge	What would happen if?
2. Explaining, and/or supporting the predictions and hypotheses	Determining the causal links leading to prediction or hypothesis	Why do you think this would happen?
3. Verifying the prediction	Using logical principles or factual knowledge to determine necessary and sufficient conditions	What would it take for it to be generally true or probably true?

The sequence of activities forms the syntax of the teaching procedures which is accompanied by underlying mental processes which Taba referred to as covert mental operations. The teacher's activity is one of moving the students from one phase to another by eliciting questions. Using her strategy, the teacher would ask questions at each task level, starting with "What?" and ending with "What does this mean?" Hunkins indicates that the "what" questions might be loosely tied to the knowledge and comprehension levels of Bloom, the "why" questions to application and analysis and the "what does it mean?" questions to synthesis and analysis. Of course, one major difference is that Taba uses cognitive tasks and three questions at each level.[19]

[17]Taba, p. 101.
[18]Taba, p. 109.
[19]Hunkins, p. 94.

Taba further advocated that the questioning at a particular level be distributed to as many students as possible before moving to the next higher stage. She felt that the premature raising of the thought to a next higher level caused a decrease in social participation and a degeneration of total class thought to solely specific knowledge.[20] She felt that even the slowest students should be involved if they are not to be lost in the interaction. Taba believed that children need the opportunity to participate at one particular plateau if they are to effectively respond to higher level questions. She also stated that premature raising of the thought level caused student participation to decline and total class thought to degenerate to specifics.[21]

Hunkins believes that the decision concerning who asks the questions should vary with the level. In the early grades, in a guided discussion, the teacher usually asks most of the questions. As the students progress through the grades, they will be expected to assume greater questioning roles. Students need to be aware that the question can be used to assist them in seeking and relating information. They also need to learn that certain types of questions provide specific kinds of information and that there is a multiplicity of questioning strategies.[22]

As an elementary teacher it behooves you to keep abreast of what research data about questioning is available and how you can use it to reflect on your teaching. Sometimes, after careful investigation, you may wish to make some changes as a result of it. A study by Wayne Herman states that questions used are 80 to 90 percent recall.[23] Parsons and Shaftel did a study involving intermediate teachers. The results of their study indicated that 43 percent of the teacher-posed questions were rhetorical; 45 percent of the questions were information recall; 9 percent were found to be leading questions, containing the answer or suggesting what the answer might be; and only 3 percent were classified as probing questions.[24]

INQUIRY

A third teaching mode is inquiry. As the questioning strategies used and the responses provided become more student-centered and less teacher-directed we find the teacher's role shifting. The teacher is faced with less predictable responses. The shift moves from product to process. The Educational Research Council of America, after fifteen years of research and development, found it very difficult to persuade teachers to change to a discussive–problem-solving method. They reported one way to break old patterns was to put the inquiry problems into

[20]Taba, pp. 123-125.
[21]Taba, pp. 125-126.
[22]Hunkins, p. 133.
[23]Wayne L. Herman, Jr., ed., *Current Research in Elementary Social Studies* (New York: Macmillian, 1969), p. 170.
[24]Theodore W. Parsons and Fannie R. Shaftel, "Thinking and Inquiry: Some Critical Issues," in *Effective Thinking in the Social Studies*, Jean Fair and Fannie R. Shaftel, eds. (Washington, D.C.: National Council for Social Studies, 1967), p. 125.

the pupil textbook pages.[25] This weakened the possibility of reserving the questions until the end of the chapter, inevitably producing the phenomenon of recall instead of inquiry.

Goldmark defines inquiry as a reflexive, patterned search, which takes questions from the substantive level, to the criteria level, to the value and assumption level, where new assumptions can be posed and new alternatives constructed.[26] She goes on to say that inquiry is a commitment to a way of behaving—to doubting, to questioning. The inquiry method is a logical structure. It is built outside the disciplines and not dependent on them except as a subject matter to which the discipline is applied.[27]

Ellis defines inquiry as a method of teaching/learning based on the premise that students should discover principles of human behavior through their own investigations. The process of how and what one learns is identified as being as important as the knowledge or product an individual acquires.[28] Through this process an individual's schema or concepts are expanded. This process is two-fold in nature. It includes the interpreting of data in terms of existing or known concepts and modifying or changing existing concepts to correspond with the information. Piaget refers to these processes as assimilation and accommodation. He firmly believes that these two functions are necessary for conceptual growth to occur.[29] It is crucial that we provide students with inquiry experiences so that they may be more autonomous and productive in their learning.

Piaget has spent a lifetime observing children. Throughout his work, he has assumed that the process of learning is more important than the product. He has also assumed that every child is unique, and goes through a series of stages of intellectual development. Piaget has come to define intelligence as one's ability to adapt to his environment. He proposes that intelligent, adaptive thinking and action develop in a sequence of stages, and that while all children go through the same stages, the age at which they do so varies, depending upon the native endowment of the child and upon the quality of physical and social experiences and environment in which the child is reared.

According to Piaget, the first stage of development of intelligence occurs between birth and two years of age. This is called the sensory-motor period. It is concerned with those abilities necessary to construct and reconstruct objects.

The second stage of development (two to seven years old) Piaget labels as preoperational, and has to do with those abilities needed for representing things. Early in this stage the child tends to identify words and symbols with the objects they are intended to represent. He is upset if someone destroys an object that he has designated to represent something else. He believes names are as much a part of objects as their color and form. By the time he is nearing this stage of

[25]English, p. 107.

[26]Bernice Goldmark, *Social Studies: A Method of Inquiry* (Belmont, Calif.: Wadsworth, 1968), p. 7.

[27]Goldmark, p. 8.

[28]Arthur K. Ellis, *Teaching and Learning Elementary Social Studies* (Boston: Allyn and Bacon, 1977), p. 74.

[29]J. J. Flavell, *The Developmental Psychology of Jean Piaget* (New York: Van Nostrand, 1963).

What are the advantages and disadvantages of a large group discussion? How does inquiry contribute to this instructional mode?

development he can clearly distinguish between words and symbols and what they represent. The child realizes that words are names arbitrarily designated. This discovery often leads to name calling so prevalent in the early school years.

Usually between seven and eleven the child reaches the next stage, called concrete operations. At this stage the child is able to "do in his head" what he would have had to accomplish through real action before. Many concrete experiences and hands-on activities are useful. At this stage children are able to deal with the relationships among classes of things and by the end of this stage they are adept at doing thought problems and combining/dividing class concepts.

Usually between ages twelve and fifteen the child reaches the last stage, which is known as formal operations. It is during this period that children think about their thoughts, construct ideas, and reason realistically about the future.[30]

While many critics argue that Piaget utilizes casual methodology and lacks scientific rigor, he has derived original ideas about children's thinking. His work seems to have real impact on teachers who have been exposed to his philosophy and they tend never again to see children in quite the same way as they had before.

Piaget believes that a principal goal in education is to create human beings who are capable of doing new things, not simply repeating what other generations have done. A second goal of education is to form minds which can be critical, can verify, and not accept everything that is offered.

[30]Case, Robbie, "Piaget's Theory of Child Development and Its Implications," *Phi Delta Kappan*, 55: 1 (September 1973), pp. 20–23.

Perhaps one of the first implications for social studies that emerges provides those who believe in readiness with some additional ammunition for their arguments. The stages of intellectual development have been discovered across a variety of tasks. They have always emerged in a definite order. The consolidation of activity and knowledge at one stage is clearly a prerequisite to activity and knowledge at the next stage. In addition, the child must restructure his world at each stage before moving on to the next. Thus a teacher cannot lead the child too much. The school's responsibility, then, is to maximize readiness-related experiences; when the child appears to be ready the teacher can introduce him to those activities which will provide the learning.

A second implication is the need for discovery learning experiences for children. If a teacher supports Piaget's theory, he or she obviously will not spend lots of time talking at young children and having them recite memorized material. It behooves the teacher to set tasks for children in which the goal is to demonstrate or apply and thus bring about a constructive mental activity. The Piagetian approach or goal would be for the child to rediscover what one has just told him and to make it a part of his life.[31]

Irving Sigel has extrapolated the propositions that he feels are most relevant to an educational strategy developed from Piaget's theory. These are as follows: (a) intellectual development is dependent on confrontations with the social as well as the physical environment; (b) intellectual development proceeds by orderly invariable sequences (stages) with transitions from stage to stage; (c) acquisition of new knowledge comes about through appropriate assimilations and accommodations resulting in equilibrated cognitive structure; (d) language is a facilitator varying in significance as a function of the developmental level of the child.[32]

In the first proposition the focus appears to be on the surroundings for learning. As the child has repeated experiences with certain objects, he begins to believe they are lasting. This then tends to change his conception of the world. Social experience is the second factor to consider. This occurs through interaction with other people and facilitates the child's language development. Piaget describes the child as moving from egocentric and individualized ways of thinking to more socially centered ways of thinking. The opportunity to exchange viewpoints and share personal experiences produces the cognitive conflict that is fundamental to intellectual development.[33]

The next consideration for the teaching strategy involves the roles of the teacher and the subject matter. Sigel says that a major thrust of a teaching strategy is to confront the child with the illogical nature of his point of view. The reason for confrontation is a necessary and sufficient requirement for cognitive growth. The child strives to reconcile the discrepancies.[34] Often this process is referred to as dissonance. The teacher must make sure that the degree of dissonance is not so

[31]Case, pp. 23–26.
[32]Irving E. Sigel, "The Piagetian System and the World of Education," David Elkind and John Flavell, eds., *Studies in Cognitive Development* (New York: Oxford University Press, 1969), p. 472.
[33]Joyce and Weil, p. 185.
[34]Sigel, p. 473.

great as to create discouragement or that the confrontation is beyond the child's stage of development.

The educational strategies developed from Piaget's theory will be reflected in the teaching modules presented in Sections A, B, and C in Part 2. Intelligence as successful adaptation will be illustrated with provisions made for creative thinking, exploratory discovery and provisions for moving from figurative to operational objectives and learning experiences. Piaget's theory of intellectual development will be handled through the use of concrete objects, pictures, simulations, and real experiences. Equilibration will be treated by providing for questioning experiences rather than giving answers, strategies for grappling with likenesses and differences, and a multiplicity of opportunities to relate the content to the child's personal experience. Socialization will be reflected by opportunities for pupils to share experiences, ideas, and reactions, as well as opportunities for them to engage in cognitive and personal problem solving. Maturation will be mirrored in the authors' attempts to fit the learning tasks to appropriate intellectual levels.

While Piaget used casual methodology to facilitate inquiry, numerous books have been written on the subject. In one of the earliest texts on inquiry published in 1968 the authors point out that there are six phases in the cognitive aspects of inquiry. Many teachers and social scientists would agree that these steps will vary in the order presented. The phases identified by Massialas, Sugrue, Sweeney, and Zevin are as follows:

1. Orientation—the child is confronted with a problem. The child needs stimulation in order to want to continue to analyze the problem and perhaps try to resolve it.
2. Hypotheses—after carefully analyzing the problem in question and securing data from the materials that are directly relevant to it, an explanatory idea or hunch is expressed, often linking two sets of events or phenomena.
3. Definition—this can take place during any phase of the inquiry process; clarification of terms takes place.
4. Exploration—next logical, or sometimes illogical, implications are explored. New ways of finding more information to test main hypotheses are encouraged.
5. Evidencing—collection of data occurs; evidence can confirm, change, or refute the hypothesis, or can come from any source as long as it is relevant to the problem.
6. Generalizing—if the hypothesis passes the empirical and logical tests of evidencing then it becomes a generalization; all possible exceptions must be accounted for.[35]

In discussing inquiry, the underlying theme that seems to emerge is *thinking*. Thinking is a high-level skill and one of the primary goals of social studies—that is, to help children think effectively. Thinking is a process in which the individual is engaged in the activity of making a series of symbolic responses. In this process, the individual is manipulating symbols which are representations of discrete or combined phenomena in his repertoire of experience. The amount of psychic energy involved is closely related to the symbolic manipulations which an individual is making. The classroom situation must be structured so that the

[35]Byron G. Massialas, Mary Sugrue, Jo Sweeney, and Jack Zevin, *Elementary Social Studies Through Inquiry* (New York: McGraw Hill, Webster Division, 1968).

children are engaged in the activity of manipulating symbols into increasingly complex patterns of meaning or ideas.[36]

Suchman suggests that one of the conditions of inquiry is access to varied experiences that permit the child to "mess around, explore, and encounter his environment." This facilitates learning about others as well as self. Secondly, the child has to be free to convert experience into meaning to formulate ideas, to engage in the process of building knowledge, to formulate new ideas, and perhaps, someday, theories.[37]

The teacher can protect the child so that the natural learning–thinking processes can function. The teacher is there to intervene and to help sharpen the concepts, often referred to as tools or content vehicles. Language and ideas can be used to further this process. Through these experiences, the teacher can be a vital force in helping the child strengthen his process of inquiry and thinking.

Inquiry lessons must be carefully planned. The teacher must plan problem situations that will initiate pupil interest, curiosity, and situations that will actively involve children in the investigations. Because the teacher will serve as a facilitator, she needs to be familiar with a wide variety of learning activities, and investigations which the children may have to use or choose from to answer questions and solve problems. In addition to learning materials and content to be learned, the teacher must be familiar with the specific process skills that will be used or developed by the children as they seek answers to their questions. The teacher will need to plan additional activities and alternatives for the very slow or very fast children. There must be a way to evaluate the results of the investigation and the learning that is to take place.

On page 70 is an example of a composite data chart containing the major objectives of a unit. The chart enables the teacher to diagnose individual strengths and weaknesses as well as group strengths and/or weaknesses. Many more ideas for evaluation will be provided in the evaluation chapter and in the evaluation section of each teaching module.

Inquiry tends to follow a general pattern. Usually inquiry begins with information followed by a series of questions. Through a discussion a problem is identified. After the problem has been identified more questions are asked or a series of "educated guesses" or hypotheses are derived. Data are gleaned from a variety of sources such as resource people, textbooks, supplemental books, films, filmstrips, experiences, newspapers, to name a few.

As we have stated numerous times, inquiry teaching and learning is very process- or skill-oriented. Processes or skills included are reading, observing, describing, measuring, comparing, contrasting, analyzing, evaluating. For more information about skills in the social studies we refer you to Chapter 5.

Another characteristic of teaching and learning through inquiry is that it is question-oriented. As the teacher sets the stage for an inquiry lesson, she needs to

[36]Jean Fair and Fannie R. Shaftel, eds. *Effective Thinking in the Classroom* (Washington, D.C.: Thirty-Seventh Yearbook of the National Council for Social Studies, 1967) pp. 123–166.
[37]Richard Suchman, "Looking at Back to the Basics," *Annual Newsletter of the ERIC Clearinghouse for Social Studies/Social Science* (January 1977), pp. 3-5.

COMPOSITE DATA CHART[38]

	Attacks Problem in Rational Manner			Organizes Data			Gathers Information				Geographic Principles			
Students' Names	Sets up hypotheses	Tests hypotheses against data	Identifies question for study	Differentiates data	Categorizes data	Generalizes data	Studies pictures	Uses maps/globes	Listens to stories	Handles artifacts	Knows cardinal directions	Identifies land/water forms	Uses map symbols to represent reality	Compares directions to known distances

Key: ☐ No evidence
         ◩ Some evidence
         ⊠ Good evidence

carefully plan the questioning strategies to be used throughout the series of lessons. Sample questions often posed are: Why? What? How? How much? What will happen if? How do we know? Can we make that assumption? Are we justified in drawing this conclusion?

The teacher should also keep in mind that she is the director or facilitator in learning. Often the teacher is referred to as a guide. The teacher should guard against being a purveyor or dispensor of knowledge. A sensitive, observant teacher will be aware of individual needs and will be able to supply a probing question, a pat on the shoulder, or a new learning material when a child bogs down. It is important that the child does not know the answers to the questions in advance. To put it another way, not all things are worth inquiring about, and if the

[38]Chart adapted from a checklist by Arthur K. Ellis, *Teaching and Learning Elementary Social Studies* (Boston: Allyn and Bacon, 1977), p. 89.

child knows the answer, pose a new and challenging problem. Textbooks can be used to verify results or to provide additional data.

Although research to date has not shown conclusively that teaching and learning by inquiry leads to greater understanding of social studies concepts and conceptual schemes, it does point to several benefits and advantages for using this technique.

Inquiry teaching is a type of instruction that stresses process and while content is subject to change the child who learns the processes or skills can retain and reuse the skills with the content most relevant for the time.

In the inquiry mode of instruction the child becomes a participant instead of being an observer or spectator. As the child involves himself he develops a sense of accomplishment and satisfaction which in turn tends to develop self-confidence, a vital part of the self-concept.

Learning by inquiry tends to teach children how to learn. It is highly action-oriented, activity-centered, and it tends to help youngsters feel comfortable with their skills or tools. Evidence tends to suggest that inquiry is one of the best teaching and learning models for promoting scientific attitudes, appreciations, and interests.[39]

Inquiry procedures tend to be in agreement with what you read earlier about Piaget and his theories about how children learn. Inquiry tends to be highly activity-oriented and this is in keeping with his ideas about direct physical experiences which are essential to learning concepts. Inquiry teaching and learning is question-centered and Piaget's work indicates that much can be learned about how children think by asking detailed questions and that such questions often have potentially creative aspects which can be used effectively in science or social studies.[40]

Inquiry activities also involve sensory experiences and Piaget believes that children's ability to deal with the broad concepts of space, time, matter and causality depend on the kind of learning that develops from direct sensory experiences.

Finally inquiry learning benefits children by providing them with skills to learn how to learn, by providing intrinsic rewards, by facilitating the use of the techniques of learning in new, often real life situations, and by aiding children in retaining information, primarily because they have personally been involved in learning and the processing of the information.

Numerous writers and researchers have developed models of inquiry. We have tested many of these with our graduate and undergraduate students. The most popular, understandable, and useful source we have found is the work of John Lee in *Teaching Social Studies in the Elementary School*.[41] Lee suggests that while the inductive process generally works better than the deductive process in elementary school, every good thinker shifts from one to the other.

[39]Edward Victor, "The Inquiry Approach to Teaching and Learning: A Primer for Teachers," *Science and Children* (Washington, D.C.: National Science Teachers Association, 1974), p. 24.
[40]Barry J. Wadsworth, *Piaget's Theory of Cognitive Development* (New York: McKay, 1975).
[41]John Lee, *Teaching Social Studies in the Elementary School* (New York: Free Press, 1974).

How can the teacher facilitate inquiry in the situation depicted in this picture?

In his book he included five models. In the first model, a question is raised and from that question a tentative answer or hypothesis is developed. Then evidence must be collected and tested against the tentative answer. When the inquirer is satisfied with the evidence, a tentative conclusion is drawn.

In the second model, a question is raised, evidence is gathered, and a proposition is inferred. The next step provides for the inquirer's skill in checking the original question against the proposition. Finally, the proposition, often referred to as a rule, is tested against new evidence.

The third model, which is largely deductive, originates with a question. Before the inquirer goes any further, he states the known rule, and from that rule an answer is inferred. The final steps provide for the inquirer to check out the accuracy of the answer by seeking additional evidence. Thus adequate evidence provides confirmation.

Lee's fourth model has been referred to as the historian's model, in that it begins with a question, data is gathered and interpreted, and finally the findings are presented.

The fifth and final model developed by Lee has been labeled the problem-solving model. Initially a question is raised. Some degree of cognitive dissonance occurs. A problem is identified. From the initial problem, hypotheses are drawn. Evidence is gathered, verified, analyzed, and interpreted. Finally, a tentative conclusion is reached and applied to the situation.[42]

Perhaps you will find one or more of these models helpful as you use the teaching modules we have provided or as you develop new ones. Remember the products of inquiry involve experiences and they involve the interaction of the learner with other learners and with social studies content. Knowledge plus inquiry skill are necessary to gather data, analyze information, and draw tentative conclusions. Then alternatives and consequences can be assessed at which time an intelligent decision can be made.

Research has shown that while even young children can use problem-solving techniques, they need to be taught.[43] Studies by Hazlitt, Heidbreder, and Isaacs, demonstrated that three-year-old children could use problem-solving techniques, when the problems were concrete, personal, and concerned with immediate situations.[44]

A wide variety of variables have been identified as having an effect on elementary children's ability to solve problems. Sieber found that children who possess a high tolerance for uncertainty are better at recognizing problems, formulating hypotheses, and gathering information.[45] Goor found that highly creative children are more adept at gathering information, using hypotheses, and applying evaluation criteria.[46] In still another study Anderson found that 70 percent of the time preschool children solved problems by insight,[47] while Klausmeier found that there is consistently better performance as children advance in age and development.[48]

While it is no doubt obvious to you by now that we believe social studies must retain a strong arm of skill/process in our ever-changing world, we do not want to close this section without warning you that there are some problems connected with this mode of teaching/learning. There is, for example, a tendency on the part of teachers to mislead children about the actual time involved in inquiry teaching. Some teachers tend to "push" inquiry at the expense of other modes of teaching and learning. Pupil reading, teacher explanation, films, television programs, and resource people are other techniques that should be included. The teacher needs to think through rather carefully which mode of instruction is most appropriate to meet a specific goal. Some educators and psychologists

---

[42]Lee, pp. 65-70.

[43]Rosemary McCartin, "The Cognitive and Affective Learning of Children," in *Focus on Geography*, Phillip Bacon, ed. (Washington, D.C.: National Council for Social Studies, 1970), p. 242.

[44]Richard J. Jantz, "Social Studies," in *Curriculum for the Preschool-Primary Child: A Review of the Research*, Carol Seefelt, ed. (Columbus, Ohio: Merrill, 1976), p. 90.

[45]McCartin, p. 243.

[46]Amos Goor, "Problem Solving Processes of Creative and Non-Creative Students," *Dissertation Abstracts* Vol. 35, 1974, p. 3517-A.

[47]Jantz, pp. 90-91.

[48]Herbert J. Klausmeier, *Learning and Human Abilities*, 4th ed. (New York: Harper & Row, 1975), p. 308.

caution that learning by inquiry is very difficult for slow learners because children of low IQ or motivation find it hard to persist in tasks that are not immediately fruitful.

Klausmeier found that children with high IQs tend to be more successful and efficient problem solvers because they are used to a more logical approach involving more analysis and verification and they tend to behave in a less random fashion.[49] Kagan found that the impulsive child involved in problem solving who is often less successful, tended to withdraw from school tasks and to develop feelings of inadequacy. The reverse was true of the child that was identified as reflective and successful. He concluded that problem solving seemed most appropriate for highly motivated children aged nine or older.[50] Keep in mind, however, that unstructured inquiry experiences that allow the child to search, experience, and explore are appropriate and meaningful for even the very young child.

Finally, you as the teacher must know your children well, have your goals clearly in mind and then assess your skill and competency in inquiry teaching.

If you can answer most of the following questions affirmatively, the chances are you have discovered this powerful tool. You might also use this instrument to assess some of your weaknesses in order to begin to correct them.

AM I AN INQUIRY TEACHER?[51]

	Regularly	Frequently	Sometimes	Seldom
As Planner				
I focus on lessons involving exploration of significant ideas, concepts, or problem areas that can be investigated at many levels of sophistication	————	————	————	————
I prepare for a broad range of alternative ideas and values which the students may raise related to a central topic	————	————	————	————
I select materials and learning experiences to stimulate student curiosity and support student investigation	————	————	————	————
I make available a wide variety of resources and materials for student use	————	————	————	————
Skill-building exercises are tied directly to ongoing learnings where they can be utilized and applied	————	————	————	————

[49]Klausmeier, p. 303.
[50]Jerome Kagan, "Personality and the Learning Process," *Daedalus*, Vol. 94 (Summer 1965), p. 561.
[51]Mary Sugrue and Jo A. Sweeney, "Check Your Inquiry-Teaching Technique," *Today's Education: NEA Journal*, Vol. 50, No. 5 (May 1969), p. 44. Used by permission of the N.E.A.

As Introducer

My introductory lessons present some problem, question, contradiction, or unknown element that will maximize student thinking ...

My aim is for students to react freely to the introductory stimulus with little direction from me ....

I encourage many different responses to a given introductory stimulus and am prepared to deal with alternative patterns of exploration

As Questioner and Inquiry Sustainer

The students talk more than I do ....

Students are free to discuss and interchange their ideas ....

When I talk, I "question," not "tell" .....

I consciously use the ideas students have raised and base my statements and questions on their ideas ....

I redirect student questions in such a way that students are encouraged to arrive at their own answers ....

My questions are intended to lead the pupils to explore, explain, support, and evaluate their ideas ....

As Value Investigator

I encourage the students to explore the implications of holding alternative value and policy positions ....

I make the students aware of personal and social bases for diversity in attitudes, values, policies ....

I encourage the students to arrive at value and policy positions of their own that they understand and can defend ....

SUMMARY

In this chapter we have discussed three basic modes of teaching and learning. The expository method tends to focus on the teacher and its main purpose is the transmission of knowledge. Since there is little interaction between the teacher and the students, it is generally felt that this method is least appropriate for early elementary children. Children at this level are believed to need concrete experiences and "hands on" materials to explore and to confront their environment.

A more widely adapted form of teaching and learning practiced in elementary classrooms is guided discussion. It is often used in situations in which the teachers feel the students are not intellectually mature enough to handle the lecture or the expository approach. Questioning strategies need the teacher's utmost consideration if he or she is to have a successful discussion or is to "stretch the minds" of the students. We mentioned Bloom's taxonomy and Hilda Taba's cognitive tasks as possible starters for developing expertise in the guided discussion.

As the questioning strategies used and the responses provided become more student-centered and less teacher-directed, we find the roles shifting and the concern becoming heavily process-oriented. We have referred to this method as inquiry. The process is felt to be as important as the knowledge the student acquires. Using this method, the child is able to convert experience into meaning and thus formulate new ideas. We believe that inquiry should be highly activity-oriented and begin with the child's own bank of experiences. Through inquiry children can personalize the learning and as they mature gradually develop responsibility for their own learning.

We have attempted to present ideas and models for using these modes of teaching and learning. As a teacher, it is your right and responsibility to assess your students and their needs, determine your curricular objectives, and make the final decision as to what teaching mode is most appropriate for a given situation.

CROSS REFERENCES TO TEACHING MODULES

In this chapter we identified three modes of instruction: expository, guided discussion, and inquiry. All of the teaching modules in Part 2 use one or more of these modes. Four modules which provide unusual opportunities for employing these modes are "Children Become Advertising Executives," "Using Leisure Time Constructively," "All of Us Are Unique Individuals," and "Exploring Human Needs."

Consumerism: "Children Become Advertising Executives" (Part 2, pp. 318–324). This module is one example that utilizes the expository method. After the students have planned, constructed, and administered a questionnaire to parents or other interested adults in an attempt to gather information about the types of advertising that influence them, it is suggested that the teacher present a mini-lecture (accompanied by illustrations) to show various techniques used in advertising. This mini-lecture is intended to provide students with a data base so that they will be able to find examples of each technique from the media.

Avocation: "Using Leisure Time Constructively" (Part 2, pp. 289–295). Designed for middle grades, this teaching module is one of several that uses questioning techniques. We suggest that with pictures or actual objects the students categorize and discuss hobbies according to doing things, collecting things, and making things.

Personal Efficacy: "All of Us Are Unique Individuals" (Part 2, pp. 304–309). Designed for lower elementary grades, this module is one example that uses lots of discussion. As a means of introducing the module it is suggested that with a cartoon display (or puppets) the following questions be discussed with the class:

1. What can you tell me about the pictures?
2. Do you see anything funny about the pictures?
3. Is there anything different about the cartoon characters?

4. Are the cartoon pictures similar in any way?
5. Which is more important, the way a person looks or the way a person acts? Why?
6. In what ways are we alike?
7. In what ways are we different?

Intercultural Relations: "Exploring Human Needs" (Part 2, pp. 363–367). Designed for upper grades, this teaching module is an excellent example of the inquiry method. We suggest that to introduce the module, the teacher show a film on the culture to be studied. The film will be shown silently in an attempt to have students sharpen their observational skills. The students are asked to list what they see and attempt to decide whether or not their observations could be found where they live. Later students are guided to generate hypotheses to be tested. Individual and group research will be stressed. Multimedia should be available so all students will meet some level of success.

BIBLIOGRAPHY

Ellis, Arthur K. *Teaching and Learning Elementary Social Studies.* Boston: Allyn and Bacon, 1977.

> The book is a valuable/practical source to teachers because the author has integrated the real world dimensions of social studies with an emerging theoretical perspective based on such precepts as active learner involvement, models of the social sciences, strategies for higher level thinking and inquiry and problem-solving techniques.

Hunkins, Francis P. *Questioning Strategies and Techniques.* Boston: Allyn and Bacon, 1972.

> This volume is a valuable resource in assisting teachers to formulate creative questioning strategies. The discovery curriculum requires questioning strategies so that children may both learn and use concepts. The author recommends the use of heuristic questions and cognitive maps in the tradition of Taba. Using the Bloom classification (*Taxonomy of Educational Objectives*) the author reminds us that the higher levels subsume the lower levels, and analysis and synthesis questions are crucial. Highly recommended.

Joyce, Bruce and Marsha Weil. *Models of Teaching.* Englewood Cliffs, N.J.: Prentice-Hall, 1972.

> Joyce and Weil seek the systematic exploration of interactions among educational purposes, pedagogical strategies, curricular designs and materials, and social and psychological theory. The authors attempt to examine a diverse range of alternative patterns upon which teachers can model their behavior.

Joyce, William W. and Frank L. Ryan, eds. *Social Studies and the Elementary Teacher: Promises and Practices.* Washington, D.C.: National Council for Social Studies, Bulletin 53, 1977.

> This publication includes the most significant articles published between 1970 and 1977 in *Social Education.* One of the three sections of the anthology is devoted to instructional strategies and techniques.

Welton, David A. and John T. Mallan. *Children and Their World: Teaching Elementary Social Studies.* Skokie, Ill.: Rand McNally, 1976.

> Chapter 6 (pp. 155–173) presents a fine account of teaching modes. The authors suggest that teaching techniques are the stuff from which teaching strategies are built. Teaching modes are discussed and many practical examples are included.

CHAPTER

4

USING DRAMATIC TECHNIQUES

GOALS

1. Recognize the importance of using various forms of creative dramatics in the elementary social studies program.
2. Become knowledgeable about the nature, function, and instructional capabilities of dramatic play, role play, and simulation, when used in elementary social studies classes.
3. Learn how to create, use, and assess dramatic plays, role plays, and simulation games.
4. Learn how to evaluate and select commercially developed simulation games.
5. Gain insights into the extent to which various forms of creative dramatics can enhance the authors' conception of the lifelong roles and organizing themes.

One of the basic premises underlying this book is that social studies instruction will have limited meaning for children unless it affords them opportunities to become *actively involved* in learning experiences that have meaning for their daily lives. This emphasis on active involvement represents a dramatic shift away from time-honored (but untested) views of teaching. Traditionally, teaching was regarded as essentially a process of imparting knowledge to young learners who spent most of the school day seated at desks that were screwed to the floor and arranged in tidy rows. Except for routine tasks, which occasionally required children to move about the room, physical activity in the classroom and conversation between pupils were discouraged—even forbidden in some instances—out of the conviction that motionless, docile, quiet children learned best. True, some deviations from this policy were condoned. The presentation of a skit, playlet, or an elaborate dramatization of the first Thanksgiving, the Pilgrims' landing at Plymouth Rock, or other special events were regarded as worthwhile and were reserved for special occasions. Using forms of dramatics in the classroom as an integral part of the social studies program was frowned upon. But this attitude is changing. Increasingly elementary social studies teachers are recognizing that various forms of creative dramatics can add exciting new dimensions to social studies classes. Among the most valuable activities of this type are dramatic play, role play, and simulation.

78

DRAMATIC PLAY

Fannie and George Shaftel remind us: "Long before children have mastered language in order to share the cultural experiences of their environment, they begin to explore the world around them through play."[1] Children want to be participants, to engage in the many activities performed by their peers, older brothers and sisters, parents, and other adults. They want to experience life. If given the opportunity, Brook, my four-year-old son, would gladly try to drive the family car, play hockey, use the garbage disposal, mow the lawn, paint the house, or do almost anything that intrigues him. Of course, Brook is not allowed to do these things; instead we try as best we can to provide him with opportunities to play at such activities as safely as possible, while minimizing damage to his surroundings. One morning, after observing the garbage men pick up our refuse, he hitched his wagon to his tricycle, loaded his wagon with newspapers and whatever he could find in the garage, and deposited them in his own "dump," a spot in the backyard. On another occasion he went to his older sister's doll house, and while manipulating Kermit and Grover, two of his Sesame Street puppets, carried on a spirited conversation regarding Grover's incompetencies. Following church services one Sunday, he collected several TV tables, turned them upside down, their legs extended upward, and with the aid of a soup ladle, proceeded to snuff his "candles," and deliver a ringing benediction.

In the first instance Brook was a garbage man; in the second, Kermit and Grover; in the third, a combination acolyte-clergyman. In all three instances he was engaging in dramatic play, reliving the roles and activities of others in his own unique, inimitable way, acquiring needed information and skills, and deriving from his play meaningful and extensive satisfaction. As a parent, I would be greatly disappointed if Brook's dramatic play experiences were to end when he enters school. Indeed, Brook would be disappointed too!

Fortunately, there are a few procedures teachers can follow to make dramatic play a powerful element in the social studies program. Unlike a drama, which has a story, characters, props, and scenery, and is intended to be acted out on a stage, dramatic play has no script, no stage (in the usual sense), and no formal props or scenery. All it has are actors (your pupils) and a stage (anywhere in your classroom or on the schoolgrounds). The word *play*, when used in dramatic play, has no theatrical connotation, since it merely indicates fun and enjoyment. As the late John R. Lee suggested, "The fun in dramatic play refers to the fun in playing and the fun in learning something you want to know."[2]

Here are a few examples from the primary grades:

Amy reads, "Juan ran out into the street to get Fuzzy. He saw a car coming, grabbed the puppy, and dashed back to the curb." Her teacher asks, "Show us how he dashed, Amy. Why did he do this?"

Fred reads, " 'Who is that trip-trapping over my bridge?' growled the ugly

---

[1]Fannie R. Shaftel and George Shaftel, *Role Playing for Social Values: Decision-Making in the Social Studies* (Englewood Cliffs, N.J.: Prentice-Hall, 1967), p. 130.
[2]John R. Lee, *Teaching Social Studies in the Elementary School* (New York: Free Press, 1974), p. 269.

Creative dramatics give children opportunities to become actively involved in social studies lessons that affect their lives.

troll." His teacher tells Fred, "O.K., let's stop the story at this point. Fred, you be the third billy goat gruff and Charlie, you be the troll. Show us what's likely to happen."

Debby solemnly reports that a police officer stopped her father for speeding. "What happened?" her classmates ask. "Here, I'll show you," she replies.

Elizabeth, after visiting a crafts show, demonstrates, using an imaginary spinning wheel, how pioneer women spun yarn.

Here are a few examples from the upper elementary and junior high grades:

"Tom, Dick, and Harry, you'll be the Red Coats. Dave, you're Crispus Attucks. The rest of you are patriots. Show how the Boston Massacre happened."

Two students demonstrate how their working model of the Panama Canal operates.

The classroom has been hastily converted into a nineteenth-century factory. Bruno, who has been designated as foreman, is overheard admonishing a worker, "If you don't get busy, I'll have to fire you."

Cortés and his small band of conquistadores approach Montezuma and his awestruck warriers. Through an interpreter, Cortés learns that the Aztecs believe him to be the reincarnation of Quetzalcoatl, their sun-god. Montezuma speaks . . .

These examples of dramatic play have several characteristics in common:

1. Each deals with social studies content.
2. The pupils are acting out roles.
3. The pupils are basing their roles on the understanding of subject matter.
4. How well they perform their roles indicates to their classmates and to their teacher what they had failed to comprehend.

Used in this way, dramatic play can serve instructional as well as diagnostic purposes. Students learn by observing each other as they engage in dramatic play. What children say and do while acting out roles give them valuable insights into the depth and quality of their own learning, and can help a teacher determine the extent to which his or her instructional goals are being achieved.

Unlike most authors of textbooks on the teaching of social studies in the elementary grades, Lee was quite enthusiastic over the advantages of dramatic play. Indeed, he formulated a set of procedures that he and his students found useful in the classroom. Below Lee describes a dramatic play activity which centers on ships and ports:[3]

Arranging the Environment

On a Friday afternoon, you have the class strip the bulletin boards, put away all old displays, and take all used books back to the library. The class leaves for home. You are about to create an arranged room environment.

Everything in this new environment will have some relationship to ships and ports. One bulletin board is filled with pictures of ships. Underneath goes a strip of tagboard on which you have printed "What do these ships carry?"

Another, but smaller, bulletin board is covered with a chart showing signal flags. Across the bottom of the chart hang four or five flags you have made from scraps of cloth. On a small table below the flags are small heaps of scrap cloth.

You cover the library table with books. In each are two or three colored markers, each inserted at a colorful picture or an exciting passage.

You set a large fish tank on the sink counter and fill it with water. You toss in a small wooden ship. Next to it you leave two metal ships (one must be large enough so that its displacement of water can be observed). You add a sign, "Why do metal boats float?" You drop a ruler and grease pencil next to the sign.

In one corner of the room you pin up, just above floor level, 6 feet of paper that will take tempera paint. Cans of paint and brushes sit nearby. Above the paper is an accurate picture of a port. In front of the paper you drop enough scraps of lumber so breakwaters and docks can be built.

Above the science table goes a picture of a lighthouse. On the table goes a set of instructions on how to build a lighthouse. Next to the instructions are batteries, wire, wood, tacks, bulbs—everything needed to build a lighthouse.

You use masking tape to hang a display. It shows men and women at work on ships and around the port. The caption asks, "What are these workers doing?"

You drop some more scraps of wood in the construction corner. Next to them go three small, dull saws, three small hammers, and an assortment of nails. You also leave a small ship that you made.

You put a song of the sea on the record player, slip on your coat, and head for home. The trap has been baited. The quarry is the interest of your pupils.

Play, Discussion, and Research

On Monday morning your class can't miss the changes in the classroom. When school

---

[3]Reprinted with permission of Macmillan Publishing Company. From John R. Lee, *Teaching Social Studies in the Elementary School.* Copyright © 1974 by John R. Lee, pp. 171-174.

begins, tell the class they may spend a little time wandering around the room, looking at things, and playing with the objects.

Give them enough time to prowl, but not enough time to satisfy their curiosity. (The interrupted pleasure is sure to be returned to eagerly.) Then ask, "Well, what do you think this is all about?"

"Boats!"

"Sailing!"

"The ocean!"

"Etc.!"

You ask, "What did you see that you liked most?"

"The boats!"

"The lighthouse!"

"The tools!"

"Etc.!"

Pick out from one-third to one-half of the class (depending on the size of the class, the amount of free space you have, and the number of toy ships available). Say, "Ok, each of you get a ship or boat, and you can play with it."

They play. You watch. The other pupils watch. You circulate among the watchers and ask quiet questions.

"What is Billy doing?"

"Why is Mary running her boat up the wall?"

"How would you do that?"

Then you shift the groups until everyone has had his chance to play with the toy ships. The class has finished its first session of *dramatic play*.

The next step is discussion of what went on during play. You will probably pursue several ideas that occurred to you as you observed the play, but I'll just use one example.

"Billy, why were you and Kathy hitting your ships together?"

"Because. I was sailing along, and she ran into me."

"Why'd you run into his ship, Kathy?"

"Because he was in my way. He should have let me by. He's a boy and I'm a girl, and boys are supposed to be polite to girls."

"What happens if two ships smash into each other out in the ocean?"

"They sink."

"The policeman comes out in a rowboat and gives them a ticket."

"What policeman?"

"Oh, you know. It was a joke."

"Do ships smash into each other on the ocean?"

"Sure, and some of them smash into ice cubes . . . uh, icebergers and sink."

"Do all the ships that are on the ocean smash into each other all the time?"

"No."

"Why not?"

"I dunno."

"How can you find out?"

"Look it up."

"Where?"

"In the books."

"How else?"

"Ask somebody."

"Who?"

"My dad."

"A sailor."

"A sixth grader."

"The principal. He thinks he knows everything."

"Ok. Who wants to work with Billy and Kathy on this question?"

And so it goes. A small research group is formed. You move on to another mistake or question or problem.

"Now, about that policeman in a rowboat. Do you really believe? . . ."

And so on.

When children play, they reflect what they know. They do some things correctly, and they make some mistakes. The mistakes are used to stimulate discussion that leads to questions that can be researched.

You do *not* say, "Billy, you are doing that wrong. Someone show him the right way." What you want is for the pupil to *find* the right way by his own (or his research group's) efforts.

You keep at these questions until everyone has elected a research group. The next day, you begin the period by asking each group to get together. Then you review, with each group, what they are trying to find out. Don't tell them! Ask them.

"Everybody set? Ok, how much time do you want?"

And off they go, some to the library table, some to the library. They will waste time this first time. Why not? They have to become acquainted with many new books. They have to find what will be useful. They skim and finger and look at pictures. You visit each group, praising and prodding. Research takes time. And you must be willing to let them take time.

Your responsibility is to be certain that they can find out. You have to be sure the answers are in materials available to them. Why else did you do your research and write that resource unit?

Of course, someone always comes up with a question you didn't, and couldn't anticipate. Then you have to dig out the answer. If third graders can't read your source, then you rewrite the source as simply as you can. I don't think I ever taught a unit of any kind where I didn't have to do some rewriting for the class.

Then, after one day or three days—however long it takes to find answers or partial answers—each group makes its report. When all are armed with this new knowledge, you go back to a play session.

Let's review for a moment. You create an environment. The class explores that environment. You let the class play with the ships. You observe the mistakes in the play. The class discusses the mistakes. Research groups are formed. Research takes place. The results of research are reported. The class plays again.

In the early stages of dramatic play you are not trying to develop major concepts. Instead, you are stimulating your pupils to find enough factual information so that during the course of their play they will apply this information. Also, you are helping your pupils to acquire the skills needed to play together and work together. A sense of responsibility, consideration of others, and courtesy are *learned* behaviors. If your pupils have not acquired these competencies, they had better well begin learning them as you embark on dramatic play.

Research skills are involved in Lee's dramatic play model. Among these are: (a) knowing what one is searching for and asking the right questions; (b) knowing where to obtain information; (c) knowing how to read for different purposes; (d) knowing how to observe; and (e) knowing how to differentiate between fact and opinion.

Lee's teaching plan includes a period or two devoted to construction activities, since he anticipates that the children will see the need for more ships or docks or lighthouses, etc. Thus new needs and problems have arisen. Initially, the children will realize that they have too few tools for everyone to build at one time. How will they share the tools? Also, since they want to build ships that resemble ships, they will need to do some independent research. Once the ships are built, they resume play.

For how long does this dramatic play adventure continue? Common sense is your best answer. When you believe that your goals have been achieved, when your children lose interest, when the level of play becomes too complex—at any of these points, it ought to be apparent to you that the time to stop has arrived.

Admittedly, Lee's model of dramatic play requires extensive preparation. Is it worth the time, effort, and patience? Fannie Shaftel insightfully notes that well-organized dramatic play can achieve these results.[4] It:

1. helps children to understand and use accurate concepts and symbols.
2. reveals the natural behavior of children.
3. develops sequence and unity in language expression.
4. discloses needs that will ensure ongoing experiences.
5. reveals new information acquired by children.
6. leads into aesthetic expression of many kinds.
7. clarifies needs for construction and research.
8. promotes interpersonal skills.
9. promotes learning without undue emotional strain.
10. provides opportunity for children to have fun.

ROLE PLAYING

In the previous section we indicated that when children engage in dramatic play, they act out different roles; sometimes they play themselves, often they play the roles of others—a boy retrieving a dog, an ugly troll, Crispus Attucks, Montezuma, a ship's captain, etc. In what ways does role playing differ from dramatic play? Dramatic play is a prelude to role play; as such, it becomes a vehicle for providing children with opportunities to act out or recreate in an unstructured and spontaneous way various human experiences. The goal of dramatic play, as Welton and Mallan suggest, ". . . is to recreate an experience so that children, as they play their various roles, get a vicarious feel for that experience, and hopefully, raise

[4]Fannie R. Shaftel, "Dramatic Play, Role-Playing, Simulations and Games," in Lavone A. Hanna, Gladys L. Potter, and Robert W. Reynolds, *Dynamic Elementary Social Studies: Unit Teaching*, 3d ed. (New York: Holt, Rinehart and Winston, 1973), pp. 249-252.

some questions that might lead to further research and investigation."[5] Lee, you will recall, believed that dramatic play is dependent on intellectual development, since pupils state their goals, conduct their own research, and validate what they have learned.[6]

In contrast, role playing tends to be more carefully organized and sequenced, and affords children a greater opportunity to grapple with a problem situation and to resolve it. Moreover, students role play before an audience, usually their classmates.

Shaftel and Shaftel advocate a nine-step sequence for role playing:[7]

1. Warm-up (teacher introduction and reading of the problem story)
2. Selecting role players
3. Preparing the audience to observe
4. Setting the stage
5. The enactment
6. Discussion and evaluation
7. Further enactments
8. Further discussion
9. Generalizing

Since we have used these procedures with our own pupils, and have witnessed their use in many other classrooms, we present below our recommendations for their use.

1. *Warming-up the group (problem confrontation).* This step sensitizes the children to the problem at hand, gets them to think about dealing with the problem, and helps them to relate the problem to their own lives. Once the problem is presented (via photographs, recordings, a story read aloud, etc.), the teacher focuses the pupils' attention on the problem, by asking such questions as, "What do you think will happen now?" or, "What would you do?"
2. *Selecting participants for the role play.* While selecting participants, use pupils who appear to have identified with the roles and who can internalize the roles. Try not to assign roles to children who have volunteered. On some occasions a teacher will assign a particular role to a pupil because he or she feels that the child needs to identify with a given role, or needs the experience of occupying for a few minutes the shoes of another.
3. *Setting the stage.* Before the role play begins, the role players should briefly plan what they are going to do. Since the act of role playing involves no script or predetermined movements, gestures, speeches, etc., this stage should take very little time, since it merely involves the general line of action that is to occur.
4. *Preparing the audience to be participating observers.* At this stage you want to insure that the nonrole players, who constitute most of your class, will be able to observe the role play intelligently. Obviously, your pupils should be good listeners and good

[5]David A. Welton and John T. Mallan, *Children and Their World: Teaching Elementary Social Studies* (Skokie, Ill.: Rand McNally, 1976), p. 291.
[6]Lee, p. 279.
[7]Shaftel and Shaftel, p. 84.

watchers. Also, as your class observes the role play, they should be considering alternative ways of dealing with the problem being role played. Why? Because in a few minutes, some of these pupils will be given a chance to present their versions!

5. *Role playing (the enactment)*. At this stage, the initial role play occurs. Your role players assume their roles, spontaneously responding to each other's words, actions, gestures, etc. Try to be understanding. Don't intrude on the role play by suggesting how the role players should act. If it is obvious that a role player is not playing his role, you might give him or her a gentle hint or prompt, but try not to do this unless you feel that it is *absolutely necessary*.

6. *Discussion and evaluation*. Immediately after the enactment, encourage your class to discuss not only what happened during the enactment, but also what is likely to occur as a consequence of the course of action taken by the role players. Elicit comments from role players and observers. Get them to compare and contrast their reactions. Remember: the observers can evaluate the enactment a bit more objectively and more insightfully because they are not as emotionally involved as the actors.

7. *The reenactment (further role playing)*. This step is one that frequently does not occur to teachers. It affords your pupils a second, or even a third chance to resolve the problems under investigation. As before, you select the role players. You may allow the original role players to play their roles again or you may assign new actors to the roles. The latter alternative makes a great deal of sense when it is apparent that new interpretations and new solutions emerge from the observers. Also, it broadens the base of pupil participation in the role-playing experience.

8. *Further discussion*. Following each reenactment, discussions should occur. It is important that those pupils who move back and forth between role player and observer can compare their perspectives in a rational manner. This enables each child to reach his own decisions regarding the viability of the solutions proposed in the role plays.

9. *Sharing experiences and generalizing*. This, the final step in role play, is a period of general discussion, of pulling together of ideas and insights gained by actors and observers. Ideally this step will help your pupils share their reactions and to generalize them to similar situations. A few well-chosen questions may be all that is needed to encourage children to generalize about their previous experiences with role playing.

SIMULATION GAMES[8]

Simulation is becoming a vital, dynamic force in the affairs of education, business and industry, the sciences, and government. Seventh-graders, role-playing Netsilik Eskimos of fifty years ago, simulate a caribou hunt. Sales trainees, employed by a vacuum cleaner manufacturer, simulate techniques of overcoming customer resistance. Biologists, using a working scale model of the San Francisco Bay area, simulate the effects of an oil spillage on marine life. Economists feed data into a computer programmed to simulate the effects of increased taxes on domestic

---

[8]Portions of this discussion were adapted from William W. Joyce, "Selecting, Evaluating, and Designing Simulation Games for Middle School Social Studies Classes," *The High School Journal* 57 (April 1974), pp. 292–311. Copyright © 1974, The University of North Carolina Press. By permission of the publisher.

Simulation games provide pupils with valuable first-hand experiences in decision-making and in oral language development.

gasoline consumption. These illustrations suggest the varied applications of simulation: education, training, research, and practical decision-making. In all of these cases simulation is used as a method for dealing with complex processes in specific situations where experimentation or analytic techniques do not exist or are not feasible. Under these circumstances simulation provides a viable alternative.

Indicative of the growing popularity of simulation in education is the emergence of: (a) new professional organizations concerned with various aspects of this field; (b) numerous books, articles, and research studies on simulations; and (c) private firms which design simulations for use in education and related fields. Concurrent with these developments has been a dramatic increase in the number and variety of simulation games designed for use in social studies classes.

Despite this evidence of interest, simulation games are not enjoying widespread popularity in elementary school social studies classes. In our opinion, this situation exists primarily because teachers are unaware of the excellent simulation games in existence and their instructional capabilities. Herein lies the rationale for this discussion.

Their are several questions which should be of concern to those social studies teachers who may desire to use simulation games in their teaching. These questions are:

1.   What are simulation games?
2.   What are their values and limitations?
3.   How can one select and evaluate them?
4.   How can teachers and students design them?
5.   What are some recommended simulation games?

What Are Simulation Games?

To define this term, one must first define its constituent elements, *simulation* and *game*. A *simulation* is a carefully controlled, yet simplified model or representation of a more complex physical or social reality. The model may be symbolic, mathematical, logical, or a combination of these. A *game* is a contest, a competitive experience regulated by established rules, wherein players seek to attain a goal, usually expressed as "winning."

A *simulation game* is a blend of simulation and games, one which stresses precise modeling of reality, role play, and competition, and is characterized by extensive interaction between players. Most simulation games used in social studies instruction are built upon models of social reality. Since these models tend to deal with issues and processes requiring students to assume roles of others (usually adults), and to make intelligent decisions affecting their play of the game as well as the play of others, social studies simulation games will involve pre-structured role play. Thus in *Democracy*, one of the better known collections of simulation games, students assume the roles of legislators and are required to make decisions reflecting the interests of their constituents. In *Generation Gap*, students role play adolescents like themselves and their parents as they plan strategies for resolving family conflicts. In the *Caribou Hunting Games*, students role play Eskimos as they plan strategies for hunting caribou. In these instances students are presented with a realistic model of a problematic social situation wherein they assume roles of persons likely to be involved in these situations, and compete against each other in attempting to resolve them.

According to these definitions, is *Monopoly* a simulation game? Admittedly, it is a game and some role play (unstructured) is present (players buy, sell, and trade real estate), but the model on which it is based and the conditions and rules under which it is played bear little resemblance to actual real estate practices. Accordingly, *Monopoly* is a game, but certainly not a *simulation game*.

It is for this reason that those games which do not simulate real-life processes and issues in an accurate manner (most games have this limitation) are not properly termed *simulation games*.

The remainder of this discussion will deal with some basic issues and practical considerations facing teachers desiring to learn more about applications of simulation games to the teaching of social studies. At various points in this discussion the terms *simulation game* and *game* will be used interchangeably, to facilitate readability. The reader will note, however, that when the term *game* is used, it refers to a *simulation game* and not to a *game* as used in the conventional sense.

What Are Their Values and Limitations?

How effective are simulation games? Despite the lack of rigorous, experimental research on classroom applications, the professional literature proliferates with claims and counter-claims concerning the efficacy of such media. Below is a series of observations indicative of the values and limitations of simulation games designed for use in elementary and junior high social studies classes. All simulation games cited for illustrative purposes are described in a later section of this chapter.

Proponents claim that simulation games possess these values:

1. *Motivation*. By their very nature, games are sources of fascination and pleasure for students of all ages. They provide a break in classroom routine, and perhaps, as Nesbitt hypothesizes, ". . . it may be that students' enjoyment of games is in some inverse proportion to their boredom with the daily fare in social studies classrooms."[9] That games strip teachers of dominant authority roles and relegate to them secondary roles as helpers or resources may be conducive to a more relaxed, psychologically free atmosphere.

2. *Efficacy*. Simulation games differ from most media in the sense that they promote active involvement in learning, and such involvement teaches students that they can control their environment and destiny. This enables them to see that causal relationships do exist between their behavior and the outcome of events. Pupils who lack confidence in themselves can learn through simulation games that their actions do make a difference.

3. *Skills*. Inherent in gaming techniques are numerous opportunities for students to reinforce and maintain inquiry and valuing skills. Successful performance in simulation games at the middle-school level is largely a function of a student's ability to engage in decision-making—examine alternative strategies, anticipate those of others, reach consensus, allocate resources, learn techniques of persuasion, cooperation, and influence-resisting.

In the debriefing process, students analyze components of the game that they have played (rules, constraints, playability, realism of roles, adequacy of materials, etc.) as well as the social or political system that was simulated. Here the ability to generalize from the gaming experience to the real world becomes a highly significant competency, one that is fundamental to competent social studies instruction.

Also related to game performance is a student's mastery of the four basic modes of communication: reading, writing, listening, and speaking. Few media offer more opportunities for students to practice these skills. Indeed, some students find that gaming is so inherently motivating as to provide a powerful inducement to improve their competencies in these areas!

4. *Responsibility*. Unlike most teacher-directed learning experiences where students feel that they are accountable only to the teacher, simulation gaming shifts the burden of responsibility to students. Errors in judgment may result, depending on the game, in hunger (*Caribou Hunting Games*), defeat at elections (*Democracy*), a labor dispute (*Labor-Management Simulation*), a loss of power over other socioeconomic groups (*Starpower*), or loss of wages (*Tin Lizzie*). In such instances, a student's desire for peer approval among teammates is likely to become a powerful incentive for him or her to play the game well.

5. *Sympathy and Empathy*. A perennial problem encountered by most teachers is the difficulty of teaching students to subvert their tendencies to be

[9]William A. Nesbitt, *Simulation Games for the Social Studies Classroom*, 2d ed. (New York: Foreign Policy Association, 1971), p. 41.

self-centered and egotistical, and instead learn to step into the shoes of others—to project themselves into the feelings, needs, problems, and aspirations of others. The role-playing component promotes this process. It has been suggested by one proponent of simulation games that players' ability to identify with their game roles is directly related to their ability to empathize with the individuals whose roles they have assumed.

6. *Group processes*. Simulation games afford teachers opportunities to study group processes in their classrooms. This has particular significance for the junior high or middle-school teacher who teaches in a departmentalized program and thus may come into contact with 130 or more students during the school day. Under these circumstances assessing individual and group behavior becomes a demanding but nevertheless important task. By carefully analyzing instances of student decision-making during the play of a game and later during debriefing, the perceptive teacher can acquire new insights into his or her students' cognitive and socioemotional development.

7. *Reality-testing*. Many simulation games provide students with chances to test realities they will later encounter in the adult world. They help students anticipate and deal with situations before they meet them by securing immediate feedback regarding the consequences of their decisions. They also help them to reevaluate their decisions and try alternative courses of action. Given these opportunities, a student is more likely to reflect upon and validate ideas when he does not have to endure their consequences in reality. Games stressing decision-making in business (*Economic Man in the Market*), collective bargaining (*Labor-Management Simulation*), politics (*Democracy*), basic consumer skills (*Shopping Game*), and human relations (*Blacks and Whites* and *Starpower*) are eminently useful in this regard.

8. *Concept Learning*. Simulation games can infuse complex, inert concepts with new life and meaning by injecting into them a sense of realism and relevance. When students play *Economic Man in the Market*, they do not merely learn about the dynamics of supply and demand, they experience them. When they play *Tin Lizzie*, they learn about craftsmen and assembly-line procedures.

9. *Flexibility*. Through judicious assignment of roles and modification of objectives, rules, constraints, scoring, and game materials, the creative teacher who uses games can accommodate the learning styles and competencies of students of varying ability. Reading retardation, by far one of the greatest barriers to learning at any level, can be compensated for by the teacher who exercises care in grouping students in a gaming situation. In the early stages of a game he may, for example, group slow readers with fast readers, to insure that all students acquire the same informational base needed to master game instructions and procedures.

Simulation games, owing to their flexibility, are compatible with team teaching, nongraded, multi- or cross-age grouping and other organizational patterns. Moreover, there is reason to believe that if the open classroom movement achieves reality, simulation games could become a vital factor in the success of this innovation.

Critics allege that simulation games have these limitations:

1. *Oversimplification*. Earlier we noted that simulation games are based on

simplified (albeit controlled) models of reality, social and physical. To make a game playable, the designer often finds it necessary to scale down a problem under study and present abstract ideas in more concrete, understandable terms. This may involve deleting certain facts, telescoping time periods and events, reducing the number of goods to be traded, simplifying computations, etc. It is argued by some critics that these changes tend to oversimplify and distort the actual situation or process being simulated, and thus cause students to acquire misinformation and misconceptions.

2. *Too motivating.* Inherent in gaming situations is the element of competition, wherein players vie with each other (or with themselves) to achieve predetermined goals. Typically social studies games are zero-sum games, wherein a player wins at the expense of his opponents. They place a high premium on goal-directed behavior expressed as "winning": influencing legislation and gaining reelection (Game 1 of *Democracy*), sustaining life (*Caribou Hunting*), making profits (*Economic Man in the Market*), assessing propaganda techniques (*Propaganda*), acquiring power over other groups (*Starpower*), or gaining competence in solving personal problems (*Generation Gap*). In these and other game-induced competitive situations students may get so intensely involved that they fail to grasp the true intent of the game as well as the meaning of the roles they are playing. If a student "loses" (from the standpoint of scoring), he or she might feel that playing the game was a waste of time or a threat to his or her self-image.

3. *"Wrong" values.* Many social situations modeled in simulation games require students to assume roles involving antisocial behavior. In *Labor-Management Simulation* students playing the role of factory supervisors are instructed to intimidate, punish, and embarrass uncooperative employees. *Blacks and Whites* gives whites financial superiority, but allows blacks to consolidate their resources, force whites to sell land at reduced prices, and obtain welfare payments and bonuses, while denying these advantages to whites. In other games success is measured by earning money or amassing votes by shrewd use of clever stratagems. Although these games require behavior which would be explicitly discouraged in most classrooms, do they teach or condone such behavior? Critics of simulation games believe that they do. Gordon demurs, maintaining that such games are value-free:

> . . . the game structures an environment in which particular behavior patterns are acceptable. In so doing, the game in no way suggests that such behavior is moral, effective, appropriate to any set of circumstances outside the game—or even that it was moral in the situation represented by the game.[10]

Some critics of simulation games argue that when students are encouraged to practice antisocial behavior in a gaming situation, it gives implied sanction to such behavior, irrespective of the intentions of the game designers. And as Nesbitt alleges, one study found that students who played a game learned ". . . a skeptical, cynical view of the world; conflict, deception were inevitable or dominant."[11] Admittedly, such a world view does reflect reality, but in the opinion of some

[10]Alice Kaplan Gordon, *Games for Growth* (Palo Alto, Calif.: Science Research, 1970), p. 34.
[11]Nesbitt, p. 61.

critics designers should take responsibility for insuring that students are not misled into believing that greed, fraud, and deception are to be valued.

4. *Dehumanizing*. Critics maintain that games dehumanize students by encouraging them to manipulate the lives of others without subjecting them to constraints and consequences similar to those operative in the real world. Arbitrarily declaring war, charging excessive prices for goods, or promoting riots may be attractive options available to the unthinking student who is well aware that in real life he or she will not be held accountable for such decisions.

In some cases personalities of players may dominate—or destroy—the simulation process. This would be a potential problem for middle-school students whose behavioral patterns are excessively peer-oriented. Peer roles can easily displace roles being simulated unless the game is designed to control for this contingency, or unless the teacher can, through judicious assignment of roles, prevent its occurrence. Imagine, if you will, the personal trauma that could result if a meek, insecure student were suddenly cast into a role demanding forceful, authoritarian behavior that was beyond his capability.

5. *Attitudes*. Do games actually change student attitudes? Do they teach students to become more sympathetic and empathetic toward the way that others feel and act? It is argued by some that there is little chance of this happening, because students rarely lose themselves in a simulation game, and they always are aware that upon termination of the game they are not compelled to endure any long-range, residual consequences of their decisions.

6. *Prerequisites*. Many simulation games require students to assume roles alien to their prior experience, and to apply skills and knowledge that they do not possess. Caribou hunters, heads of state, department store managers, congressmen, city officials, delegates to a constitutional convention, factory supervisors and workers—these are but a few of the roles inherent in simulation games designed for the upper elementary grades. How much prior knowledge about these roles and the context in which they are played would a student need to possess in order to successfully play the game? Some critics assert, "Too much!" One proponent of simulation games maintains that a well-designed game will provide players with carefully delineated role profiles and rules, will carefully control interaction between players to insure adherence to roles and rules, and will begin slowly to enable players to become familiar with roles and rules. But, the critics argue, most games do not take into account the values and predispositions students bring to the gaming situation.

Proponents also acknowledge that some students possess certain experiences and skills which enhance their performance. Presumably the calculating, perceptive, entrepreneurial type of student already possesses skills which should make him a successful negotiator in *Labor-Management Simulation*. Similarly, the literate student versed in techniques of persuasion and compromise should become an able congressman in *Democracy*. But some critics reason that most students do not possess these competencies, and those that do have an unfair advantage over others!

7. *Classroom control*. Simulation games pose a serious threat to rigid, tradition-bound, authoritarian teachers who equate learning with the acquisition

of facts. Such teachers are likely to find themselves incapable of accepting the new role that simulation games require of them: a helper, a facilitator, a co-learner with students. Even more flexible, open-minded teachers are likely to encounter problems in using simulation games in their social studies teaching. Games require time, usually a minimum of two or three instructional periods. Games afford students far more freedom of speech and movement than other media. At first, many students are incapable of using this newly gained freedom, and accepting the responsibility that should accompany it. Classrooms will be noisy. Students will mill about in a purposeless manner. The teacher will need to explain and reexplain rules and procedures *ad nauseum,* or so it seems. Critical game materials may vanish. Room arrangements (the authors defy any teacher to use a simulation game in a 20 × 20 foot classroom with thirty-five desks bolted to the floor!), teaching schedules, discipline problems, unsympathetic parents, teachers, and administrators—all these grim facts of life seem to militate against effective use of simulation games. Are they worth the effort? Proponents say they are; opponents say they are not.

How Can One Select and Evaluate Them?

Admittedly, it is more difficult for teachers to select and evaluate simulation games than other media. Despite some arguments to the contrary, the simulation movement is in its infancy. This is evidenced by the limited number of high-quality simulation games designed for classroom use, by the dearth of rigorous, comprehensive researches, and by the reluctance of publishers to incorporate simulation games into their social studies program. The conclusion is fairly obvious: Simulation games are not being widely used in schools in general and in social studies classes in particular. In our opinion, this situation will improve once teachers *become aware of the strengths and weaknesses of simulation games, and are willing to experiment with them in their classrooms.* But before such experimentation can begin, it is essential that teachers learn how to select and evaluate games.

SELECTION

The first step involves securing copies of simulation games. If the school district has recently purchased a new social studies textbook series or a multimedia program, it is likely that a few games will be included with such material, or will be available for purchase as optional, ancillary material. In most cases, however, teachers will need to look elsewhere for simulation games.

Unfortunately, there is no extant publication comparable to *Consumer Reports* magazine, containing critical, no-holds-barred, empirically based analyses of simulation games and recommendations for their use. Two exemplary publications of the Social Science Education Consortium do provide brief, incisive, and in some cases, critical reviews: *Learning with Games: An Analysis of Social Studies*

Educational Games and Simulations[12] and *Social Studies Curriculum Materials Data Book.* [13] These are the finest publications of their type available, and should occupy a prominent position in the professional libraries of social studies teachers. Of decidedly less value to social studies teachers (owing to their lack of performance data on simulation games) are two other publications: Klietsch's *Directory of Educational Simulations, Learning Games and Didactic Units,* [14] and Zuckerman and Horn's *Guide to Simulation Games for Education and Training.* [15] Broader in scope than the two SSEC publications, these are descriptive compendia of simulations covering the fields of education, business, industry, and the sciences.

Once a committee of social studies teachers and administrators has assembled a collection of simulation games, initial decisions need to be made with regard to their instructional value *vis-á-vis* other media. At this point the basic question facing each teacher is "Which media (or combination) will enable me to most effectively teach the lifelong roles and supportive concepts which undergird our social studies curriculum? Will textbooks be most useful? Tradebooks? Films?" Before deciding to use a game in preference to other media, it is imperative that teachers weigh the anticipated benefits of all available media.

Assuming that one has decided to use simulation games, other questions arise: What do I want the games to do for my students? Motivate them? Introduce a concept? Sensitize them to the parameters of a problem at hand? Teach certain valuing or inquiry processes? Help students achieve closure on a given issue? Involve them in a moral dilemma?

EVALUATION

When the intended use of simulation games has been established and documented and specific games have been identified, the task of evaluation begins. Typically this involves specifying criteria for assessment, assigning verbal or numerical weightings to each criterion, and applying them. Ideally all games under consideration should be assessed by more than one person, to insure that they receive as fair and as comprehensive an evaluation possible.

The following criteria, adapted from Niemeyer's pioneering study,[16] are offered for the express purpose of assisting you in evaluating simulation games for use in your social studies classes.

---

[12]*Learning with Games: An Analysis of Social Studies Educational Games and Simulations* (Boulder, Colo.: Social Science Education Consortium, 1974).

[13]*Social Studies Curriculum Materials Data Book* (Boulder, Colo.: Social Science Education Consortium). Revised annually.

[14]Ronald G. Klietsch, *Directory of Educational Simulations, Learning Games and Didactic Units* (St. Paul, Minn.: Instructional Simulations, 1969).

[15]David W. Zuckerman and Robert E. Horn, *The Guide to Simulation Games for Education and Training* (Cambridge, Mass.: Information Resources, 1970).

[16]Roger C. Niemeyer, "Simulation-Gaming in Pre-Service Teacher Education: A Case Study," unpublished doctoral thesis, Michigan State University, 1972. Adapted by permission of the author.

Background	1.	Is the background information, *i.e.*, type of pupil, school setting, and social studies curriculum for which the simulation game is designed adequate?
Objectives	2.	Are the objectives of the simulation game set forth in clear, unambiguous terms? Are the game objectives amenable to evaluation?
Teacher Instruction	3.	Are there adequate instructions for use by the teacher in preparing for and conducting the simulation game? Are such instructions clear, precise, and understandable?
Players	4.	Is there a complete listing of minimum, maximum and/or optional players?
Role Profiles	5.	Are role descriptions (players' goals and resources) complete?
Scenario	6.	Is basic information base (background information regarding situation to be simulated and preliminary instructions for players) adequate?
Materials	7.	Is there a complete listing of all hardware (name tags, play money, tokens, gameboards, etc.) needed to make the game operational? Are all materials present?
Rules	8.	Are the rules simple and specific? Are they consonant with the social reality under simulation? Are they flexible enough to enable players to make alternative decisions?
Interaction Sequence	9.	Are options and moves available to players consistent? Does order of play provide for continuous involvement of players?
Sequence	10.	Is the organization of the simulation game sequential? Is it related to the rules, choices, and moves?
Scoring	11.	Does the simulation game state clearly and precisely how to determine the extent to which players have attained their objectives?
Chance	12.	Are chance factors, if present, proportionate to their presence in the reality under simulation?
Debriefing	13.	Is a debriefing guide included? If so, do debriefing questions interface with the objectives of the simulation game? Do they stress cognitive as well as affective learnings of players?

How Can Teachers and Students Design Them?

Developing simulation games as a class activity is a demanding, yet rewarding experience for students. Admittedly, the final product may be too easy or too difficult, too time-consuming or too brief, but these disadvantages are outweighed by the personal benefits students acquire while engaged in the process of game development. Not only do students develop skills in seeking and validating information about the situations to be simulated, they also improve their writing skills as they set forth rules, constraints, and game procedures. Equally significant, the intellectual demands of designing games require students to become scientists as they stretch their intellect and imagination while identifying, manipulating, and integrating the parameters of the game and the situation under study. Indeed, it may be that the process of designing simulation games is a more worthwhile learning experience for students than merely playing them!

Although the professional literature encourages game development by students, few authors describe precisely how this can be done. Shelly has designed and validated instructional materials and strategies for teaching students techniques of game design. Below is a brief description of Shelly's instructional model.[17] The reader will note that although the components described below

[17]Ann Converse Shelly, "Total Class Development of Simulation Games," *Social Education* 37 (November 1973), pp. 687–688. For a more comprehensive discussion see Ann Converse Shelly,

appear in sequential order, in reality students will need to move back and forth from component to component as the simulation game takes shape.

Topic: What process (reconciling parent-child conflicts, establishing prices for goods, passing a law) do you want to teach, assess, or sensitize students to? In most cases it will be a decision-making process involving weighing alternatives, predicting consequences, etc.

Objective: What is the purpose of the simulation game? What should students be able to do as a result of playing the game? The answers to these questions can be expressed behaviorally as performance objectives.

Simplified Model: Think of a specific situation in which the process you have chosen is used. Describe that situation as completely as possible. Tell what happens, the order of events, who and what are involved. From this description a complete picture of the situation to be simulated should emerge.

Players and Resources: What is involved in the situation described above? Make your list as complete as possible by associating players with their resources (money, good will, votes, real estate, etc.).

Player Decision Guides: What decisions are open to each player? What are the possible results? List these for each player.

Game Goal: State as simply as possible what the goal of each player and/or group of players is *for the game*.

Rounds: Go back to the simplified model and identify breaks in the action. What seem to be natural rounds? How much time should be allocated to each? Do you wish to impose on players crises, new laws, rule changes, etc.? If so, state them.

Debriefing Questions: These questions are to be discussed at the conclusion of the simulation game. Be certain to cover all intended learning specified in your objectives. Do not overlook players' emotional reactions and attitude changes. These questions should focus on events that occurred during the game and on social realities related to the game.

Materials: In this section you and your students assemble the information acquired in response to the preceding questions, and create the final form of the game.

Scenario: Using the simplified model, write a brief statement to introduce the game to and set the stage for the players. Also at this point your students might wish to decide on a title for the game.

Player Profiles: Write a description of the role(s) to be assumed by each player or group of players. Include game goals, decision topics, and resources of each role. This provides the players with personalities to role play.

Rules: What can the players do? What can't they do? Make your list of rules as simple, concise, and complete as possible.

Game materials: List all physical objects the players will need to play the game. These could be dice, tokens, information sheets, maps, game boards, etc.

Game Director Guide: Write a statement indicating all basic information that the game director will need. Be certain to include suggestions to facilitate play of the game.

"Total Class Involvement in Simulation Game Development," unpublished doctoral thesis, Michigan State University, 1973. Adapted by permission of the author.

Some Recommended Simulation Games

Below are descriptions of simulation games recommended by the author for use in upper elementary social studies classes. These games are recommended because they exhibit most of the following characteristics:

1. They have received high ratings from those who have used them.
2. They can be integrated into school social studies curricula.
3. They can be modified to fit the needs of a given social studies class without compromising the models they are based upon.
4. They are available at low cost.
5. They do not require special training of teachers and students using them.
6. They are nonzero sum, with players competing against themselves.

BLACKS AND WHITES

Grade Levels: 7 and higher.

Lifelong Role: *Occupation* (via Human Equality and Intercultural Relations)

Description: Developed by Robert Sommer and Judy Tart, and marketed by *Psychology Today* magazine, *Blacks and Whites* is a board game which seeks to sensitize students to minority racial discrimination practices. Players, assuming roles of blacks and white, purchase real estate to maximize their wealth. The game is designed to prohibit blacks from purchasing cheaper properties, thus making it difficult for them to acquire power and prestige. By consolidating their financial resources and welfare and tax benefits, blacks can overcome these disadvantages and compete effectively against whites. In addition, the game provides for bartering between blacks and whites.

Materials: Game sheet describing rules and player roles, game board, play money, dice, pawns, deeds, and opportunity cards.

Number of Players: 3 to 9

Playing Time: Two consecutive 50-minute periods are needed, although players may at their option continue the game.

Recommendations: Basic reading and computational skills are needed. Although assignment of roles in a racially mixed class may be problematic for some teachers overly concerned about student reactions to the game, these writers feel that such contingencies should not prevent any teacher from trying the game. Once students have played *Blacks and Whites* for the first time, they should be encouraged to rewrite the rules. The game designers not only encourage such changes, but structured the game to allow for this.

Publisher: The Headbox
Educational Products Division
P. O. Box 4762
Clinton, Iowa 52732

CARIBOU HUNTING GAMES

Grade Levels: 5 and higher

Lifelong Roles: *Occupation* and *Personal Efficacy* (via Morality)

Description: The *Caribou Hunting Games* are two board games originally designed by Jerry L. Fletcher, Donald A. Koeller, and David S. Martin[18] as an integral element of *Man: A Course of Study*, a social studies program created by Educational Development Corporation, Inc., and currently marketed by Curriculum Development Associates, Inc. Originally *Man: A Course of Study* was designed for fifth and sixth graders, but increasingly the program is gaining popularity in the middle school. The games consist of *The Bow and Arrow Hunting Game* and *The Crossing-Place Hunting Game*. Since the latter game is a more sophisticated version of the former, it is described here. The purpose of *The Crossing-Place Hunting Game* is to afford players experience in combining basic components of an Eskimo caribou hunt—inukshuk building, cooperation among hunters, and kayak placement—into an overall strategy. Among the variables to be considered by players are speed of hunter and prey, caribou behavior when frightened, kayak placement, and migration routes of caribou. Using sheets of highly stylized paper representing a map of a ten-square mile area of Canada's Pelly Bay region (Simpson Peninsula), three players (two hunters and a third player who moves the caribou herd) simulate a caribou hunt.

Materials: Game maps, dice, rule sheets, Eskimo cards, black and red pencils (or crayons), and a teacher's guide entitled *The Netsilik Eskimos at the Inland Camps*.[19] These materials are not sold apart from *Man: A Course of Study*.

Number of Players: 3

Playing Time: Game can be played through to conclusion in one 50-minute class period, although designers strongly recommend that the game be played three times to enable each player to play every role.

Recommendations: In the lessons preceding the game, students: (a) study attributes of men and caribou, tools available to men, and an ethnographic account of bow and arrow hunting; (b) play *The Bow and Arrow Hunting Game*; (c) view films of an actual crossing-place hunt; and (d) study Eskimo hunting techniques. Since *The Crossing-Place Hunting Game* functions as an integrating learning experience and was designed expressly for *Man: A Course of Study*, it is unlikely that teachers not using this program would find the game useful to their students—the game's content would be too foreign to their students' experiences. The writers included this game in this chapter because it is one of the most imaginatively, carefully designed and researched learning games in existence, and should serve as an exemplary model for those teachers desiring to teach their students techniques of game design.

Publisher: Curriculum Development Associates, Inc.
1211 Connecticut Ave., NW
Washington, D.C. 20036

DEMOCRACY

Grade Levels: 7 and higher

Lifelong Roles *Citizenship* and *Personal Efficacy* (via Morality)

[18] A revealing description of experiences encountered by these authors while developing the Caribou Hunting Games appears in Jerry L. Fletcher, Donald Koeller, and David S. Martin, "The Caribou Hunting Games," in Michael Inbar and Clarice Stael (eds.), *Simulation and Gaming in Social Science* (New York: Free Press, 1972), pp. 159–172.
[19] *The Netsilik Eskimos at the Inland Camps* (Cambridge, Mass.: Educational Development Center, 1970), pp. 46–49, 56–60.

Description: *Democracy* is the title of a set of eight simulation games developed by James S. Coleman for Academic Games Associates, Inc., of Johns Hopkins University. The games were first published in 1966 and later were revised in 1969. Arranged in order of complexity, the *Democracy* games simulate elements of the legislative processes employed by the U.S. Congress. In the basic version, Game 1, students role play Congressmen as they initiate and press for passage of legislation consistent with desires of their constituents. Games 2 and 3 simulate citizen involvement in the legislative process, and games 4 to 8 deal with more complex ideas and processes.

Materials: Coordinator's and student manuals, cards denoting constituency, age, sex, marital status, region, issue, and worksheets and checklist.

Number of Players: 6 to 11

Playing Time: The first three games require an hour apiece for play if students have received previous preparation during the previous day or in the morning (if played in the afternoon). Games 4 to 8 tend to require two to three class periods each.

Recommendations: In these writers' opinion, the *Democracy* games are an extremely effective means of teaching students and teachers the work of legislatures. Games 1 to 3 can be used effectively with seventh graders. Game 1 is particularly ideal for use with sixth or seventh graders who have never played simulation games. Games 4 to 8 can be used with advanced seventh graders, or can be deferred until eighth or ninth grade. No previous knowledge of subject matter is required for successful play of *Democracy*. If possible, players should be seated in a circle or around a large table.

Publisher: Western Publishing Company, Inc.
School and Library Department
850 Third Avenue
New York, NY   10022

ECONOMIC MAN IN THE MARKET

Grade Levels: 4 to 8

Lifelong Role: *Occupation* (via Consumerism)

Description: Originally *Economic Man in the Market* (hereafter referred to as *Market*) was a basic component of the Elementary Economics Project materials developed by the Industrial Relations Center of the University of Chicago. Currently the game is sold separately by Benefic Press as part of a three-week unit on consumer economics. The game's purpose is to teach principles of supply and demand. Players are divided into retailer and consumer teams. Retailers seek to maximize profits by selling food products at profitable, yet competitive, prices. Using a $10.00 budget, consumers attempt to purchase the most food at the lowest cost.

Materials: Coordinator's manual, retailer and consumer envelopes (containing rules, order lists, play money, menus, price lists, shopping board, etc.).

Number of Players: Game is designed for use by an entire class.

Playing Time: Five 50-minute class periods, allowing for the game to be played twice.

Recommendations: A large room with movable furniture is necessary for effective play of *Market*. Admittedly, considerable reading is required of students, but the teacher can easily assist students in digesting reading material. Many teachers using this game report that their students use it as a model for creating economics games of their own, usually based on local business firms. In our opinion, *Market* is by far the finest game of its type available, and should be a valuable aid for teachers desiring to provide instruction in the emerging field of consumer education. The cost of this game is not excessive, if the game is used by several social studies classes.

Publisher:	Benefic Press 10300 West Roosevelt Road Westchester, IL 60153

GENERATION GAP

Grade Levels:	6 and higher
Lifelong Role:	*Family Membership* (via the Human Life Cycle)
Description:	*Generation Gap* was created by Erling O. Schild and Sarane S. Boocock for Academic Games Associates, Inc., of Johns Hopkins University, and published in 1969 by the Western Publishing Company. This game attempts to meet a critical need: to help students deal with common problems affecting parent-adolescent relations. The game centers on issues involving completion of homework, getting a haircut, wearing makeup, curfews, and sharing household responsibilities. Students pair off, and, assuming family roles, seek to resolve conflicts regarding these areas.
Materials:	Coordinator's manual, playing boards, issue cards, satisfaction cards, score sheets, and alphabetical letters.
Number of Players:	6
Playing Time:	One 50-minute class period.
Recommendations:	Although designed for middle-school students, *Generation Gap* can be modified for use with older or slightly younger students. Students and teachers can easily learn to play this game, as rules and procedures are clearly and concisely presented; also, required reading and mathematical skills are minimal. On several occasions these writers observed parents and students playing *Generation Gap* at PTA functions. Reactions from participants were extremely positive. This game can serve as a worthwhile beginning activity for a unit on interpersonal relations.
Publisher:	Western Publishing Company, Inc. School and Library Department 850 Third Avenue New York, NY 10022

LABOR–MANAGEMENT SIMULATION

Grade Levels:	6 and higher
Lifelong Role:	*Occupation* (via Morality)
Description:	Designed by Erwin Rausch, *Labor–Management Simulation* is described in the teacher's guide for Scott, Foresman's "Promise of America" series. This game, published in 1971,

seeks to teach students to become aware of the problems and concerns of labor and management, understand why and how workers organize, and experience the give-and-take of collective bargaining. Three roles are simulated: supervisors, workers, and union stewards. The game is contrived so that workers become dissatisfied with working conditions and organize.

Materials: A specimen set of materials (instructions, shape checker forms, and shape sheets) is included in the description of the game. Copies of these materials will need to be reproduced for student use. Play money, the only essential component not included, will need to be purchased by the teacher.

Number of Players: The game is designed for use by an entire social studies class.

Playing Time: Two consecutive 50-minute class periods.

Recommendations: *Labor-Management Simulation* may present problems for students with reading disabilities, owing to the lengthy statements to rules and procedures. However, with a minimum of effort, teachers can rewrite instructions so as to clarify them. Included in this simulation are instructions requiring supervisors to browbeat, embarrass, and punish uncooperative workers, behavior which commonly occurred in factories at the inception of the labor movement, but which some teachers may regard as inappropriate for a classroom. These elements can be deleted from the simulation game without unduly compromising the game's intent. Despite these potential limitations, teachers report that this game affords students unique opportunities to learn about labor-management relations—a concept which usually receives only incidental treatment in most social studies textbooks.

Publisher: Scott, Foresman and Company
1900 East Lake Avenue
Glenview, IL 60025

PROPAGANDA

Grade Levels: 8 and higher

Lifelong Role: *Personal Efficacy* (via the Media)

Description: *Propaganda* was designed by Robert W. Allen and Lorne Greene and field-tested in the Nova Schools, Ft. Lauderdale, Florida. The purpose of this game is to teach players to recognize propaganda techniques employed by attorneys, politicians, advertisers, and others, and differentiate emotional appeals from actual content of the idea. Over 50 propaganda techniques are presented through 240 examples. After players have completed their analysis, they can collect their own examples of propaganda and play a more sophisticated game.

Materials: Coordinator's manual, score chart, technique prediction dial cards, technique example cards.

Number of Players: 3 to 7

Playing Time: Very flexible. Approximately one hour required to master techniques used in the game. Typically length of play based on time limit or maximum score.

Recommendations: Preparations (roughly one hour) could occur outside of class. Once game begins, minimum teacher direction is needed. Game can be used in English, speech, and social studies classes—and in other courses stressing oral language. Teachers using this game report that students encounter difficulty in recalling definitions and examples of propaganda techniques, and recommend that duplicate lists of definitions and examples be prepared and distributed to students for use during play of the game. The game can be played in an average classroom without modification.

Publisher: Wff 'N Proof Company
Box 71-BA
New Haven, Conn. 06501

STARPOWER

Grade Levels: 6 and higher

Lifelong Role: *Personal Efficacy* (via Government and Politics and Morality)

Description: *Starpower* was designed by R. Garry Shirts and published by the Western Behavioral Sciences Institute in 1969. The game simulates the acquisition, uses, and abuses of power in a three-tiered society. Players can achieve upward mobility by acquiring wealth through trading with other players. Once the society has been established, the group with the most wealth is given the right to establish game rules which the other groups regard as unfair, self-serving, and autocratic. Typically a revolt ensues against the rules and rule makers, terminating the game.

Materials: Coordinator's manual, plastic chips, name cards for class of 25.
Number of Players: 15 to 40

Playing Time: Continuous two- to three-hour block of time.

Recommendations: This is by far the most effective simulation game we have ever used with middle-school students, owing to the high level of excitement and involvement it creates. *Starpower* can be used with nonreaders and slow learners. No reading or writing is required and mathematical computations are very simple. A large room is needed for effective play of the game. Teachers using *Starpower* should know their students well and should be prepared to help students handle the game's effect on their emotional behavior. The game should be played in one session. Debriefing questions are extremely useful as points of departure for self-analysis, and for helping players generalize from game experience to social realities of American society. Teachers can reduce cost of game materials by purchasing sample set ($3.00) and then using this as a guide for preparing their own student materials.

Publisher: Western Behavioral Sciences Institute
1150 Silverado Street
La Jolla, CA 92037

TIN LIZZIE

Grade Levels: 3 to 6

Lifelong Roles: *Personal Efficacy and Occupation*

Description: Designed for use with *Inquiring about Cities,* the third level of the *Holt Databank System, Tin Lizzie* simulates the construction of Model-T cars. During the course of the simulation the classroom becomes a make-believe automobile factory. The simulation occurs in three stages: (a) students assemble paper cars, using the nonassembly line or craftsman method; (b) students assemble cars, using the assembly line approach, with specific, specialized jobs assigned to individuals; and (c) half of the class builds cars under the craftsman approach, while the other half builds cars under the assembly line approach. Both modes are then compared in terms of efficiency.

Materials: Template ditto masters, which facilitate the production of multiple sets of patterns used in building the model cars, a sound filmstrip, and a recording.

Number of Players: Entire class.

Playing Time: Three or four class periods.

Recommendations: The purpose of the game is to teach pupils about different methods of production. That an art activity (cutting out patterns, coloring cars, and gluing components together) is involved should make this simulation an enjoyable experience for all children—especially those who have reading problems. There is an element of competition involved, as pupils receive $25.00 in play money for each car they produce, but this zero-sum feature is incidental and does not in any way limit the effectiveness of this simulation. The follow-up discussion is crucial, as it covers such topics as division of labor, specialization, the monotony of the assembly line, pride in workmanship, etc. Children who have used *Tin Lizzie* tell us that this is one of the most enjoyable parts of their social studies work.

Publisher: Holt, Rinehart and Winston
                         383 Madison Avenue
                         New York, NY 10017

SUMMARY

Social studies instruction will have limited meaning for children unless it enables them to become actively involved in learning experiences that have meaning for their daily lives. Dramatic play, role playing, and simulation games are extremely useful in this regard.

Dramatic play can consist of short reenactments of various human experiences that children encounter in their social studies program, or it can consist of a series of preplanned, organized experiences conducted over an extended period of time. When used in the latter sense, dramatic play enables children to gain a sense of responsibility toward themselves and others, state their learning goals, conduct research, and validate what they have learned. When used effectively, dramatic play is synonymous with fun—fun in playing and fun in learning what one desires to learn.

Role playing is more carefully organized and structured than dramatic play, and gives children an opportunity to thoroughly explore a problem situation and to resolve it. Although elementary teachers conduct role plays in different ways, most good role plays utilize a three-step procedure: the preparatory stages, the enactment or role-playing action, and follow-up discussion. Throughout the role-play experience teachers should refrain from interfering, and should make a special effort to encourage the audience to judge the roles being played and not the personalities of young actors and actresses.

Simulation games can make many valuable contributions to the elementary social studies program, if teachers become aware of their instructional capabilities, and make an effort to select, revise, and adapt them for their pupils.

Although a spirited debate is raging over the real or imagined advantages and disadvantages of simulation games, our experiences with them and the reports we have received from classrooms tend to support their use. Moreover, we are of the opinion that the real instructional pay-off from simulation games occurs when pupils design, use, and evaluate their own.

CROSS-REFERENCES TO TEACHING MODULES

All of the teaching modules in Part 2 stress the use of various forms of creative expression. Three modules which provide unusual opportunities for employing dramatic play, role play, and simulation are "The Energy Problem Is Our Problem," "New Insights into Aging," and "Participating in the Legislative Process."

Energy: "The Energy Problem Is Our Problem" (Part 2, p. 332).

The primary goal of this teaching module, designed for the middle grades (approximately 4 to 6), is to teach pupils about our existing and potential sources of energy, the causes of our energy crisis, and how they can become directly involved in solutions to our energy problems. Stressed in this module are the use of learning games and a variety of dramatic play experiences. Geography and economics contribute content to this module.

Human Life Cycle: "New Insights into Aging" (Part 2, p. 355).

Designed for the middle grades, this teaching module stresses that aging is a natural, inevitable process affecting everyone, that elderly people have unique physical, social, and emotional needs, and that elderly people can perform a vital, productive role in society—if we allow them to. Through dramatic play and role-play activities the module propels children into real-life situations involving the elderly. Content for this module is drawn primarily from sociology, anthropology, and social psychology.

Government and Politics: "Participating in the Legislative Process" (Part 2, p. 344).

This upper-grade (approximately grades 5 to 8 or 6 to 8) teaching module is designed to teach the need for laws, law-making functions of state legislatures and Congress, and the process by which a bill becomes a law. A significant element in this module is the simulation game, *Democracy*, which gives pupils first-hand experiences in the legislative process. Content for this module was drawn from the fields of political science and history.

BIBLIOGRAPHY

Books

Abt, Clark C. *Serious Games*. New York: The Viking Press, 1970.
A general overview of the theoretical and practical aspects of games written by a leading exponent and innovator.

Chapman, Katherine, J. E. Davis, and Andrea Meier. *Simulations/Games in Social Studies: What Do We Know?* Boulder, Colo.: Social Science Education Consortium, 1974.
An especially insightful analysis of the instructional capabilities of simulations and games.

Gordon, Alice Kaplan. *Games for Growth.* Palo Alto, Calif.: Science Research, 1970.
Gordon's perceptive, well-organized treatment of procedures for designing simulations strongly recommends it.

Hanna, Lavone A., Gladys L. Potter, and Robert W. Reynolds. *Dynamic Elementary Social Studies: Unit Teaching* (3d ed.). New York: Holt, Rinehart and Winston, 1973.
An extremely practical, usable text that covers a wide variety of learning activities. A definite must for your professional library.

Lee, John R. *Teaching Social Studies in the Elementary School.* New York: Free Press, 1974.
Chapters 16 and 19 are treasure troves of information on dramatic play and role playing, respectively. If you lend Lee's book to a colleague, it may never be returned.

Shaftel, Fannie R. and George Shaftel. *Role-Playing for Social Values.* Englewood Cliffs, N.J.: Prentice-Hall, 1967.
Clearly this is by far the *most* significant book on role playing that has been published for many years.

Social Education, 38 (March 1974), pp. 283–294.
Articles by Everett T. Keach, Jr., Joseph P. Stoltman, Earl C. Bagley, and David A. Pierfy present insightful analyses of simulation games, their development, use, and relationship to the elementary social studies curriculum. An absolute must!

Social Science Education Consortium. *Social Studies Curriculum Materials Data Book.* Boulder, Colo.: SSEC.
Published annually, this is a gold mine of information regarding materials used in teaching the social studies. Review of simulations tend to be relatively uncritical, but are highly descriptive.

Stadsklev, Ron. *Handbook of Simulation Gaming in Social Education.* University, Ala.: Institute of Higher Education, Research and Services, University of Alabama, 1976.
This two-volume publication, consisting of a textbook and a directory, is probably the best resource for teachers who wish to explore the capabilities of simulations. The textbook is easily understood and used.

Inexpensive Materials

Big Rock Candy Mountain: Resources of Our Nation
Dell Publishing Company, Inc.
750 Third Avenue
New York, NY 10017
A spinoff from *The Whole Earth Catalog.*

Elementary Teachers Guide to Five Curriculum Materials

Educators Guide to Free Social Studies Materials
Educators Progress Service, Inc.
Randolph, Wis. 53956
Should be in your school's professional library.

Materials List: A Useful List of Classroom Items
That Can Be Scrounged or Purchased

Educational Development Center
55 Chapel Street
Newton, Mass. 02160
An inexpensive but useful "idea" list.
Warman, Richard S. (ed.) *Yellow Pages of Learning Resources.*
The MIT Press
Massachusetts Institute of Technology
Cambridge, Mass. 02142
Let your fingers do the walking toward numerous learning resources found in most communities. This book will disappear from your book case if you're not careful; it's that valuable.

SKILL DEVELOPMENT

GOALS

1. Reexamine the role of skills in the social studies curriculum.
2. Gain new insights into the skill program as a part of the total curriculum and more specifically the role of skills in social studies instruction.
3. Determine the strengths and weaknesses of the skills program as a separate entity versus teaching skills as an integral part of social studies; update the existing program accordingly.
4. Gain new insights into the difference between using skills and teaching them; assess existing patterns of skill development, and revise instruction accordingly.
5. Review the four categories of social studies skills: Inquiry (critical thinking or problem solving), communication skills, map reading, and group work or social skills, and rethink the purposes of each.

It is generally acknowledged that public and professional interest in skills in the content areas has substantially increased during the last decade. The reasons are varied, reflecting in part: (a) growing legislative pressures at the state level; (b) emergence of new professional viewpoints; (c) mounting public concern about reported serious deficiencies in skill performance, particularly in the case of the economically and culturally disadvantaged, with growing distress concerning the "average" child; and (d) the availability of funds to support research and training for a "back-to-basics" approach.

These reasons suggest that a credibility gap exists between what schools say they are producing and what the public believes they are producing. Many taxpayers believe that the schools are inefficient and ineffective. They see too many kids who have not mastered such basic skills as using a telephone directory, keeping track of money in a checking account, or reading a city map. They want the schools to teach such fundamental skills while developing children's capacities to be humane and responsible citizens. All of these circumstances are leading to more demands for educational accountability. Certainly one aspect of instruction that can be measured is skill development. This emphasis on skill development encourages teachers to help their students move toward becoming more effective, mature adults, able to grapple with their life roles and problems inherent in a changing society.

Our rationale for increased attention to social studies skills in grades K–12 is based on the following assumptions:

1. In the past, too much attention has been given over to content which is very often learned at the figurative level and never made operational.
2. Skills are needed to identify, select, organize, evaluate, and apply information relevant to the study of a problem.
3. Skills have the potential of producing competencies needed for survival in a rapidly changing world.
4. Skill development can help children be more responsible for their own learning.
5. Skills are becoming increasingly more important because scientific knowledge is doubling every decade.
6. The vast amount of new instructional materials available to kids places more demands on skill development than ever before; yet too frequently we assume that kids have already mastered such basic skills as reading and effective discussion techniques.
7. Skills are indeed one dimension of the social studies curriculum that can be measured, both formally in school, as well as informally in out-of-school real-life situations.

While we are not at all sure what jobs will be available for the kids of today, we are certain that skills will be essential for them to gain the minimum of economic security, social maturity, and independence. Skill competencies can do more than help an individual acquire a job—they will also become important in interpersonal relationships within the family structure as well as outside of it, in leisure activities, in citizenship roles, and in perceptions of self.

Skills cannot be isolated from the rest of the educational process. While they can be dealt with as discrete entities for purposes of clarity, they are really inextricably related to content and attitudes. They can be defined as tools essential in performing a physical, mental, or emotional task. If taught properly, they can be transferred from one situation to another. They can be refined with practice and with the child's maturity.

TEACHING SKILLS

While you might philosophically agree with the authors that skills are important and should be taught, you might be facing the same problem that thousands of other teachers are facing: "How do I teach skills and everything else I'm supposed to do?" This is a major concern, and one not easily answered. The first thing that you must do is *decide on your priorities*. Ask yourself these questions: "Does the social studies content that I teach interest me or the kids?" "How much of the existing content taught in isolation will be retained?" "Could I teach content and skills together?" "If I'm teaching a unit on 'Families,' could I teach the skill of locating information at the same time that I teach the concept that families differ in size and composition?" Perhaps you could teach essay writing in conjunction with a unit on community. There are unlimited possibilities, especially if you plan to integrate language arts and social studies. Obviously this approach would take large amounts of planning to make sure that each subject area is getting adequate balanced coverage.

Another approach is to teach skills apart from other existing content and reinforce the skills when appropriate, in social studies, language arts, reading, and the other content areas. There are several skills programs that can be used in this slightly more isolated format. A good example (for map and globe skills exclusively) is the Nystrom Map and Globe materials. The authors of this material have identified a scope and sequence for map skills in the elementary grades, and have designed appropriate exercises for the student. We feel that whether you use this more isolated approach or the integrated one, the important thing is that you teach skills and relate them to existing content, and even more importantly that you relate them to real-life situations.

If you have made the decision to teach skills, your next concern no doubt will be, "Where do I begin?" To date there is no research to give us the answers about precise grade placement of skills. The wide range of students within any given classroom seems to indicate that instruction should be far more individualized than ever before. The continuity of skill development is essential as skills build on each other and, to some extent, can be practiced concurrently.

In one Michigan school system, teachers have taken this awesome concern very seriously. They decided that skill development should be a top priority, not only in social studies, but across all content areas. Each content area specialist in high school, middle school, as well as committees of elementary school teachers perused all instructional and testing materials related to skill development. They listed all the skills that were taught and all the skills that were used in each content area. Needless to say, they produced lengthy lists with lots of overlap. Their next step was to make some arbitrary decisions based on their findings about the subject areas and the grade levels responsible for *introducing and teaching* the skills, and the areas and grade levels responsible for *giving practice* in using the skills. In addition, the teachers designed practical experiences for using the skills both in and out of school. Their next step is to develop informal evaluation procedures to check student performance and progress. A master chart is being developed by the curriculum coordinator of this school district to provide a graphic view of their skill development. It will look something like Table 5–1 on page 110.

The Michigan school system is convinced that it is must identify the skills that should be introduced, taught, and used and also feel that with cooperative planning, implementation will be possible. Not only do they want to implement the systematic teaching of skills, they also want to show students in concrete ways how the skills will contribute to their lives both in and out of school.

Your response to the above might be "That sounds great, but what happens to content? I can't stuff anything else into the already bulging curriculum." We would predict that the Michigan school teachers in this district might respond as follows: "Having a stockpile of knowledge may be necessary and useful for a productive and successful life, but it is insufficient. Learning how to learn and having the tools to do so are essential for all humans." These teachers, therefore,

Table 5–1 SCOPE AND SEQUENCE CHART OF SKILLS

Skill To Be taught	Content Area Responsible for Teaching Skill	Practical Application	Strategy To Be Used	Skill To Be Used	Content Area Responsible for Using It	Practical Application	Strategy To Be Used	Evaluation
12								
11								
10								
9								
8								
7								
6								
5								
4								
3								
2								
1								
K								

are identifying concepts out of their existing texts and tying in the organizing themes to add relevancy. In addition they are adding the skills they have been charged to teach or use. A third-grade teacher might select the topic community from the text. She adds consumerism for relevancy, teaches the skill of interviewing, and uses or reinforces listening. To some of you the previous example probably sounds like a panacea. You might feel that you could not get the teachers at your grade level to agree on anything, far less an entire staff. Perhaps you have never even talked to high school social studies teachers. Quite obviously, we would hope that plans could be made for K–12 staff meetings that really begin to "carve out" ways to systematically build a skill program. For the time being we suggest that you carefully examine the texts and evaluation materials that you use in your classroom and identify the skills that are being taught, used, or reinforced. Make yourself a chart similar to the one that the Michigan teachers are developing and jump in with both feet.

If by now we have convinced you to develop a skills component in your curriculum, the next step is to write it down in a way that will be operational for you and useful when you communicate with parents and administrators. When you have developed your plan in writing you are ready for the third step, which is probably the most difficult—implementation.

Is teaching or implementing skills really that hard? Think about this for a moment: "What skill did I teach today?" "How?" Did you really teach the skill or did the kids merely try to use the skill? Herber argues that too many teachers are what he calls "assumptive" teachers, who assume that their students already possess the reading, writing, and thinking skills necessary to complete assigned learning activities. These teachers make little attempt to diagnose the degree of the child's mastery prior to instruction. Consequently, when many kids achieve poorly, the teacher often blames the content rather than the real cause, which is inadequate mastery of skills needed to grapple with the content.[1]

Herber believes many teachers feel that they do teach basic skills in their classes; however, he says actually they may be having the kids use these skills or testing for them instead.[2] Recently we polled a class of thirty teachers. We asked each to identify one skill that they taught during a given week and tell explicitly how it was developed. Much to our chagrin, and theirs too, twenty-nine had used or tested the skill with worksheets or exercises and only one had actually taught a skill. In many, many cases teachers merely require students to use whatever skills they have in order to accomplish content related objectives.

To teach skills rather than merely asking children to use the skills requires deliberate attention to the skills themselves—drawing, of course, content from one or more sources. It is essential that teachers provide guidance, direction, and assistance to children in how to *use* the skill. According to Barry Beyer, effective skill teaching requires two things: (a) knowledge of the essential steps or opera-

[1]Harold Herber, *Teaching Reading in Content Areas* (Englewood Cliffs, N.J.: Prentice-Hall, 1970), pp. vi–viii.
[2]Herber, pp. vi–viii.

tions which constitute the skill (developed by demonstration, explanation, and reflection); and (b) doing the skill (developed by guided practice).[3]

One common strategy that Beyer suggests as a means of helping children learn new skills and refine existing ones is as follows:

1. Read about, tell about, or show the skill.
2. Explain the steps involved in using the skill.
3. Demonstrate the skill.
4. Practice the skill numerous times on a variety of data or examples.
5. Reflect on and summarize the skill and its components.[4]

For example, if you were attempting to teach paragraph writing, you could proceed as follows:

1. Read paragraphs that are well organized. You might even read one that is not well organized and compare them. How are they different? Give kids written examples of good and bad paragraphs.
2. Write a paragraph on the blackboard. Explain the steps. You might use Beyer's "Hamburger" idea. He indicates that a well-organized paragraph contains the topic sentence which presents the key idea—this is the top roll. It has a bottom roll which attempts to wrap up or summarize what the writer has attempted to communicate in the paragraph. The "hamburger meat" of the paragraph really consists of the information given to clarify, explain, support, or exemplify the main idea. The condiments (onions, mustard, catsup, etc.) make the meat more tasty. These correspond to the details and examples used to explain the facts.
3. Select a subject that is of interest to students and demonstrate the writing of a paragraph. Write the paragraph on the blackboard. If you do not have a blackboard, place it on the overhead on a large sheet of paper. The important thing is that everyone must see the demonstration and the finished product in total.
4. Have the kids write several paragraphs, using social studies subjects they are studying. Hopefully included in the content will be one or more of the organizing themes inherent in each of the life roles. For example, if you are studying Japan, think of ways ecology or the life cycle relates to the Japanese and their cultural setting.
5. Periodically reflect with the students what they have learned about writing paragraphs. Have them compare some of their paragraphs over time. Have them analyze the work of another writer. Then summarize the skill and its components through a class discussion.[5]

It should be clear from the above five steps that skills consist of organized and coordinated activities that are built up gradually through repeated experiences.[6] For our purposes we will look at social studies skills as mainly cognitive

[3] Barry Beyer, "Teaching Basics in Social Studies," *Social Education*, Vol. 41, No. 1, (February 1977), p. 98.
[4] Beyer, p. 98.
[5] Beyer, p. 98.
[6] David Legge (ed.), *Skills* (Baltimore: Penguin, 1970), p. 22.

and affective abilities based on one's experiences, aptitude, knowledge, and practice. We are not in any way saying that there is a body of skills unique to social studies; rather we believe that the skills used in social studies cut across all content areas.

While there are many ways of categorizing skills used in social studies, we will arbitrarily identify four major ones—namely, critical thinking and problem solving, which we will refer to as inquiry; communication skills; map reading skills; and group work or social skills. We will describe some skills inherent in each category, and provide some helpful hints for implementing these skills. We hope you will use the results of our attempt as a skeletal framework and fill in the missing parts. No skills will be labeled for the disadvantaged because we feel that too often labeling causes teachers to ignore the manifold differences among pupils. The most important thing is to assess children's development and take them from that point forward, keeping in mind always that there is no one approach to meet the diverse needs of diverse students. We hope that the ensuing discussions will provide you with a framework on which to construct your skills program.

INQUIRY: CRITICAL THINKING OR PROBLEM SOLVING

As we discuss the inquiry skills (critical thinking and problem solving), keep in mind that different students learn in different ways. Some students prefer group inquiry/problem-solving activities while others prefer to work independently. Some children gain most from structured inquiry while others seem to be most successful when they create their own structure. Some seem to learn best from such visual materials as pictures, films, and other media, while others learn more from reading. Some children need many concrete examples, while others are ready for more abstractions. Some kids prefer and do best with the manipulation of spatial problems while others find these the most difficult. All of these learning styles of students can and should be accommodated in inquiry/problem solving. A popular inquiry model that can include diverse learning styles includes the following steps:

1. Recognition or identification of a problem
2. Developing hypotheses
3. Data collection
4. Data analysis
5. Drawing "tentative" conclusions and reassuring hypotheses

While frequently the steps are not easily separated or appear in a different order, you as the teacher should be aware of the unique characteristics and special problems associated with various stages. For more information about this inquiry model or several others that can be implemented we refer you to Chapter 3.

Recognition or Identification of a Problem

There are several key items to remember in this initial stage:

1. The child cannot apply his past experiences until he recognizes that there is a problem.
2. The child needs to learn to point out the critical issues within a problem.
3. The teacher needs to stimulate the children's interests so that they really want to learn. Use all kinds of imaginable resources.
4. The problem must not be so difficult that it goes beyond the student's level of understanding. Keep in mind that within any given class there are wide differences among achievement levels.
5. The problem or issue needs to have a direct relationship to the children's lives and their concerns. It should be seen as a part of the real world.
6. The problem selected should be important and not so narrow that it will merely reinforce the narrow views already held by students.
7. The problem should help students realize that what they thought they knew is not totally accurate, or it should help them become aware of how much more there is to know.
8. In presenting the problem, vary the format from unit to unit to avoid boredom.[7]

Developing Hypotheses

After a problem has been identified, a hypothesis can be defined as a speculation or hunch. This is helpful in finding a solution to a problem. Helpful questions might be: "What do I know?" "What do I suspect is true about the topic?" With early elementary school children, questions are frequently posed instead of hypotheses. Teachers have found that by providing related topics or experiences children are helped through the initial stages of solving the problem. Keep in mind also that some children hypothesize or question first, then go back and identify the problem. Various interest and ability groups can be accommodated through these avenues.

During this stage of hypothesizing and questioning, idea generation skills are probably the most important because the direction for further investigation or research is usually set at this point. If a student's idea seems farfetched or impossible, the teacher needs to ask a series of probing questions to help the child focus and clarify his ideas. The following are key points to keep in mind when helping children work through this:

1. Have pupils ask questions if they cannot think of hypotheses.
2. Behavior and social phenomena are emphasized instead of individuals or institutions. Insure that data are not heavily infused with values because it will be impossible or extremely difficult to test them.
3. After exhausting ideas for relevant hypotheses, group the hypotheses, and put them aside for later refinement and clarification.

[7]Drawn from June R. Chapin and Richard E. Gross, *Teaching Social Studies Skills* (Boston: Little, Brown and Company, 1973), pp. 154–164.

4. Make sure that during this stage you allow students to clarify their own values.
5. Good hypotheses should be based upon sound reasoning.
6. As an alternative to total class participation in the generation of hypotheses or questions, allow students to work in groups.
7. Make sure that children realize that all hypotheses need not be accepted and emphasize the fact that they can learn just as much if they reject the hypothesis. The students, of course, need to be able to demonstrate at some later time why their original hunches were correct or incorrect.
8. Keep in mind that many students have not been rewarded in the past for asking questions or proposing ideas.[8]

These eight points, while not all inclusive, should provide direction as you guide students in using some of the more up-to-date social studies text materials and/or the modules provided in Sections A–C of our text. There seems to be an increased emphasis in new social studies materials to encourage—better yet, urge—students to develop and test their own hypotheses or questions. Therefore, you need to be flexible and you need to keep your kids interested and reward them for their promising ideas.

Data Collection

After hypotheses have been formulated you and your students need to ask, "How researchable are these ideas or questions?" This question may not be answered in total at the outset and often during the process the hypotheses have to be refined, modified, or discarded. Students must consider the evidence that will help to explain, solve, describe, or clarify a hypothesis or question. Students or groups must work out some information-selecting processes that will help them answer or solve the problem under study. While young children are less capable than older students in gathering data, they can learn how to become better observers of social phenomena; invariably teachers have demonstrated that even children in the lower grades are able to use elementary research techniques with success.

Many factors determine how open the process of collecting data will be. If "packaged material" is used, obviously there are limitations on the scope of the investigation, because the data from which the child can draw a "tentative" conclusion has been preselected and somewhat limited. Typically, however, these "prepackaged" materials give a variety of source documents, pictures, cassette tapes, and other resources and from this material the teacher can guide the children into comparing, contrasting, analyzing statistics, assessing value conflicts, etc. Three popular and excellent examples of such programs are *Holt Databank System, Man: A Course of Study,* and *Family of Man.* While you need to recognize the limitations of these approaches and modify them to your specific teaching styles, certainly materials such as artifacts, games, first-rate films, tapes, maps, documents and other manipulative materials provide a greater data base than the typical teacher could locate.

[8]Drawn from June R. Chapin and Richard E. Gross. *Teaching Social Studies Skills* (Boston: Little, Brown and Company, 1973), pp. 164–171.

Whether you use "prepackaged" materials, gather your own by tapping all available resources, or use a combination of the two, it is vital that the materials offer more than one point of view or interpretation. In real life, data does not come all sorted out and layered according to different points of view. In fact, people are bombarded with information coming from television, books, newspapers and journals, and from other people; therefore, it seems critical that students learn to locate, observe, sort out, organize, and analyze the data surrounding them.

Probably the most important thing for students to learn from this often exciting but difficult process is that the library sources, their own texts, and their own personal fieldwork give data about a very small portion that is known about any particular topic. Students must become aware that they are thus dealing with biased information, since all points of view are not presented and, therefore, conclusions are "very tentative"; it is often impossible to arrive at valid generalizations. Part of the real value of having students gather their own data is to help them become increasingly more critical of the validity of their sources as well as those of the experts.[9] The following key points will be helpful in guiding children through this phase:

1. The major objective is not the particular data gathered or the hypothesis, but rather the skill and attitudes that are developed in collecting the data and drawing conclusions.
2. Using the scientific method of data collection requires that data gathering be objective and unbiased. While all people in a group cannot be questioned, for example, social scientists use the research technique of sampling to select a portion, or sample, that accurately represents the total population.
3. The need to choose a data sample is important if the student's research involves watching and listening to people, asking questions through interviews, and asking people for information through questionnaires or inventories.
4. While engaging in direct observations, students need to be aware of what they are looking for and the degree to which a group of students can agree on what they are observing. For example, if we are studying the organizing theme, human equality, by observing prejudices shown toward women in the work force, then each student must clearly know what is meant by the term, prejudice, what they are looking for when they say prejudice, and what specific behaviors would be classified as such.[10] The Michigan Elementary Social Science Education Program, published under the title *Social Science Laboratory Units*,[11] can serve as a good resource.
5. One useful technique for collecting data is the interview, a face-to-face interaction during which time the interviewee or respondent responds orally to the questions.
6. Another useful technique for gathering data is the questionnaire, a written set of questions which can be mailed to respondents; the questionnaire does not involve social interaction.

[9]June R. Chapin and Richard E. Gross, *Teachig Social Studies Skills* (Boston: Little, Brown, 1973), pp. 178–179.

[10]Drawn from June R. Chapin and Richard E. Gross. *Teaching Social Studies Skills* (Boston: Little, Brown and Comany, 1973), pp. 178–181.

[11]Ronald Lippitt, Robert Fox, and Lucille Schaible, "Social Science Laboratory Units, Teacher's Guide" (Chicago: Science Research, 1969).

7. Careful planning is necessary for designing questions for an interview or question-naire. There are basically four formats available for the respondent's answers. The first is the *forced* choice in which the respondent must select from several alternatives. The second is the *scale question* in which the respondent answers by taking a position. The third is *rank order,* and the fourth is *open ended* in which the respon-dent can answer any way he wishes.

8. The following criteria should be used to evaluate the questions for the interview or questionnaire before any formal field research is done *unless the purpose of the activity is to have children find out the weakness* in their instrument: (a) the data that are desired in the end must be decided upon explicitly; (b) the group of people identified to respond must be qualified and willing; (c) the questions must be clearly understood.

9. A well prepared worksheet should be developed to enable ease and accuracy in recording data. All data should be double checked.[12]

10. During coding, the following criteria should be followed: (a) each answer should fit into only one category; (b) the classification process should be reliable so that the different people more or less agree on where each response should be classified; (c) categories that help to answer the original hypotheses should be established; (d) too many categories should be avoided. Usually after eight or ten, it becomes too difficult to remember all of them.[13] The authors urge you to pay careful attention to this section as numerous opportunities for data gathering are found in the modules—Sections A, B, and C.

Data Analysis

After the data have been gathered from the various sources and have been tabulated in some form, students must attempt to put meaning to the evidence. This process is referred to as data analysis. The following analytical skills will be drawn upon:

1. Evaluating the sources of information
2. Distinguishing between fact and opinion
3. Distinguishing between primary (first hand) and secondary (second hand) sources.
4. Distinguishing between fact and value statements[14]
5. Identifying relevant and irrelevant information

If these skills are new to students, it might be wise to teach them in isolation first, then practice with the data that the individual or class has gathered.

Some skills that students will need to draw upon in analyzing data gathered from textbooks, library materials, interviews, questionnaires, or other sources include: comparing and contrasting (looking for likenesses and differences among

[12]June R. Chapin and Richard E. Gross. *Teaching Social Studies Skills* (Boston: Little, Brown and Company, 1973), p. 183–

[13]June R. Chapin and Richard E. Gross. *Teaching Social Studies Skills* (Boston: Little, Brown and Company, 1973), p. 188.

[14]June R. Chapin and Richard E. Gross. *Teaching Social Studies Skills* (Boston: Little, Brown and Company, 1973), p. 190.

data), using promising concepts to make inferences from new data, using both inductive and deductive reasoning, and verifying the feasibility or accuracy of the data.

As students attempt to verify the feasibility or accuracy of the data, make sense out of them or try to see connections among the data, they need to zero in on a form of analysis. A very simple design for classifying data is to put all evidence that appears to uphold the hypothesis in one pile and all the evidence that appears to reject the hypothesis in another pile. From there the student or class can ask why or what characteristics appear associated with one set of facts or opinions. Other questions include: Can they be organized into additional categories? Which data represent evidence? Which data fail to represent evidence? Interpretations? Conclusions? What evidence appears irrelevant? Weak?[15]

Classification of data has received attention in some of the social studies projects. For example, the "Taba Program" published by Addison-Wesley emphasizes that concepts are learned through enumerating and categorizing. Listening, grouping, and labeling are used over and over to teach concepts or generalized bodies of attributes associated with the symbol for a class of things, events, or ideas. See Table 5–2 for an illustration of this.[16]

Following this task in the Taba scheme, the students must infer and generalize about the data. The third task consists of applying previously learned generalizations and facts to explain unfamiliar phenomena. The fourth task concerns the explanation of feelings, and the fifth task deals with interpersonal problem solving. The sixth and final task addresses the analysis of values. We refer you back to Chapter 3 for more detail.

After the data have been classified a statistical analysis can be applied. Elementary-school children can compute mean, median, and modes as well as grapple with such information as, "60 percent of their sample was in favor of storm windows as an energy saving device, 30 percent disapproved, and 10 percent really didn't care; or that the average number of television serials viewed by women at home during the afternoon on blocks of X, Y, and Z was 10.5 per week."

A fine resource for the teacher interested in statistics for the classroom is a text by Townshend and Burke, entitled *Statistics for the Classroom Teacher*.[17] Helpful hints for teaching data analysis include the following:

1. Integrate social studies and mathematics for teaching/learning graph construction/ analysis. Use real-life problems whenever possible!
2. Help students in becoming more aware of classifications and how they permeate into the world around us.

[15]Drawn from June R. Chapin and Richard E. Gross. *Teaching Social Studies Skills* (Boston: Little, Brown and Company, 1973), pp. 188–191.
[16]Alice Duvall, Mary C. Durkin, and Katharine C. Leffler, *The Taba Social Studies Curriculum, Grade Five: United States and Canada—Societies in Transition* (Reading, Mass.: Addison Wesley, 1969), pp. xxii.
[17]Edward A. Townshend and Paul J. Burke, *Statistics for the Classroom Teacher* (New York: Macmillan, 1967).

TABLE 5–2 DEVELOPING CONCEPTS[1]

LISTING, GROUPING, AND LABELING

This task requires students to group a number of items on some kind of basis. The teaching strategy consists of asking students the following questions, usually in this order.

Teacher Asks:	Student	Teacher Follow Through
What do you see (notice, find) here?	Gives items	Makes sure items are accessible to each student For example: Chalkboard Transparency Individual list Pictures Item card
Do any of these items seem to belong together?	Finds some similarity as a basis for grouping items.	Communicates grouping. For example: Underlines in colored chalk Marks with symbols Arranges pictures or cards
Why would you group them together?[2]	Identifies and verbalizes the common characteristics of items in a group.	Seeks clarification of responses when necessary.
What would you call these groups you have formed?	Verbalizes a label (perhaps more than one word) that appropriately encompasses all items	Records
Could some of these belong in more than one group?	States different relationships	Records
Can we put these same items in different groups?[3]	States additional different relationships	Communicates grouping

[1] Alice Duvall, Mary C. Durkin, and Katharine C. Leffler, *The Taba Social Studies Curriculum—Grade Five: United States and Canada—Societies in Transition* (Reading, Mass.: Addison-Wesley, 1969), p. xxii.
[2] Sometimes you ask the same child "why" when he offers the grouping, and other times you may wish to get many groups before considering "why" things are grouped together.
[3] Although this step is important because it encourages flexibility, it will not be appropriate on all occasions.

3. Help students make sense of and see relationships between data.
4. Use existing concepts to search for new data and in organizing new/existing data.[18]

Drawing Conclusions and Reassessing Hypotheses

After the data have been analyzed and interpreted to the best of the students' abilities, they are ready for the final task of inquiry or problem solving, namely drawing a "tentative" conclusion. It is "tentative" in the sense that it involves working with limited data. From the tentative conclusion the initial hypotheses, hunches, or questions can be reassessed. Teachers need to help students realize that tentative conclusions and assessment of hypotheses can really only be made when the data sample is representative of the identified population and the data analysis has been carried out in a systematic, reliable way. Students must be willing to accept the fact that inquiry does not yield final answers. They need to foster, always, a critical attitude toward hypotheses and generalizations.

Students are constantly asked to accept, modify, or reject a hypothesis. *The Taba Social Studies Program*[19] is a good example of a social studies project that stresses the need for students to try to generalize at the end of their inquiry experience. Students are asked to interpret, infer, and generalize about the data. To make a generalization the inquirer makes assumptions about all members of the class or objects. It is most difficult to make a statement that always holds true; therefore, as we stated earlier, a generalizable fact is often made about a subgroup. Students need lots of practice in working with data to enable them to see the inherent difficulties in generalizing about a given sample.

Social action is another aspect that is often connected with generalizing, drawing tentative conclusions, and reassessing hypotheses. This would be especially true if you use our organizing themes approach. Inquiry training should help students attain essential insights for drawing "tentative" conclusions, using the best rules of action, with of course attention being directed toward alternatives and consequences. Action may only be a letter to the grocer telling him that his prices are not competitive with the supermarket and if he wants the student's business he will have to lower the prices. Advocates of this position feel it is psychologically necessary for children to think about social action after an inquiry experience. *The Unified Sciences and Math Project*,[20] developed by Educational Development Center, has social action built into each of its real-life problems and philosophically supports the notion that children should feel that what they do *does make a difference.* Our lifelong roles–organizing themes approach would be supportive of this in that what we teach should help children be more adaptive in their life roles. Throughout this text the authors refer you to Sections A–C in Part 2 for specific examples of how social action can be implemented in the social studies program and be an integral part of students' lives.

[18]Drawn from June R. Chapin and Richard E. Gross. *Teaching Social Studies Skills* (Boston: Little, Brown and Company, 1973), pp. 203–204.
[19]*The Taba Curriculum Development Project* (Reading, Mass.: Addison Wesley, 1969–1972).
[20]Educational Development Center, "Unified Sciences and Mathematics Project" (Newton, Mass.: Educational Development Center, 1975).

To summarize this section on drawing conclusions and reassessing hypotheses we suggest you consider the following as you plan for inquiry lessons in your classroom:

1. Make sure that students gather "representative" data.
2. Make sure students realize that they are dealing with "limited" data.
3. In guiding students as they draw "tentative" conclusions, make sure they carefully and reliably analyze data.
4. Try to assess the motivational level of students. If they are working with real-life data, are they ready to take some sort of action on the problem?
5. Have students examine their hypotheses for possible social and value implications. Will these affect the tentative conclusions?
6. At the conclusion of each inquiry experience, ask students if generalizations are possible as a result of their study.[21]

While critical thinking, inquiry, and problem solving are vitally important to the social studies, communication skills likewise play an equally important part. The next section will consider this body of skills and how they can be used in social studies instruction.

COMMUNICATION SKILLS

Attention to communication skills in teaching social studies yields rich returns in subject matter outcomes. Michaelis reminds us that the more efficient the child is in the use of these skills, the more easily he can acquire social studies concepts; and the more concepts built into the social studies, the more effective the child will be in the communication of ideas.[22]

Through attentive listening to conversations, discussions, debates, explanations, and reports in a social studies class, the child can add to his ideas and interests. By listening to directions given for reading assignments, visual aids, as well as for studying maps, landscapes, and artifacts the child can improve his work in individual and small group activities. The child is able to improve his ability to observe and discover by explaining what he has seen to his teachers and peers. By improving his skills in asking questions, the child is able to clarify and eventually acquire new desired knowledge.

Through the use of reading and the other work study skills the child is able to gain information and check ideas gained from research in the field. The child is also able to become a more independent problem solver, because he is able to gain information through the printed word. Often the solution or partial solution to a given problem leads to new questions and thus to new motivation. Skill in the use

---

[21]Drawn from June R. Chapin and Richard E. Gross. *Teaching Social Studies Skills* (Boston: Little, Brown and Company, 1973), pp. 199–200.
[22]John U. Michaelis (Ed.), *"Social Studies in Elementary Schools." Thirty-second Yearbook of the National Council for Social Studies* (Washington, D.C.: National Council for Social Studies, 1962).

of the library, especially the reference books and the card catalog, gives the child unlimited opportunities for advancing research and study.

Children who are actively engaged in inquiry have unlimited opportunities to use writing skills in social studies. They can keep all kinds of records which assist them in making comparative studies. They list their plans for their field research; they record their notes or logs; they draw maps or diagrams; and they prepare reports of their results. In addition, they often write letters in an attempt to acquire more information. For all of these reasons and many more, writing too, seems vital to social studies.

The following pages, which were taken from the 32d Yearbook of the National Council for Social Studies, will provide an outline of the common communication skills taught in grades 1–8.[23] Keep in mind that the grade level for teaching and reinforcing these skills should be adjusted to meet the needs and individual differences of the particular students you have in your classroom. Ideally, it would be wise for your school system to develop a scope and sequence chart of skills similar to the one we mentioned earlier. This would involve subject area and the level where the skill will be taught and subject areas and the level where the skills will formally be reinforced. This should in no way restrict other teachers from using the skills in their teaching.

Many of the skills identified on the following pages will be used in the teaching modules found in Sections A–C. As you modify the modules to meet the needs of your children, we are sure you will find many other skills equally as appropriate.

COMMUNICATION SKILLS[24]

Speaking and Listening Skills

I. Primary grades, 1–3. The child:
1. Participates increasingly in informal conversation, taking his turn, listening with courtesy, and saying something of interest (e.g., as children inspect a display table or new books on a unit).
2. Contributes to group and class discussion, showing increasing ability to listen thoughtfully, to stay with the topic, and to ask pertinent questions.
3. Asks and answers simple questions with increasing skill, determining what information is wanted, wording the question to obtain a clear answer, making brief statements that are to the point (e.g., before, during, or after a field trip; or visit of a guest speaker).
4. Follows simple directions, listening intently, noting the sequence of steps, and being sure he understands the directions before trying to carry them out (e.g., directions for a project such as preparing a bulletin board on animals that graze; recording on a slate or plastic globe Columbus' route when he discovered America).
5. Gives short, clear oral reports, sticking to his subject, using good, clear language of his own, and

---

[23]Michaelis, pp. 177–187.
[24]Michaelis pp. 177–187. The list of skills is used with the permission of the National Council for Social Studies.

presenting ideas worth listening to (e.g., explaining a social studies concept, how something is done, or what was learned from a travel story).

6. Shows skill in social situations (e.g., inviting a parent to tell of a country he has visited, inviting another class to see a dramatization or hear reports of what has been learned; using the telephone to obtain needed information).

7. Attends a radio or television program, listening attentively for a specific purpose (e.g., for general background on wild animals; to learn what some other part of the world looks like; to enjoy a historical story).

II. Intermediate grades, 4–6. The child:

1. Makes an effort to get interesting material for conversation (e.g., through observing, listening, interviewing, and reading both in and out of school).

2. Speaks clearly and directly, using appropriate social studies vocabulary with understanding and correct pronunciation.

3. Notes discrepancies and gaps in the information his classmates offer orally.

4. Differs courteously with the views of others; when necessary, gives evidence from authorities in support of his own view.

5. Asks pertinent questions to gain understanding and to draw out the reticent and unresponsive pupil; does not monopolize the discussion.

6. Accepts increasing responsibility for the reasonableness and accuracy of what is said.

7. Times his contribution so that it relates to what has preceded and carries the discussion forward; contributes to real thinking together.

8. Gives accurate directions for locating a place on the globe or map.

9. Gives particular attention to time expressions such as "meanwhile," "a decade," and "ancient," and to the location of the places being discussed.

10. Listens for important facts and ideas to be remembered; tries to retain these.

11. Serves successfully as a discussion leader, both of small groups and of the entire class (e.g., draws out the ideas of classmates, keeps the discussion progressing, summarizes the main ideas).

12. Outlines and organizes ideas in advance of giving an oral report.

III. Upper grades, 7–8. The child:

1. Follows the thought of the speaker; listens with an open mind; thinks through and weighs the ideas; grasps significant facts and ideas.

2. Uses social studies language effectively to explain, to describe, to inform, and to narrate.

3. Uses material from an increasing variety of sources in both conversations and discussions.

4. Points out false ideas and inadequacies of facts clearly and calmly.

5. Brings discussion back to the subject by restating the problem for clarification.

6. Changes the topic of conversation tactfully if it becomes unpleasant or unproductive for the class.

7. Interrupts courteously and sets others on the right track when points are misinterpreted.

8. Gives brief, concise summaries of what is heard.

9. Makes more detailed outlines preparatory to giving an oral report (e.g., lists topics and subtopics in proper sequence for presentation); reorganizes and restates information in his own words.

10. Uses simple parliamentary procedures efficiently (e.g., presides over a group discussion, carries out duties of class officers, participates in making decisions by voting orally and in writing, abides by the results, understands the points of views of minorities).

11. Conducts an interview with an adult in his home or at his place of business (e.g., introduces himself, states the purpose of the interview, asks questions in meaningful sequence, takes notes, expresses appreciation for the interview).

12. Organizes and presents the findings of an interview, giving an interesting and enlightening account of what was learned.

Reading Skills

I. Primary grades, 1–3. The child:

1. Locates needed material within books (e.g., locates stories by examining the table of contents; peruses material to find the answer to a question; indicates it by placing a marker in the book).
2. Understands and interprets short, easy-to-read social studies material (e.g., recalls important concepts as a background for understanding; recognizes the meanings of words; reflects on what is read; rereads when necessary).
3. Reads orally to an audience with accuracy, fluency, and understanding (e.g., to present new ideas, prove a point, answer a question).
4. Reads extensively with pleasure and interest simple stories containing the travel element and easy informational accounts.

II. Intermediate grades, 4–6. The child:

1. Makes use of simple bibliographies in locating social studies material.
2. Locates needed references on shelves in a children's library.
3. Finds sources of social studies material by using the table of contents, index, and list of maps.
4. Evaluates a book in terms of the purposes for which it is needed (e.g., Does it give enough material to satisfy the purpose? How recent is this material? What questions does it leave unanswered?).
5. Understands social studies material of appropriate difficulty and interprets it accurately (e.g., knows words that are more or less unique to social studies; gathers ideas from the accompanying maps, charts, diagrams, and illustrations).
6. Follows the logical organization of a simple social studies selection (e.g., notes topic headings, uses them as aids in comprehension and selection of central ideas, sees paragraph organization, recognizes the progression of ideas).
7. Skims and reads material rapidly as an aid in selecting important ideas to remember.
8. Organizes the ideas in relation to the question or other purpose of the reading.
9. Reads widely with interest and understanding narrative and other materials of suitable reading difficulty, including children's literature on the subjects being studied.

III. Upper grades, 7–8. The child:

1. Finds sources of material by using the parts of a book including simple appendices and items mentioned in II–3 above; consults bibliographies at the ends of chapters in social studies books.
2. Uses efficiently atlases, geographic handbooks, yearbooks, and other references such as *The World Almanac* and yearbooks of the Department of Agriculture.
3. Locates material through the use of the card catalog in elementary and junior high school libraries.
4. Checks sources of information for reliability on such bases as competence and objectivity of author, sources of data, etc.
5. Adapts his reading techniques to his purposes for reading.
6. Understands and interprets accurately tables and graphs found in social studies material.
7. Thinks critically concerning the ideas given in social studies material; begins to recognize propaganda and bias.
8. Reaches valid generalizations on the basis of material read; applies these in interpreting new content.
9. Synthesizes information from several sources for his own use; classifies the pertinent facts and ideas in a desired order.
10. Makes more elaborate preparation for giving a report (e.g., carries on wide reference reading; studies pertinent maps and data such as rainfall or temperature data; makes notes of ideas to be remembered; decides upon the best form for the report—outline, narrative, or exposition).
11. Reads widely for information as well as pleasure.

Study Skills

I. Primary grades, 1–3. The child:
   1. Follows directions to locate information in classroom books (e.g., turn to page 26, find the picture of the fireman).
   2. Works and studies successfully by himself or in a small group as required by the study situation or the directions of the teacher.
   3. Alphabetizes items according to first letters (e.g., forest, fog, highway, health).
   4. Begins to use children's encyclopedias to satisfy curiosities (e.g., pictures of airplanes, old cars, people in other lands).
   5. Reads simple picture maps, giving information about a place or region (e.g., the public buildings in our town, the kinds of crops on our farms).
   6. Interprets pictures in simple library books and in classroom textbooks (e.g., pictures of workers and their activities).
   7. Sees the connection between reading matter and the accompanying illustrations.
   8. Interprets symbols and signs met in everyday living (e.g., stop and go signals, super-market and gas station signs).

II. Intermediate grades, 4–6. The child:
   1. Uses the table of contents to see whether a book covers a broad general topic (e.g., Africa, transportation, Indians).
   2. Uses the index to locate specific information (e.g., Nile River in a book on Africa, airplanes in a book on transportation, Iroquois in a book on Indians).
   3. Uses the dictionary for help in spelling and for definitions of new words (e.g., Does torrid have one or two r's? What is the meaning of reservoir?).
   4. Uses the almanac to locate specific information (e.g., population of New York City, salary of the President).
   5. Makes accurate alphabetical listings (e.g., fog, forest, health, highway).
   6. Interprets pictorial maps, charts, and graphs presenting facts about a country or a region (e.g., population, products, natural resources).
   7. Consults a variety of materials to locate needed information (e.g., highway maps, travel folders, and scenic pamphlets).
   8. Reads the captions of pictures, charts, and graphs for a fuller understanding of pictorial materials.
   9. Sees the relationship between personal and individual study and the work of the group (e.g., fits an individual report into a unit of study of the class).
   10. Listens carefully to study directions as they are given (e.g., asks only for explanations of directions, not a repetition of them).
   11. Makes note of the important items in classroom assignments.
   12. Takes notes successfully for future study or reference (e.g., from reading or from reports given by other children).

III. Upper grades, 7–8. The child:
   1. Knows the more general sources of information, turns to them for needed data, and uses them intelligently (e.g., dictionary, encyclopedia, almanac).
   2. Distinguishes between sources of information and selects the proper one to locate specific data (e.g., almanac and encyclopedia).
   3. Reads and uses special graphs and charts (e.g., charts and graphs of population, rainfall, government expenditures).
   4. Uses captions and accompanying reading matter for a complete understanding of pictorial materials (e.g., always reads the caption when studying a chart).
   5. Makes graphs and charts to illustrate concepts and to convey information to others (e.g., a circle

graph of the sources of the tax dollar, a bar graph to show the population growth of the United States).

6. Begins to use adult periodicals such as news magazines, to get current information on a topic; reads editorials.
7. Discriminates among several newspapers with respect to reliability of news coverage (e.g., reads accounts of the same events in several newspapers).
8. Keeps notes for future reference for reports and study (e.g., notes from reading of library materials).
9. Budgets time wisely (e.g., daily budgeting of time to complete daily study, weekly or monthly budgeting of time to meet deadlines on projects and reports).

Library Skills

I. Primary grades, 1–3. The child:
1. Identifies the letters of the alphabet and learns their proper sequence (as a preliminary skill essential in using dictionaries, encyclopedias and other materials which are alphabetically arranged).
2. Arranges simple words or names by the initial letter.
3. Uses alphabet books and picture dictionaries.
4. Handles books carefully in removing them and returning them to the shelves.
5. Holds books properly (e.g., large picture books flat on the table).
6. Turns pages correctly (e.g., by upper right hand corner of page).
7. Uses a book mark to mark his place in a book.
8. Understands a simple classification of books on the library shelves (e.g., "Easy," "Picture," "Easy Fiction," and "Fairy Tales").
9. Locates these books on the shelves by the classification number on the spine of the book (e.g., E, P, EF, 398).
10. Recognizes the title page in a book.
11. Identifies pertinent information on the title page (e.g., author, title, illustrator, publisher).
12. Demonstrates good citizenship by sharing books, respecting the rights of other children and by assuming his share of responsibility for making the room a pleasant place in which to read and work.

II. Intermediate grades, 4–6. The child:
1. Applies his knowledge of the alphabet to facilitate the use of reference books.
2. Identifies the parts of a book (e.g., the table of contents, index, glossary, list of illustrations and maps, appendix, preface, and introduction).
3. Uses the foregoing information as he seeks material for assignments from his classrooms.
4. Uses the dictionary to obtain information about words (e.g., definition, spelling, syllabication, and pronunciation).
5. Shows a growing understanding of the special features of the dictionary (e.g., gazetteer, special plates, obsolete words, foreign words, biographical dictionary, abbreviations, and phrases).
6. Begins to use the Dewey Decimal Classification scheme to locate books in the library (e.g., all ten general classifications, with some specific sub-headings such as: 910 Geography, 973 U.S. History).
7. Locates entries in the card catalog and interprets them correctly (e.g., author, title, subject, "See" and "See Also" cards).
8. Begins to use the classification number on the catalog card to locate books on the shelves.
9. Uses children's encyclopedias efficiently in locating and gathering information (e.g., becomes familiar with arrangement, scope, contents, illustrations, indexes, cross-references, letter-guides, and special features).

10. Consults more than one encyclopedia to compare material on the same subject; notes the copyright date whenever up-to-date information is sought.
11. Assumes greater responsibility in the care and maintenance of library resources.
12. Learns to use some of the resources of the public library.

III. Upper grades, 7–8. The child:

1. Locates place names and statistical information in atlases and gazetteers.
2. Understands the arrangement, scope, and use of different kinds of atlases (e.g., geographical, political, historical).
3. Uses the glossary of geographical terms.
4. Uses specialized maps and charts (e.g., airways, world explorations, tables of oceans, mountains, climate, races, resources).
5. Uses the index or lists of maps in an atlas to locate the required map.
6. Uses reference books that supply concise information about places, things, events, people, and progress (e.g., handbooks, almanacs, yearbooks, and manuals: *The World Almanac, Information Please Almanac, Statesmen's Yearbook, Statistical Abstract of the U.S.*, municipal manuals, state manuals); notes whether material is up-to-date.
7. Uses special indexes to locate poetry, plays, and short stories (e.g., Brewton's *Index to Poetry* and *Subject and Title Index to Short Stories for Children*, published by The American Library Association).
8. Consults current materials as sources of information (e.g., newspapers, magazines, pamphlets, clippings, pictures, bulletins).
9. Uses lists and bibliographies on current subjects.
10. Discovers sources of free and inexpensive materials.
11. Examines and evaluates newspapers as source of information (e.g., compares several newspapers; learns to evaluate coverage, editorial policy, special features, propaganda, sources).
12. Consults a variety of magazines for reference (e.g., pictorial, scientific, news, literary, special).
13. Locates needed material in magazines through use of the *Readers' Guide to Periodical Literature.*
14. Consults many different sources of biographical information (e.g., books, dictionaries, encyclopedias, directories, yearbooks, Webster's *Biographical Dictionary, Current Biography, Who's Who in America*).
15. Selects information pertinent to a problem (e.g., makes a plan for selecting information before starting to read; decides how information is to be used; reads material through quickly to see if it is appropriate; re-reads the material and takes selective notes).
16. Records information efficiently (e.g., identifies topic sentence in each paragraph; identifies key words that support topic sentence; records only pertinent ideas).
17. Demonstrates maturity by his consideration of others and his independence in finding and using a wide variety of materials.
18. Uses the resources of the public library intelligently.

Writing Skills

I. Primary grades, 1–3. The child:

1. Dictates ideas in such form that the teacher can record them on the board (e.g., captions for pictures, maps, diagrams, lists of items such as the seasons and ways men make a living; experience records).
2. Copies written material accurately; adds an original sentence or two, on occasions, to make the material his own (e.g., a group composition; a short letter written to ask permission for a trip; questions to be answered from observations made outside of school).
3. Does own writing with the teacher's help in deciding what to say and how to say it, in spelling

words correctly, using capital letters, and simple punctuation marks where needed (e.g., one, or a few, new facts learned; directions for reaching his home; explanatory labels for articles on exhibit).

4. Contributes ideas for more ambitious forms of writing which the teacher and children together compose on the board (e.g., field trip, standards to guide a discussion).

II. Intermediate grades, 4–6. The child:

1. Develops a sense of order or sequence in thinking and the writing that follows.
2. Does original writing with the teacher's guidance (e.g., stories about the dairy farmer or what I know about the oceans of the world).
3. Copies material correctly when needed (e.g., notebook record; quotation to be read to the class).
4. Prepares good written explanations to accompany maps, exhibits, and models (e.g., displays for Open House).
5. Uses suitable expression for various purposes (e.g., when preparing a list, includes similar items only; uses the right form and tone for a thank-you note; writes sentences to give summary statements of facts).
6. Makes increasing use of self-help materials such as simplified dictionaries, English textbooks for matters of form (e.g., report on an interview, record of observations made, business letter).
7. Keeps accurate records for particular purposes (e.g., of rainfall measured in a pail left outside, of temperatures, of interviews, of books read in preparation for a report).
8. Makes adequate preparation for written reports (e.g., rough notes based on observations and reading, a simple plan for the writing).
9. Checks his writing and corrects errors so far as possible before seeking the teacher's help.

III. Upper grades, 7–8. The child:

1. Cooperates effectively in the preparation of written reports, working with one or more classmates (e.g., contributes to the report; reads it critically; corrects parts that are not clear; considers best form of statements; corrects mis-spellings; selects illustrations, maps, models, and the like to make the report more concrete; times the report; cuts it if necessary).
2. Makes more elaborate preparation for writing a report (e.g., carries on wide reference reading; studies pertinent maps and data such as rainfall or temperature data; makes notes of ideas to be remembered; decides upon the best form for the report such as outline, narrative, or exposition).
3. Shows less dependence upon the teacher in his own written composition and gradually improves it (e.g., better paragraph construction, ability to write a longer composition, improved titles, more precise use of words, greater range of social studies ideas).
4. Makes simple, needed bibliographies in good form (e.g., author, title, pages, copyright date).
5. Habitually proofreads and corrects his own writing before submitting it to the teacher.

Many educators would agree that parallels are frequently seen between success in the communication skills and good grades in social studies. Traditionally there have been positive correlations between reading skills and social studies.[25] Good readers have tended to have the advantage in social studies. Most of the national social studies projects and textbook series have assumed that all children already know how to read at grade level. Two exceptions are Follett's history book entitled *The American Nation: Adventure in Freedom*[26] and Fenton's social stud-

---

[25]June R. Chapin and Richard E. Gross. *Teaching Social Studies Skills* (Boston: Little, Brown and Company, 1973), p. 23.
[26]Jack Abramowitz, *American Nation: Adventure in Freedom* (Chicago: Follett, 1975).

ies book at the junior high level, *The Americans.* [27] Both books were developed for slow learners. Many of the other social studies projects include not only a textbook but also pamphlets, books, case studies, and documents all of which rely heavily on the reading skills. Thus a significant question emerges and as yet remains to be answered: What can be said of the readability of these materials which bear the influence of a decade of curricular reform?

There are several readability formulas that can serve as valuable tools for the classroom teacher in determining the readability level of available materials. The SMOG Readability Formula provides a gross measure. The readability is determined by word length. A teacher using this formula must be aware of its limitations, since other factors besides word length can influence readability. These factors include: abstract concepts, sentence length, syntax, and specialized vocabulary. For a more complete explanation of the SMOG procedure, refer to an article by Harry McClaughlin entitled, "SMOG Grading–New Readability Formula."[28]

The Fry Readability Technique is another useful tool. In using it, the teacher must be concerned with the number of words, number of sentences, and number of syllables. For more information refer to *Readability: An Appraisal of Research and Application* by Jeanne Chall.[29]

A third tool for measuring readability is the CLOZE Procedure. In using that technique the instructor selects random passages from material whose difficulty is being evaluated. Every fifth word in the passage is deleted and replaced by a line of standard length. Students are asked to fill in the blanks by guessing from context or remaining words what the missing word should be. For more information on this technique locate the article by Bormuth entitled, "Readability: A New Approach."[30] In addition, we invite you to review Chapter 2 of our text for more details about these formulas.

Research using readability formulas for assessing difficulty of curriculum materials continues to be viewed as meaningful. In 1973, Johnson and Vardian applied four readability formulae to the assessment of sixty-eight social studies texts for grades one to six. Their findings suggest that there is a persistent tendency to publish elementary social studies texts at readability levels above grade level. Their study disclosed for the intermediate texts a readability range within texts from two to twelve years.[31]

Readability research in the social studies should become more sensitive to the problem of concept loading. The increasing emphasis in social studies upon

[27]Edwin Fenton (Ed.), *The Americas: A History of the United States* (New York: American Heritage, distributed by Holt, Rinehart and Winston, 1970).

[28]Harry G. McClaughlin, "SMOG Grading—New Readability Formula," *Journal of Reading,* XII, 8, pp. 639–646.

[29]Jeanne S. Chall, *Readability: An Appraisal of Research and Application,* Bureau of Educational Research Monographs No. 34 (Columbus: Ohio State University, 1957).

[30]J. R. Bormuth, "Readability: A New Approach," *Reading Research Quarterly* (Spring, 1966), 1:79–132.

[31]Roger Johnson and Ellen B. Vardian, "Reading, Readability, and the Social Studies," *The Reading Teacher,* 26 (February 1973), pp. 483–488.

more concepts and methodologies from all the social sciences and the issues inherent in each suggests that students must learn more specialized vocabularies, abstract concepts, and frames of reference. Thus readability is one of the variables to be considered.

While the authors do not have an answer to this problem, we do believe that the relationship between concept learning in the social studies and reading performance is a highly significant topic. We believe that more emphasis needs to be placed on experience-based concept development. We believe that this can be accomplished by providing youngsters with real-life experiences with the organizing themes and life roles, by providing lots of direct, hands-on experiences, by including a wide range of support visual and audio materials, and by utilizing lots of supplemental reading materials. Bruno Bettelheim recently pointed out that weakness in reading ability often stems from boredom with the content of the reading matter.[32] In support of this thinking is a recent report published by the Educational Research Council in America. After surveying fifteen years of research, the authors report the following:

1. The vivid content and challenge in the material often outweigh the need for strict attention to official standards of reading level.
2. The teacher who discusses the content of a section of a textbook before asking the students to read it gets better results educationally then the teacher who requires the reading before class discussion.
3. It is a mistake to use the social science period as a kind of extended remedial reading lesson. For pupils with reading difficulties, the teacher should teach social studies content and use the textbook as an aid, not as an additional chore.
4. Conscientious teachers attempt to instill total mastery of the subject matter in the youngsters. This has been found to be a great mistake in an area that is so vast and complex as the social studies. It has been found that excessive "mastery" at one stage may block expansion and utilization of basic concepts and skills at later stages. It is believed that mastery of the facts is often mastery of a very imperfect and inadequate set of information.[33]

In conclusion, we would like to offer some helpful hints for reading and the other communication skills as they relate to social studies:

1. Whenever possible use literature to enrich the social studies and to broaden the data base.
2. Utilize books about individuals of different ethnic groups or social classes as a means of sensitizing your students to the problems of others.
3. Observe and evaluate your students during oral reading sessions and in their written work. You will then be able to identify those children who have reading difficulties.
4. Devise a systematic plan to help children who have problems in reading.
5. Gather as much multiage reading material—textbooks, supplemental texts, paperbacks, and magazines—as you can; use it as a means for providing for individual differences.

[32]Raymond English, "Ten Discoveries about Basic Learning," *Social Education*, Vol. 41, No. 2, (February, 1977), p. 106.
[33]English, p. 106.

6. Try always to orient children to what they are going to read. Discuss–read–discuss seems to be a workable format.
7. Help children to see how their own frame of reference and set of experiences affects the interpretation of what they read.[34]

Hints for teaching listening and speaking include:

1. Help children develop an acute awareness for the amount of listening and speaking they do, both in and out of school.
2. Identify what it is you want pupils to listen for.
3. Provide students with material that is worth listening to.
4. Allow children (initially) to communicate in a language they already know. This is especially true for the culturally different child.[35]

Hints for teaching speaking skills include:

1. Use a variety of speaking formats: debates, panels, and round table discussions.
2. Help children discover the types of speaking abilities required in and out of school.
3. Provide guidelines for making an oral presentation. Include students in preparing guidelines.
4. Emphasize the positive aspects of the student's oral presentation.[36]

Hints for teaching writing skills include:

1. Stress the fact that students need to have background information about the subject before they begin writing.
2. Use a variety of formats for writing; stress ideas more than mechanics.
3. Discuss with students the rationale for writing and help them find out about writing opportunities both in and out of school settings.
4. Encourage students to keep logs as a means of expression and to increase writing power.[37]

While we have only scratched the surface, in terms of suggestions or hints for utilizing the communication skills in the social studies, we hope you will refer to your favorite authors in the area. We invite you once again to refer to some of our teaching modules for using communication skills in your social studies lessons. We would now like to direct your attention to map and globe skills.

[34]Drawn from June R. Chapin and Richard E. Gross. *Teaching Social Studies Skills* (Boston: Little, Brown and Company, 1973), p. 45.
[35]Drawn from June R. Chapin and Richard E. Gross. *Teaching Social Studies Skills* (Boston: Little, Brown and Company, 1973), 69–71.
[36]Drawn from June R. Chapin and Richard E. Gross. *Teaching Social Studies Skills* (Boston: Little, Brown and Company, 1973), p. 82.
[37]Drawn from June R. Chapin and Richard E. Gross. *Teaching Social Studies Skills* (Boston: Little, Brown and Company, 1973), pp. 100–101.

MAP AND GLOBE SKILLS

A third vital area of skills in social studies as it relates to life in and out of school is the area of map and globe skills. Perhaps the most important idea relative to mapping is that map concepts for elementary children should initially be introduced in a concrete way and should relate to the child's experience. This is a mighty big challenge because map and globe skills are fundamentally abstract, and deal with ideas about space and symbols.

Some school systems adopt a separate map and globe package for use in the classroom while other districts attempt to integrate map and globe skills with the total social studies curriculum. The authors believe that these skills should be taught within a program whether separate or integrated, which provides for systematic development of both skill and knowledge, and which leads to a better understanding of the world in which we live. Ideally map and globe skills should be developed according to some scope and sequence established by the school system. In a total school plan, a chart (see Table 5–1 of this chapter) should indicate at what grade level each skill should be introduced and taught and where each should be reinforced. The content vehicles—organizing themes or textbook topics—will provide the data source through which these skills can be developed.

A well planned program should consist of a scope and sequence and provisions for readiness if it is to be effective. In the lower elementary grades children should also be provided with the widest possible exposure to their own

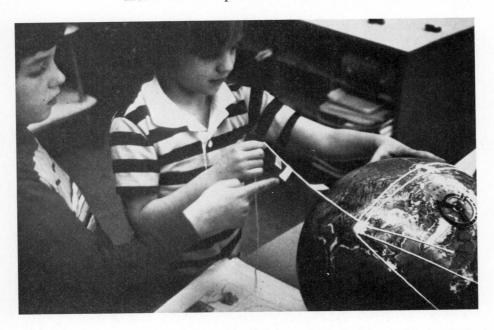

At what age do you think children should be taught to estimate distances using the great circle routes?

environment—to land features, for example. Using field trips as a means of giving kids concrete experiences with maps can be effective. Children must know what is meant by river, lake, hill, or island to understand the meaning of symbols on a map. Short walks can be extremely effective as a means of providing children with opportunities to observe physical and cultural features. Many geographic educators advocate that students map the areas visited. A sand box is popular for this type of mapping because it is a flexible means of illustrating a concept which can be easily formed and easily changed in a brief period of time. Another technique the authors have used effectively with young children to help them begin to develop concepts of physical features is creative dramatics. After children have observed the physical features, let them imagine they are those features. It's great fun! Some children even express themselves orally. How do you suppose a mountain would talk? How would a waterfall feel? What might it say?

As children advance in mental development and experiences, they will be able to utilize their desks, classrooms, bedrooms, yard, street, neighborhood, and community as data sources for mapping.

By the time the child reaches third or fourth grade, he will probably be introduced to flat maps. He should be made aware of the following: (a) a map is flat and cannot show real roundness; (b) all maps have some distortion; (c) the legend or key explains what each symbol means; (d) the scale of the map controls the degree we can generalize.

As the student matures he can be challenged by visualizing the local environment from a spatial perspective, by constructing base maps from aerial photographs, by hypothesizing from map data, and by translating oral and written information to maps. The Ellis text entitled *Teaching and Learning Elementary Social Studies*[38] has an excellent chapter, "Strategies for Making and Interpreting Maps," on this topic. It is an excellent source for elementary teachers. We firmly believe that success in map and globe skills lies in teaching these skills as they relate to the child's environment first, and then gradually beginning to read and interpret maps that deal with faraway places.

While there is no "master" scope and sequence chart for map and globe skills, you can use pages 134–137 of this text as a guide for the development of the program for you. Keep in mind as you use this material that the child's maturity level, individual differences, and realm of experience are all factors that affect the success of the program.

We hope you can use the scope and sequence of map and globe skills as a guide. To facilitate the use of this list we offer the following hints that you might find helpful as you develop the map and globe skills component of your social studies program:

1. Provide children with concrete experiences that relate to maps and globes. If the ideas fit into the experiences of children, they will be more highly motivated.
2. Actual mapping experiences are the most useful means of "tapping" local resources.

[38]Arthur K. Ellis, *Teaching and Learning Elementary Social Studies* (Boston: Allyn and Bacon, 1977), pp. 261–281.

REPRESENTATIVE LIST OF MAP AND GLOBE SKILLS
FOR GRADES 1 THROUGH 6[39]

Grade 1

Indicates directions by pointing and gesturing toward persons and objects in his environment.

Uses such relative terms in indicating direction as *this way, that way; to the right, to the left; in front of, in back of;* etc.

Understands that in the early morning the sun is first seen in the east, appears to be nearly overhead at noon, and is last seen in the west during the late afternoon.

Orients large-scale maps of the classroom and playground with existing objects in the classroom and on the playground.

Uses relative terms in expressing distance: *short, long, near, far, nearby, faraway,* etc.

Indicates location by pointing and gesturing.

Uses relative terms in expressing location: *here, there, over here, over there, above, below, near, far,* etc.

Distinguishes between land and water masses on maps and globes; recognizes that there is more water than land on the earth's surface.

Describes the location of his home in relation to such natural and man-made features of his environment as sidewalks, streets, hills, railroad tracks, streams, ponds, wooded areas, etc.

Observes that land surfaces in and around his local community tend to be uneven.

Watches a stream and notes the direction in which water flows; discovers that water tends to flow from higher to lower levels.

Observes natural and man-made features in and around his neighborhood; describes and draws pictures of these features.

Uses pictures, drawings, films, or aerial photographs to identify familiar places in and around his local community.

States that the colors used on a given map were selected arbitrarily and have nothing to do with the way an area appears in reality.

Grade 2

Finds wind direction by observing the effects of wind on weather vanes, trees, flags, puddles, lakes, etc.

Uses the terms *north* and *south* to show he knows that *north* is in the direction of the north pole and that *south* is in the direction of the south pole.

Using a globe, discovers that north–south lines extend from pole to pole.

Demonstrates understanding of distance by pacing off the dimensions of his classroom, by counting the number of city blocks from one place in his neighborhood to another, or by pacing off distances around his neighborhood.

Estimates the length of a mile while walking or riding in a car or on a bicycle and then compares his conception of a mile with the actual length of a mile.

Compares the actual length of a city block with a block as shown on a map.

Recognizes that long distances on the ground can be represented by short distances on a map.

Studies different sized maps of his classroom showing the same area and objects; recognizes that the same area can be represented by maps of different sizes.

Explains that maps should be drawn to scale if they are to be accurate representations of the earth's surface.

Tells why large-scale maps of his neighborhood tend to be more accurate than small-scale maps.

---

[39]Abstracted from William W. Joyce, *The Development and Grade Placement of Map and Globe Skills in the Elementary Social Studies Program*, unpublished doctoral dissertation, (Evanston, Ill.: Northwestern University, School of Education, 1964).

Locates his desk and other familiar objects on a map of his classroom.

Constructs a map of his neighborhood, showing the location of familiar places and then indicates on this map the routes he takes in going from his home to these places.

Constructs floor maps of his home neighborhood and local community by using models, drawings, and photographs depicting features of the landscape.

Recognizes the differences between land and water forms shown on maps and globes.

Grade 3

Explains that when he locates any one direction (north, south, east, or west), he can then locate the other directions.

Finds direction by observing shadows.

Uses the terms *up* and *down* to show he knows that *up* is the direction away from the center of the earth and that *down* is the direction toward the center of the earth.

Uses the terms north, south, east, and west in telling a person how to go from one place in his neighborhood to another.

Using a globe, demonstrates how it is possible to travel toward the north or south poles from any other points on the earth.

Compares maps and globes, observes that the earth and a globe are similar in shape, and that globes are more accurate representations of the earth than are maps.

Locates the continents and ocean basins on maps and globes; discovers that the size and shape of continents and ocean basins is shown differently on maps and globes.

Locates the north and south poles on a globe and map of the world; discovers that the north pole is the farthest point north on the earth and the south pole is the farthest point south.

Using a world map and a globe, locates North America, the United States, his home state, and home town.

Using a street map of his local community, locates his home neighborhood, his home, and other familiar places.

Using a globe and a world map, locates countries, continents, and bodies of water studied in class.

Describes, in terms of direction and travel time, the location of his home in relation to such familiar places in the neighborhood as his school, a friend's home, the fire station, etc.

Identifies features of the terrain which impede or facilitate travel in his home neighborhood and local community.

Using maps and globes, describes the location of land masses in relation to water areas.

Locates the United States in relation to North America; to the Atlantic, Arctic, and Pacific Oceans; the Gulf of Mexico; the equator, and the north and south poles.

Using maps, recognizes semipictorial symbols which depict rivers, lakes, coastlines, islands, mountains, roads, cities, railroads, etc.

Grade 4

Using a globe, discovers that east–west lines are parallel to the equator, to each other, and encircle the earth.

Orients street maps of his local community to aerial photographs of the same area.

When comparing different kinds of maps, notes that north is not always at the top of the map—it depends on the location of the north pole. (For example, north would lie at the top of a mercator projection, but would lie at the center of a polar projection.)

Locates north, south, east, west, northeast, northwest, southeast, and southwest on maps and globes.

Demonstrates that distance along the ground can be calculated in terms of feet, yards, miles, etc.

Measures and records distances in terms of inches, feet, yards, miles, etc.

Using a globe, locates the four hemispheres and the equator.

Studies simplified maps of his local community and makes such observations as:

1. Gas stations are generally located at busy intersections.
2. Recently built schools are generally located in residential sections of town.
3. Shopping districts are generally located in main thoroughfares and are usually close to public transportation.
4. Many streets are laid out in north–south and east–west directions.

Using a map of the world, locates the equator, the poles, rivers, lakes, islands, peninsulas, the Arctic and Antarctic Circles, and north–south and east–west lines.

Compiles a list of places visited during trips taken by his class and by his family and then, using a road map, locates these places with reference to each other and to such natural features as lakes, rivers, mountains, etc.

Describes the location of his home community in relation to natural and man-made features of the environment, to transportation routes and facilities, and to nearby communities.

Describes the location of communities and nations studied in class in relation to natural and man-made features of the environment, to transportation routes and facilities, and to other communities and nations.

Using maps, locates cities, countries, and continents studied in relation to the poles, equator, and Arctic and Antarctic Circles; discovers interrelationships among location and climate, weather and terrain.

Using maps, locates important cities, countries, and continents studied in class; discovers interrelationships that exist among location and commerce, transportation routes, etc.

Using maps, identifies more complex semipictorial symbols which depict falls and rapids, deltas, dams, canals, deserts, swamps, etc.

Draws a map of his local community, using either conventional semipictorial symbols or his own symbols to represent natural and man-made features.

Compares different kinds of maps with regard to the use of color; discovers that color may be used to designate elevations of land or the depth of water, to represent political boundaries, and to show rainfall, population, temperature, and other similar data.

Compares different kinds of maps with regard to keys or legends; recognizes that keys or legends indicate the meaning of symbols used on maps but that the same symbol may mean quite different things on different maps.

Compares text descriptions in social studies textbooks with accompanying maps.

Uses maps and globes to secure specific information; selects the best map for the purpose at hand.

Reads a map and infers the relationships suggested by the data shown. (For example, the factors determining the location of cities, manufacturing centers, crop and livestock production, political boundaries, recreation facilities, etc.)

Grade 5

Uses the terms *northeast*, *northwest*, *southeast*, *southwest*, in referring to directions in his classroom and around the neighborhood.

Reads a compass to find directions.

Uses the terms *upstream* and *downstream* to show that he knows that *upstream* means going toward the source of the stream and against the current, and that *downstream* means going toward the mouth of the stream and with the current.

Uses the north arrow on maps as a directional finder.

Estimates, then measures, the dimensions of his classroom; draws a floor plan of the classroom to scale, with all measurements in inches.

Estimates, then measures, the dimensions of his schoolyard; draws a map of the schoolyard to scale, with all measurements in feet or yards.

belonging, and success. The same students should *not* always be leaders, nor should all the less capable be placed in a group. The best groups are usually heterogeneous; thus students can learn from each other and be able to recognize the worth of each individual contribution and become concerned over the less fortunate.

There is also the "numbers question" that frequently enters into a teacher's decision in grouping. In considering a pair or two, keep in mind the following phenomena:

1. Interactions are limited to exchanges between two members.
2. There are many opportunities to share feelings and ideas.
3. These provide the maximum for student input because there is little waiting time.
4. One potential weakness is the limitation of ideas and viewpoints.
5. There is a tendency for high tension and emotion between the pairs.
6. There is a tendency to avoid disagreement.
7. There is a high exchange of information.
8. There is a tendency for deadlock.[41]

If you are considering a group of three, consider the following:

1. These are often effective in short-term discussions, especially when one member is the arbitrator, the focus of the discussion, or the observer.
2. There is a potential unstable arrangement because there is the possibility of excluding one member.
3. There exists the possibility of the power of the majority over the minority.[42]

In considering odd- versus even-numbered groups keep in mind the following:

1. There tends to be more disagreement in even-numbered groups than in odd-numbered groups due to formation of subgroups of equal size.
2. The most satisfying group size tends to be five as the 2:3 ratio or division provides support for minority members and a group of five is large enough for stimulation and small enough for participation and personal recognition.[43]

Whatever form of group you establish, keep in mind these points for smoother group functioning:

1. Beginning groups need early success. Plans should be kept simple and reporting progress and evaluating should be a part of each day's procedure. Plan with the total group ways in which they can work together. Set up the directions so everyone knows what is to be done. Establish a specific way that reporting will be done at the *end* of each class period. For example, at the end of social studies period on a given day, the chairperson may need to report on the most unusual thing the group learned,

[41]David A. Welton and John T. Mallan, *Children and Their World* (Skokie, Ill.: Rand McNally, 1976) pp. 368–372.
[42]Welton and Mallan, pp. 368–372.
[43]Welton and Mallan, pp. 368–372.

the thing it feels will be of most interest to the class, or the most unbelievable thing, etc.

2.   Groups should constantly be made aware of the importance of each child's contribution. It is crucial that the room atmosphere be conducive to free discussion and acceptance of each child's method of participation.

3.   Guidelines should be firmly established at the onset. They should include: what to do, where the materials can be located, individual student's responsibility, standards of behavior, and time to work.

4.   Frequent regrouping tends to give more opportunities for leadership, tends to prevent formulation of cliques, and assists the outsider in being accepted in the group. Regrouping also gives the teacher an opportunity to observe the children in a variety of situations.

5.   Groups should share and get advice from the total class.

6.   Summarizing activities should always take place in a total group setting.

An extremely helpful tool in group work is the use of charts as a point of departure or when difficulties in group functioning arise. It is interesting to see the student's perceptions through these charts. They are useful in discussing or reviewing the various roles and responsibilities of group members.

COMMITTEE CHAIRPERSON	**COMMITTEE MEMBERS**
1. Keeps the main idea in mind 2. Gets ideas from all members 3. Sees that each member has a job 4. Is fair and doesn't talk 5. Urges everyone to do his best 6. Says "our" not "my" committee	1. Work together 2. Know what to do 3. Divide the work 4. Do each job well 5. Discuss problems 6. Plan the report carefully

WORK PERIOD	**A GOOD LISTENER**
1. Plan our work 2. Get information 3. Do our jobs quietly 4. Help each other 5. Keep a log 6. Put materials back	1. Pays attention 2. Asks important questions 3. Adds information 4. Takes notes 5. Makes helpful suggestions

In addition to using charts for discussions or as reinforcers for the development of group/social skills, they could be modified and used in self-assessment. For example, at the end of a work period, the committee chairperson might have to complete the following checklist:

CHAIRPERSON CHECKLIST	Always	Sometimes	Never
1. Did I keep the main job in mind?			
2. Did I get ideas from all members?			
3. Did I see that each member has a job?			
4. Was I fair?			
5. Did I watch the amount of talking I did?			
6. Did I urge everyone to do his best?			
7. Did I say "our" rather than "my" committee?			

This is merely one example that can be used. Committee members' charts could likewise be developed. The teacher could fill out a similar one for evaluation purposes.

Assessing group work and individual performance and progress must be an ongoing process. As groups become more sophisticated they will require more planning by both the teacher and the students if in fact they are to continue to develop and to remain stimulating. Keep in mind that you want to help students develop content understandings as well as to learn how to:

1. get information
2. use various research resources
3. distinguish between important and unimportant facts
4. apply facts from one context to another
5. use committees as resources to each other
6. use audio visual aids in individual groups
7. make reporting interesting
8. develop discussion techniques

Group work, as you no doubt have experienced, is no panacea for the ills that beset social studies or any other curricular area. It has, however, a great deal to offer if handled properly. Group work will no doubt become even more productive as our knowledge of group phenomena broadens. As is true of various methods of instruction, results often depend more upon the discriminating and wise use of the method than upon the method itself.

In using group work for the development of social skills we offer the following suggestions for your consideration:

1. Make sure that group members can work together and that most of the energies of the group are directed toward the group task rather than diverted into activities necessary to resolve internal group problems.
2. The membership of a group should be based on both willingness and ability to participate in the enterprise in which the group is engaged.
3. The group should contain only as many members as are needed to accomplish the task.

4. Plan group work for your class in such a way as to facilitate the maximum development of group skills in the course of the year's work.

SUMMARY

An emphasis on skill development affords teachers yet another opportunity to help students to become more effective members of society, able to grapple with the problems confronting them in their daily lives. If students possess skills or tools they are able to uncover, process, and interpret data and to apply relevant information to a new problem situation in a meaningful way. With the explosion of knowledge upon us, skills have the potential for producing the competencies for our survival. Perhaps most importantly, they can help children take a more active role in their learning.

Skills can be taught apart from the content or, more effectively, perhaps, they can be taught as an integral part of it. In this chapter we have identified four categories of skills: inquiry (critical thinking and problem solving), communication skills, map reading, and group work or social skills. Inquiry is very complex. It is usually used in situations in which typical reactions or former answers do not suffice or work effectively, and a new approach is needed. While there is an identifiable series of steps, problem solving seldom occurs in a cut and dried process, and different individuals vary in their approach and style of thinking.

Communication skills include listening, speaking, reading, and writing. Much of the social studies program in most school systems takes place through listening and speaking. These skills are mutually dependent upon language development. Certainly these skills are essential to enable the child to acquire social studies concepts which in turn allow the child to communicate effectively. Reading and writing likewise play a vital role, and are tools that are essential both in and out of school throughout life.

The third category includes map and globe skills. Since these are comprised of abstractions, it behooves the teacher to provide concrete methods and materials for teaching them in a way that relates to the child's immediate surroundings. Begin with the child's immediate environment. Utilize his room at home, his house, yard, street, neighborhood as data sources for mapping. Build on what the child knows. As the child matures he can be challenged with more of the complexities and begin to see the relationship of his environment to the continent and global world.

The fourth category of skills includes group work skills, often referred to as social skills. Learning to work cooperatively in groups is an individual process. It involves a readiness stage, continuous growth at varying rates of speed, and sequential step-by-step development.

It is vital that skills be identified for teaching purposes and for reinforcement. These skills are lifelong tools that will be used in and out of school in even the most far-reaching situation. While content will change over time, skills will remain stable and lasting.

CROSS REFERENCES TO TEACHING MODULES

In this chapter we identified four major types of skills as an integral part of a social studies program: problem solving/inquiry skills, communication skills, map and globe skills, and social/group skills. Four modules which provide unusual opportunities for employing skill development are "The American Family—Pioneer and Present," "Challenging Sex-Role Stereotypes," "The Community As a Resource for Physical Fitness," and "Children Gain Insight into Aging."

Family Membership: "The American Family: Pioneer and Present" (Part 2, pp. 266–272). Inquiry skills are used extensively in this teaching module. Students are asked to investigate their family backgrounds. Where did they come from? How did they live? What kinds of customs and traditions did they possess? How did they satisfy their basic needs? Genealogy is introduced and utilizing family members as resource people is encouraged. A trip to a museum is suggested in an attempt to have students compare and contrast life of pioneer families and families today. A data retrieval chart is included as a means of recording information so that comparisons can be made and tentative conclusions drawn.

Human Equality: "Challenging Sex-Role Stereotypes" (Part 2, pp. 350–355). This teaching module uses reading, writing, speaking, and listening. Students are asked to make lifelines depicting their lives to date and to add pictures to represent what they would like to be in the future. They are encouraged to share their lifelines with their peers and to discuss the likenesses and differences among themselves. They are asked to complete surveys, view a film entitled "Free To Be You And Me," go to the library to gather information and ideas about the changing roles of males and females in society, and to invite grandparents or older adults to class to discuss what it was like when they were growing up in terms of role expectations of males and females. Letter writing is included and as a culminating activity we suggest students write and present a play comparing a typical day in the life of a modern man or woman with the life of a man or woman thirty years from now.

Avocation: "The Community As a Resource for Physical Fitness" (Part 2, pp. 295–303). Designed for upper grades this teaching module provides unlimited opportunities for mapping. In the module, one activity calls for the student to explore through surveys, telephone directories, and maps the types of physical activities that are available in their community. Students are then asked to secure or make a large map of the community and locate where each activity does or potentially could occur. The map is to serve as a major source of information for the students and community. For gifted students we suggest they explore the availability of physical leisure activities within the state and nation. During the module the students will be encouraged to visit the places located on the map and where possible to participate in the leisure activities available.

Human Life Cycle: "New Insights into Aging" (Part 2, pp. 355–362). This middle-grade teaching module is one example in which social skills are used. Students are asked to make a list of adjectives or descriptions that fit the individual or group's image of "what old people are like." Then they are asked to gather data to determine whether or not their perceptions are accurate. In another lesson students are asked to divide into two groups—old people and helpers. Props will be used to help transform students into old people. Groups will be subdivided and role plays will be planned, presented, and discussed.

BIBLIOGRAPHY

Chapin, June R. and Richard E. Gross. *Teaching Social Studies Skills*. Boston: Little, Brown, 1973.

    This book presents the basic social studies skills that students must learn in school. The authors incorporate many specific suggestions for using these skills in a K–12 program. Examples from many social studies programs and projects are provided.

Kurfman, Dana G. (Ed.). *Developing Decision Making Skills*. Forty-seventh Yearbook of the National Council for Social Studies, 1977.

    This yearbook considers the more traditional social studies skills within the context of decision making. The major skills identified include thinking, information gathering, group process, and socialization skills.

Lunstrum, John P. "Reading in the Social Studies: A Preliminary Analysis of Recent Research," *Social Education*, Vol. 40, No. 1 (January 1976), pp. 10–18.

    Through an analysis of significant research primarily in the past 6–8 years, the author attempts to identify and clarify new developments, persistent issues, and critical needs of reading in the social studies.

Lunstrum, John P. "Improving Reading in the Social Studies," *Social Education*, Vol. 42, No. 1 (January 1978), pp. 8–27.

    The special section of the journal is designed to demonstrate what practical measures teachers in elementary and secondary schools can use in their classes to expand vocabulary, improve concept development, strengthen critical reading, relate children's backgrounds to reading assignments, adapt texts to reading abilities, and stimulate interest in reading abilities.

Welton, David A. and John T. Mallan. *Children and Their World: Teaching Elementary Social Studies*. Skokie, Ill. Rand McNally, 1976:

    Chapter 8 (pp. 199–228) of this text contains a fine account of managing skills based instruction: The access skills. The authors include reading, observation and listening as basic access skills.

VALUES AND
VALUES PROCESSES

GOALS

1. Assess the proposition that social studies, by its very nature, deals with the teaching of values and value processes.
2. Gain insight into problems which typically confront teachers, when dealing with various approaches to values education.
3. Describe the nature, purpose, advantages, and disadvantages of values clarification approaches to values education.
4. Design appropriate values clarification strategies for use in the elementary social studies program.
5. Describe the nature, purpose, advantages, and disadvantages of Kohlberg's moral reasoning approach to values education.
6. Design appropriate moral dilemmas for use in the elementary social studies program.
7. Assess situational variables which are likely to affect the use of values clarification and moral reasoning strategies in the elementary classroom.
8. Gain insights into the contribution that approaches to values education can make to an elementary social studies program reflecting the authors' conception of the lifelong roles and organizing themes.

That values are in fact being taught in our schools is self-evident. Every instructional decision that you make reflects your standards or criteria of goodness, worth, or beauty. The standards or criteria that guide your thoughts, feelings, and actions become your values. You arrange the desks in your room so that those children who disturb each other are separated. You elect to read aloud to your children excerpts from White's *Charlotte's Web* in an effort to expose your children to the mysteries of life and death. You arrange for your children to bake gingerbread cookies, in an effort to expose them to the concepts of producer and consumer (we are producers when we make the cookies; we are consumers when we eat them). You teach your children the correct procedures to follow when the fire alarm sounds. You play recordings of nineteenth-century Black folksongs sung by slaves as they worked in the cotton fields. You decide against admonishing a pupil for being late for school, because you are aware that her parents leave home for work at 7:00 AM, and that she must get her younger brother and sister off for school. In all of these instances your behavior as a teacher reflects the values you hold.

Unfortunately, most teachers do not teach about values in a purposeful, systematic way. This may be ascribed to the long-standing tradition in American education to relegate value-laden topics to home and church. Traditionally parents and teachers regarded such topics as personal matters, but in recent years educators have acknowledged that home and church have been notoriously unsuccessful in teaching children about values. Moreover, the incidence of drug usage, alcoholism, shoplifting, and violent crimes committed by juveniles has caused an alarmed public to decry the breakdown in morality among our youth, and to demand that educators make a concerted attempt to teach values and morality in our schools.

Few areas of the curriculum have been more directly affected by this mandate than the social studies. Perhaps this is to be expected because this area of the curriculum, particularly as taught in the elementary grades, is heavily impregnated with values questions. For example, an integral element in the primary-grade social studies curriculum is a broad range of subject matter which explicitly stresses positive interpersonal relationships and such values as honesty, sincerity, responsibility, punctuality, resourcefulness, patriotism, and the like. In the upper-grade social studies program, values tend to be presented more implicitly, but unfortunately in too many instances they have been ignored or subverted by teachers who stressed the learning of inert accretions of facts, dates, and events. Imagine if you will how a fifth-grade teacher could teach about World War II without confronting students with President Truman's decision to use the atom bomb on Hiroshima and Nagasaki. Or how this teacher could refuse to expose students to the values which impelled Dr. Martin Luther King to endure tear gas, high-pressure fire hoses, attack dogs, assassination attempts, and imprisonment in the name of the Civil Rights movement. In the past teachers have ignored the values inherent in Truman's use of the atom bomb and in Dr. King's advocacy of civil rights; moreover, we suspect that today many teachers continue to ignore these topics for a variety of reasons, not the least of which is the controversy that such topics may evoke.

Another reason can be ascribed to teachers' inability to deal with values-laden topics. Many of our teacher-training institutions provide inadequate instruction in values education; moreover few school districts attempt to correct these deficits by providing in-service instruction in this area. Admittedly, some enterprising teachers who have not had such instruction will of their own accord attempt to correct this deficit through self-instruction. But these teachers (bless them all!) are in the minority. Is it not surprising that few teachers actually attempt to deal with values in a forthright, systematic manner?

Fortunately this situation is beginning to change. Values education is gradually gaining acceptance as a legitimate element in American schools (despite the back-to-basics movement) largely through the efforts of a growing number of psychologists, social psychologists, sociologists, political scientists, and philosophers. Their efforts, directed in part toward developing ways of teaching about values in our schools, have led to the creation of various philosophies, and in some instances, theories of values education. These, in turn, are being translated into a variety of instructional materials and programs available for purchase by schools. As interest in values education grows, it becomes increasingly important that elementary teachers of the social studies become knowledgeable about the instructional capabilities of various approaches to values education, and to use discretion in their selection and use.

There are various types of approaches to values education. Those that appear to have the greatest significance for the K–8 social studies curriculum are listed (alphabetically) below.

Developing Understanding of Self and Others (kits published by American Guidance Service)

Dimensions of Personality (pupil texts and workbooks published by Pflaum/Standard)

Focus on Self-Development (kits published by Science Research Associates)

Human Development Program (teachers' guides published by the Human Development Institute)

Moral Reasoning (a theory of moral development pioneered by Lawrence Kohlberg and articulated through a series of cassette-filmstrips entitled *First Things*, and produced by Guidance Associates)

Values Clarification (an approach to values education presented in books and articles conceived by Louis Raths, Merrill Harmin, Leland Howe, Howard Kirschenbaum, and Sidney Simon)

The first of these materials listed above, *Developing Understanding of Self and Others*, is best known under its acronym, DUSO. The DUSO materials consist of several kits consisting of story and songbooks, records, cassettes, posters, puppets, and a teacher's guide. The lower-level (or primary-grade) kit, *DUSO 1*, develops such themes as "Understanding and Accepting Self," "Understanding Feelings," and "Understanding Emotional Maturity." *DUSO 2*, an upper-level kit, centers on themes such as "Toward Self-Identity: Developing Self-Awareness," "Toward Emotional Stability: Understanding Stress," and "Toward Responsible Choice-Making: Understanding Values." A heavily moralistic and manipulative child guidance program, DUSO might be accused of violating its principles and exhortations.

Dimensions of Personality is a series of grade 1–6 texts and workbooks variously entitled "Now I'm Ready" (grade 1), "I Can Do It" (grade 2), "What about Me" (grade 3), "Here I Am" (grade 4), "I'm Not Alone" (grade 5), and "Becoming Myself" (grade 6). Although a relatively bland program, *Dimensions* does give teachers opportunities to improvise and experiment.

Focus on Self-Development consists of three kits which center on three stages of self-development: awareness, responding, and involvement. Record-filmstrips, records, photos, and activity books are included in the kits, which are designated by their publisher as guidance materials.

The *Human Development Program*, better known perhaps as "Magic Circle," is another guidance program. It focuses on three themes: awareness, mastery, and social interaction. The magic circle technique involves arranging pupils in circles and encouraging them to discuss topics germane to the program's themes. The teacher's guide clearly specifies the ground rules for these discussions and how they are to be conducted. Some teachers may resent the highly specific directions and regimen of this program.

The last two approaches cited above, *Moral Reasoning* and *Values Clarification*, tend to be the best known, most widely used, and most controversial. Moreover, they deal more directly with values education and appear to have greater relevance for the social studies program than the others. For these reasons, both approaches will be explored in depth throughout the remainder of this chapter. Since both approaches are undergoing revisions, of necessity the ensuing discussion is a report on their status when this chapter was written.

VALUES CLARIFICATION

No discussion of the role of values in the elementary social studies curriculum would be complete unless it included the values clarification approach advocated by Louis Raths, Sidney Simon, Leland Howe, Merrill Harmin, and Howard Kirschenbaum. One of the most widely used approaches to values education, values clarification stresses the *process* of valuing rather than the teaching of certain values. Proponents describe this approach as

> . . . a form of questioning, a set of activities or "strategies," and an approach toward subject content, all of which are designed to help individuals learn a particular valuing process and to apply that process to value-laden areas and moral dilemmas in their lives.[1]

Further, proponents maintain that the valuing process, a central element in this philosophy, has these advantages:

> [It] helps individuals (and groups) to develop and clarify their values in such a way that they are more likely to: (a) experience positive values in their own lives; and (b) act more constructively in the social context.[2]

Values and Teaching, Raths, Harmin, and Simon's seminal text on values clarification, describes the valuing process as consisting of three dimensions (choosing, prizing, and acting) and seven subprocesses which must occur when a value is acquired:

Choosing: (1) freely
           (2) from alternatives
           (3) after thoughtful consideration of the consequences of each alternative
Prizing: (4) cherishing, being happy with the choice

---

[1] Howard Kirschenbaum et al., "In Defense of Values Clarification," *Phi Delta Kappan*, 58 (June 1977), p. 743.
[2] Kirschenbaum, p. 743.

Acting: (5) willing to affirm the choice publicly
         (6) doing something with the choice
         (7) repeatedly, in some pattern of life[3]

This conception of the valuing process, attributed to Raths, has been extended by Kirschenbaum to embrace five dimensions (thinking, feeling, choosing, communicating, and acting) and eighteen subprocesses:[4]

TABLE 6-1   KIRSCHENBAUM'S CONCEPTION OF THE VALUING PROCESS

THINKING

1. On many levels [e.g., Benjamin S. Bloom *et al.*, *The Taxonomy of Educational Objectives: Handbook I, The Cognitive Domain* (New York: David McKay, 1956)].
2. Critical thinking [e.g., Louis Raths, Selma Wasserman, Albert Jonas, and A. M. Rothstein, *Teaching for Thinking* (Columbus, Ohio: Merrill, 1967)].
3. Divergent thinking [e.g., S. J. Parnes, *Creative Behavior Guidebook* (New York: Scribners, 1967)].
4. Moral reasoning [e.g., Lawrence Kohlberg, "The Child as a Moral Philosopher," *Psychology Today* (September, 1968)].

FEELING

5. Being aware of one's feelings [e.g., Carl R. Rogers, *On Becoming a Person* (Boston: Houghton Mifflin, 1961)].
6. Discharging distressful feelings [e.g., Harvey Jackins, *The Human Side of Human Beings* (Seattle: Rational Island Publishers, 1965)].
7. Experiencing positive self-concept [e.g., Arthur W. Combs, D. L. Avila, and W. W. Purkey, *Helping Relationships: Basic Concepts for the Helping Professions* (Boston: Allyn and Bacon, 1971)].

CHOOSING

8. Goal setting
9. Data gathering
10. Considering alternatives
11. Considering consequences
12. Choosing freely

COMMUNICATING

13. Sending clear messages, including public affirmation [e.g., Thomas Gordon, *Parent Effectiveness Training* (New York: Peter Wyden, 1970)].
14. Empathic listening [e.g., Carl R. Rogers, *Client-Centered Therapy* (Boston: Houghton Mifflin, 1951); Thomas Gordon, *Teacher Effectiveness Training* (New York: Peter Wyden, 1975)].
15. No-lose conflict resolution [e.g., Gordon, *Parent Effectiveness Training*].

ACTING

16. Repeatedly
17. Consistently
18. Skillfully, competently

---

[3]Louis E. Raths, Merrill Harmin, and Sidney B. Simon, *Values and Teaching* (Columbus, Ohio: Merrill, 1966), p. 30.

[4]Howard Kirschenbaum et al., "In Defense of Values Clarification," *Phi Delta Kappan,* 58 (June 1977), p. 744. Copyright 1977 by The National Humanistic Education Center. Reprinted by permission. For a

Kirschenbaum's five-dimensional conception of the valuing process retains two of Raths' dimensions (choosing and acting), rejects one of Raths' dimensions (prizing), and adds three new dimensions (thinking, feeling, and communicating). Despite these differences, Raths' and Kirschenbaum's conceptions tend to be in accord with the goal of values clarification, which is to add more positive value to our lives.

Proponents of values clarification have devised a series of activities designed to teach students to learn a particular valuing process and to apply it to value-laden issues or problems confronting them in their daily lives. Below are but a few examples.

The Clarifying Response

Basic to Raths' three-dimensional conception of values clarification is the clarifying response—a method of responding to what a student says or does not say. This method encourages people (in this case your pupils) to think about the choices they have made, what they regard as important, or their life goals, etc. Below is an example of a student–teacher exchange in which clarifying responses are used.

Teacher: Bruce, don't you want to go outside and play on the playground?
Student: I dono. I suppose so.
Teacher: Is there something that you would rather do?
Student: I dono. Nothing much.
Teacher: You don't seem much to care, Bruce. Is that right?
Student: I suppose so.
Teacher: And mostly anything we do will be all right with you?
Student: I suppose so. Well, not anything, I guess.
Teacher: Well, Bruce, we had better go out on the playground now with the others. You let me know sometime if you think of something you would like to do.[5]

As you read the above exchanges, observe their brevity. The teacher does not want to probe too deeply, moralize, or criticize; to do so might place the student on the defensive. Rather, the teacher is trying to get the student to examine his behavior and thoughts, with the expectation that he will clarify for himself what he values.

Activities

Since the publication of *Values and Teaching*, Raths' colleagues have published a series of books containing numerous values clarification "strategies" or activities for use in the classroom. One of the most comprehensive compilations is *Values*

free listing of materials available on values education, write The National Humanistic Education Center, 110 Spring St., Saratoga Springs, N.Y. 12866.
[5]Louis E. Raths, Merrill Harmin, and Sidney B. Simon, *Values and Teaching*, 2d ed. (Columbus, Ohio: Merrill, 1978) p. 55. Reprinted by permission of the publisher.

Clarification: A Handbook of Practical Strategies for Teachers and Students,[6] by Simon, Howe, and Kirschenbaum. This publication contains seventy-nine "strategies," each of which is tied in with one or more of Raths' seven processes of valuing. A few of these strategies are described below, to give you a feeling for the range of options available to you and your pupils.

The *rank-order* strategy gives pupils practice in choosing among alternatives and in explaining their choices in terms of priorities. Here are a few examples selected from *Values Clarification: A Handbook of Practical Strategies for Teachers and Students:*[7]

When playing house, would you rather be the
    _____ mother
    _____ father
    _____ baby
Which would be hardest for you to do?
    _____ show a bad paper to your parents
    _____ walk away from a fight
    _____ wait your turn when you have something exciting to say
What would you do if someone hit you?
    _____ tell the teacher
    _____ hit him or her back
    _____ walk away

The *value sheet* is a provocative story or statement, and a series of questions for pupils to think, write, or talk about. Below is one example of how the value sheet can be used with elementary pupils.

1. What does friendship mean to you?
2. If you have friends, did you choose them or did they get to be your friends by accident?
3. In what ways do *you* show friendship?
4. How important do you think it is to develop and maintain friendships?
5. If you plan to make any changes in your ways, please say what changes you will make. If you do not intend to make any changes in your ways, write "no changes."[8]

Value sheets for students could include selections from biographies, poetry, news reports, interviews—nearly any subject matter that deals with value-laden topics relevant for the lives of your students.

The *value continuum* requests students to designate their positions on issues or topics presented on a continuum from one extreme to its opposite. Then they

---

[6]Sidney B. Simon, Leland Howe, and Howard Kirschenbaum, *Values Clarification: A Handbook of Practical Strategies for Teachers and Students* (New York: Hart, 1972).

[7]Sidney B. Simon, Leland Howe, and Howard Kirschenbaum, *Values Clarification: A Handbook of Practical Strategies for Teachers and Students* (New York: Hart, 1972), pp. 86–87. Reprinted by permission of the publisher.

[8]Louis E. Raths, Merrill Harmin, and Sidney B. Simon, *Values and Teaching,* 2d ed. (Columbus, Ohio: Merrill, 1978), pp. 97–98. Reprinted by permission of the publisher.

are invited to tell the class their reasons for their positions. If they do not wish to disclose their reasons, they may pass. Below are a few examples:[9]

What do you do with your money?

: :

Hoarding Hannah— won't spend a penny

Handout Helen—spends it all or gives it all away. Never has enough left for necessities.

How do you like teachers to relate to you?

: :

Super-buddy—lets us do anything

Compulsive moderate— yells constantly, but doesn't do anything to stop us

Very strict and punitive. Beats us for a grammatical error

How much do you watch TV?

Blurry-eyed Bill— : : : : : : : : : : : : : : : : : No-knob Ned—
never turns it off   never turns it on

This is a mere sampling of the numerous values clarification strategies devised by Raths and his colleagues. If you desire to design your own (as Raths and his coworkers would recommend), we strongly suggest that you consult the texts listed at the end of this chapter.

Criticisms

In recent years proponents and opponents of values clarification have mounted a spirited debate over the real and imagined strengths and weaknesses of this approach. Since space limitations preclude us from subjecting values clarification to vigorous analysis, we will confine our discussion to major criticisms that have been raised by social studies educators and by social scientists. These criticisms focus on the scope of this approach, definitional problems, effects on students, and supportive theory and research.

Scope.   Shaver and Strong argue that values clarification is not a decision-making process, since it focuses on but one dimension—clarifying one's commitments. Further, these authors maintain that the limited focus of values clarification precludes it from dealing with two fundamental responsibilities of the school, improvement of thinking and decision-making skills, particularly those involving

[9]Sidney B. Simon, Leland Howe, and Howard Kirschenbaum, *Values Clarification: A Handbook of Practical Strategies for Teachers and Students* (New York: Hart, 1972), pp. 122, 125. Reprinted by permission of the publisher.

ethics.[10] Fraenkel elaborates on this limitation by alleging that while values clarification seeks ultimately to make students more aware of their own and others' values, it does not go beyond this: ". . . in effect, it teaches that self-awareness is an end in itself. Such an aim . . . teaches that all values are the same, that no value is any better than any other—only different."[11]

One of Kohlberg's criticisms centers on what he regards as the value-free or relativistic thrust of values clarification proponents. He indicts their philosophy on the grounds that the goal of values education—self-awareness—stems from a belief in ethical relativity held by many proponents of values clarification. According to Kohlberg, teachers are to stress that "our values are different," not that one value is more adequate than others, and if this emphasis is systematically pursued, students will become relativists who believe that there is no "right" moral answer. He cites a potential consequence: "For instance, a student caught cheating might argue that he did nothing wrong, since his own hierarchy of values, which may be different from that of the teacher, made it right for him to cheat."[12]

Definitional Problems. The term, "value," as defined by proponents of values clarification, has been sharply criticized by social studies educators. Originally Raths defined "value" as individual beliefs, attitudes, or feelings that satisfy the seven criteria of: (a) having been freely chosen; (b) having been chosen from among alternatives; (c) having been chosen after due reflection; (d) having been prized and cherished; (e) having been publicly affirmed; (f) having been incorporated into actual behavior; and (g) having been repeated in one's life.[13] Shaver and Strong take issue with this definition on the grounds that it: (a) obscures the distinction between emotive and cognitive meanings, and thus ignores the different functions of each; (b) fails to distinguish between value judgments and their underlying principles (a distinction they regard as important to making and analyzing decisions); and (c) ignores what is known about the development of standards and principles.[14]

Fraenkel takes issue with Raths' and his colleagues' emphasis on the process of valuing. In his opinion, "This emphasis virtually excludes any stated awareness by the advocates of the need for knowledge about and understanding of the *facts* required to deal intelligently with value issues."[15] Fraenkel uses the topic, sex education, to illustrate his point. He argues that before one can begin to determine what children should be taught about sex, an extensive amount of information needs to be assembled: facts about conception, reproduction, and abortion, facts about emotions, facts about sexual customs and taboos, facts about changing attitudes toward sexuality, etc. That values clarification implies that an emphasis

[10]James P. Shaver and William Strong, *Facing Value Decisions: Rationale-Building for Teachers* (Belmont, Calif.: Wadsworth, 1976), p. 119.
[11]Jack R. Fraenkel, *How To Teach about Values* (Englewood Cliffs, N.J.: Prentice-Hall, 1977), p. 45.
[12]Lawrence Kohlberg, "The Cognitive-Developmental Approach to Moral Education," *Phi Delta Kappan* 56 (June 1975), p. 673.
[13]Raths, Harmin, and Simon, 1st ed., p. 30.
[14]Shaver and Strong, p. 120.
[15]Fraenkel, p. 46.

Building a medieval castle can trigger exciting speculation about the values held by people far removed in time and space.

on *process alone* can help students to deal with issues in values questions is in Fraenkel's opinion, grossly misleading.[16]

A related definitional problem could be created by Raths' and his colleagues' insistence on the fulfillment of the seven conditions cited earlier. Are, for example, values always freely chosen? Aren't some, perhaps many, values acquired as an unconscious consequence of human experience? If one has never acted on a value, can we conclude that he or she has not acquired the value? Fraenkel questions whether people *always* need to publicly affirm what they value—even when it may be foolish or even dangerous to do so. He concludes, "Isn't that asking for more than most people can produce?"[17] Other requirements stated by Raths appear equally confusing. What is meant by "acting repeatedly," or "choosing after thoughtful consideration of the consequences of each alternative"? Unfortunately, proponents of values clarification appear reluctant to provide specific answers to such questions.

Effects on Students.   The previous discussion has reviewed some of the basic criticisms lodged against values clarification. These criticisms have centered on the alleged misuses of the term, "value," and on presumed defects in conceptions of the "process of valuing." At this point, it is appropriate to consider criticisms regarding the consequences of values clarification, when used in the classroom.

[16]Fraenkel, pp. 46–47.
[17]Fraenkel, p. 44.

One of the most devastating indictments against values clarification was issued by John S. Stewart,[18] who alleged that value clarifying activities encourage students to *conform* to certain values, rather than to acquire their own set of values. This critic is concerned over the effects of the values continuum on students who fervently desire peer approval. Would these students be likely to publicly affirm an extreme position on an emotionally laden issue involving, for example, stealing, lying, cheating, sexuality, religion, etc.? Stewart claims that these extreme positions on the values continuum are ". . . so value-specific, and/or emotionally loaded as to preclude them as legitimate alternatives for public affirmation . . ."[19] According to Stewart, even the middle choice on a values continuum may be equally unacceptable, owing to the implications that a student may draw from its wording.

Fraenkel regards the values clarification model as ". . . a personal authentication model," one that aims to help students to become more knowledgeable of their own personal commitments. As such, he believes that values clarification offers little help to students confronted with dilemmas where personal commitments often conflict:

> Suppose that an individual has been taught from childhood to be both loyal and honest. She has internalized and become committed to these values. Suppose that she has observed one of her friends taking money from another student's purse and later is asked by one of her teachers—whom she respects and admires—if she knows anything about the theft. Should she be loyal to her friend and say nothing? Should she be honest and tell the teacher what she has seen? Or should she pursue another alternative? How does she decide? The values clarification model gives little help to individuals dealing with such dilemmas.[20]

Theory and Research. Is values clarification a legitimate theory? Is there a sound body of research which documents the claims of values clarification proponents? Stewart, one of the harshest critics, maintains that ". . . values clarification has accepted, and remained committed to, an inadequate theory it inherited from Louis Raths—a theory that is philosophically indefensible and psychologically inadequate."[21] Further, he suggests that Raths and Simon may have exaggerated when they claimed that their theory of values clarification is derived from the writings of John Dewey. In Stewart's opinion, this claim may reflect a misunderstanding of Dewey's thought: When values clarification proponents adopted Dewey's ideas, they did so unsystematically and with no regard for their original context. Shaver and Strong note, ". . . little of what one might call a 'theory' is spelled out, beyond a few assumptions underlying their basic approach."[22]

Fraenkel is in accord with these critics; he stresses that there is no values theory underlying values clarification, because the writings of its proponents do

[18]John S. Stewart, "Clarifying Values Clarification: A Critique," *Phi Delta Kappan* 56 (June 1975), p. 685.

[19]Stewart, p. 685.

[20]Fraenkel, p. 45.

[21]Stewart, p. 686.

[22]Shaver and Strong, p. 118.

not contain: (a) interrelated, testable propositions suggesting relationships likely to exist in the real world; and (b) propositions capable of explaining why certain events occur, and which predict future occurrences. Fraenkel concludes that values clarification literature is devoid of such propositions:

> At best, one finds only a few assumptions by authors as to *how* values develop. These assumptions do not in any way help to explain why they develop this way. Nor do the assumptions predict how individuals with certain values are likely to act in a given situation. They don't tell what to do when values conflict or even how—or if—the holding of a *particular* value affects the development of other values. All these are considerations one might reasonably expect a theory of values to provide some ideas about.[23]

The quality of research cited in support of values clarification has been criticized by Stewart. He is particularly critical of the research cited in Chapter 10 of the seminal values clarification text, *Values and Teaching,*[24] by Raths, Harmin, and Simon. Stewart found that many of these studies extolled the virtues of values clarification, but were characterized by subjective claims of teachers and/or researchers, inconclusive findings, and research designs fraught with problems.

Despite these criticisms, Superka and Johnson's insightful analysis of research on values clarification does lend credence to the effectiveness of values clarification strategies, when used in the classroom. These authors concluded:

> The research, although inconclusive, does provide some basis for the authors' claim that students who use values clarification become less apathetic, less flighty, and less conforming as well as less overdissenting.[25]

One possible explanation for these encouraging conclusions may be, as Stewart suggests, the values clarification researchers' inability to control variables which may have influenced the results of their studies.[26] It may be that the *circumstances* under which the values clarification studies were conducted produced results that would have occurred whether or not values clarification strategies were used. Presumably the increased individual attention accorded the subjects, the creation of a more open, humane classroom climate, the change from one method of instruction to another, or even the newness of values clarification could have produced similar results. Too often researchers who desire to study the effects of a new approach to instruction overlook the insidious, often unmeasurable effects of such factors.

Rebuttal

Proponents of values clarification are mounting a vigorous counterattack against the critics. Through various publications, presentations given before professional

[23]Fraenkel, p. 43.
[24]Raths, Harmin, and Simon, *Values and Teaching.*
[25]Douglas Superka and Patricia Johnson, *Values Education: Approaches and Materials* (Boulder, Colo.: ERIC Clearinghouse for Social Studies and the Social Science Education Consortium, 1974), unpaged.
[26]Stewart, p. 687.

and lay groups, and through instructional materials designed for students and teachers they attempt to convince educators that their philosophy of values merits a legitimate position in school curricula. Unfortunately some advocates of values clarification prefer to describe their philosophy in glowing, superficial, often evangelistic terms; others fail to respond directly to criticisms regarding the theoretical foundations or the methodology of values clarification, or the quality of the values clarification research. An article co-authored by Sidney B. Simon and Polly deSherbinin, and entitled "Values Clarification: It Can Start Gently and Grow Deep,"[27] typifies the glib, messianic, hard-sell approach used by some values clarification advocates.

In an article entitled, "In Defense of Values Clarification,"[28] authors Kirschenbaum, Harmin, Howe, and Simon attempt to set the record straight. These progenitors of the values clarification movement deal with these criticisms: (a) that values clarification is value free and relativistic; and (b) that the theoretical and research base of values clarification is inadequate.

Kirschenbaum and his colleagues acknowledge that their philosophy is relativistic to the extent that each student's views are treated with equal respect, but that relativism stops at this point. They maintain that: (a) irrespective of their views, all students who participate in values clarification exercises are asked further clarifying questions, to facilitate the development of their values; and (b) that the values clarification process promotes the value of prizing, choosing, and acting (as defined by Raths), or thinking, feeling, choosing, communicating, and acting (as defined by Kirschenbaum). Further, they claim that:

> . . . values clarification promotes certain types of thinking, feeling, choosing, communicating, and acting. Thinking critically is regarded as *better than* thinking non-critically; considering consequences is regarded as *better than* choosing impulsively or thoughtlessly. Choosing freely is considered *better than* yielding passively to authority or peer pressure. And so on.[29]

Kirschenbaum and his co-authors go a step further, arguing that their valuing processes are better than their counterparts:

> Here again, certain value judgments are implicit in each process. If we urge critical thinking, then we value *rationality*. If we promote divergent thinking, then we value *creativity*. If we support moral reasoning as Lawrence Kohlberg defines it, then we value *justice*. If we uphold free choice, then we value *autonomy* or *freedom*. If we encourage "no-lose" conflict resolution, then we value *equality*.[30]

Advocates of values clarification claim that there is a growing number of studies that support their hypotheses. In addition to the twelve early studies reported by Raths, Harmin, and Simon in 1966,[31] they cite twenty-three addi-

[27]Sidney B. Simon and Polly deSherbinin, "Values Clarification: It Can Start Gently and Grow Deep," *Phi Delta Kappan*, 56 (June 1975), pp. 679–683.
[28]Howard Kirschenbaum, et al., "In Defense of Values Clarification," *Phi Delta Kappan*, 58 (June 1977), pp. 743–746.
[29]Kirschenbaum, et al., p. 744.
[30]Kirschenbaum, et al., p. 744.
[31]Raths, Harmin, and Simon.

tional studies reported by Kirschenbaum in 1977.[32] Although Kirschenbaum and his associates acknowledge that the results of these studies are far from conclusive and that their designs are far from perfect, they state that roughly 80 percent of them ". . . lend credibility to the assertion that use of the valuing process leads to greater personal value (e.g., less apathy, higher self-esteem, etc.) and greater social constructiveness (e.g., lower drug abuse, less disruptive classroom behavior, etc.).[33]

Moreover, Kirschenbaum claims that if one views values clarification within the context of his expanded conception of five dimensions and eighteen subprocesses, there is even greater research support for this approach.[34] You will recall that his conception of the valuing process (see Table 6–1) contains references to existing theories or philosophies regarding socioemotional behavior. Do these references support one or both of the goals of values clarification? Even the most casual inspection of these references forces us to question this sweeping claim. For example, Kirschenbaum cites Kohlberg's moral reasoning as an example of a subprocess of the dimension of thinking. Would Kohlberg condone this application of his work? Before responding, we suggest that you reread his objections to the relativistic thrust of values clarification which appeared earlier in this chapter. Would Benjamin Bloom, S.J. Parnes, or Carl Rogers acquiesce to this application? Unfortunately, these authors and their colleagues who are not involved in the values clarification movement have not publicly affirmed the extent to which their theories support Kirschenbaum's conception of values clarification. Until these scholars are heard from, we are unable to determine whether their theories are consistent with the spirit and intent of Kirschenbaum's provocative and insightful conception.

Despite the vociferous attacks aimed at values clarification, and despite the reluctance of its defenders to respond to these criticisms,[35] we cannot summarily condemn this approach to values education. Those who currently are in the vanguard of this movement have designed many exciting, worthwhile activities for the classroom (see Sections B and C in Part 2). That much needed research on values clarification continues suggests that the necessary documentation may be forthcoming. Nevertheless, we urge you to be aware of the inherent limitations of the values clarification approach, and to be wary of the glittering promises expressed by some of its promoters.

Personal Coat of Arms and Lifelong Roles

Here is one example of an exercise that we adapted from one values clarification text,[36] and have used in our social studies classes. The purpose of the exercise is to

[32]Howard Kirschenbaum, *Advanced Values Clarification* (La Jolla, Calif.: University Associates, 1977).
[33]Kirschenbaum, et al., p. 745.
[34]Kirschenbaum, et al., p. 744.
[35]We urge the reader to peruse Simon's cavalier response to Stewart's harsh criticisms of values clarification, as reported in *Phi Delta Kappan* 56 (June 1975), p. 688.
[36]Simon, Howe, and Kirschenbaum, *Values Clarification: A Handbook of Practical Strategies for Teachers and Students*, pp. 278–280.

encourage students to think about their goals in life, their achievements, and the image of themselves that they would like to convey to others. As such, this exercise provides students with an excellent introduction to the lifelong role of personal efficacy.

To begin the exercise, the teacher gives each student a large piece of tagboard or construction paper and an outline of a coat of arms (or has them copy it from the blackboard). Next, the students are asked to do five things:

1. Draw a picture of an activity that you are good at.
2. Draw a picture of an activity that you really want to be good at.
3. Draw a picture showing the one activity that you hate to do the most.
4. Draw a picture showing how you helped someone else with a difficult activity.
5. Below your coat of arms write three words that you would like people to say about you.

As your pupils begin work on their personal coats of arms, stress that the quality of their artwork and spelling are unimportant. What is important is that the pupils follow your directions, know what their pictures express, and can briefly describe their coats of arms to the class (if they wish), when they are completed.

At the conclusion of the assignment, you may elect to have your pupils share with you or in small groups their coats of arms, explaining the meaning of the pictures and words. One alternative is to ask the janitor or custodian of your school to hang each child's coat of arms directly over his desk. Displayed in this way, the coats of arms can exert a powerful effect on you, the teacher: They provide you

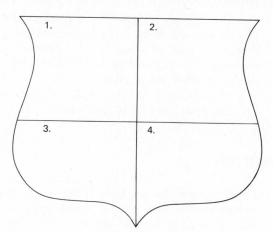

FIGURE 6–1 A PERSONAL COAT OF ARMS

with a constant reminder that your pupils are individuals, each possessing his own set of goals, aspirations, and achievements. We must warn you, however, that for various reasons, some pupils will not want their coats of arms displayed, and thus we urge you to *respect their wishes*. This exercise should not become an art show; if it does, the exercise becomes self-defeating. Moreover, our experience demonstrates that some pupils may deliberately copy ideas from their classmates in an effort to produce coats of arms that are acceptable to you. If this happens, stop the lesson, explain again the purpose of the exercise, and continue.

Our former students who have used this exercise report that it does an excellent job of exposing pupils to the lifelong role of personal efficacy, for it asks them to take stock of themselves and to consider their personal achievements as well as their aspirations. Also, the exercise gives each child an opportunity to express himself in a unique way, without being forced into writing sentences and paragraphs. Finally, the exercise can be easily modified to include other kinds of questions, some of which center on other lifelong roles:

1. If you were given a million dollars, what would you do with it?
2. What is a belief that your family lives by?
3. What value do you want all of mankind to live by?
4. What is your greatest weakness? Your greatest strength?
5. What is your family's greatest accomplishment?
6. What is one thing that your friends could do to make you happy?
7. What freedom do you value the most?
8. What kind of job would you like to have when you grow up?

Some teachers have used variations of this exercise in studying about famous people and significant events. For example, one class, working in small groups, designed coats of arms for a nineteenth-century American family traveling westward in a wagon train. Other classes have designed coats of arms for Reverend Martin Luther King, Thomas Edison, and for Presidents Lincoln, Kennedy, Nixon, and Carter. In these instances, the coats of arms produced amazing insights into the goals, successes and failures, and aspirations of the people under study.

MORAL REASONING

Lawrence Kohlberg is the preeminent exponent of the moral reasoning approach to values education, just as Raths and his coworkers are readily identified with values clarification. This approach has been widely disseminated through a multitude of conferences, seminars, professional publications, and instructional programs for children and youth. It is extremely difficult to undertake a point-by-point comparison of the two approaches, since each operates from a different set of assumptions, lays claim to different historical antecedents, and utilizes different instructional methods. Rather than attempting such a comparison, we prefer to describe moral reasoning apart from values clarification, so that the strengths and weaknesses of Kohlberg's approach to values education can be judged on their own merits. As with our previous discussion of values clarification, space limitations preclude us from rendering a penetrating, in-depth analysis of moral reasoning, and thus we are compelled to confine our discussion to the basic tenets of this approach, as reported in the extant professional literature.

According to Kohlberg, the purpose of the moral reasoning approach is to stimulate students into developing more complex patterns of moral reasoning. Basic to this approach is a six-stage conception of moral development. Teachers who use Kohlberg's approach present (via a written story, film, or filmstrip) their students with a hypothetical or factual story involving a moral dilemma. Next, the students are encouraged to decide what the characters should do in an attempt to resolve the dilemma, and to defend their positions. The class then divides into small groups to discuss their positions, with the teacher moving from group to group, gently probing the pupils' reasoning. Following group discussions, the teacher asks the pupils to reconsider their positions, in an attempt to determine whether they have revised their viewpoints. Kohlberg maintains, and his research tends to corroborate his theory, that these group discussions expose pupils to higher levels of reasoning, which has the effect of stimulating pupils to reach the next stage of moral development.

Following are the essential details of a moral dilemma in *First Things: Values*,[37] a series of sound filmstrips based on Kohlberg's work:

> A father takes his children to the circus. Upon their arrival, he learns that he does not have enough money to pay for their admission. But the entire family could be admitted if he lied about the age of one of the children. Since the family lives a great distance from the circus, it would be impractical to return home for the money. If he pays the required admission fees, one of the members of the family will be unable to attend. Should the family return home, because they don't have sufficient money for their tickets? Should the father explain their predicament to the ticket seller, in the hope that he would allow the entire family to attend the circus, with the understanding that the father would pay for the balance of the ticket later? Should the father lie about the age of one of the children, so that the entire family can attend the circus? Should the child for whom the father cannot afford a ticket be required to wait outside the gate while the others attend the circus?

Presumably by participating in small-group discussions of these and other courses of action, a pupil will be encouraged to take a position, defend it among his peers, consider the positions taken by other members of his group, and advance in his moral reasoning ability.

Historical Antecedents

Kohlberg traces the philosophical lineage of moral reasoning back to the writings of John Dewey and particularly to the stage theory of Jean Piaget. He refers to his philosophy as a "cognitive–developmental approach," one that is consistent with

---

[37]Lawrence Kohlberg and R. L. Selman, *First Things: Values* (Pleasantville, N.Y.: Guidance Associates, 1972–1973).

that which was initially explicated by Dewey in his seminal works, *Ethics*[38] and *Democracy and Education: An Introduction to the Philosophy of Education*.[39] Kohlberg explains that he uses the term "cognitive," because it acknowledges ". . . that moral education, like intellectual education, has its basis in stimulating the *active thinking* of the child about moral issues and decisions."[40] He uses the term, "developmental" ". . . because it sees the aims of moral education as movement through moral stages."[41]

Kohlberg reminds us that Dewey posited three levels of moral development: (a) the premoral or *preconventional* level of behavior motivated by biological or social impulses with consequences for moral behavior; (b) the *conventional* level of behavior in which the individual uncritically accepts the standards of the group; and (c) the *autonomous* level of behavior in which one's conduct is guided by his or her own assessment of the goodness of his purposes, and refuses to accept the behavioral standards of the group without reflection. Further, Kohlberg notes that these three levels correspond roughly to his three levels of moral reasoning: the preconventional, the conventional, and the principled.[42]

A second and more pronounced influence on Kohlberg's conception of moral reasoning was the stages of cognitive development in children postulated by Jean Piaget. While Dewey's thoughts tended to be highly theoretical, Piaget's were based on data and impressions gleaned from actual interviews of children and from observations of children engaged in playing games for which rules had been established.

Fraenkel's insightful analysis of Piaget's stages may enhance our understanding of them. According to him, the first stage alone (premoral) is a blind-obedience stage where a child's conception of right and wrong is governed by what his parents permit or forbid him to do. He defines the second stage (heteronomous or conventional, if one uses Dewey's wording) as an "interpretation-of-rules" level, when a child learns that the spirit or intention of a rule is more important; and the third stage is an "interpretation-of-the-act" stage during which the child acquires a feeling of personal or ethical responsibility for his or her behavior.[43]

Since the second and third stages are most relevant for elementary students, we will explore them in greater detail, by citing examples of student behaviors for these stages. Piaget's second and third stages can be explained in terms of children's concepts of control, justice, and responsibility. Instead of designating these stages as conventional (or heteronomous) and autonomous, these authors prefer to use Piaget's "morality of constraint" and "morality of cooperation,"

---

[38]John Dewey and James H. Tufts, *Ethics* (New York: Henry Holt and Company, 1908).

[39]John Dewey, *Democracy and Education: An Introduction to the Philosophy of Education* (New York: Macmillan, 1916).

[40]Lawrence Kohlberg, "The Cognitive-Developmental Approach to Moral Education," *Phi Delta Kappan* 56 (June 1975), p. 670.

[41]Kohlberg, p. 670.

[42]John Dewey, "What Psychology Can Do to the Teacher," in Reginald Archambault, ed., *John Dewey on Education: Selected Writings* (New York: Random House, 1964), cited by Kohlberg, "The Cognitive-Developmental Approach to Moral Education," p. 670.

[43]Jack R. Fraenkel, *How To Teach about Values* (Englewood Cliffs, N.J.: Prentice-Hall, 1977), p. 52.

respectively. Below are examples of pupil behaviors at these stages. Examples for concepts of control and justice were adapted from the work of Jantz and Fulda.[44]

CONTROL

1. Morality of Constraint

    A classroom rule states that pupils should walk in a straight line and remain silent while going to the library. Sally, a seven-year-old, was asked, "Were you a good girl in school?" She replied, "No, good girls walk in a straight line and I walked next to Annette and talked to her."

    At this stage children believe that it is their duty to obey authority. They do not analyze rules; instead, they regard them as revealed and imposed by adults. Obedience to a rule or to an adult is good.

2. Morality of Cooperation

    Six 7th graders are playing basketball. As four additional players join the game, the rules are changed. Now they use the full court and both baskets instead of half the court and one basket.

    At this stage a child's perception of control changes from that imposed by adults or superiors to an authority of equals. Authority is mutually agreed upon by a child and his peers, or rationally agreed upon with an adult. Rules are no longer sacred and inviolable, but can be changed by mutual agreement.

JUSTICE

1. Morality of Constraint

    Ramon, a first-grader, is asked, "What should happen if you don't follow the rules while playing football?" His answer: "You're kicked out of the game and miss recess for a whole week."

    A child's concept of justice at this stage requires that the letter, not the spirit, of the law be followed. Piaget believes that children regard violations of the law as extremely serious offenses. A child's intentions are of little consequence when passing judgment on the behavior of others. It is the direct consequence that counts.

2. Morality of Cooperation

    Jean, a fifth-grader, is asked "What happens when you break the rules while playing

---

[44]From Richard K. Jantz and Trudi Fulda, "The Role of Moral Education in the Public Elementary School," *Social Education* 39 (January 1975), pp. 25–26. Adapted by permission of the National Council for the Social Studies.

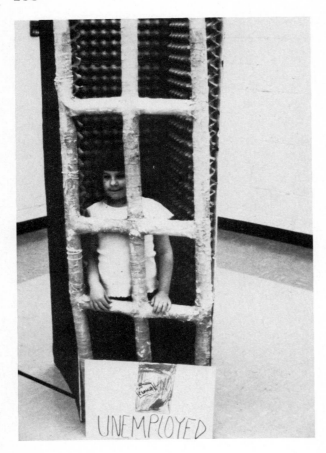

UNEMPLOYED

Is it likely that this pupil's concept of justice is changing? If so, in what ways?

football?" Her response: "Your team is penalized. The ball's moved back five or fifteen yards, depending on the penalty."

As the child moves from a morality of constraint to a morality of cooperation, his/her concept of justice expands from a punitive view to one of restitution. In the above example, Jean sees no need for a playmate to be punished because she has broken the rules of football; instead, she sees the need for her team to be assessed a penalty, one that restores the opportunity of the other team to score.

RESPONSIBILITY

1.   Morality of Constraint

Six-year-old Ann invites her friends to play with dolls at her house. Before they arrive, she decides to help her mother bake cookies. When her friends arrive, Ann tells them to come back another time when she's not busy helping her mother. Ann's friends leave, very disappointed, and angry with Ann.

When Ann decided to bake cookies with her mother, she intended to honor her obligation to her friends. She was more concerned with the immediate prospect of baking cookies. Her friends could not conceive of Ann's intentions; they were primarily concerned over the *consequence* of Ann's actions. They viewed Ann's responsibility in cold, objective terms.

2. Morality of Cooperation

Thirteen-year-old Jane invites her friends to listen to records at her house. Shortly before they arrive, Kevin, Jane's boyfriend, appears without warning. As her friends arrive, Jane tells Kevin that she'll have to excuse herself, because she'd arranged to see her girl friends. As Kevin leaves, he arranges to see Jane later that day.

Kevin's actions reveal that he understands the motives behind Jane's decision, for they were prompted by a previous commitment that Jane had made. If he wants to keep Jane's friendship, he will accept the consequences of Jane's decision.

These examples reveal that moral thinking and intellectual development are interrelated, and that they occur at stages. Moreover, as Piaget's studies suggest, children are consistent in their level of moral judgment; they move toward the next higher stage (never backward), and their thinking at a higher stage encompasses lower stage thinking.

This discussion explored the two major historical antecedents of Kohlberg's stage theory, Dewey's and Piaget's conceptions of moral stages of development. As you examine Kohlberg's conceptions of moral reasoning as articulated through his stage theory, we urge you to keep in mind these precursors, for they provide you with a basis for grasping the essence of Kohlberg's conceptions, and should enable you to apply them in your teaching.

Kohlberg's Stage Theory

Kohlberg's theory of moral reasoning grew out of his efforts to redefine and validate Dewey's and Piaget's stages of reasoning. Since 1955 Kohlberg and his associates have studied, through longitudinal and crosscultural research, the moral reasoning of children and adults, initially in the United States and later in Turkey, Canada, Great Britain, Israel, Taiwan, Yucatan, Honduras, and India. The subjects (ages 10, 13, 16, and 20), after being presented hypothetical moral dilemmas centering on key issues regarding punishment, affectional relations, authority, contract, property, life, civil liberties, and conscience, were then interviewed regarding their responses to the dilemmas. Their responses were classified into six groups, according to the reasons they gave. From these studies Kohlberg found that there are three levels of moral development: the preconventional, the conventional, and the postconventional, and that within each of these three levels are two stages, thus yielding a total of six stages. Kohlberg's levels and stages of moral development are described in detail below.[45]

[45]This discussion is a synthesis of ideas expressed in Lawrence Kohlberg, "The Cognitive-Developmental Approach to Moral Education," *Phi Delta Kappan*, 56 (June 1975), p. 671–677; Edwin

Level 1. Preconventional Morality

At this level sanctions and motivations for one's behavior are *external*. Children's impulses to satisfy their personal needs are modified by punishments, rewards, or exchange of favors.

Stage 1. Punishment and Obedience Orientation

Self-interest is identical to rule-following. Authority and rules are obeyed to avoid punishment or the threat of punishment. Justice is regarded as "an eye for an eye, a tooth for a tooth." Retaliation becomes an automatic response, regardless of intention or motive. Typically children in grades K–3 are at stage 1, but evidence of stage 1 behavior exists in the junior high (or middle school) and to some extent in high school.

Stage 2. Instrumental Relativist Orientation

A child at this stage conceives of a right as that which satisfies his own needs, and occasionally the needs of others. Reciprocity is defined as "You scratch my back and I'll scratch yours," not as loyalty, gratitude, or justice. Stage 2 begins about grade 3, when it begins to dominate stage 1 by late elementary and early junior high grades. Despite this, stage 2 is a powerful force in the morality and decision making of adolescents in high school. The morality of the market place and politics (log-rolling, for example) are significant elements of stage 2 moral development. Some people remain at this stage throughout their lives.

Level 2. Conventional Morality

At this level the individual's behavior is motivated by a desire to maintain the expectations of his family, friends, or nation—for its own sake—regardless of immediate and obvious consequences, in order to avoid social criticism. Thus, sanctions on one's behavior are external, but motivations on one's behavior are internal. One seeks not only to conform to expectations of others, but also strives to be loyal to them and to support and maintain them.

Stage 3. Interpersonal Concordance Orientation

Behavior at this stage is characterized by a "good boy—nice girl" orientation. The individual equates good behavior with whatever pleases or helps others, and with what others approve of. At this stage, the individual regards justice as that which makes everybody happy, and which meets everyone's approval. He or she conforms to stereotypic images of "acceptable" or "natural" behavior. Often behavior is judged by one's intentions ("He means well," or "She thought that she was doing the right thing."). Stage 3 behavior normally begins to occur at about ages ten or eleven, but is more prevalent and predominant beginning at ages twelve or thirteen. Many people never advance beyond this stage.

Stage 4. Law and Order (or Conscientious) Orientation

At this stage the individual is oriented toward authority, fixed rules, laws, duty, and maintenance of the social order for its own sake. He is motivated to escape feelings of guilt or blame by behaving in a way that is consistent with standards established by recognized authorities. Stage 4 behavior begins manifesting itself around ages fifteen to seventeen, sometimes a bit earlier. This tends to be the modal stage for the United States, and a terminal stage for many people.

Fenton, "Moral Education: The Research Findings," *Social Education*, 40 (April 1976), pp. 189–193; William W. Joyce (Ed.), "Moral Education in the Elementary School: A Neglected Responsibility," *Social Education*, 39 (January 1975), pp. 23–39; and in Ronald E. Galbraith and Thomas M. Jones, "Teaching Strategies for Moral Dilemmas," *Social Education*, 39 (January 1975), pp. 16–22.

Level 3. Postconventional Morality
Basic to this, the highest level, is the individual's acceptance of the moral principles that control his actions. Since these principles have validity apart from the authority of groups or persons with which he identifies, sanctions and motivations governing his behavior are internal.

Stage 5. Social Contract Orientation
This stage is the "official" morality of the United States Government and Constitution. It is oriented toward individual rights and standards of behavior that have been critically examined and agreed upon through democratic processes by our society. The individual who is at stage 5 espouses the legality of our laws and constitutional guarantees, but stresses the importance of changing laws, after rationally considering their impact on the welfare of society. Where no laws apply, a stage 5 person's obligations are based on free agreement and contract. Persons at this stage are in their middle or late twenties.

Stage 6. Universal Ethical Principle Orientation
This, the highest stage in the Social Contract Orientation, defines what is right as a matter of conscience in accord with ethical principles that are logically comprehensive, universal, and consistent. An individual at this stage attaches the highest value to justice, the value of human life, equality, and dignity. A mere fraction of the population is at this stage. It tends to occur in the late twenties or thirties or later.

At the risk of oversimplifying the six stages described above, it should be noted that the *reasons* people give for moral decisions often give insight into the central meanings of these stages. Shaver and Strong draw our attention to the differences in justification cited by Kohlberg:

Stage 1: Obey rules to avoid punishment.
Stage 2: Conform to obtain rewards, have favors returned, and so on.
Stage 3: Conform to avoid disapproval, dislike by others.
Stage 4: Conform to avoid censure by legitimate authorities and resultant guilt.
Stage 5: Conform to maintain the respect of the impartial spectator judging in terms of community welfare.
Stage 6: Conform to avoid self-condemnation.[46]

Although Kohlberg acknowledges that maturity of moral judgment is not highly correlated with verbal intelligence, he maintains that cognitive development in Piaget's stage sense has far greater significance for moral development than correlational studies would suggest. Once a child learns to speak, he has three periods of cognitive development ahead of him: preoperational, concrete operational, and formal operational. When he is about seven, he enters the concrete operational period; at this point he can make logical inferences and apply them to concrete problems. As an adolescent, he enters the stage of formal operations; by now he can solve various types of logical problems including deductive hypothesis testing, and complex verbal and hypothetical problems.

[46]Lawrence Kohlberg, "Indoctrination versus Relativity in Value Education," *Zygon* (1972), pp. 297–298, cited in James P. Shaver and William Strong, *Facing Value Decisions: Rationale-Building for Teachers* (Belmont, Calif.: Wadsworth, 1976), pp. 126–127.

Kohlberg believes that since moral reasoning *is reasoning*, a person's ability to engage in advanced moral reasoning is contingent upon his ability to engage in advanced logical reasoning, and that a person's stage of logical reasoning imposes limits on the moral stage that he is capable of attaining.[47]

Fenton has presented eleven generalizations drawn from Kohlberg and his colleagues' research into cognitive moral development. We hope that they will crystalize your thinking on this topic.

1. People think about moral issues in six quantitatively different stages arranged in three levels of two stages each.
2. The most reliable way to determine a stage of moral thought is through a moral interview.
3. A stage is an organized system of thought.
4. An individual reasons predominantly at one stage of thought and uses contiguous stages as a secondary thinking pattern.
5. These stages are natural steps in ethical development, not something artificial or invented.
6. All the people move through these stages in invariant sequence, although any individual may stop at a particular stage.
7. People can understand moral arguments at their own stage, at all stages beneath their own, and usually at one stage higher than their own.
8. Higher moral stages are better than lower ones.
9. Stage transition takes place primarily because encountering real-life or hypothetical moral dilemmas sets up cognitive conflict in a person's mind and makes the person uncomfortable.
10. Deliberate attempts to facilitate stage change in schools through educational programs have been successful.
11. Moral judgment is a necessary but not sufficient condition for moral action.[48]

Moral Discussions

Since moral discussions are the basic instructional device used to promote moral reasoning in the classroom, it is important that one acquires an understanding of the methods and procedures for conducting such discussions before attempting to apply Kohlberg's theory to the classroom. Galbraith and Jones[49] and Beyer[50] have designed models for conducting moral discussions.

A film, "Who Needs Rules?"[51] provided the basic content for a moral dilemma designed by Galbraith and Jones. The film presents two problematical situations in which children are asked to decide whether they will obey or break a rule. In the initial situation Steve and Connie encounter a stray puppy. Steve is

[47]Lawrence Kohlberg, p. 671.
[48]Edwin Fenton, "Moral Education: The Research Findings," *Social Education*, 40 (April 1976), pp. 189–193. Reprinted by permission of the National Council for the Social Studies.
[49]Ronald E. Galbraith and Thomas M. Jones, "Teaching Strategies for Moral Dilemmas," *Social Education*, 39 (January 1975), pp. 16-22.
[50]Barry K. Beyer, "Conducting Moral Discussions in the Classroom," *Social Education*, 40 (April 1976), pp. 194–202.
[51]"Who Needs Rules?" (Chicago: Encyclopedia Britannica Corporation, 1972).

determined to keep it, but Connie reminds him that a rule of their apartment building expressly forbids pets. But Steve is worried about the puppy, and wants to take the puppy to his apartment so that he can feed it. Although Connie shares Steve's concern over the puppy, she reminds Steve about the rule, and worries that their family will be evicted should a pet be discovered. A basic conflict arises over Steve's desire to care for the puppy and Connie's practical view of the potential consequences. At this point the teacher is to turn off the projector, and encourage the pupils to decide what they would do in this situation.

Galbraith and Jones' teaching plan is divided into six stages:

1. *Warm-Up Questions*: These stimulate the children's thinking about their own experiences with lost puppies, apartment building rules, their own pets, and animal shelters.

2. *Presentation*: This stage consists of showing the segment of the film described above.

3. *Initiating Questions*: Once the teacher has clarified the essential elements of the story, she asks a series of questions concerning the action(s) that Steve and Connie should take, the reasons why apartment buildings have rules against pets, whether Steve and Connie should break the rule, whether Steve and Connie should tell anyone about their puppy, and the course of action that these children should follow so that they can save the puppy. Galbraith and Jones encourage teachers to seek many answers to the initiating questions, and to frequently ask pupils to react to their classmates' responses. The teacher can ask additional initiating questions, use a small-group strategy, or introduce a story expansion.

4. *Small-Group Strategies*: Galbraith and Jones suggest three types of small-group strategies. These include; (a) *role taking*—working in small groups, the students might, for example, role play Steve, Connie, their parents, and the apartment manager; (b) *illustrating the ending*—working in groups of three, the children draw pictures of how the story should end, and then explain these pictures to the class; and (c) *listing reasons*—groups of three or four pupils are asked to list and defend two or three courses of action that Steve and Connie should pursue or should not pursue. Galbraith and Jones note that at the conclusion of a group strategy, the teacher should encourage the pupils to discuss what happened in their small groups, and the pupils' rationales for the positions taken in their groups.

5. *Story Expansion*: Galbraith and Jones suggest teachers may wish to add a chapter to the story when the basic dilemma does not succeed in creating a conflict for the pupils, or when the pupils appear to have terminated their discussion. For example, the apartment manager confronts the family with the news that he has learned that Steve and Connie are keeping a puppy hidden in the building, and reminds them of the "no pet" rule.

6. *Probe Questions*: These questions might deal with whether it was fair of Steve and Connie to bring the puppy home, whether the children should tell their dad about the puppy in the storeroom, whether they should tell the apartment manager about the puppy, etc. Note that probe questions use the word *should*; they center thinking on moral reasoning to the extent that pupils are asked to decide on the right or correct thing to do.[52]

---

[52]From *Moral Reasoning: A Teaching Handbook for Adapting Kohlberg to the Classroom*, by Ronald E. Galbraith and Thomas M. Jones, pp. 172–180. Published by Greenhaven Press, Minneapolis, Minnesota, 1976, and reprinted with their permission.

Lifelong Roles and Organizing Themes

The previous example illustrates how the lifelong roles of family membership and personal efficacy can be taught through the medium of moral discussions. Similarly, personal efficacy can be taught through experiences that children encounter in their daily lives. Should a child report a friend whom he observed shoplifting, breaking a window, cheating on a test, lying, defacing property of others, etc.? Should a pupil allow a classmate to copy his social studies assignment? Should he tell his parents that his older brother had an accident with the family car? Situations such as these are replete with compelling, real-life dilemmas which, when analyzed in terms of their potential consequences, enable children to reexamine, test, and modify their personal goals or standards.

Another fertile source of moral dilemmas is the subject matter taught in today's social studies programs. Weaver, for example, suggests the development of case studies focusing on moral dilemmas that confronted significant figures in the history of our nation. Among the moral decisions cited by this author are President Truman's decision to use the atom bomb against Japan, Reverend Martin Luther King's fearless advocacy of nonviolence during the Civil Rights movement, and President Lincoln's decision to go to war to preserve the Union, and various decisions involving treaties that our government made with Native Americans between 1789 and 1871, and broke when our national or regional interests were at stake.[53] To these we may add such significant presidential decisions as Lincoln's suspension of the writ of *habeas corpus* during the Civil War, Roosevelt's issuance of Executive Order 9066, which ordered the internment of 110,000 Japanese–Americans during World War II, and Carter's advocacy of the Panama Canal Treaty. Or consider the instructional payoff of using events in recent US history as a source of moral dilemmas. Duffey noted that the moral decisions facing Elliot Richardson, Archibald Cox, Judge John Sirica, and other central figures in President Nixon's "Saturday Night Massacre" of the Watergate Era would provide appropriate content for moral dilemmas centering on recent US history.[54] These topics would have profound relevance for the lifelong roles of citizenship and personal efficacy, which could be developed through such organizing themes as government and politics, law, and morality.

Moral dilemmas can add another dimension to a pupil's understanding of the lifelong roles and organizing themes. Consider for a moment the moral dilemmas that you might develop when studying energy conservation in your classes. At various times a pupil might observe older members of his family tampering with the household water, gas, or electric meter, joyriding in the family car, driving at an excessive speed, watering the lawn during a water shortage, or engaging in numerous other activities that waste our precious energy resources. Clearly, moral dilemmas of this type add new meaning and purpose to the lifelong role of family membership when studied within the context of the organizing theme, energy.

[53]V. Phillips Weaver, "Moral Education and the Study of United States History," *Social Education*, 39 (January 1975), pp. 36–39.
[54]Robert V. Duffey, "Moral Education and the Study of Current Events," *Social Education*, 39 (January 1975), pp. 33–35.

Critique

Despite the compelling appeal of Kohlberg's theory of moral development, and despite its reliance on the theories of Dewey and Piaget, several basic criticisms have been advanced by social studies educators and social scientists. These center on the universality of Kohlberg's moral stages, his belief in the superiority of higher-stage reasoning over lower-stage reasoning, and the demands that his theory places on classroom teachers.

Universality. Shaver and Strong challenge Kohlberg's claim that his stages are adequate global descriptions of moral development; moreover, they question whether it is appropriate to impose on students a Western, individualistic conception on the world. They write, "There is ample reason to be cautious about assuming that he has struck on *the* description of moral development for *all* people."[55] Fraenkel is of a similar mind, and questions whether Kohlberg's research data drawn from five cultures "support the inference that the concept of justice—fundamental to the reasoning inherent in the higher stages (5 and 6)—is endorsed by all cultures."[56] Peters criticizes Kohlberg for his failure to acknowledge that there are various *definitions* of morality, of which morality of justice is but one. For example, he cites a morality of courage displayed by train robbers, the old "virtue" of Machiavelli's *Prince*, and the romantic type of morality displayed by D. H. Lawrence.[57]

Various questions have been raised regarding the adequacy of the research which Kohlberg cites in support of his theory. After reviewing such research, Kurtines and Greif reported in 1974 that there were insufficient findings to support Kohlberg's claim that individuals always develop through the same moral stages and in an invariant order, and his advocacy of the efficacy of his "one stage higher" challenges.[58] Another scholar, Simpson, claimed that the research which Kohlberg cites in defense of his theory demonstrated that people move through the six stages in invariant sequence only at stages two, three, and four.[59]

Despite the alleged inadequacies of this research, it is important to bear in mind that most of the studies that we have cited or alluded to were conducted over the past ten years; some are even older. By the time you read these words, there is a possibility that studies conducted in the interim will provide better documentation of Kohlberg's theory and its application.[60]

Higher-Stage Reasoning. Kohlberg claims that higher-stage reasoning is different from and better than lower-stage reasoning. Scriven[61] and Fraenkel[62] allege that it is impossible to prove this. If children who reason at lower stages are

---

[55]Shaver and Strong, p. 129.

[56]Fraenkel, p. 72.

[57]Richard S. Peters, "A Reply to Kohlberg," *Phi Delta Kappan*, 56 (June 1975), p. 679.

[58]W. Kurtines and E. B. Greif, "The Development of Moral Thought: Review and Evaluation of Kohlberg's Approach," *Psychological Bulletin,* 81 (1974), pp. 453–470.

[59]Elizabeth L. Simpson, "Moral Development Research: A Case Study of Scientific Cultural Bias," *Human Development* 17 (1974), pp. 81–106.

[60]For a list of recent and forthcoming publications that may rebut some of these criticisms, see Edwin Fenton, "A Response to Jack R. Fraenkel," *Social Education,* 41 (January 1977), pp. 56, 58, 60–61.

[61]Michael Scriven, "Cognitive Moral Education," *Phi Delta Kappan,* 56 (June 1975), pp. 689–694.

[62]Fraenkel, pp. 72–73.

unable to understand higher-stage reasoning, why should they want to accept higher-stage reasoning as superior to that of their own, and strive to elevate their reasoning? And, as Fraenkel notes, "If 'higher' is not 'better,' then there doesn't seem to be any justification for trying to 'improve' the reasoning of children by helping them move through the stages."[63]

Peters alleges that Kohlberg's theory does not take "good-boy" morality (stage 3) seriously enough. He regards this as a serious limitation: Since few people advance beyond stages three and four, it is important that people function effectively at these stages. Peters warns:

> The policemen cannot always be present, and if I am lying in the gutter after being robbed it is somewhat otiose to speculate at what stage the mugger is. My regret must surely be that he had not at least got a conventional morality well instilled in him. Theoretically, too, the good-boy stage is crucial; for at this stage the child learns from the inside, as it were, what it is to follow a rule. Unless he has learned this well (whatever it means!), the notion of following his *own* rules at the autonomous stage [i.e., level 3], Postconventional Morality is unintelligible.[64]

Do Kohlberg's theory and research not only underestimate the extreme importance of stages three and four, but also acknowledge the inability of most people to attain the conventional level of morality?

Demands on Teachers and Students.   Several critics of moral development have questioned the ability of teachers to lead productive moral discussions and the ability of pupils to benefit from them. Since Kohlberg insists that to maximize the effectiveness of moral communications in the classroom, the developmental level of the teacher's verbalizations must be one stage ahead of the child, one may question whether most teachers have this ability. Admittedly, this requirement should not be problematical for teachers of young children, but it could begin to become a problem in upper elementary and secondary grades, where some students are likely to be operating at higher stages of moral reasoning than their social studies teachers. Of far more significance for elementary teachers and their pupils are the implied demands of the moral dilemmas and the class discussions. Since most of the dilemmas are presented as case studies involving specific instances, it is likely that some—perhaps many—pupils will not find the dilemmas interesting or applicable to them. Moreover, one must question whether the majority of elementary- and middle-school pupils are capable of benefiting from intellectually demanding (often protracted) moral discussions which may run longer than most lessons. We hope that Kohlberg's supporters and colleagues will deal with this problem by producing for the elementary grades moral dilemmas and instructional plans that attempt to take these realities into account. Unless this is done, moral discussions at these levels may be beyond the capabilities of most students.

---

[63]Fraenkel, p. 72.
[64]Richard S. Peters, "A Reply to Kohlberg," *Phi Delta Kappan*, 56 (June 1975), p. 679. Reprinted by permission of Phi Delta Kappa.

SUMMARY

This chapter is based on the assumption that elementary and junior high school social studies programs are heavily impregnated with values. The question facing teachers is not, "*Should* I teach values?" but, "*How* do I deal with values?" Two widely used and potentially productive views of values education that appear to have special relevance for the teaching of social studies are values clarification and moral reasoning.

The primary architects of values clarification are Raths, Harmin, Simon, Howe, and Kirschenbaum. They have designed activities and instructional procedures in an attempt to assist individuals and groups to develop and clarify their values. Presumably a student who has clarified his values will be more likely to experience positive value in his life and act more constructively in the social world. Critics have questioned the scope of values clarification, definitional problems, its effects on students, and its theoretical and research foundations. Despite these criticisms, we support the use of values clarification strategies in elementary social studies classes. Nevertheless, we urge teachers to become aware of the limitations of this approach, and to be wary of the glittering promises offered by a few of its overly enthusiastic promoters.

The moral reasoning approach of Lawrence Kohlberg is descended from the writings of John Dewey and especially from Jean Piaget's pioneering research on the cognitive development of children. According to Kohlberg, the purpose of his moral reasoning approach is to stimulate students into developing more complex patterns of moral reasoning. He posits a six-stage conception of moral development, which he claims to have validated through studies undertaken in the United States and in various foreign nations. Basic to this conception is the idea that the individual's growth through the six stages is sequential, invariant, and occurs in all cultures.

Critics have challenged the individualistic, Western bias of Kohlberg's stage theory, the adequacy of the research that is offered in support of the theory, and the logic that underlies Kohlberg's claims regarding the superiority of higher-stage reasoning over lower-stage reasoning. In addition, we expressed concern over the demands that moral discussions tend to impose on pupils and on teachers.

Both approaches to values education can make many valuable contributions to the social studies, especially when used with our conception of the lifelong roles and organizing themes. As these approaches are refined and applied to the classroom, we have every reason to expect that their instructional capabilities will become increasingly apparent.

CROSS-REFERENCES TO TEACHING MODULES

Values and values processes are integral elements of the teaching modules presented in Part 2 of this text. Some of the modules deal with values in an indirect, implicit fashion, while others accord them more direct, explicit attention. Four modules described below illustrate the various ways in which this topic can be handled in the classroom.

Occupations: "Initial Exposure to Careers" (Part 2, p. 275). This teaching module, designed for the lower grades (K–3), helps children to become aware of various jobs that exist in their daily lives, and stresses the values inherent in the work ethic. Children learn to assume new responsibilities at home and at school, and gain first-hand exposure to the concept, interdependence. Sociology and economics are stressed in this module.

Ecology: "Cleaning Up the Local Environment" (Part 2, p. 324). Designed for the lower grades (K–3), this teaching module is intended to give children direct, first-hand experience with ecological problems in their immediate environments. By gathering litter and trash from the schoolyard and environs, and by considering this material in terms of its threat to health and safety, pupils learn about the importance of maintaining an unpolluted environment. Moreover, at the conclusion of the teaching module, they take constructive action designed to keep their schoolyard litter-free, and to recycle litter. Such activities become a consequence of the value analysis activities that permeate the module.

Morality: "Using Moral Dilemmas" (Part 2, p. 381). This module focuses on problems that many upper-grade (grades 5–8 or 6–8) pupils are likely to encounter in their daily lives: shoplifting, vandalism, and stealing. By discussing the moral questions implicit in these problems and then by creating defensible, viable solutions to them, pupils gain valuable experiences in moral reasoning. At the conclusion of the module pupils are encouraged to go a step further: to write out moral dilemmas affecting their own lives. Social psychology provides content for the module, which treats values implicitly.

Personal Efficacy: "Self-Identity and Personal Worth" (Part 2, p. 309). This teaching module, created for use in the upper grades (5–8 or 6–8), seeks to encourage pupils to express their views about various topics which affect them. Values clarification strategies are employed throughout the module, as pupils consider their needs, preferences, goals, and aspirations. Self-inventories, individual and group interviews, autobiographies, and creative dramatics are used to help pupils better understand themselves and their relations with others. Social psychology contributes content to this module, which covers the personal dimension of valuing.

BIBLIOGRAPHY

Fraenkel, Jack R. *How To Teach about Values: An Analytical Approach.* Englewood Cliffs, N.J.: Prentice-Hall, 1977.
      Aimed more toward the secondary than toward the elementary level, this slender volume contains a penetrating critique of values clarification and moral education. Chapters 5 and 6 present suggestions for building a comprehensive values education program.
Galbraith, Ronald E. and Thomas M. Jones. *Moral Reasoning: A Teaching Handbook for Adapting Kohlberg to the Classroom.* Minneapolis: Greenhaven Press, 1976.
      This book is precisely what its title implies. If you want to learn how to write and use moral dilemmas in your class, this is the book for you.

Kirschenbaum, Howard, Merrill Harmin, Leland W. Howe, and Sidney B. Simon. "In Defense of Values Clarification." *Phi Delta Kappan,* Vol. 58, June, 1977, pp. 743–746.

This article presents a lucidly-written, persuasive rationale for the values clarification approach. Kirschenbaum's new five-dimensional conception is the authors' frame of reference.

Metcalf, Lawrence E. (Ed.). *Values Education.* Forty-first Annual Yearbook of the National Council for the Social Studies, 1971.

What a prosaic title for a mind-stretching, yet eminently useful book! Rationales, strategies, and procedures for values education are discussed in a well-organized, insightful manner.

Simon, Sidney B., Leland Howe, and Howard Kirschenbaum. *Values Clarification: A Handbook of Practical Strategies for Teachers and Students.* New York: Hart, 1972. Seventy-nine values clarification strategies are presented clearly and succinctly. Before using these deceptively simple strategies, we urge you to become familiar with the philosophical foundations and purposes of values clarification.

Superka, Douglas and Patricia Johnson. *Values Education: Approaches and Materials.* Boulder, Colo.: ERIC Clearinghouse for the Social Studies and the Social Science Education Consortium, 1974.

One of the most frequently cited articles on values education, this does what most articles fail to do: gives you a broad perspective on the topic.

EVALUATING LEARNING

GOALS

1. Determine when it is appropriate to use behavioral objectives as a basis of evaluating social studies learning.
2. Understand the nature, function, and use of preliminary, formative, and summative evaluation processes.
3. Recognize the role of mastery tests in the evaluation process.
4. Learn how to design and use objective test items, essay test items, observational tools, and attitudinal measures.

Earlier chapters demonstrated how you can use various instructional materials and teaching strategies in your social studies classes. At this point we are ready to explore another crucial stage in the teaching–learning process, evaluation of student achievement.

Evaluation of achievement in any school subject is never an easy matter. The social studies present unusual evaluation problems. There seem to be three basic reasons for this: (a) the newer social studies programs tend to stress complex intellectual skills that are difficult to evaluate; (b) teachers often lack the competencies needed to evaluate the acquisition of these complex skills; (c) teachers do not make a serious effort to acquire the requisite evaluation competencies. We will examine these reasons in order.

EVALUATION PROBLEMS

Increasingly, the newer elementary social studies programs stress the acquisition of a broad range of competencies including map and globe reading, social skills, critical thinking and problem solving, and the like. Implicit in such competencies are higher order thought processes that cannot be effectively evaluated by hastily constructed off-the-top-of-the-head tests or other procedures. Unfortunately, authors of commercially produced social studies programs are not evaluation specialists; thus they are unwilling or unable to create evaluative measures that help teachers to determine the extent to which their pupils are meeting the goals of their social studies program. (Admittedly, the McGraw-Hill and Houghton-

Mifflin social studies programs, and others identified in Chapter 2 are notable exceptions to this rule, since competent evaluation specialists were involved in their creation.) This should not amaze you. Social studies educators have never been closely identified with the field of evaluation and measurement. Moreover, we suspect that had it not been for several recent trends in American education, social studies educators might be even less evaluation-minded than they are at present.

Here we allude to the growing interest in teacher and pupil accountability, competency-performance-based instruction, and the return to the so-called "basics." These trends embrace evaluation as a key, pivotal element in the teaching–learning process, and stress the use of measurement techniques, in concert with carefully designed behavioral objectives.

Teacher Education Gets an "F"

If the newer social studies programs do not provide teachers with adequate evaluation techniques or even assistance in their development and use, then, of necessity the burden of responsibility lies squarely on you and your fellow teachers. Are you capable of responding to this challenge? Most preservice teacher education programs attach little importance to evaluation of learning in the elementary grades. Indeed, we agree with Gaines' contention that the type of evaluation competencies that a teacher needs in order to assess the cognitive and affective skills typically taught in elementary social studies classes are more complex, more sophisticated than those developed in most undergraduate-level evaluation courses, *when such courses are in fact taught.* [1]

The professional literature tends to give credence to our suspicions. Roeder's study, "Teacher Education Curricula—Your Final Grade is F," is particularly important in this regard. In his nationwide survey of colleges and universities that operated preservice teacher education programs in elementary education, Roeder found that, of the 860 institutions that responded to his questionnaire, 57.6 percent had no required course in measurement and evaluation, while only 10 percent did not require art methods courses, and 12.7 percent did not require music methods courses. [2] Roeder's conclusion is discouraging: ". . . most prospective elementary teachers are better prepared to conduct impromptu art and music lessons than they are to evaluate pupil performance." [3] If you are taking or have taken a course in evaluation of learning—particularly an evaluation course which centers on achievement in the elementary school subjects—you are among a select few.

A course in evaluation is usually an integral part of many M.A. programs. But in too many instances such courses share with their undergraduate counter-

---

[1] W. George Gaines, *Measurement and Evaluation in Social Studies: Reality or Myth,* Unpublished paper, November 21, 1973.
[2] H. H. Roeder, "Teacher Education Curricula—Your Final Grade Is F," *Review of Educational Research,* 38 (1968), pp. 141–143.
[3] Roeder, p. 141.

parts (when they exist) one common characteristic: they are general in scope and give limited specific attention to evaluation of learning in school subjects—particularly the social studies.

Will You Get an "F"?

The preceding discussion has suggested that today's new social studies programs require teachers to possess evaluation skills that many—perhaps most—of them lack. Is this an unreasonable demand? We would like to think not. Our experience as former elementary teachers and our frequent visits to elementary classrooms suggest that one of the basic reasons why elementary teachers find it difficult to evaluate the social studies achievement of their pupils is their negative attitude toward the concept of evaluation. The reasons for this are obvious: The role of the elementary teacher is becoming progressively more demanding. Not only are teachers (like yourself, perhaps?) expected to handle more complex curricula in the social studies and in at least six other school subjects, including mathematics, reading, language arts, science, the fine arts, and physical education, they also are expected to fill out more reports and handle more nonteaching tasks than ever before. And, looming over their heads is the ever-present threat of losing their jobs, should there be a cutback in funds. Since evaluation of student learning is at best a rigorous, complicated task, is it any wonder that legions of teachers are not exerting the effort needed to become competent evaluators?

There is another problem which prevents elementary teachers from becoming competent evaluators. Lacking adequate training in evaluation, teachers tend to evaluate their pupils' achievement in social studies in much the same way that their own achievement was evaluated when they were in school. Teachers who possess this mind set are likely to equate evaluation with the giving of tests. When they cannot devise an appropriate test, they feel that they are incapable of evaluating achievement. When they do devise what they regard as an appropriate test, it is often based on a narrow range of objectives which tend to encompass such lower order thought processes as the ability to recall, list, or recognize bits of factual information. Below are a few examples of such objectives:

> Recall five important dates of the American Revolution.
> Identify famous Americans by name, when shown their pictures.
> List the major causes of the Civil War.
> Arrange the following wars in order of occurrence: Civil War, Revolutionary War, World War II, French and Indian War, War of 1812.

Although a pupil's attainment of these objectives can be measured by objective tests, do the scores obtained from such tests provide a sound basis for giving grades? We think not. There are far more important objectives for the study of US history than those listed above, aren't there?

Clearly poor evaluation is often a consequence of poorly stated objectives, or no objectives at all. Consider for a moment the first-grade teacher who is attempting to determine the extent to which her pupils have benefited from instruction on respecting the property of others. How should she proceed? Give a paper-and-pencil test? A questionnaire? Conduct an interview? In most instances none of these techniques would be satisfactory. Before we can select the appropriate technique, we'll need to spell out the behavior that is implied by the words "respect the property of other children." Authorities on behavioral objectives would ask us to state the conditions under which the behavior is to occur, the actual behavior that we are seeking, and the standards by which we would judge the behavior. This suggests that we must define our objectives as explicitly and as precisely as we can.

Is it worth the time and effort to do all of this? Under some conditions, yes; under other conditions, probably no. If we really want to find out whether the pupils are learning to respect the property of others, let us define what this behavior really means and then look for instances where it is occurring. Presumably a child who possesses this competency will exhibit behaviors such as these:

1. When he wants to borrow something from another pupil, he'll ask for permission. Then he'll return it in good condition when he's finished with it.
2. When he sees a scarf lying in the playground, he takes it to his teacher, or to the lost-and-found area of the school. If he thinks that Mary lost the scarf, he'll give it to her.
3. If a child sees a classmate taking something that doesn't belong to him, she'll try to convince him that he shouldn't do this.
4. She will not mark her books or desk—indeed, she might even convince others not to do this.

Granted, these are but a few behaviors that would be manifested by the child who is learning to respect the property of others. Would it be worthwhile to state these in the form of a behavioral objective? Is it essential that the teacher be able to specify the conditions under which a child respects the property of others, the specific behaviors that can be ascribed to respecting the property of others, and the standards or criteria by which such behaviors are to be assessed? If your answer is "yes," we suggest that you forget about teaching first graders, and secure a job writing behavioral objectives, for you have missed the point of this discussion: Under some circumstances clearly stated objectives are indispensable guides to evaluation; under other circumstances they are not.

Please do not construe this as a denunciation of behavioral objectives. There are some instances where they should be of great value to you in teaching. Assume for a moment that you want your fourth graders to know how to read symbols appearing on a map of their local community. What does this mean for their behavior? Under what conditions are they to know how to read the map symbols? Which symbols are they to know? By rewriting this task as a behavioral objective, you and your pupils can see precisely what is involved in reading map symbols shown on a map of the local community.

A clearer statement of this task might be, "Using a city map, the pupil will point to and tell the meaning of symbols for interstate highways, state highways, city streets, bridges, railroad crossings, schools, airports, police stations, fire stations, and parks." The *condition* (using a city map) and the *standard* (all ten symbols identified above) are apparent; the *task* (point to and tell the meaning of) should be equally apparent. Such a statement is clear, specific, and behavioral. It gives you a clear-cut, unambiguous basis for evaluation.

Not all of our social studies objectives need to be stated in this way. It is your responsibility to decide when it is appropriate to state your objectives in terms of the desired behavioral changes that you are seeking. Remember also that you only have a limited amount of time available for developing behavioral objectives. For this reason we suggest that you develop behavioral objectives only for the more significant, *measurable* competencies that you desire your pupils to acquire. More generalized statements of objectives should be adequate for other competencies.

Thus far we have said very little about the selection, development, and use of evaluative measures. We have postponed this topic until later in this chapter because of our strong conviction that the teacher who desires to become a capable evaluator of her pupils' social studies achievement must first of all understand the purpose and function of instructional objectives, and the critical role that objectives play in the teaching–learning process. The teacher who possesses this understanding, and is willing to expend the effort needed to master the technical skills of creating evaluative measures, need not worry about receiving an "F" in evaluation.

If you wrote an objective describing how you'd want your pupils to cross the street, would you include the conditions, standards, and the task? Why?/Why not?

THE EVALUATION PROCESS

Evaluation as used here is a process by which you obtain information regarding the extent to which your social studies goals have been achieved, and use this information as a basis for further planning and instruction. At various stages in this process you will need to make value judgments regarding the instruction you have provided. You should base your value judgments on various measurement devices you used and on informal impressions you acquired. The most commonly used measurement device is the objective test, a device that is administered for the purpose of finding out the extent to which students have attained one or more instructional objective. Bear in mind that *evaluation* and *measurement* are not synonymous. We regard measurement as a key element in the evaluation process, nothing more. Since the term, evaluation, is the broader and more inclusive element of teaching and learning, we will deal with it first, and forego our discussion of measurement until later in this chapter.

Embedded in our definition of evaluation are several extremely significant ideas. The first centers on the word, *process.* We regard evaluation as an ongoing process, one which begins prior to actual instruction and continues throughout and following instruction. These stages are presented in the diagram below.

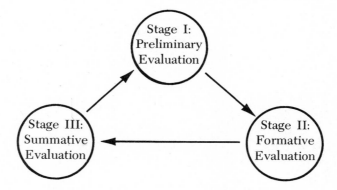

Notice the cyclical process depicted in the above diagram. Each of the three stages has a particular, unique purpose, yet is dependent upon the preceding stage.

Stage I: Preliminary Evaluation seeks to determine how much and what type of instruction is needed. It centers on the question, "Do my pupils have the skills, concepts, and attitudes needed to learn the new subject matter that I'm going to teach?" To a great extent, preliminary evaluation enables you to ascertain your pupils' readiness for the new instruction. If it appears that they lack this readiness, you may find it necessary to defer such instruction until you have adequately prepared them for it.

Suppose that you and your first graders are studying the lifelong role of family membership through the organizing theme, consumerism. To this end you have constructed a unit on consumer skills. Many of the activities in the unit involve the collection and analysis of data regarding the buying habits of your pupils' families. These research activities are to be undertaken by pupils working together in small groups.

To assess your pupils' work skills, you assign them to small groups and give each a specific assignment to be completed in the next forty minutes. As the class begins work, you quietly move about the room, carefully observe their behavior, and give help as needed. Below are examples of the type of pupil behavior that you might be looking for.

Do they organize the task and delegate responsibility?
Do they listen to each other's ideas?
Do they assume roles of leaders and followers?
Do they share materials?
Do they stick to the task?
Do they help each other?
Do they seek help from you when they reach an impasse?

Let us assume that twenty minutes after the group work has begun, you observe the following behaviors among members of the groups:

Arguments erupt in two groups.

Simultaneously three girls come to you in tears, complaining that "the boys in their groups are bothering them."

Members of one group are quietly working on their arithmetic assignment.

For some mysterious reason, Fred has vanished from the face of the earth.

Two boys leave their group to feed Felix, the class gerbil.

Three groups are industriously working on their consumer projects.

A girl is methodically removing the wings of a bee that flew into the room, while others observe with bored stares.

Members of one group are intently staring at the clock.

Clearly, the import of these behaviors suggests that your pilot project in group work skills is not succeeding. There are several options open to you:

1. Forget about the group work activities in your consumer unit, but start the unit anyway.
2. Go ahead with the group work activities and pray that eventually the kids will shape up.
3. Plan to get sick when you initiate the unit, and let the substitute handle the group projects.
4. Defer any further group work until you've restored law and order and taught the requisite group work skills.

If you selected options 1, 2, or 3, put down this book, forget about your teaching career, and apply for a job as a zookeeper. At least the animals won't complain to you about the behavior of their peers. If you selected the fourth option, give yourself a pat on the back, for you have grasped the essential purpose of Stage I: *to find out the extent to which your pupils are ready for new instruction, and to plan this instruction accordingly.*

Stage II: Formative Evaluation occurs while instruction is in progress— usually at the point where you are ready to terminate the study of a unit or miniunit. Your purpose in conducting formative evaluation is to find out the degree to which your instructional objectives are being attained. You use this knowledge as a basis for modifying your objectives and/or teaching strategies.

Suppose that while studying the lifelong role of personal efficacy, your sixth graders have been probing the purposes of laws, their effect on our daily lives, and the importance of obeying them. At the beginning of this instruction your pupils expressed extensive cynicism regarding our legal system; some were openly antagonistic toward police officers. To help your pupils understand why they hold these attitudes, you have involved them in a variety of learning activities calculated to help them understand the need for laws and their enforcement, and the ways in which our legal system can be improved.

At this point you want to ascertain the extent to which your sixth graders' attitudes toward the law have changed as a result of your instruction. Which of these approaches would you use?

1. Give a paper-and-pencil test on basic principles of constitutional law.
2. Conduct a mock trial centering on a sixth grader who was charged with shoplifting.
3. Administer a few short, open-ended questions centering on problematic situations involving assault and battery.
4. Arrange for your pupils to simulate experiences typically encountered by police officers in dealing with juveniles.
5. Administer an instrument designed to assess your pupils' attitudes toward the police, attorneys, and judges.

If you rejected the first approach and accepted any of the others, you're on target with respect to formative evaluation. The first option is unacceptable because it is unrelated to your instructional goal (to teach your pupils to reassess their attitudes about the need for laws and their enforcement) and is beyond the capabilities of sixth graders. Would *you* like to take such a test? The other options are acceptable because they can help you to determine the extent to which the desired attitude changes have occurred; as such, they constitute a few ways in which you can apply formative evaluation.

Obviously you could use other evaluative strategies to ascertain the extent to which the desired attitude changes have occurred, but the basic point that we are making here is that the strategies you use should be appropriate for your instructional goals. If it is apparent that your pupils have not achieved these goals, you will need to reexamine them and the teaching strategies you have employed. Perhaps the goal imposes excessive demands on you and your pupils, perhaps it cannot be attained by most of them, given the time and effort you have expended.

But if the goal is important, it will be necessary for you to try additional approaches; if you and your pupils have reached an impasse, you might return to this topic at a later, more opportune moment.

Stage III: Summative Evaluation occurs at the conclusion of a grading period. If used properly, this stage in the evaluation process will enable you and your students to "get the big picture," to acquire a panoramic view of what was accomplished during the grading period, and to use this information in planning for the next grading period.

Suppose that during the previous grading period your social studies instruction centered on the lifelong role of personal efficacy, and you have taught several units, including one on our legal system. You used formative evaluation strategies to determine the degree to which your objectives have been attained, and now you and your students are about to embark on summative evaluation. Since you want to get a broad overview at this point of what was accomplished during the previous grading period, you will want to review the goals that you had established for your unit on our legal system and the results of the evaluation strategies that were employed. Below are some questions you will want to ask:

1. Were the goals of the unit worthwhile? Realistic? Attainable? Accurately stated?
2. If we were studying this unit again, would we change our goals? If so how?
3. Did our teaching strategies promote the attainment of our goals? If not, in what ways should these strategies be changed?
4. Did the evaluation strategies give my pupils and me the information we wanted? If not, in what ways would we change them?
5. Did my pupils enjoy their work? Did they relate this study of the law to their personal experiences?
6. Did our study of the law yield any clues for our new work in the next grading period? Are there ways in which I can interrelate this with the new concepts I'll be teaching?

These questions are the essence of summative evaluation, for they enable you to draw together the data gleaned from the previous grading period, and use this information as a basis for planning the next grading period. You might have observed, for example, that your pupils excelled when role playing police officers, law-breakers, attorneys, and judges, and that they greatly enjoyed this learning experience. On the other hand, you might find that the procedural aspects of simulated or mock trials proved too difficult for your kids to handle. Perhaps your pupils continue to experience difficulty in assuming responsibility for working together in small groups. Or some children in your room might have writing problems that are interfering with their ability to write fair, easily understood laws. Armed with this knowledge, you can make the necessary adjustments needed to insure that over the next grading period your subsequent work in social studies will be as meaningful and rewarding as possible.

It is at this point where our three stage, cyclical conception of the evaluation process acquires its self-renewing characteristics. If the summative stage is to be accomplished, you will have answered such key, pivotal questions as "What goals were reached?" "What skills were mastered?" "How far did we go with that concept?" "Did I make adequate provision for my slow learners?" Once you have gained this knowledge, you and your students are ready to move ahead into the next grading period, where Stage I becomes operative again.

Decisions, Decisions, Decisions

The preceding section stressed that evaluation is an ongoing, cyclical process, one that consists of a series of discernable, interrelated stages. At each stage you will need to make many significant decisions regarding your social studies instruction. At Stage I you will have to decide whether your pupils are ready for the new instruction that will be forthcoming. At Stage II you will need to decide whether your instructional objectives have been attained. And at Stage III you will need to make some decisions regarding the nature and extent of the instruction that you will be providing during the next grading period.

Since these decisions must be based on pupil information you have gathered, the information itself becomes an extremely significant matter. There are two questions confronting you: "How do I obtain this information?" and "On what basis can I assess this information?" Clearly these questions imply the need for a referent, one that gives perspective and meaning to the information, and thereby enables you to use such information as a sound basis for rational, informed decision-making.

Imagine that your pupils are ready to embark on the study of their local community. Before beginning instruction you want to determine the extent to which they possess certain map reading skills that will be indispensable to them as their work begins. To obtain this information you give your pupils small maps of the area to be studied and twenty paper-and-pencil questions which test their ability to orient the map and compute directions, read symbols, and locate specific places.

After correcting the tests, you notice that Charlie has successfully answered 16 of the 20 items on the test. How well has Charlie performed? To interpret this score, you need a referent or standard of comparison.

If you built your own map skills test, you could compare Charlie's score with the average score for your entire class. If you used a standardized test (a commercially prepared test that is administered and scored under uniform conditions) you could compare Charlie's score with the average score attained by a nationwide sample of kids who are of the same age and in the same grade as Charlie. These two bases for comparison (Charlie's class and a nationwide sample) serve as your referents. Since the referents are scores obtained from groups of pupils, they become norms against which you can compare Charlie's score. This process of making such comparisons is called *norm-referenced evaluation*.

Suppose that Charlie's class attained an average score of 12 on the 20-item test. What conclusion might you draw regarding Charlie's score? Presumably the test was difficult, and the fact that Charlie got 16 correct answers suggests that he scored well above the class average.

There are other ways in which we could interpret Charlie's score. One commonly used approach is called *self-referenced evaluation.* Suppose that you gave your class the same map skills test on two occasions—before you began your instruction on the local community and after the instruction was well underway. Since you are concerned over the progress that Charlie has made in acquiring the map skills, Charlie's score on the pretest serves as your referent. The process of comparing the two scores is called *self-referenced evaluation.*

Criterion-referenced evaluation is a third method that might be used. It consists of making comparisons between information about an individual and a performance standard or criterion—typically one that is stated in the form of a behavioral objective. Suppose that you give your pupils a few different maps of your local community, with the expectation that they will use these as sources of information about past, present, and future developments in the community. After they have carefully studied the maps, you want to find out the extent to which the pupils have used these maps in a meaningful way. Below are a few behavioral objectives that you might use.

> The pupil will correctly answer ten short-answer questions dealing with the location of important places in the community.
>
> Given a current street map and a street map made in 1930, the pupil will correctly identify five of those areas of the city which have become developed since 1930.
>
> Given a recently made aerial map, the pupil will correctly locate Sexton High School, Capital City Airport, the Capitol Building, Grand River Avenue, and Potter Park.
>
> Given a street map made in 1900, the pupil will compute in miles the length of Grand River Avenue. The pupil's computation will be accurate to within one-quarter mile.

These objectives would enable you to use criterion-referenced evaluation techniques, because they clearly and precisely specify the respective behaviors you would be looking for. Notice that of the four examples, *only the first one* involves giving a paper-and-pencil test. Surprised? You shouldn't be. We want you to see for yourself that actual *performance* of a learning task (in this case, using maps) is a form of testing, one that can be a more effective evaluative technique than merely giving a paper-and-pencil test—provided the behaviors you are seeking are *observable.* Admittedly, it might be awkward and time consuming for you to take each pupil aside and ask him to perform the tasks indicated in these objectives, but for many pupils (particularly those who are notoriously poor test takers) this may be the only way in which you can ascertain whether these kids are attaining the objectives that you have established for them.

The Tyranny of Testing(?)

The professional literature proliferates with scathing denunciations of testing. For years, critics have argued that since standardized achievement tests and tests of mental ability are designed for white, middle-class children, they cannot possibly take into account the social, cultural, and economic backgrounds of children who belong to minority groups. Their protagonists respond with equal vigor, by maintaining that it is possible to produce tests that minimize such differences.

While this debate rages, other critics are attacking achievement tests as used in our elementary classrooms. They attack these tests primarily on the grounds that they guarantee failure or near-failure to a high percentage of children. Since achievement tests are designed for the purpose of measuring the extent to which pupils have met a given set of objectives, it becomes inevitable that these tests will yield different scores for different pupils. And when their pupils' achievement test scores are tightly clustered, some teachers go into a mystical trance, produce a curve, and manipulate the scores until grades of *A*, *B*, *C*, *D*, and *F* can be assigned to children. Under these circumstances it is likely that some children who receive low grades—perhaps far more than we would imagine—label themselves as failures, convinced that they are not smart enough to do well in school. Is it any wonder that testing has been labeled by some of the more mercurial critics as tyrannical, destructive, or inhuman?

Testing will continue to be a fact of life in our elementary schools; indeed there is very little that we can say on these pages that will convince the power structure of our educational establishment that the misuse of testing should be abandoned. All we ask of you is this: Carefully consider the strengths and limitations of tests, and when you construct and administer them, try to be as fair to your pupils as you can. When your pupils do well on a test, give them high grades rather than attempting to superimpose a fictitious curve. When the scores for your class are widely dispersed, the test may be too easy; but that's your problem, isn't it? When your class does not do well on a test, consider the factors involved. Perhaps the items were too difficult, perhaps you did not devote sufficient time and effort to the instruction that the test was supposed to cover, or perhaps your items were too vague or had technical flaws. Once you have discovered why some children did not score well on the test, do your utmost to help them understand why they made mistakes, and how they should respond to certain types of test items. *In short, teach them to become competent test takers!* If you do, your children and their parents will bless you!

Mastery Tests: A Viable Alternative?[4]

Since you are expected to administer standardized tests of achievement and mental ability, we have argued that it is imperative that you deal with them fairly, honestly, and compassionately. But yet, there is another form of test that should not only enable your pupils to become more directly involved in the teaching–learning process, but should also help them to share responsibility for their learning. We are referring to the mastery test, an evaluative measure that is acquiring greater acceptance than ever before by teachers and administrators.

Mastery tests are quite different from achievement tests. They are designed

---

[4]Many of the basic ideas for this discussion of mastery tests were gleaned from conversations with the late John R. Lee, and from his book, *Teaching Social Studies in the Elementary School* (New York: Free Press, 1975). For his valuable contribution we are immensely grateful.

Short mastery tests, when administered frequently in class, enable pupils to become directly and continually involved in the teaching-learning process.

with the expectation that nearly all of your pupils will pass the test. If, say, half of your pupils do not meet a minimal standard of passing the first time, they will retake the test. Typically mastery tests are criterion-referenced, short (contain a few carefully constructed questions), based on one or two instructional objectives, and given frequently (generally a few times a week). Instead of receiving grades, the pupils know immediately whether or not they pass.

The child who does poorly on achievement tests may find that a mastery test helps him to regard learning as his personal goal, a goal that is within his grasp. Of course, a few pupils will find it difficult even to meet the minimal standards of performance that you establish for your mastery tests. Don't despair; there is hope. More about this soon.

Mastery learning and testing promotes a pupil–teacher partnership, wherein both of you strive to identify the source of the pupil's problem and the teacher helps to remediate it. Or, perhaps the pupil works with another student who has passed the test. He or she retakes the test and if the score has improved, the progress ought to be apparent. If the child still has not quite met your minimal standard of performance, you again review the test, and if you are satisfied that he or she is working up to capacity, you move on to the next bloc of content. The results of this approach will amaze you. Mastery testing does involve heavy investments of time, patience, and understanding, but it's worth it!

Below is an example of a mastery test item for the primary grades. The objective for this item is, "Given a series of pictures showing tools, the pupil will identify the one tool that is used by a gardener."

Directions: Draw a line around the tool that is used by a gardener.

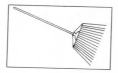

This item could be presented as a part of a paper-and-pencil test, or could be presented orally. If the latter method is used, you would read aloud the directions and present each child with a picture of the four tools.

For the upper grades you might try other types of mastery test items. Assume that your behavioral objective reads, "Given a statement regarding the closing of an air base, the pupil will select one result that is most likely to occur."

Directions: Mark the statement that best completes the sentence below.

Sawyer Air Base is located in a sparsely populated section of the country. If this air base were closed, employment in the area would be most likely to:

1. Stay the same
2. Increase
3. Decrease

These are but two examples of mastery test items that you could use. In the following section we will present numerous examples of a wide variety of items.

OBJECTIVE TEST ITEMS

This section centers on the creation and use of objective test items. We will restrict our discussion to three commonly used test items—matching, alternate choice, and multiple choice—since these are among the most appropriate and popular items used in measuring social studies achievement in the elementary grades. Omitted are fill-in-the-blank and short answer items, as they are not as appropriate for inclusion in social studies mastery tests. Not only do these items lack reliability, but often it is difficult to state them in clear, unambiguous terms. Also, pupils with limited writing ability (young children in particular) may find that these items are too difficult for them to handle. Despite these reservations, we have included a few examples of them in the modules presented in Sections B and C.

Often, matching, alternate choice, and multiple choice test items are labeled as "objective" items. In a sense this is a misnomer, because the process of selecting the subject matter to be tested involves considerable subjective judgment by the teacher. Indeed, the only aspect of so-called "objective" items that might be regarded as truly objective is the act of scoring pupil responses.

If you page ahead to the sample test items, you will note that we wrote more than one set of sample items for each type of measurement exercise. We did this deliberately, in an attempt to convince you of the range of options available to you.

Matching

Matching exercises consist of two lists which are presented to the pupil, who is required to match or pair up each item from one list with an item from the other list. Some evaluation experts look askance at matching exercises. They maintain that such exercises lack the flexibility of multiple choice tests, to the extent that they require the test builder to use items with common properties (names, processes, events, objects, etc.). What our colleagues forget is that a well-constructed matching test will contain a range of options from which the pupil chooses, in attempting to match terms and definitions, important persons and their contributions, events and dates, etc. As you will observe in some of the following examples, the matching process can indeed test for higher order reasoning ability.

MATCHING TEST ITEMS: ECOLOGY

Directions: For each word in column 1, choose the statement from column 2 that best defines it. Write the letter on the line in front of the question number. Do not use any definition more than one time. There are more definitions than you will need.

1	2
a 1. dredge	**a.** Device mounted on a barge and used in cleaning the bottom of lakes and rivers.
h 2. holding tank	**b.** Grass clippings, plants, weeds, garbage arranged so that they can be recycled.
c 3. septic tank	**c.** Tank for storing sewage from homes and small businesses.
e 4. sanitary landfill	**d.** Tank used in storing fertilizer.
b 5. compost pile	**e.** Burial ground for garbage and rubbish.
	f. Machine used in recycling scrap metal.
	g. Device for removing pollutants from air.
	h. Tank used in storing sewage on a boat.

MATCHING TEST ITEMS: ENERGY

Directions: Match each source of energy in column 1 with the way in which it is produced in column 2. Write the letter on the line in front of the question number. Some of the forms of energy may be used more than once.

	1			2
a,c,d	1.	oil	**a.**	drilling
a,c,d	2.	gas	**b.**	digging
b	3.	coal	**c.**	manufacturing
c	4.	gasoline	**d.**	collecting
d	5.	solar heat		
c	6.	kerosene		
b	7.	peat		
c	8.	steam		
c	9.	water power		
c	10.	electricity		
c	11.	helium		

MATCHING TEST ITEMS: ECOLOGY

Directions: Match each part of a car that reduces pollution in column 1 with the result from column 2 that it will most likely produce. A result may *not* be used more than once. Write the letter of the result on the line next to the part of the car.

	1			2
d	1.	filters	**a.**	Carries engine exhaust away from under car.
e	2.	catalytic converter	**b.**	Reduces engine noise level inside and outside of car.
b	3.	muffler	**c.**	Reduces road noise inside of car.
a	4.	tail pipe	**d.**	Removes pollutants from air, gasoline, and oil in car's engine.
c	5.	insulation	**e.**	Removes pollutants from car's exhaust.

Alternate Choice

Alternate choice items require the test taker to consider two choices. He is presented with a statement, a story, a diagram, an advertisement, or some other form of stimulus and is asked to decide whether it is true or false, fact or opinion, good or bad, an example or a nonexample, whether the evidence is sufficient or insufficient, etc. There are various types of alternate choice items. Typically these include true–false, yes–no, right–wrong, or accept–reject items. Since true–false items are by far the most widely used variety, the following discussion centers on them. Nearly all of our comments about true–false items apply to other forms of alternate choice items.

Why are true–false items so popular? It would appear that they are quickly and efficiently administered, easily constructed, easily scored, and useful for obtaining a lot of information in a short time. But most of these alleged advantages are open to question. First, it is difficult to construct items that are clearly, unequivocally true or false, without some form of qualification. Second, since true–false items tend to deal primarily with low-order cognitive processes involving the recall, comprehension, and application of factual information and the interpretation of such information, a relatively narrow range of subject matter can be included. Thus, there is a danger that, unless true–false items are carefully written, they will deal with trivia, and that the correct responses might be based on the value judgments of the author of the items. Finally, the element of guessing is a serious problem of true–false items.

Despite these objections, Robert L. Ebel, an internationally recognized authority on measurement and evaluation, regards the prejudice against true–false testing as superstition. In his textbook, *Essentials of Educational Measurement*,[5] Ebel insists that true–false items can become highly effective means for evaluating various levels of cognitive learning, when the writer follows these procedures in building such items:

1. Direct attention to an important segment of knowledge.
2. Select a worthwhile proposition to test.
3. Convert the proposition into a test item.[6]

Those who are interested in pursuing Ebel's approach to the construction of true–false items should consult his textbook, one of the most widely accepted publications in the field of measurement and evaluation. We are reluctant to deal here with the specifics of Ebel's procedures, as it appears that they are more appropriate for use with students in the secondary grades.

Below are some suggestions that we hope will be of value to you in constructing true–false and other alternate choice test items:

[5]Robert L. Ebel, *Essentials of Educational Measurement* (Englewood Cliffs, N.J.: Prentice-Hall, 1972).
[6]Ebel, pp. 173–175.

1. Use only statements that are clearly true or false, fact or opinion, examples or nonexamples, or that can elicit definite yes–no responses.
2. Keep your statements short, direct, and specific. Try to focus them on one central idea.
3. Do not—we repeat—do not pull statements directly from textbooks or other class material. Often they encourage guessing or uncritical responses from your pupils.
4. Refrain from giving tests that consist entirely of alternate choice items; rather, place such items within a test that includes a variety of cognitive measures.
5. Do not use negative statements, as they will confuse your pupils.
6. Try to keep your items roughly the same length, to avoid telegraphing the correct answers.

Following are a variety of alternate choice test items which focus on the organizing theme, consumerism. As you read the items, see if they are constructed in accordance with these suggestions.

ALTERNATE CHOICE TEST ITEMS: CONSUMERISM

Directions: Draw a circle around the *T* if the statement is true. Draw a circle around the *F* if the statement is false.

Ⓣ F 1. The Federal Trade Commission tries to protect us against false advertising.

Ⓣ F 2. "Listerine fights bad breath" is an example of a weasel claim.

T Ⓕ 3. It is important for you to know if a hockey stick that you want to buy has been approved by a professional hockey player.

Ⓣ F 4. If a person feels that a store has cheated him or her, he/she can sue the store in small claims court.

Ⓣ F 5. Different brands of ten-speed bikes sold at the same price do not differ in quality.

Ⓣ F 6. Mr. and Mrs. Williams, a retired couple, are more likely to live in a mobile home than are Mr. and Mrs. Brink and their eight children.

T Ⓕ 7. A radio is more expensive to operate than a color TV set.

T Ⓕ 8. Smokers are as likely to get cancer and heart disease as nonsmokers.

Ⓣ F 9. If Americans ate less beef, there would be more grain available to feed the starving nations of the world.

YES–NO TEST ITEMS: CONSUMERISM

WOW!!!
GRAND OPENING!   GIGANTIC SALE!

25-inch TV Sets
Beautiful picture. Fine piece
of furniture.
Hurry! They won't last at this
price. $199.95
Honest John's TV Shop
123 Scruffy Road

After reading this ad, Pete and his dad hurried over to Honest John's. "You really don't want this TV," the salesman pleaded. "The set is used, is five years old, and doesn't have a factory warranty. If it breaks down in thirty days, I'll try to get it fixed for you." Pointing to another TV, the salesman said, "I'll sell you this brand new set. It's got a five-year warranty, and it's a steal at only $499.95."

Directions: Draw a circle around the word, *Yes,* if your answer to the question is yes. Draw a circle around the word, *No,* if your answer to the question is no.

 No   1.   Was Honest John using bait-and-switch advertising?

 No   2.   By using such words as "beautiful picture," and "fine piece of furniture," was Honest John puffing the TV set?

Yes   3.   Was the salesman's offer to "try to get the set fixed" a binding contract?

Yes   No   4.   If Pete's dad bought the used TV set and it broke down in a few days, would the manufacturer be likely to repair the set free of charge?

ALTERNATE-CHOICE TEST ITEMS: CONSUMERISM

Directions: Below is a list of reasons why you might want your parents to buy a certain brand of breakfast cereal. If you believe that a reason is excellent, mark an *e* on the line next to the reason. If you think a reason is poor, mark a *p* next to it.

___p___   1.   I like the color of the box.

___p___   2.   I like the way that it is advertised on TV.

___p___   3.   There is a prize in the box.

___p___   4.   There are special offers on the box.

___p___   5.   The cereal is sugar-coated.

___e___   6.   The price is reasonable.

___e___   7.   The box says that the cereal has no preservatives.

___p___   8.   My friends eat this cereal.

___e___   9.   My doctor says that this cereal is good for me.

Multiple Choice

One of the most widely used (and abused) tests of cognitive learning is the multiple choice test. Items in this test consist of a stem, a correct alternative choice, and incorrect alternative choices, or distractors. The stem is an introductory statement (usually a question or incomplete sentence), ideally written in concise, precise terms. Usually there are three, four, or five alternative choices, each of which should be related to the stem, conceptually and grammatically. Of these, one should stand out as the best or most correct alternative choice.

Below is an example of a multiple choice test item. Read it carefully. Is it a good item? A bad one? Why? Why not?

In which of these sections of a newspaper are you *most* likely to find more opinion than fact? } Stem

1. weather)
2. sports   } Incorrect alternatives
3. classified)
4. editorial } Correct alternative

In the above example the stem, correct alternative, and incorrect alternatives are identified. Notice that the stem provides pupils with all of the basic information that they should need. "Editorial" is the correct alternative because it is the best possible answer: There is bound to be more opinion than fact expressed in a newspaper's editorial page or section than in the other sections listed as alternatives. We could have jeopardized the item, had we used "cartoon" as an alternative, since cartoons could be correctly interpreted by kids as purveyors of opinion. "Financial page" might be similarly interpreted, and thus would be a poor alternative.

Following are additional examples of multiple choice items which have been answered correctly. All of them center on the organizing theme, media. As you read over these items notice that all of them contain four alternatives (one correct alternative and three incorrect alternatives or distractors). We have deliberately limited the number of alternatives because of our conviction that to add additional ones would impose an unreasonable burden on students.

MULTIPLE CHOICE TEST ITEMS: MEDIA

Directions: Choose the best answer to each question. Then draw a circle around the number in front of your answer.

1. The forests of Canada are *most* important to companies that make:
   1. TV sets
   2. cars
   3. shirts
   (4.) newspapers
2. A person whose main job is to find out news is a:
   (1.) reporter
   2. printer
   3. typist
   4. proofreader

3. Which of these inventions is of *least* help to a disc jockey?
   1. record
   2. microphone
   (3.) camera
   4. studio

4. If you wanted to buy a dog, which part of a newspaper would you check?
   1. letters to the editor
   2. movie section
   (3.) classified section
   4. comics

5. Which of these magazines would be *least* likely to report recent news?
   1. Time
   (2.) National Geographic
   3. Newsweek
   4. US News & World Report

6. Which of these businesses is protected under the First Amendment to the US Constitution?
   1. dairy farm
   (2.) TV station
   3. gas station
   4. gun shop

7. Eyewitnesses reported that in a recent race riot in the Union of South Africa, soldiers clubbed and teargassed Black men, women, and children. This was not shown or mentioned in a recent film made by the government of that nation. This is an example of:
   (1.) censorship
   2. salesmanship
   3. sportsmanship
   4. gamesmanship

8. John Peter Zenger was brought to trial in 1735 by the royal governor of New York because he:
   1. threatened to overthrow the government
   2. refused to sign a loyalty oath
   (3.) criticized the governor
   4. printed dirty books

9. Which of these is used by *most* Americans?
   (1.) AM radio sets
   2. CB radio sets
   3. TV sets
   4. walkie-talkies

10. When a dictator tries to control the minds of citizens, he will begin by taking over the nation's:
   1. clothing stores
   2. shopping centers
   (3.) newspapers
   4. hotels

Admittedly, it is difficult to build good multiple choice test items. Writing a stem that provides sufficient pertinent information, but is not too wordy, is a skill that few of us learn immediately. Nor is the skill of writing plausible distractors or maintaining logical and grammatical consistency throughout the item.

Lest we discourage you from responding to these challenges, here are several hints you will find useful. First, write your stem and your correct answer simultaneously. Next, carefully analyze both question and answer to insure accuracy and clarity. Finally, write your distractors. Do they flow from the stem? Are they believable but incorrect, or not as good as the correct alternatives? Are any distractors weird, odd-ball alternatives? If so, get rid of them! Are the distractors roughly the same length? If not, either shorten-lengthen them, or if that's not feasible, throw them out and write new ones.

Here's a final hint: Take a good look at the standardized achievement tests that are used in your school. Invariably you will find that most of the multiple choice items included in these tests will be good ones.

Once you get the hang of writing and using these multiple choice items, it ought to be apparent to you that these items are flexible, for they can be used in evaluating various types of learning. This is a distinct advantage over many of the other types of objective test items. Also, bear in mind that multiple choice items can be scored objectively; this mitigates the effects of guessing—a characteristic of true–false and other alternative response items.

ESSAY TEST ITEMS

Essay questions can be of considerable value, when used with middle- and upper-elementary grade children (grades three to eight or four to eight). Mehrens and Lehmann have identified ten types of questions which might be asked on an essay test.[7] For each of their ten types we have written an essay question centering on the organizing theme, our legal system.

1. Comparison of two things:
   In what ways are rules and laws alike and different?
2. Decision (for and against):
   Suppose that there is a law in your state that you cannot ride a motorcycle until you are sixteen years old. Is this a fair law? Explain your answer.
3. Cause or effects:
   Why do stores have signs posted which read, "Shoplifters will be prosecuted"?
4. Explanation of the use or exact meaning of some phrase or statement in a passage:
   A sign in front of a store reads, "Parking Reserved for Handicapped." Explain what the sign means.
5. Analysis:
   It is dark and you are riding your bike without any lights. Why is this dangerous?
6. Statement of relationships:

[7]William A. Mehrens and Irvin J. Lehmann, *Measurement and Evaluation in Educational Psychology,* 2d ed. (New York: Holt, Rinehart and Winston, 1978), pp. 207–208.

Why are older children instead of younger children on your school's safety patrol? Explain your reasons.

7. Discussion:
Explain what a lawyer and a judge do in the courtroom.

8. Reorganization of facts:
Tell the steps that you would follow if your dog had been stolen.

9. Formulation of new question (problems and questions raised):
Suppose that there were no laws against smoking. How would this affect the health of people?

10. Criticism (as to the adequacy, correctness, or relevancy of a pointed statement):
"Pupils can come to school only when they want to." Tell what is good and bad about this statement.

Essay tests have several advantages and disadvantages. First, they are easier to prepare than objective tests. Second, they are the only tests that help you to determine the extent to which your students can create answers to questions and write them in understandable English. Finally, they test your pupils' ability to produce rather than merely select the correct answer. On the other hand, essay tests provide minimal coverage of the content to be tested. Second, they do not promote reader reliability—a particularly acute problem in the case of pupils in the middle- and upper-elementary grades. These pupils tend to vary considerably in their writing skills, and thus it becomes quite difficult for teachers to grade essay tests with consistency. A related problem is presented by the variability in pupils' reading skills at these levels. As the good reader will be more inclined to understand the essay questions than the poor reader, so will the good writer be better able to respond to essay questions than the poor writer.

Below are a few guidelines to follow in writing and administering essay questions:

1. Write your questions with care. Make them clear, concise, and understandable.

2. State your questions so that they fit your objectives and indicate the content to be covered. Do not make them so vague that your pupils cannot grasp their intent, or so specific that they conclude that there is but one acceptable answer.

3. Before writing the questions decide whether you will grade them in part on spelling, grammar, penmanship, clarity of expression, and other writing skills. If you do not take these factors into account, be prepared to make allowances in your grading for your poor readers and writers.

4. At the beginning of the test, inform your pupils of your expectations, how the test will be scored, and the amount of time allocated to the test. Then briefly discuss the questions to insure that your pupils understand what is expected of them.

5. Try to restrict your exam to a series of short, specific essay questions, each of which can be answered in a brief paragraph. How many questions you will include will be dependent on your estimate of the capabilities of your students, the content to be tested, and the importance that you attach to the test.

6. Before giving the test, write down what you would regard as the best answers to each of your essay questions. The mere act of doing this can disclose some inherent deficiencies in the questions, but more important, the answers can serve as standards for grading your pupils' responses.

7. Once you have graded and returned the essay tests, discuss them with your pupils—as a total class and individually as necessary. If you find that a given question was misinterpreted by many of your pupils, do not blame them—blame yourself! Admit that you were in error, throw out the question, and make any adjustments in grades that seem fair under the circumstances. (Incidently, this guideline applies equally to objective tests.)

8. Earlier we urged you to teach your pupils how to take tests. This suggestion is especially important in the case of essay tests, which tend to impose greater intellectual demands on pupils than other methods of evaluation.

Before ending this discussion, permit us to issue two warnings. The first centers on the misuse of testing, the second, on the limitations of tests. Increasingly, we have noted that tests, if misused, tend to cause adverse side effects in children. Teachers who use tests as a means of intimidation or punishment ("Class! If you don't quiet down, I'm going to give you a test"), as a ploy to make their pupils work harder ("Tomorrow I'm giving you a real tough test. You'd better study hard for it"), or for countless other reasons *unrelated to actual student achievement* are perpetrating a serious injustice. When used for these purposes, tests can generate in pupils negative attitudes toward testing, toward teachers, toward their schoolwork. Similarly, the principal or supervisor who evaluates the effectiveness of his teachers on the basis of their pupils' scores on achievement tests is behaving in a grossly unprofessional manner, for he is violating the intent of such tests. Unfortunately some administrators follow this practice when evaluating nontenured teachers.

Our second warning concerns the inherent limitations of tests. They do not and cannot take into account a student's motives or effort. The amount of time and effort expended by a student in preparing for a test, his ability to read the test items, his desire to do well on the test, how he felt on the day of the test—these and countless other factors cannot be quantified in a test score. It is precisely for this reason that we urge you to be humane, understanding, and compassionate when giving tests and interpreting your pupils' test scores. Try to find out *why* some pupils did not perform as well as others. The reasons can be of great value to you in future testing situations.

OBSERVING PUPIL BEHAVIOR

Throughout the school day you constantly observe how your pupils behave in a wide variety of situations—while working in small groups on a task-oriented activity, presenting an oral report, discussing or debating a given issue, engaging in role play, dramatic play, or in a simulation game. You observe that some pupils dominate an activity, while others assume a more passive role. Still others appear to be uninvolved in some activities, and prefer instead to disturb the rest of the class. Too often these are fleeting impressions that quickly vanish as your attention abruptly shifts to other more pressing matters.

Fortunately, evaluation experts have designed observational instruments and techniques which enable you to record and specify aspects of pupil behavior that give you important insights into the teaching–learning process. Among the better known and more widely used are participation charts, checklists, rating scales, and anecdotal records. Their construction and use will be explored below.

Participation Charts

All of us want our pupils to voluntarily participate to the fullest extent in a variety of activities—indeed, this is an essential ingredient of successful social studies teaching. Participation charts can be helpful to you in evaluating the nature and extent of your pupils' participation in reports, discussions, projects, instructional games, dramatic play, and similar activities undertaken by pupils working in task-oriented groups.

Below is an example of a participation chart developed and used by an elementary teacher whose pupils had been studying how elderly people are affected by the aging process. This study, taught as a part of the organizing theme, the human life cycle, centered on the various physical, social, and emotional problems confronting elderly people. To promote the exchange of ideas, the teacher had divided the class into small discussion groups of three to five pupils each. As the children discussed problems of the elderly, the teacher used the following participation chart (based on the writings of Mehrens and Lehmann)[8] in evaluating their participation in the discussion.

| | MEMBERS OF GROUP | | | | |
Contribution	Mary	Otto	Sue	Fred	Shawn
Supplies important new ideas	X		X	XX	XX
Supplies new ideas of minor importance	XX			XXX	XXX
Unsure of pupil's contribution		X			
Supplies irrelevant ideas	X		XXX	X	X
Contribution is disturbing to the group			XX	X	

Below are several guidelines for using participation charts.

1. Use these charts only with small groups of children. It is impossible to make effective use of this observational device with large groups.

[8]Mehrens and Lehmann, pp. 350–351.

2. Your role is that of observer—not a participant. When using this technique, try to be unobtrusive.
3. Record pupil behaviors as they occur. Do not wait until the end of the discussion to use your participant chart, as you may forget significant pupil behaviors.
4. Use the data obtained from this technique for constructive purposes. Discuss with individual pupils your findings. Try to ascertain why they prefer to participate in some types of activities and not in others. Offer helpful suggestions for improvement.
5. Bear in mind that these types of charts are not intended to show a pupil's motives for participation or nonparticipation in a given activity. Rather, they are used only to determine the extent of their participation.

Checklists

These types of observational tools are designed to determine the presence of certain pupil behaviors—not their quality, duration, frequency, or intensity. The most effective checklists are simple in format, easy to use, and force you (the observer) to focus your attention on specific behaviors that you desire to observe. Below is an example of a checklist that was created by a teacher whose pupils were studying the organizing theme, intercultural relations, as taught through the life-style of the Balinese, a culture residing in the Indonesian Archipelago. As the children were completing their work on a scale model of a Balinese village, the teacher used the following checklist in assessing the behavior of her students:

> Cooperated with others
> Willingly shared ideas and materials
> Willingly followed directions
> Accepted suggestions
> Put away construction materials after using them
> Sensitive to the needs of others
> Assumed responsibility for completing tasks
> Was proud of his/her work

Below are several guidelines for using checklists:

1. Carefully identify the pupil behaviors to be observed. Restrict your observations to these behaviors.
2. Do not try to observe several pupils simultaneously. It is preferable to observe one pupil at a time.
3. If you cannot observe certain behaviors on your checklist, leave those parts of the checklist blank. Hunches and guesses are of little value.
4. Use the information obtained from checklists as a basis for conferences with individual pupils. By all means discuss with pupils the positive behaviors that you've noted, and do your best to make any criticism as constructive as possible.

Rating Scales

Unlike checklists and participation charts, which reveal the presence of certain pupil behaviors, rating scales produce quantitative information about the behavior under observation. Moreover, they can be used with large numbers of students.

Despite their advantages, rating scales share with other observational techniques one common limitation that cannot be ascribed to objective tests: They lack reliability and validity.

Imagine that you have taught a series of lessons on problem-solving skills and that you desire to rate each pupil's attainment of each of the skills. Below is a rating scale that may prove useful to you.

Skill	Rating				
Identifies problem worthy of investigation	1	2	3	4	5
Formulates testable hypotheses	1	2	3	4	5
Collects pertinent data needed to solve problem	1	2	3	4	5
Analyzes and interprets data	1	2	3	4	5
Draws conclusions from data	1	2	3	4	5
Reassesses original hypotheses	1	2	3	4	5

1 = Excellent
2 = Above Average
3 = Average
4 = Below Average
5 = Poor

As you use this scale, you base your judgments on information and data gathered while you taught the problem-solving skills. Student projects, test data, conferences with pupils, and observations will enable you to make these evaluative judgments.

If you are teaching a self-contained class in the lower- and middle-elementary grades (K–5 or K–6), you should be able to assign reasonably accurate ratings to your pupils' problem-solving skills, as your class size probably will range from twenty-five to thirty-five pupils. If you teach the upper-elementary grades (5 to 8 or 6 to 8), in a departmentalized school program, it will be very difficult for you to rate with precision your pupils' problem-solving skills. Under these circumstances you are likely to be working with 125 to 150 or more students—a reality which will make it very difficult to use the rating scale described earlier. In this case it might be better to rely on tests as your primary evaluation tool, as they will provide you with more reliable, more valid data.

Below are guidelines for the use of rating scales.

1. Ratings should not be based on guess-work. If your information about a pupil's performance or trait is inadequate, do not attempt to rate such behaviors on a rating scale.
2. Construct rating scales so that they are simple and easily used. A scale of 1 to 5 should be adequate for elementary pupils.

3. Rate your pupils individually. Do not rate them by groups, even though some groups of two or three students may appear to be exhibiting very similar behaviors.
4. Discuss your ratings with individual pupils. Use pupil conferences for diagnostic as well as evaluative purposes. Help your pupils to see what your ratings imply for their behavior.

Anecdotal Records

These observational devices enable you to record specific incidents of pupil behavior over a period of time. Interpersonal relations, the development of language, geographic, or problem-solving skills, contributions to class discussions and changes in interest patterns of pupils are among the many types of behaviors that can be described in anecdotal records. In these instances anecdotal records, if carefully written, give you specific information regarding pupil behavior at a given time and place. Note, however, that your interpretation of these incidents and suggestions for improvement should be kept separate from specific incidents. Below are examples of incidents described in anecdotal records.

> *Monday, January 12, 10:00 am:* While we were simulating an assembly line, Juan began arguing with Fred. Before I could intervene, they were hitting each other. I separated both boys and moved them to opposite sides of the room. Peace reigns.

> *Monday, January 12, 3:30 pm:* The conflict between Juan and Fred has persisted unabated throughout the day. At lunch time and during recess (morning and afternoon) they resumed their battle. I have called their parents about this. They promised to speak with their boys this evening.

> *Tuesday, January 13, 4:00 pm:* Fred and Juan have not openly resumed their hostilities. On occasions they continue to glare at each other. I've spoken to our principal about the problem. The boys' parents will meet with the principal and me at 9:30 tomorrow morning.

Obviously these records are incomplete, for they do not reveal the sequel to Fred and Juan's conflict. But they do typify anecdotal records. Note that these records describe the setting in which the behavior occurred. Note also, that the teacher tried to refrain from interpreting the incidents. Had this teacher failed to provide this information, it is likely that the causes of Fred and Juan's hostility toward each other could be misinterpreted. Below are guidelines for using anecdotal records.

1. Describe each incident and its setting as clearly and as precisely as you can.
2. Record only important incidents that appear to be a part of a pattern of behavior. As the significance of these incidents becomes apparent to you, attempt to take constructive action.
3. Do not confine your anecdotal records to negative behavior of pupils. Both positive and negative behaviors—if deemed significant—should be noted.
4. Keep your principal, your guidance counselor, social worker, or other appropriate personnel informed of problems revealed in your anecdotal records. Involve them in the problem and in its solution.

Granted, anecdotal records are time-consuming to write, and the data recorded in them tend to be less reliable than data obtained from other observational tools and techniques. Despite these limitations, they do enable you to focus your attention on the individual pupil, and can yield highly meaningful descriptions of growth and development occurring in specific settings. In this sense, anecdotal records give you a more complete, first-hand description of a pupil's behavior than other observational devices.

MEASURING ATTITUDES

Until recently, teachers of the social studies have not made a serious, concerted effort to evaluate the affective learning of their pupils. This is not surprising, since attitudes are, by their very nature, extremely difficult to identify and measure. Moreover, as Carswell reminds us, ". . . the measuring instruments that are used in affective evaluation are more complex, less reliable, and certainly quite different from those we are familiar with in cognitive measurement."[9] But there is another possible explanation: generations of teachers believed that once they had attempted to teach attitudes toward patriotism, honesty, respect for the rights of others, or lawful behavior, their work was finished. They saw no need to develop instruments to determine whether such attitudes were in fact acquired by their pupils, because they felt that this type of learning was not amenable to measurement.

These beliefs are beginning to change. Increasingly we are learning of new approaches toward evaluating the affective learning of elementary pupils. This section will explore the capabilities of three approaches to evaluation of affective learning: Likert Scales, Semantic Differential Scales, and Unobtrusive Measures.

Likert Scales

Typically when this type of instrument is used, it asks pupils to express the extent to which they agree or disagree with a series of statements regarding what is, what was, or what should be. Usually a five- or seven-point scale is used, with the most positive response given the highest number and the most negative response given the lowest number. Below are examples of statements which might be used in teaching about the organizing theme, our legal system.

[9]Ronald J. B. Carswell, "Evaluation of Affective Learning in Geographic Education," in *Evaluation in Geographic Education*, 1971 Yearbook of the National Council for Geographic Education (Belmont, Calif.: Fearon, 1971), p. 107.

LIKERT SCALE: OUR LEGAL SYSTEM

Directions: Tell how you feel about these statements by making an X at the place on the line which best tells your feelings.

1.   If you don't like a law, you should obey it anyway.

1	2	3	4	5
strongly agree	agree	undecided	disagree	strongly disagree

2.   Policemen treat poor people differently than they treat rich people.

1	2	3	4	5
strongly agree	agree	undecided	disagree	strongly disagree

3.   If a student sees kids breaking windows in the school, he should tell the principal.

1	2	3	4	5
strongly agree	agree	undecided	disagree	strongly disagree

Directions: Draw an X on the face which best tells how you feel about the sentence.

4.   Most people who break the law are never caught.

Of these four examples, two contain positive statements (1 and 3) and two contain negative statements (2 and 4). In scoring these items, you would use a 5-point scale, with "strongly agree" responses receiving a 1 for items 1 and 3 (positive items) and "strongly disagree" receiving a 5 for items 2 and 4 (negative items). Below are some guidelines for building Likert Scales.

1.   Write as many positive as negative statements.
2.   Write each statement in the language of your pupils. Make your sentences as simple and as short as you can.

3. Your statements should express a definitely positive or definitely negative attitude.
4. Relate your statements to attitudes for which you require information.

Semantic Differential Scale

This instrument can be used in rating pupils' attitudes toward concepts that are basic to your social studies program. Typically when pupils use a semantic differential scale, they will rate concepts on simple rating scales, each consisting of adjective pairs (good–bad, strong–weak, unfair–fair, etc.), arranged on continuum. Below are examples of semantic differential items which might be used in evaluating elements of a pupil's beliefs regarding the organizing theme, government and politics. We have deliberately included more items than you would typically use, to enable you to see the many types of adjective pairs. Under most circumstances six to ten pairs ought to be sufficient for your purposes. Bear in mind also that your pupils' vocabularies must be taken into account when you select these items.

SEMANTIC DIFFERENTIAL SCALE: GOVERNMENT AND POLITICS

Directions: Mark an X in the space which best shows what each of these ideas means to you.

GOVERNMENT

Good	——	——	——	——	——	Bad
Closed	——	——	——	——	——	Open
Valuable	——	——	——	——	——	Worthless
Strong	——	——	——	——	——	Weak
Careful	——	——	——	——	——	Reckless
Impersonal	——	——	——	——	——	Personal
Necessary	——	——	——	——	——	Unnecessary
Clean	——	——	——	——	——	Dirty
Responsive	——	——	——	——	——	Unresponsive
Greedy	——	——	——	——	——	Generous
Considerate	——	——	——	——	——	Inconsiderate
Wasteful	——	——	——	——	——	Saving

PRESIDENT

Forward-looking	——	——	——	——	——	Backward-looking
Weak	——	——	——	——	——	Strong
Vague	——	——	——	——	——	Specific
Stupid	——	——	——	——	——	Smart
Caring	——	——	——	——	——	Uncaring
Decisive	——	——	——	——	——	Indecisive
Exciting	——	——	——	——	——	Dull
Hard-working	——	——	——	——	——	Lazy
Generous	——	——	——	——	——	Greedy

Arrogant	—— —— —— —— ——	Humble
Uninspiring	—— —— —— —— ——	Inspiring
Responsible	—— —— —— —— ——	Irresponsible
Competent	—— —— —— —— ——	Incompetent
Unethical	—— —— —— —— ——	Ethical
Wasteful	—— —— —— —— ——	Frugal

POLITICS

Clean	—— —— —— —— ——	Dirty
Fair	—— —— —— —— ——	Unfair
Serious	—— —— —— —— ——	Funny
Unimportant	—— —— —— —— ——	Important
Useful	—— —— —— —— ——	Useless
Crooked	—— —— —— —— ——	Straight
Necessary	—— —— —— —— ——	Unnecessary
Complex	—— —— —— —— ——	Simple
Unchallenging	—— —— —— —— ——	Challenging
Unproductive	—— —— —— —— ——	Productive
Inspiring	—— —— —— —— ——	Uninspiring
Immoral	—— —— —— —— ——	Moral

VOTING

Serious	—— —— —— —— ——	Silly
Careless	—— —— —— —— ——	Careful
Necessary	—— —— —— —— ——	Unnecessary
Informed	—— —— —— —— ——	Uninformed
Closed-minded	—— —— —— —— ——	Irresponsible
Biased	—— —— —— —— ——	Unbiased
Futile	—— —— —— —— ——	Worthwhile
Patriotic	—— —— —— —— ——	Unpatriotic
Intelligent	—— —— —— —— ——	Stupid
Uninvolved	—— —— —— —— ——	Involved
Disloyal	—— —— —— —— ——	Loyal
Committed	—— —— —— —— ——	Uncommitted

To score the four semantic differentials presented above, assign a value of 5 to the most positive rating and 1 to the least positive. For example, when scoring the committed–uncommitted adjective pair in the final scale, *Voting*, assign a 5 to the space nearest to *committed* and a 1 to the space nearest to *uncommitted*. To score the entire scale (consisting of twelve adjective pairs), note that the pupil could receive a total score ranging from 12 to 60 points.

You can use this scoring system to calculate a mean value for each adjective pair for your class. To figure the total score for the entire scale, sum the means for the individual adjective pairs. Or, you may wish to follow Carswell's recommendation and analyze the data, using a profile. All you need to do is plot on the original semantic differential scale the class mean for each adjective pair. If you plot these means on the scale for pre- and post-administrations of the instrument, you will probably see an interesting pattern emerge.[10]

Here are some guidelines for constructing a semantic differential:

1. Select the concepts to be evaluated. Insure that they are significant ones.
2. Use clear, appropriate, bipolar adjective pairs.
3. Insure that the positive end of the adjective continuum varies so that you don't develop in your pupils a predisposition to respond in certain ways.

Unobtrusive Measures[11]

This discussion of measures for appraising the affective learning of your students would be incomplete if it failed to describe unobtrusive techniques. You will recall that when the preceding techniques are used, the pupils are aware that their overt and covert behaviors are being evaluated; indeed, in many instances they are conscious of the attitudes they are revealing. Unobtrusive measures do not have this characteristic, as the pupils with whom they are used are unaware that their behavior is in fact being evaluated, and they are not directly involved in the evaluation process.

Below are questions that, if answered, will enable you to use unobtrusive measures. Note that most of these questions can be answered by you, while others can be answered by parents of your pupils. Perhaps the easiest way to use these measures is by asking questions that yield numerical answers. Thus, you might ask, "How many pupils:

discuss their social studies projects at the dinner table, watch a TV show related to the projects

prematurely wear out social studies materials

spend their free time using a social studies interest area

complete social studies assignments ahead of time

seek extra help from you

play hooky on days when special social studies projects are scheduled

ask to stay after school, to work on social studies projects

ask to take social studies materials home with them

check out and read library materials related to your social studies projects

tell their classmates about out-of-school discussions related to their social studies classes?"

[10]Carswell, pp. 123–125.

[11]For insightful discussions of unobtrusive measures, see Eugene J. Webb, et al., *Unobtrusive Measures; Nonreactive Research in the Social Sciences* (Skokie, Ill.: Rand McNally, 1966), p. 124; and Carswell, pp. 128–129.

All of these questions presuppose voluntary pupil behavior. For example, your pupils do not watch a TV show that is related to a current social studies project because you asked them to; on the contrary, they behave in this way because they want to. Also note that the responsibility for asking questions and recording answers rests entirely on your shoulders. The moment a child is aware of your purpose in asking these questions, the process ceases to be unobtrusive, and the accuracy of the responses becomes questionable.

Unobtrusive measures are particularly productive as far as evaluation is concerned, when used in concert with approaches described earlier. They enable you to check on information obtained from rating scales, checklists, observational procedures, interviews, and other affective measures. Admittedly, they do require time and effort and they lack precision, but they do yield information not generally available through conventional approaches.

SUMMARY

Assessing social studies learning is at best difficult and time-consuming. The newer elementary social studies programs stress the teaching of complex cognitive skills, but unfortunately, teachers appear to lack the competencies needed to evaluate the acquisition of these skills. Moreover, these teacher competencies are not being taught systematically and purposively at the pre- and in-service levels. Herein lies the rationale for this chapter.

We regard evaluation as a process by which teachers obtain information about the extent to which their social studies goals have been achieved, and use this information as a basis for further planning and instruction. This process consists of three sequential stages. At Stage I—Preliminary Evaluation, teachers seek to determine how much and what type of instruction on a given topic is needed. At Stage II—Formative Evaluation, teachers attempt to determine the degree to which their instructional objectives are being or have been attained. They use this knowledge as a basis for modifying their objectives and teaching strategies. Stage III—Summative Evaluation, occurs at the end of a grading period, when teachers assess what was accomplished since the previous grading period, and use this information in planning their instruction for the next grading period.

Three references or standards of comparison are useful in interpreting a pupil's test scores: norms based on overall class performance or on a larger sample (statewide or national, for example), the pupil's previous score on the same test, and criteria or performance standards usually based on behavioral objectives. These are designated respectively as norm-referenced, self-referenced, and criterion-referenced evaluation. All three are of value in interpreting pupil test scores.

Achievement tests, teacher-made and standardized, will continue to be given in our schools, despite their inherent deficiencies, and despite their suscep-tibility to misuse. We urge you to become competent in building and administering these tests, to be fair and compassionate when interpreting the results, and to make a special effort to teach your pupils to become proficient test-takers.

Mastery tests, consisting of a few carefully written objective items, are designed with the expectation that nearly all of the pupils in a given class will pass them. They directly involve teachers and their pupils in the teaching–learning process. When a pupil fails a mastery test, the teacher reviews the material with the child, who then retakes the test. Since mastery tests are given frequently—usually immediately following the teaching of a new skill or concept—and since they are not as threatening to pupils, we regard them as more useful than achievement tests in evaluating social studies learning. Especially appropriate for inclusion in social studies tests—mastery and achievement—are three types of items: matching, alternate choice, and multiple choice. Despite arguments to the contrary, these items, if carefully constructed, can test higher order thought processes, and can function as reliable and valid tools of evaluation.

Essay test items, consisting of short, specific questions, can be used in the middle- and upper-elementary grades. Since these items ask pupils to construct answers to questions and to write them in coherent English, they place a premium on language skills, and can penalize those students who are particularly deficient in writing skills. Allowances for this must be made by the teacher.

There are a variety of observational tools available for assessing the status or changes in pupil behavior. Among the more useful are participation charts, checklists, rating scales, and anecdotal records. Although all of these lack reliability and validity, often they yield valuable insights into pupil behavior that cannot be obtained from conventional objective tests.

Of particular value to the elementary social studies teacher are three tools for assessing pupils' attitudes: Likert Scales, Semantic Differential Scales, and unobtrusive measures. Likert Scales ask pupils to express the extent to which they agree or disagree with a series of statements regarding what is, what was, or what should be. Pupils responding to Semantic Differential Scales rate concepts on a series of adjective pairs, each of which is a direct opposite. Unobtrusive measures enable teachers to assess in-and-out-of-school behavior of pupils. These three tools produce information not generally obtained through the more typical approaches described above, and when used judiciously, can add a significant dimension to the evaluation process.

CROSS-REFERENCES TO TEACHING MODULES

The teaching modules which appear in Part 2 include provision for the use of objective test items, essay test items, and instruments for observing pupil behavior and for measuring pupil attitude changes. Below is a partial listing of those modules in Part 2 which use many of these approaches to evaluation.

Energy: "The Energy Problem Is Our Problem" (Part 2, p. 332). This module, designed for middle-grade (4–6) pupils, uses an objective test designed to measure pupils' knowledge of forms and sources of energy, and a checklist for assessing their problem-solving skills.

Ecology: "Cleaning Up the Local Environment" (Part 2, p. 324). Designed for lower-grade (K–3) pupils, this module uses several evaluation techniques, including a graph (closely resembling a rating scale) for recording litter found around their school, various checklists for recording types of litter collected, and a participation chart for recording pupils' study habits observed during the lesson.

Media: "Children's TV Viewing Habits" (Part 2, p. 373). This module asks upper-grade (5–8 or 6–8) pupils to respond to a log entitled "Accounting for Myself." This self-evaluation device enables pupils to account for their activities during the course of a typical day.

Occupations: "Occupations and Human Equality" (Part 2, p. 282). In this module, upper-grade (5–8 or 6–8) pupils are evaluated through anecdotal records, as they study about changing career opportunities for males and females. These records would be designed expressly for the purpose of assessing changes in stereotypic thinking of pupils.

Consumerism: "Children Become Advertising Executives" (Part 2, p. 318). This module, designed for middle-grade (4–6) pupils, employs a variety of evaluation approaches, including objective measures, questionnaires, oral quizzes, personal logs, and "I learned" techniques. Of these, the "I learned" approach has exceptional possibilities, for it enables pupils to state in writing what they learned about advertising techniques. The teacher then can evaluate these statements by superimposing on them a simple rating scale.

BIBLIOGRAPHY

Buros, Oscar K. *Mental Measurements Yearbook.* Highland Park, N.J.: Gryphon Press. Published periodically, this yearbook contains references, descriptions, and applications of various types of tests. The most recent yearbook, the eighth, was published in 1978.

Ebel, Robert L. *Essentials of Educational Measurement.* Englewood Cliffs, N.J.: Prentice-Hall, 1972.
We regard this as our bible in measurement. If we can convince you to acquire this book for your personal library, you'll thank us.

Joyce, William W. (Ed.). "Informal Assessment of Social Studies Learning." *Social Education,* Vol. 40 (November–December 1976), pp. 567–582.
Articles by Myra T. and John G. Herlihy and Janet Hanley Whitla present a variety of practical approaches to evaluating pupil achievement.

Mehrens, William A. and Irvin J. Lehmann. *Measurement and Evaluation in Education and Psychology* (2d ed.). New York: Holt, Rinehart and Winston, 1978.
This book deserves to be in every professional library. It is a readable, eminently useful text written by two of the foremost authorities in their field.

Wick, John. *Educational Measurement: Where Are We Going and How Will We Know When We Get There?* Columbus, Ohio: Charles E. Merrill, 1973.
Authors of social studies methods texts consistently give this book an A+ rating. It is witty, highly informative, and packed with practical ideas. What more could one ask of any book in this area?

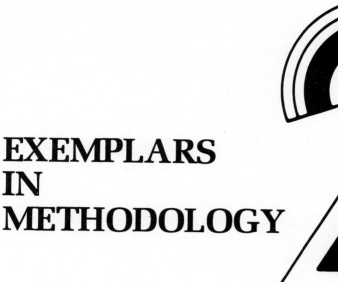

EXEMPLARS IN METHODOLOGY

This part focuses on the methodology, the how-to-do-it, of social studies instruction. You will recall that the chapters in Part 1 explored a wide range of topics impinging on your role as an elementary social studies teacher, and defined our conception of the lifelong roles and organizing themes. Part 2 attempts to show how this information can be applied directly to the teaching–learning process. There are three sections in this part. The first, *Designing and Using Teaching Modules*, demonstrates how you can design and use teaching modules in your social studies classes. As used here, a module is a comprehensive teaching plan which functions much like a combination lesson plan–teaching unit. The second and third sections, *The Lifelong Roles: Exemplars for Teaching* and *The Organizing Themes: Exemplars for Teaching*, present a series of teaching modules designed for average, below average, and advanced students. Following each module is a subsection entitled *Classroom Results,* which reports the results of actual classroom use of the module.

Section A
DESIGNING AND USING TEACHING MODULES

GOALS

1. Explore in depth advantages of using the lifelong roles and organizing themes as a point of departure for revising existing social studies programs or for designing new programs.
2. Acknowledge the fundamental importance of careful, thoughtful planning of social studies lessons.
3. Become knowledgeable about the purpose of teaching modules, how they can be designed and used, and their relation to the lifelong roles and organizing themes.
4. Become aware of the essential differences between original teaching modules and reteach versions of these modules.
5. Become capable of designing and using teaching modules consistent with the perceived abilities, prior experience, and needs of elementary pupils.

In this section we will attempt to show how you can incorporate the lifelong roles and organizing themes into your existing social studies program. A key element in this process is the teaching module, a comprehensive instructional plan consisting of a series of detailed lessons, suggestions for their use, and a listing of necessary instructional materials. A teaching module is far more than a conventional daily lesson plan, for it contains more detail and is intended for use over a period of several days or even several weeks. In this sense the teaching module resembles the conventional teaching unit. Yet it differs from a unit in that it contains specific day-to-day lessons that are spelled out precisely. Indeed, when several teaching modules are taught in sequence, they become the equivalent of a carefully detailed, carefully sequenced teaching unit, one that combines the qualities of daily lesson plans.

"HOUSE FOR RENT"

If you look at Tables A–1 and A–2 on pp. 221–228 you will notice that they present illustrative modules on the lifelong role of Family Membership, as taught through Ecology and Energy, two of the ten organizing themes. The modules center on the problems faced by the Kinneys, an American family attempting to rent a house in another community. A cursory glance at these modules may reveal that they are more highly structured than most lesson plans that you have encountered before. We have presented our illustrative modules in this way to impress on you the fact that careful, methodical planning is essential to good teaching, and to insure that you will clearly understand the techniques of designing and using instructional modules.

The basic elements of the modules are:

    I.   Grade Level
    II.   Special Materials
    III. Time
    IV. Concept(s)
    V.   Objective(s)
    VI. Entry Behavior Indicator(s)
   VII. Teaching Procedures
  VIII. Evaluation

At this point we are going to take you on a quick tour through the modules presented in Tables A–1 and A–2. Note that Table A–1 consists of one module to be taught in two sessions, while Table A–2 presents one module to be taught in one session. Let us take one section of the module at a time.

Note that we have designated the module in Table A–1 as the *Original Version,* because it presents a basic, foundation learning experience, one that could serve as a prerequisite for subsequent modules on this topic. The other designation, *Reteach* (Table A–2), is reserved for subsequent modules designed for children, who for various reasons might not successfully complete the *Original* module. But if you have the same teaching problems as 99.9 percent of your colleagues and if 99.9 percent of your children have various learning problems, you will find that some of them (hopefully only a few) will need to devote additional time and effort to completing the *Original* module—particularly if you regard it as extremely important. On the other hand, if all of your pupils are among the .1 percent who can successfully complete the *Original* module, great! But please let us know the secret of your success so that we can pass it on to others. For the majority of teachers, the *Reteach* module can be of great help in their attempts to reach the slower pupils.

I. Grade Level. Here we merely indicate whether the module is appropriate for lower elementary (grades K–2 or K–3), middle elementary (grades 3–5 or 4–6), or upper elementary (grades 5–8 or 6–8) levels. We use these broad categories in preference to precise grade levels, primarily because we are reluctant to pinpoint precise grades for any of our modules. Indeed, we would prefer that you make this determination.

II. Special Materials. Here we have designated those materials—teacher- and/or pupil-made, or commercially prepared—which are essential for satisfactory completion of the module. In Table A–1 we specified these types of materials: copies of the story, *House for Rent,* and original and revised maps of the neighborhood for pupils; a transparency of the pupil maps for the teacher. Of course, other special materials (trade books, charts, filmstrips, records, tapes, etc.) might be added to the list, should you desire to extend this module (we hope you will!).

III. Time. This is an estimate of the amount of time you and your pupils will need. In Table A–1 we suggested that a thirty to forty minute session and a forty to fifty minute session be allocated to the module, but of course some classes will need more time, others less. In Table A–2 we suggested a fifty-minute period. Typically it is best to allocate short chunks of time to modules for primary-grade children (owing to their short attention span) and longer chunks of time to modules for older children. Since Tables A–1 and A–2 are designed for the middle- and upper-elementary grades, we have allocated longer blocs of time than for younger pupils.

IV. Concepts. As used here, concepts are clusters of meanings individuals attach to categories of objects, activities, qualities of objects and activities, or abstractions. Usually these clusters are expressed as nouns. The modules in Tables A–1 and A–2 focus on the organizing theme *Ecology and Energy*, and stress the concepts *Energy Cost, Pollution, Safety*, and *Decision-Making*.

V. Objectives. What behavioral changes do you want to produce in your children as a result of their experience with the module? Under what conditions will these changes occur? What minimal standards of performance have you established for your pupils? These are the basic questions which should be considered here. Do not get us wrong—we are not proposing or even hinting that you arbitrarily stipulate for your pupils a rigid, unyielding set of specifications that all must meet, for to do so would suggest that we are encouraging you to treat your children as robots possessing the same interests, and capable of learning at precisely the same rate in precisely the same manner. Unfortunately such thinking is characteristic of the fringe of the behavioral objective movement. Indeed, its activities have precipitated a flourishing Help-Stamp-Out-Behavior-Objectives counter movement now rampant in many school districts.

What we are merely trying to say is that if your lesson is an important one, it behooves you to plan it carefully, and in so doing careful specification of the behavioral changes you want the lesson to produce must be made. Viewed from this perspective such changes should become a flexible standard of achievement to aim for, not a straitjacket. Keep this in mind as you read the objectives we have stated in Tables A–1 and A–2.

One more thing to remember: your *objectives* should interrelate with the remainder of the module (*i.e.*, see items VI, VII, and VIII below). This suggests that the objective should take into account the entry behavior of your pupils (VI), should give direction and purpose to your teaching procedures (VII), and should be amenable to evaluation (VIII). Let us explore these relationships in greater detail.

VI. Entry Behavior Indicators. While planning any new learning experience, it is important to assess the children's stages of readiness, or entry behavior, as they begin the module. Such an assessment would take into account those previous experiences in- and out-of-school, and special competencies which your children would need to possess before beginning work on the module.

In the case of Table A–1, it would be desirable for some of your children to have recently moved to a new neighborhood, as their recollections of this experience could sharpen their perceptions regarding the desirable and undesirable features of the new neighborhood. In the second module (Table A–2), which is designed for pupils who failed to successfully complete the *Original* module, we have specified entry behavior which focuses directly on a major stumbling block for pupils: the ability to visualize map symbols and to apply this skill to a problematic situation.

The second type of entry behavior includes those skills, understandings, or attitudes deemed essential to satisfactory completion of the module. Note the types of competencies listed for Number VI of Tables A–1 and A–2. Obviously, it is important for you to know the extent to which your pupils possess these competencies, but rather than subjecting them to exhaustive testing (this is a good way to kill off pupil interest even before you begin the module), a brief warm-up lesson or two should help you assist your pupils' readiness for the module. And if it appears that most of your pupils find it difficult to read the case study, "House for Rent," or to interpret the type of map included in the module, it is probably best for you to get busy and teach the requisite reading or map skills before beginning work on the module. If only a few kids have this problem, don't worry! You can structure the teaching procedures so as to accommodate this deficiency by mixing your more advanced pupils with your slower pupils. The same proposition applies to those kids who find it difficult to work with others on group decision-making tasks.

VII. Teaching Procedures. In this section you spell out in step-by-step order the procedures you intend to follow in teaching the module. If you read over this section of Tables A–1 and A–2, you will notice that we have spelled out our teaching procedures in considerable detail, to minimize any misunderstanding regarding the meaning of this section. This is a far more detailed description than you would care to write, as we suspect that your version of this module would consist of short, carefully written notes. This is fine, as long as you write modules for your exclusive use. But bear in mind that there will be occasions when another regular teacher, your principal, or a substitute teacher will be taking over your class. For this reason it is probably better to make your modules more complete than daily lesson plans, but not as complete as ours.

A suggestion: If you really want to impress your student-teaching supervisor, principal, or other administrator who may be expecting to observe your teaching on short notice, casually whip out a duplicate copy of your module, give it to him or her to read over, and use the time to collect your wits before beginning your lesson. This technique works most of the time, but when it doesn't, you still have these options: (a) grab the textbook and assign several pages to be read silently; (b) announce to your visitor that you must leave school to visit a sick great-grandmother; or (c) give a spelling test.

Irrespective of how much detail you intend to state in item VII, remember that the primary purpose of this section of the module is to translate your objective into action, by providing procedural guidelines to follow in teaching the lesson.

VIII. Evaluation. What evaluative strategies will be of value to you? Are some better than others? Under what circumstances? "Give a test!" you loudly proclaim. Unfortunately, most of us are likely to respond in this fashion—if only because our experience in school has conditioned us to think this way. Admittedly under some circumstances the use of tests as an evaluative procedure is appropriate—particularly when the lesson you are teaching involves mastery learning of basic facts or skills. If, for example, your module is designed to teach your kids the names and relative locations of the fifty states, to use a grid system in locating places on a map, or to recount the major points in the *Declaration of Independence*, a mastery test might be the most effective evaluative technique available. On the other hand, there are other evaluative techniques, which when properly used, can give you better, more precise indicators of the extent to which your pupils are attaining the behavioral objective you have established for them. A few of the endless variety of evaluative techniques available to you include observing your pupils in a dramatic play situation, while on a field trip, while completing a mural, during a role play; interviewing your pupils one at a time; asking them to complete an unfinished story, fill out a checklist, rating scale or questionnaire, write a poem, construct a diorama.

The process of selecting the most appropriate evaluative technique is largely a function of what you desire your kids to learn. Accordingly, if your objective is carefully written—to the extent of specifying what is to be learned, the conditions under which the learning is to occur, what is to be learned, and your criteria for determining success following performance—you have many cues to use in formulating your evaluative procedures. In Tables A–1 and A–2 the basic procedures are observation and discussion. As an observer, you have a threefold task: to observe what your pupils say and do before, during, and following their group meetings. In these instances you cannot expect to render an accurate assessment unless you know beforehand precisely what to look for. In Table A–1, the reasons for and against renting the house are stated. These are not the only reasons, but they are indicative of the quality of the children's reasoning; accordingly, they serve as indicators of achievement.

Also note that the adequacy of the reasons for and against renting the house is to be jointly assessed by pupils and the teacher. This removes the teacher from the position of being judge and juror, and enables her to serve as a co-inquirer with her pupils. If practiced over a period of time, such an evaluative procedure is bound to encourage pupils to assume greater responsibility for their learning. And is not this one of our prime functions as teachers?

Illustrative Teaching Modules

TABLE A-1 "HOUSE FOR RENT" (ORIGINAL VERSION)

LIFELONG ROLE: FAMILY MEMBERSHIP
ORGANIZING THEMES: ECOLOGY AND ENERGY

I. **Grade Level**
    Middle and Upper
    Elementary

II. **Special Materials**
    For Pupils: copies of the story, *House for Rent*, and map (original and revised version) of the neighborhood in question.

    For the Teacher: a transparency of the map (original and revised versions).

III. **Time**
    One 30–40 minute session
    One 40–50 minute session

IV. **Concepts**
    Energy Cost
    Pollution
    Safety
    Decision-Making

V. **Objective**

Using data obtained from the story, *House for Rent*, and from a map of the neighborhood, pupils working in groups will reach and defend decisions regarding the desirability of the Kinneys' renting the house in question.

VI. **Entry Behavior Indicators**

Pupils who have recently moved to a new neighborhood should be prompted to share this experience with their classmates. Encourage these pupils to relate the factors which prompted their parents to select the house, condominium, apartment, or mobile home where they now reside. In addition, pupils should be capable of: (a) reading the story with understanding; (b) locating places on the maps and interpreting semipictorial map symbols; (c) working together on a decision-making task.

VII. **Teaching Procedures**

First Session

  A. Open the class by asking your pupils, "Have any of your families bought or rented a house, apartment, condominium, or mobile home lately? What did you look for in the home? In the neighborhood? Did you consider more than one place to live? Why? Why not?" As pupils volunteer information, record on the chalkboard what they consider to be desirable features of a home and neighborhood. Devote 5–10 minutes to this initial warm-up session.

  B. Distribute copies of the case study, *House for Rent*, and the original version of the map. Have pupils read the case study and map silently, then discuss them orally, to insure that they grasp the basic information presented in both documents. Then project the map transparency on your overhead projector, to insure that your pupils have correctly read the map.

  C. Redirect pupils' attention to their list of desired features of a home and a neighborhood. Ask them to use these features as criteria in judging the desirability of the home and neighborhood in Little Chute. As the discussion ensues, pupils may recognize the inadequacy of the information presented in the case study and map—indeed, some pupils may observe that the map and story raise more questions than they answer! If this happens, don't despair. Redirect their attention to the basic information presented, and refrain from adding new information. Conclude the session by asking for a tentative decision on renting the house in question.

Second Session

  A. Supply pupils with the revised version of the map. Ask, "Does this map do a better job of answering your questions? Why? Why not? What new information is presented? Is it helpful? In what ways?"

  B. Once you're satisfied that your pupils are beginning to see that there are advantages and disadvantages to residing in the neighborhood depicted on the revised map, divide your pupils into groups of 4–7 members each. Ask each group to appoint a chairperson (boy or girl) and a secretary (boy or girl). Instruct the pupils as follows:

1. "Your job for the remainder of the period is to answer the question, 'Should the Kinneys rent the House?' Each group is to answer this question and produce a list of reasons for their answer. Be sure to consider reasons *for* and *against* renting the house."

2. "The secretary of your group is to make a list of the reasons for your decisions and to give it to the chairperson."

3. "Your chairperson is to keep your discussion moving, and at the end of class, to report to the class the results."

C. As the group meetings begin, move from group to group, to insure that all pupils understand what they are to do. Refrain from giving advice to your pupils.

D. Following the group meetings, the chairpersons of each group will orally report and defend the decisions reached by their groups, using the information provided by the secretaries.

VIII. Evaluation

Evaluation centers on two behaviors: (a) the pupils' ability to reach and defend decisions regarding the advisability of the Kinneys' renting the house; and (b) the pupils' ability to defend their decisions. Inherent in this process are four concepts: *energy cost, pollution, safety,* and *decision-making.*

Energy Cost. This concept is to be developed during the first session. You will want your pupils to consider: (a) the cost of electricity and natural gas in Little Chute, as compared with Milwaukee, where the Kinneys had formerly resided; (b) that the Little Chute house is well insulated; and (c) that the cost of electricity, gas, and water is increasing nationwide. Here is an excellent opportunity for your pupils to apply their reading and math skills to real-life situations, as they explore the cost factors involved in renting the home. If they can use these cost factors as a basis for determining whether the Kinneys should rent the house—*i.e.*, whether they can afford it—the pupils will have succeeded in demonstrating their knowledge of the concept, energy cost.

This concept of energy cost should reappear during the second session, as the cost of living in the house is weighed against the condition of the neighborhood. Thus, you will want to observe whether your pupils do indeed make this comparison.

Pollution and Safety. The extent to which the pupils are acquiring these concepts is evidenced by their ability to conclude from the map that there are features of the neighborhood which cause pollution and create hazards for people living there. This ability to read, interpret, and then generalize from data on the map is essential to satisfactory completion of the module.

During the first session, you will want to observe whether the pupils can generalize from the data on the map, and recognize the limitations of the data presented in the story and on the map. During the second session they are using an expanded version of the map, and therefore are presented with more data for use in grappling with the pros and cons of renting the house. Accordingly, the real meat of this lesson is in the second session, which will require far more attention evaluation-wise.

At the conclusion of the small-group meetings, note the reasons the pupils cite *for* renting the house: close to the railroad, fire station, stores, etc., and *against* renting the house: busy street (traffic hazard, noise, dirt, ugly signs, exhaust fumes);

railroad tracks (noise, dirt, vibrations); gas and fire stations (noise, traffic); lack of play areas nearby. Bear in mind that the advantages of living in the house (space, privacy, well insulated, etc.) might outweigh any disadvantages of living in the neighborhood.

As these reasons pro and con are given by the chairpersons of each group, refrain from interjecting your personal opinions. Remember, your major task is to encourage your pupils to hypothesize about the consequences of features of the immediate environment for the quality of life in the neighborhood.

Decision-Making. Once it becomes apparent to your pupils that they've reached defensible decisions about the rental of the house, spend several additional minutes in assessing their competencies as decision-makers. Ask these questions (pupils could respond to some orally, to others in writing):

1. *Of the chairpersons:* How easy was it for you to keep the discussion moving and directed toward the problems presented in the case study? Did you have any problems? If so, what were they? Would your behave differently if you worked with another problem of this type? With another group? If so, how?

2. *Of the secretaries:* Was it easy or hard to take notes on the decisions reached by your group? Why? Why not? Did you like your assignment? Why? Why not?

3. *Of the other pupils:* Did you feel comfortable in your group? Did your group work well together? Did you stay on the subject? Was your group the right size? Did you learn from others in your group? Did everyone get a chance to speak? Is it better to work with others or alone on a problem of this type? How did others in your group behave toward you? Did they listen when you spoke? Did your chairperson and secretary do a good job? Did you cooperate with them?

By the conclusion of this session you should have obtained sufficient evidence indicating that your pupils regard decision-making, as practiced in their groups, as a process that is learned through practice.

CASE STUDY: "HOUSE FOR RENT"

Ms. Kinney lives with her children in a small, cramped apartment in Milwaukee, Wisconsin. She is divorced from her husband and is raising her three children, Kevin, aged eight, Mary, eleven, and Fred, fourteen.

She has accepted a new job in Little Chute, a small Wisconsin town. In two weeks she must move to Little Chute, to begin her new job.

After leaving her children in the care of their grandmother, Ms. Kinney drove to Little Chute to find a home to rent. After looking at several houses, she finally found one that appealed to her. It was large enough for their needs, well-insulated, in good condition, and within walking distance to her new job. Also, the rent seemed reasonable.

Mr. Vanderwall, the owner of the house, told Ms. Kinney that she had two days to decide if she wanted to rent the house, as he knew several other families that were interested in the house. She knew that there were very few houses for rent in Little Chute, and that the rent for Mr. Vanderwall's house was lower than for any of the other houses she had seen.

Before Ms. Kinney reached a decision, she and her children estimated the yearly cost of living in Mr. Vanderwall's house and the cost of living in the Milwaukee apartment. Here are the estimate yearly costs:

	Little Chute House	Milwaukee Apartment
Rent	$3,600	$3,200
Gas	740	300
Electricity	360	200
Water	100	no charge
Total	$4,800	$3,700

While the Kinneys were comparing these costs, Ms. Kinney showed her children a map that she had drawn of the neighborhood where the house was located. If you were Kevin, Mary, or Fred, would you want your mother to rent the house?

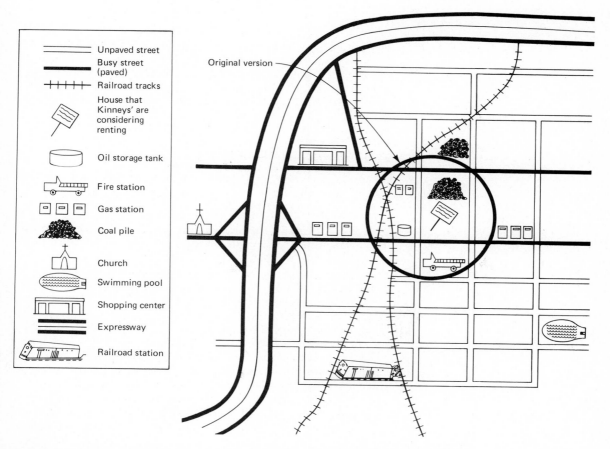

Figure A–1 MS. KINNEY'S MAP. Area encircled is original map. Total map is revised version.

TABLE A–2   "HOUSE FOR RENT" (RETEACH VERSION)

LIFELONG ROLE: FAMILY MEMBERSHIP
ORGANIZING THEMES: ECOLOGY AND ENERGY

The purpose of this module is to help you reteach those portions of the original module (Table A–1) which are most likely to present difficulties for your pupils. For illustrative purposes, we have assumed that for some pupils a major source of difficulty is the ability to: (a) read and comprehend the case study; and (b) visualize realities represented by map symbols. Until pupils attain these competencies, they will be unable to reach a defensible decision regarding the rental of the house.

I.	**Grade Level** Same as in Table A–1	**II.**	**Special Materials** Same as in Table A–1
III.	**Time** One 50-minute period	**IV.**	**Concepts** Same as in Table A–1

V.   **Objective**
Using data obtained from the story, *House for Rent*, and from the revised version of Ms. Kinney's map, pupils, working independently, will demonstrate their ability to generalize about: (a) the energy costs involved in renting Mr. Vanderwall's house; and (b) the effects of busy streets, unpaved streets, oil storage tanks, railroad tracks, fire and gas stations, and vacant stores on the quality of life in the neighborhood under study.

VI.   **Entry Behavior Indicators**
Pupils failed to successfully complete the original module (Table A–1). Presumably the source of their problem is the ability to: (a) correctly read the case study; or (b) interpret the symbols on Ms. Kinney's maps; or (c) hypothesize regarding the effects of the realities of these symbols on the quality of life in the neighborhood.

VII.   **Teaching Procedures**
   A.   Begin the lesson by distributing among your pupils the original and revised versions of Ms. Kinney's map, and the story, *House for Rent*. Then briefly review with your pupils the essential elements of the story. As you do this, record on the chalkboard the most significant elements of the story.
   B.   Place on the overhead projector your transparency of Ms. Kinney's maps. Ask the pupils to identify on their individual maps each symbol of importance (busy street, fire station, railroad tracks, etc.).
   C.   When all relevant symbols have been correctly identified, ask each pupil to make a list of the good and bad characteristics of the realities depicted by each symbol. Upon completion, ask each pupil to orally report this information. As pupils report, record their responses on the chalkboard.
   D.   Conclude the lesson by asking each pupil to add to their maps five new symbols, each representing some positive changes they'd like to see in this neighborhood. Upon completion, have each pupil orally present his own revised version of Ms. Kinney's map.

VIII.   **Evaluation**
The focal point of your evaluation is your pupils' ability to visualize how the reality represented by map symbols actually appears. Since the group of students with

whom you'd be working on this reteach version would be a segment of your class, it should not be difficult for you to carefully monitor their performance during various stages of the module. Below are examples of questions you might consider:

A. Can pupils discern the essential elements of the case study?
B. Can pupils correctly translate the map symbols and visualize what they represent?
C. Can pupils see the positive and negative characteristics of the realities represented by the symbols?
D. Do each of the five new symbols represent positive changes to the neighborhood? Does each pupil adequately explain his rationale for creating his symbols?
E. Did the pupils work effectively individually?

"THE BREAKFAST INDUSTRY"

There are additional ways of using our modular approach, when teaching pupils about the lifelong roles. Tables A–3 and A–4 contain illustrative teaching modules designed for primary-grade pupils, and center on the role of breakfast cereal in their lives. A cursory examination of Table A–3 reveals that while our teaching

If you took your class to a nearby supermarket, how could you use the breakfast cereal display as a learning laboratory?

module, "The Breakfast Industry," uses the same format as Tables A–1 and A–2 ("House for Rent"), the module is divided into three separate instructional periods, which occur on a Thursday (exploring personal preferences is stressed), Friday (taste, packaging, and advertising are stressed), and the following Monday (investigating TV ads, packaging and labeling are stressed). If taught in this sequence, the components of the module can serve as a mini-unit of instruction. Indeed, it would be quite easy for you to expand this module into a unit of even longer duration.

Table A–4 is a reteach version of the module presented in Table A–3. We have included this version because it is very likely that some of your pupils will encounter difficulties when they are taught the original module in Table A–3. Indeed, when we field-tested the original module, we noted that a few children found it difficult to read, interpret, and classify information found on cereal boxes, and to draw conclusions from this information. We also noted that in some classes, younger children had problems when working in small, task-oriented groups. Note that we have cited these problems under item IV of the module (Entry Behavior Indicators), as a reminder.

Illustrative Teaching Modules

TABLE A–3 "THE BREAKFAST INDUSTRY" (ORIGINAL VERSION)

LIFELONG ROLE: PERSONAL EFFICACY
ORGANIZING THEMES: CONSUMERISM AND MEDIA

Your purpose in using this module is to sensitize your pupils to the role that advertising plays in determining their desire to eat a given type of food (breakfast cereal) and their preferences for given brands of cereal. As you read the module, note the extent to which communication skills impinge on completion of the behavioral objectives.

To avoid redundancy, items I–IV are listed for the first period only. These sections would apply to the other periods as well.

Thursday (First 30-minute period)

Module No. 1: *Exploring Personal Preferences*

I. Grade Level Lower Elementary	**II. Special Materials** 1. Packages of 4–6 of the most popular brands of breakfast cereal. 2. 35–40 (depending on size of class) small transparent bags. 3. Audio tape recordings of TV cereal ads.
III. Time One 30–minute period (Thursday) Module #1 One 30–minute period (Friday) Module #2 One 30–minute period (Monday) Module #3	**IV. Concepts** Personal preferences Advertising Packaging and labeling Product information Taste Invention

V.   **Objective**

Pupils will orally state: (a) why they eat breakfast cereal; (b) their favorite brands of cereal; (c) the reasons for their brand preferences; and (d) a plan of action for exploring how their preferences are determined by advertisers of cereal.

VI.   **Entry Behavior Indicators**

Pupils should be capable of reading brand names of breakfast cereals, and recalling and discussing sources of information by which they are exposed to brands of cereal.

VII.   **Teaching Procedures**

A few days before you begin, send home with your pupils a brief note describing the purpose of the project (teach children the effects of advertising on their breakfast cereal preferences), and how parents can assist you (encourage their children to watch Saturday morning TV cereal commercials and help them read the information printed on cereal packages in the home).

A.   Ask your pupils whether they eat breakfast cereal and why; then to identify their favorite brands of breakfast cereal, and to explain why they prefer certain brands over others. As pupils volunteer answers, carefully record this information on the chalkboard (brand names and reasons).

B.   Once their preferences and reasons are recorded, encourage your pupils to assess the *validity* of their reasons. Refrain from expressing your personal opinions regarding their reasons. At this point it is essential that the pupils be encouraged to talk freely, to challenge each other's reasons.

VIII.   **Evaluation**

A.   Once it is apparent that your pupils are beginning to validate their reasons for eating cereal and preferring one brand over another, go back to the chalkboard and record their reasons in order of importance. There is bound to be some confusion at this point, but bear in mind that you should be evaluating the degree to which your pupils can express *why* they prefer one brand over another.

B.   Your next step is to help your pupils determine whether there is a better cereal than another. "Taste the cereal, read the printing on the package, study how the cereals are advertised on TV"—these are among the suggestions that should come from your pupils.

Friday (Second 30–minute period)

Module No. 2: *Taste, Packaging,* and *Advertising*

V.   **Objective**

Pupils will orally identify cues they used in identifying brands of cereal and describe characteristics of cereal packaging and TV advertising affecting their preferences for given brands of cereal.

VI.   **Entry Behavior Indicators**

Pupils should be capable of working together (in small groups) on task-oriented activities (taste-testing), describing characteristics of cereal packages, and distinguishing between types of information printed on outsides of cereal packages.

VII.   **Teaching Procedures**

Come to school armed with original packages of 4–6 of the most popular brands of cereal identified the previous day. Before the pupils arrive, pour equal amounts of the cereal into plastic bags. Code each bag so that only you know the brand name of its contents; keep the cereal packages hidden.

A. Group your pupils into tasting stations (4–5 desks per station). As each pupil tastes the contents of each bag, ask him to note the brand name on a piece of paper. The taste-testing completed, have one child from each station report the results of his group. As results are reported, record them on the chalkboard.

B. As you list the findings on the chalkboard, ask your pupils to reveal the cues they used in identifying each cereal by brand name.

C. Ask your pupils to reevaluate the importance of taste in determining cereal preferences. Some—perhaps many—will confess that taste is relatively unimportant. Are there more important reasons? What are they?

D. Distribute the packages from which you obtained the cereal for your taste tests. Ask your pupils to carefully examine the packages. What information is printed on the package? Is the package itself an important factor? *Should* the package be an important factor? Again, try to refrain from passing judgment, but reintroduce the idea of product information.

E. Are there other kinds of information that tell us why we should buy certain brands of cereal? Invariably someone in your class will suggest TV commercials as a source worth investigating. Ask your pupils to carefully watch the commercials that will appear on TV tomorrow (Saturday). Do they provide product information? What do you like about the commercials? What don't you like? Why?

VIII. **Evaluation**
Evaluation should center on the cues your pupils used in identifying the cereal by brand name (number VII, item B), and on the information obtained by studying the *cereal packages* (number VIII, item C).

Cues: Taste, texture, shape, color, and possibly smell.
Cereal packages: size, shape, color, use of illustrations, special offers, gifts inside the box, nutritional data, price.

Monday (Third 30-minute period)

Module No. 3: *Inventing TV Ads, Packaging and Labeling*

V. **Objectives**
Pupils will orally report findings gleaned from observation of TV cereal ads and cooperatively invent their own brands of cereals, design packages for the cereal, and create their TV cereal ads.

VI. **Entry Behavior Indicators**
Pupils should be capable of distinguishing between product information and extraneous information on cereal packages and in TV ads, and capable of working together on task-oriented activities (designing packages and TV ads).

VII. **Teaching Procedures**
A. Discuss with pupils the characteristics of TV ads they observed over the weekend. Stress length of ads, use of cartoon figures, claims, etc.

B. Play your audio tape recordings of the TV ads. What did pupils like and dislike about the commercials?

C. Discuss the characteristics of honest and dishonest advertising used on TV and on cereal packages. Record this information on the chalkboard.

D. Devote your art and language arts classes during the balance of the week to inventing brands of cereal and designing packages for these products; if equipment is available, have the TV ads videotaped for follow-up evaluation.

VIII. **Evaluation**

A. Evaluation should center on the cereal boxes and on the TV ads.

B. Work with your pupils in establishing a set of evaluative criteria. Are cereal packages: colorful, eye-catching, easy to read? Do they contain product information?

C. Are the TV ads persuasive? Do they present product information? Do they resort to gimmickry?

D. While engaged in the projects, did the pupils consider the morality of using honest and dishonest advertising techiques? If so, what did they conclude?

E. Did the pupils apply their reading, writing, and listening skills to the design of the packages and the TV ads? Did they enhance their competencies in these skills?

F. Did the pupils express concern over the need to regulate advertisers who bamboozle, deceive, or mislead the public?

TABLE A–4 "THE BREAKFAST INDUSTRY" (RETEACH VERSION)

LIFELONG ROLE: PERSONAL EFFICACY
ORGANIZING THEMES: CONSUMERISM AND MEDIA

The purpose of this module is to help you reteach those portions of the previous modules which are likely to present difficulties for your elementary pupils. Note that number VIII, Evaluation, is incorporated within number VII, Teaching Procedures, because evaluation should occur *as the lession is taught*—not at the end of the lesson—in this module.

I. **Grade Level**
Lower Elementary

II. **Special Materials**
1. Empty packages of breakfast cereal used in previous modules. Packages should be sprayed with clear lacquer, so that they can be easily marked and erased.
2. Red and black crayons
3. Box of Kleenex
4. Audio tape recorder–player.

III. **Time**
One 30-minute period

IV. **Concepts**
Product information
Advertising

V. **Objective**
While examining packages of their favorite brands of breakfast cereal, pupils will

report their observations, then generalize regarding the extent to which the cereal packages determine their preferences for these brands of cereals.

VI.   **Entry Behavior Indicators**
Pupils have encountered difficulties in attempting to successfully complete modules 1–3. These difficulties involve the ability to read, interpret, and classify information and draw conclusions. Pupils can work together in small groups.

VII.   **Teaching Procedures**
A.   Organize your pupils into research teams of three or four members, then distribute among the teams several empty cereal boxes and a supply of Kleenex. Pupils will supply their own crayons.
B.   Ask your pupils to carefully study each package, and observe use of color, illustrations, and printed information. Then ask pupils to mark directly on the cereal packages as follows: red for information which tells about the cereal inside and black for information unrelated to the cereal inside. Move among your pupils, providing assistance as needed. Encourage them to use the Kleenex to erase their marks if they change their minds.
C.   (At this point you'll need your tape recorder-player.) Once it appears that your pupils have marked all of the cereal packages, ask each team to report its findings. Move from team to team, tape-recording the reports (or better yet, have a pupil do this). Then play back the audio tapes. As this happens, record the basic ideas on the chalkboard.

Evaluation: As pupils report their observations, note whether they mention these characteristics: size, shape, and color of package, illustrations, special offers, notices regarding "gifts" inside the package, price, and information regarding nutritional and food content of the cereal (sugar, starch, artificial color, preservatives, etc.). As pupils cite these characteristics, ask them to describe their meaning, to insure against empty verbalization.
D.   Ask your pupils to evaluate these characteristics in terms of their importance to them. Try to get the kids to describe each package as a totality and as a combination of various types of information.

Evaluation: Have pupils vote on those characteristics which have the most powerful appeal to them, and then explain why they voted as they did. For example, if they gave special offers a high rating, find out whether the kids sent in for these offers, what they received, how long it took, whether they were pleased or disappointed, etc.
E.   Conclude the lesson by asking your pupils to state what they learned from the lesson. Tape their responses. Are cereal packages important to them? Why? Why not? Was the information on the outside important to them?

VIII.   **Evaluation**
Ask, "How important are the cereal packages?" "Which is more important, the cereal inside, or what's on the outside?" "Is the advertising on cereal boxes honest?" "If not, what can we do about it?"

"EVALUATING PORTABLE RADIOS"

As breakfast cereal is a basic element in the lives of younger children, so do portable radios occupy a prominent position in the leisure-time activities of older kids. Thus our final illustrative teaching module, "Evaluating Portable Radios," is especially appropriate for the middle or junior high grades. This module centers on the lifelong role of Avocation, as taught through the organizing theme, Consumerism. This concept is articulated through the concepts of Product-testing, Warranty, and Decision-making.

You will notice that we have allocated teaching procedures to a thirty-minute period and to two forty-minute periods. Ideally these periods would occur in three consecutive days, owing to the departmentalized nature of most junior high or middle school programs. But since social studies classes at these grade levels may not be scheduled on consecutive days, we have merely identified these as three instructional periods.

Note also that we have not included a reteach version of the original teaching module. This was not an oversight. We omitted the reteach version because originally we felt that it was unnecessary. If you believe otherwise (some of our graduate students, particularly those who are experienced teachers, might agree with you), we suggest that reteach versions might be designed to assist those students who find it difficult to: (a) read the operating instructions and warranty information for their portable radios; or (b) prepare and present oral and written reports; or (c) work together in task-oriented groups. Now it appears that we have been too presumptuous. We have fallen into the trap of believing that most pupils in the upper elementary grades (5–8 or 6–8) possess these competencies, when in reality many students at this level do not. Therefore, we urge you to regard Table A–5 (Evaluating Portable Radios) as incomplete to the extent that it will, under most circumstances, require a reteach version. But rather than designing an illustrative module for this purpose, we would prefer that you do this. If you have carefully read this chapter, we are convinced that you should be fully capable of designing an excellent reteach version of the module in Table A–5.

Illustrative Teaching Module

TABLE A-5   "EVALUATING PORTABLE RADIOS" (ORIGINAL VERSION)

LIFELONG ROLE: AVOCATION
ORGANIZING THEME: CONSUMERISM

Your purpose in using this module is to teach your students to become competent decision makers in the market place. Although the module centers on portable radios, you can, with minimal effort, revise the module to accommodate such consumer goods as tape recorder–players, TV sets, CB radios, etc.

I. **Grade Level**
   Upper Elementary

II. **Special Materials Required**
   1. AM–FM portable radios, operating instructions and warranty information. One radio to be supplied by the teacher, others by students.
   2. Large portable projection screen or portable chalkboard, and 3–4 tables.

III. **Time**
   One 30–minute period
   Two 40–minute periods

IV. **Concepts**
   Product testing
   Warranty
   Decision-making

V. **Objective**
   After conducting independent tests of AM–FM portable radios, students will submit oral and written reports of their investigations.

VI. **Entry Behavior Indicators**
   Students should be capable of reading operating instructions and warranty information for AM–FM portable radios, and capable of working together on task-oriented activities.

VII. **Teaching Procedures**
   Before beginning this module, bring to school an inexpensive AM–FM portable radio, preferably one which operates on batteries.

First 30–Minute Period

A. Show your radio to the students. Ask them whether they think it was a good buy and why. As students begin responding, record on the chalkboard their responses. Encourage them to cite positive and negative reasons.

B. After a few minutes it should be apparent that any assessment of a product should include its performance. But how can we determine how well this radio performs? At this point your students should suggest that they try it out. Pass the radio among your students, encouraging them to carefully examine and play it at their desks, elsewhere in the room, and outside the school building.

C. As students begin noting characteristics of the radio, add these to the list on the chalkboard. By now their list should include such criteria as:

   1. Is it easy to tune?
   2. How good is the sound?
   3. How durable is it?
   4. Is it attractive looking?
   5. How much did it cost?
   6. Does it operate on batteries and on AC current?
   7. How well does it perform in different locations?
   8. How long do the batteries last?

D. At this point (or earlier) students will mention the virtues and limitations of radios they have at home. Capitalize on this by suggesting that they compare this radio with their own. Give your students the following assignment for the next class meeting:

   "Bring to school your own radio, as well as operating instructions and warranty information. This will help us test these radios. Label the radios and literature with your names."

Second 40–Minute Period

A. Begin the class by reviewing the criteria the students listed at the previous class. Any new criteria? (Warranties and instructions will be among the topics suggested.) If so, be sure to add them to the list on the chalkboard.

B. Discuss ways of testing the radios. Introduce the idea of *objectivity* in testing for sound quality, absence of static, clarity, etc.

C. Place the radios behind the portable screen or chalkboard. Tune each radio at the same station and at roughly the same volume. Play each radio separately as members of the class judge it according to the performance criteria suggested earlier. Have the students independently rate each radio against the criteria on a 1–3 scale. Then sum the numerical ratings for each radio.

D. At the conclusion of the testing, reveal the radios and their respective operating instructions and warranty information. Depending on the number of radios available, group the students into small teams. After giving one radio to each team, ask each team to write a brief report of their investigation. Students will begin the reports during this class period and complete them as a part of their language arts class. Ask students to build their reports around the criteria listed on the chalkboard and to add others as needed. Prior to the next class, examine students' initial drafts of reports. Suggest revisions.

VIII. **Evaluation**

Evaluation should center on the oral and written reports. Below are suggested criteria for assessment of the reports:

1. How valid were the criteria?
2. Were the criteria applied accurately?
3. Did the criteria include results of product tests as well as operating and warranty information?
4. Did students differentiate between and among the importance of the criteria?

How you grade these papers is up to you, but we strongly encourage you to assign to the papers a social studies grade (based on content) and a language arts grade (based on form, style, grammar, and above all, communicability). If another teacher is responsible for providing language arts instruction to your students, you should enlist his or her support before teaching this module, and carefully work out with this teacher details of the project.

Third 40–Minute Period

Each student team will present a brief oral report on its investigation. Encourage each member of the team to participate in the report. Use the criteria indicated above as well as the criteria of *communicability* and *organization:* have students presented the results of their investigations clearly, concisely, to facilitate understanding?

SUMMARY

We proposed that the five lifelong roles can serve as major organizers of content for your existing social studies program. Further we proposed that the ten organizing themes can add meaning and direction to your teaching, when taught within the framework of the lifelong roles. Admittedly, it is not necessary to use all ten themes when teaching each of the roles. The particular concepts that you stress are dependent on the instructional goals that you and your pupils have established, the readiness and ability of your students, the availability of instructional materials, and your own capabilities.

Teaching modules are designed to help you to organize social studies content into specific lessons. A teaching module is a comprehensive instructional plan consisting of a series of detailed lessons, suggestions for their use, and a listing of necessary instructional materials. A module specifies the approximate grade level where lessons are to be taught, special materials required, estimated time needed, concepts to be stressed, pupil objectives, entry behavior indicators, teaching procedures, and evaluative procedures. There are two types of teaching modules, original ones which are initially taught to an entire class, and reteach versions, which are later taught to those students who had difficulty with the original version.

Our experiences in field-testing these modules and our feedback from hundreds of teachers who are using them has convinced us that under many circumstances, reteach modules should be taught following original modules. In most classes there will be some pupils who are incapable of satisfactorily attaining the behavioral objective of a given module. For example, they may be encumbered by reading or writing deficits, they may lack certain inquiry skills, they may lack the requisite experiential background, or they may have problems in working independently or in small groups. Once it is apparent to you that this indeed is the case, we urge you to design and use a reteach version of your module.

The illustrative modules presented in this chapter were intended solely for illustrative purposes. The modules that you design for your pupils will be less comprehensive and less detailed than ours. We hope that our presentation of these modules will convince you that an essential ingredient in successful teaching is careful, thoughtful planning. If our approach to the design and use of teaching modules assists you in this quest, this chapter will fulfill its intended purpose.

Section B

THE LIFELONG ROLES: EXEMPLARS FOR TEACHING

GOALS

1. Learn how to apply the authors' concept of lifelong roles to selection, planning, and evaluation of instructional materials (prepared or teacher-made).
2. Gain greater insight into ways of involving parents and community in the planning, instruction, and evaluation of children.
3. Identify concepts and skills developed in school that affect the lives of children immediately as well as throughout life.
4. Gain new ideas for "hands-on" materials and strategies that cost little or no money yet allow children to be real problem solvers and at the same time use lifelong skills.
5. Learn how to interrelate the affective and cognitive domains that ultimately lead toward more intelligent decision making.
6. Formulate new ideas for helping children grapple with social studies problems within their lives and help them begin to see that what they do to solve the problems can make a difference.
7. Utilize the prototype modules or exemplars as "seeds" for developing plans for each individual classroom according to the needs and interests of the children in an attempt to improve the human condition.
8. Through the "Classroom Results," gain insights into problems, considerations, and suggestions for use of all or part of the modules in the individual classroom.

As we have stated in the preceding chapters, the lifelong roles can serve as major organizers of content for your social studies instruction. The concepts that you stress will be determined by the instructional goals established by you and your students, the readiness and abilities of your students, the available instructional materials, and your expertise.

The purpose of this section is to present sample teaching modules for each of the life roles. It is not intended for you to use all of these modules or for you to feel compelled to implement them in their identical form. Rather it is our hope that you will read them, react, and reflect, and then modify the existing modules or develop your own using the appropriate concepts, objectives, methodology, materials, and evaluation procedures.

The chapter is divided into five sections—citizenship, family membership, avocation, occupation and personal efficacy—each of which deals with a lifelong role. A general statement has been developed for each of the sections. Following each statement the reader will find two sample modules. Each will be preceded by an introductory statement in an attempt to assist the reader in visualizing where such a module might fit into the existing curricula. Following each module a "Classroom Results" report will be given to share responses from teachers who have field-tested the modules. We reiterate once more that these modules are examples, that they are to be modified to meet individual class needs and that the modules addressing the life roles and organizing themes can be used to develop new curricula or to add "spark" and relevancy to an existing program.

Citizenship

If our schools are to put into practice what they hope to achieve in the making of responsible citizens, more than incidental learning opportunities need to be provided. A systematic and relevant program is necessary to insure that children have experiences within the realm of this lifelong role. The experiences must be seen by the child as an integral part of life—experiences that can be operationalized *now*.

To do this the teacher and school system must undertake a careful analysis of what would constitute a responsible citizen in a democracy. The following objectives developed by the authors can serve as a guide:

1. Given the human need for individuality and rights and responsibilities of being an individual, a person demonstrates citizenship by valuing and upholding the values of the community.
2. Given the human need for individuality and rights and responsibilities of being an individual, a person demonstrates citizenship by acquiring all sides of information.
3. Given the human need for individuality and rights and responsibilities by being an individual, a person demonstrates citizenship by deliberating—seeking out others with different positions.
4. Given the human need for individuality and rights and responsibilities of being an individual, a person demonstrates citizenship by exercising power.
5. Given the human need for individuality and rights and responsibilities of being an individual, a person demonstrates citizenship by evaluating consequences.

After identifying the behaviors exhibited by responsible citizens and agreeing that there is a need to prepare students to participate in a democratic society the teacher must then take another careful look at the classroom. One of the most widely used texts in elementary social studies identifies the main objective of social studies as the same for the total school program—the development of democratic citizens: "The perpetuation of our way of life, its values and ideals, depends almost entirely on the success of society in educating its members in democratic principles and democratic action."[1] Michaelis provides a statement regarding the classroom. He says that the teacher must be aware of the kind of behavior which is consistent with democratic values.[2] Implicit in that are

[1]Jarolimek, John, *Social Studies in Elementary Education* (New York: Macmillan, 1967), p. 6.
[2]Michaelis, John U., *Social Studies for Children in a Democracy* (Englewood Cliffs, N.J.: Prentice-Hall, 1972), p. 239.

responsibility, respect, creativity, cooperation, and open-mindedness. Each unit of work or teaching module that is planned should contribute to one or more of these categories of behavior.

The following sample teaching modules reflect these democratic values. These have been field-tested by classroom teachers. You will note that citizenship must be experienced. It can be experienced through participation, discussion, role-play, simulation, writing, reading, reflection, and negotiation to whatever degree possible, that is appropriate to child's level.

MIDDLE

First-Hand Experiences in Citizenship

This teaching module is designed for pupils in middle-elementary grades. Typically at these levels students will study some aspect of political science, which is referred to in most texts as citizenship. The primary objective is to help students come to respect the rights and responsibilities of each individual. The module provides opportunities for students to become personally involved by asking that the students take a look at their own rights and responsibilities and then take a look at what happens when an individual oversteps his bounds. This leads to consideration as to why we need rules and laws. Suggestions are made for a variety of activities such as devising a child's Bill of Rights, developing a coat of arms, writing creative stories, and keeping journals. The local community and the section of the social studies text concerned with citizenship, rules, laws, or government could provide excellent resource material. By the end of the module the student will have opportunities to use the information that he has gathered and attitudes that he has formulated to practice citizenship in and out of school.

I.   Grade Level: Middle Elementary

II. Special Materials:
   A.   Art materials for bulletin board caption, example:
      "Your Right To Swing Your Arm Ends Where My Nose Begins"
   B.   Magazine pictures depicting rights, responsibilities, cooperation
   C.   Role-playing cards (See item VII, Teaching Procedures)
   D.   Learning Center Materials—Examples:
      1.   A copy of the Bill of Rights, cards indicating an individual's rights and cards giving various situations in which rights are being violated. Match the situations with the rights that are being violated.

Bill of Rights	Freedom of Speech	You are taken to jail for voicing your opinion.

2. Who am I? The child can explore his or her outside and inside. Sample activities for this exploration of the outside include: (a) How am I different from this picture? (Provide pictures and a mirror.); (b) What do I see in the mirror? Draw my body. What are my features? (Using the mirror have the child describe in writing his or her characteristics. The child may want to attach a drawing or a colored photo.) Sample activities for exploring the inside are: (a) Values—list the things you prize the most or make a personal coat of arms. Share it with a friend; (b) Write a paragraph describing what it feels like to be afraid; (c) Take a trust walk. (Establish trust in a friend.) Have a friend blindfold you and then the two of you take a walk. Discuss your reactions. Record your feelings; (d) Build a lifeline using a string to represent your life and all the important aspects and people in it.

E. Cooperation Games*
   Dimensions of Cooperation

   Objectives
   To stimulate the group to analyze some aspect of the problem of cooperation in solving a group problem.
   To sensitize the members to some of their own behavior which contributes toward or hinders solving group problems.

   Materials
   Individual tables that will seat five participants.
   One set of "instructions" for each five people participating and one for the leader.
   One set of "squares" for each five people participating. (See directions for making the sets of squares.)

   Room Arrangement
   If appropriate, tables should be arranged in advance with groups of five chairs around them and with a packet of the necessary materials on each table. The tables should be spaced far enough apart that the various groups cannot observe the activities of the other groups. The members then take chairs as they enter. If this is not appropriate, tables and chairs may be arranged after the leader's introduction.

   Discussion
   This exercise involves so much interest and feeling that the group discussion usually carries itself though the leader may need to guide

---

*Adapted from an article entitled "An Experiment in Co-operation," *Today's Education*, Vol. 58, No. 7 (October 1969) p. 57.

the focus of comments or may wish to add points from his own observations.

The discussions should go beyond relating experiences and general observations. Some important questions are: How did members feel when someone had completed his square correctly and then sat back with a self-satisfied smile on his face? What feelings did they think he had? How did members feel about the person who couldn't see the solution as fast as the others? Did they want to get him out of the group or help him?

When the discussion is under way, the leader may wish to raise questions which stimulate the participants to relate their feelings and observations to their daily work experiences.

DIRECTIONS FOR MAKING A SET OF SQUARES

A set of five envelopes containing pieces of cardboard which have been cut in different patterns and which when properly arranged will form five squares of equal size is needed. One set should be provided for each group of five persons. Since classes average from twenty-five to thirty persons, it is suggested that the leader make five sets.

To prepare a set, cut five cardboard squares of equal size, approximately six-by-six inches. Place the squares in a row and mark them as below, penciling the letters A, B, C, etc., lightly so they can later be erased.

The lines should be drawn so that when cut out, all pieces marked A will be of exactly the same size, all pieces marked C, of the same size, etc. By using

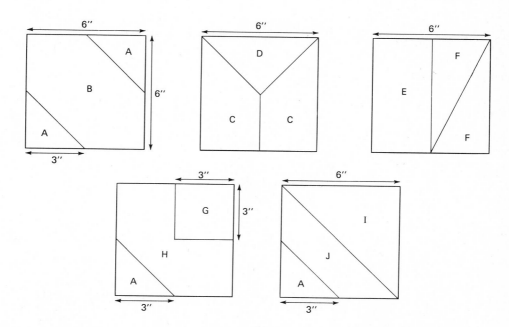

multiples of three inches several combinations will be possible that will enable participants to form one or two squares, but only one combination is possible that will form five squares six-by-six inches.

After drawing the lines on the six-by-six–inch squares and labeling them with lower case letters, cut each square as marked into smaller pieces to make the parts of the puzzle.

Mark each of the five envelopes A, B, C, D, and E. Distribute the cardboard pieces in the five envelopes as follows:

Envelope A has pieces a, b, a.

B	c, c, d
C	e, f, f
D	a, h, g
E	a, j, i

Erase the penciled letter from each piece and write, instead, the appropriate envelope letter as Envelope A, etc. This will make it easy to return the pieces to the proper envelope for subsequent use when a group has completed the task.

[Use the overhead projector for slow learners to demonstrate the activity or work with a small group verbalizing each transaction.]

INSTRUCTIONS TO THE CLASS

In this package are five envelopes, each of which contains pieces of paper for forming squares. When the signal to begin is given, the task of your group is to form five squares of equal size. The task will not be completed until each individual has before him a perfect square of the same size as that held by the others.

Specific limitations are imposed upon your group during this exercise:
1. No member may speak.
2. No member may ask another member for a card or in any way signal that another person is to give him a card.
3. Members may, however, give cards to other members.
   (Have gifted children describe how the outcome of the cooperation activity relates to daily life. Have them keep a log that describes when they use cooperation in out-of-school situations.)

    Debriefing Questions:
1. How did you feel when you could not get the puzzle piece that you wanted?
2. How did members in your group function?
3. If you had problems, why did they occur?
4. If you didn't have problems, why not?
5. What are the advantages of cooperating? Disadvantages?

F.   Film—"Why We Have Laws" (Shiver, Gobble, and Snore)—By Learning Corporation of America, 711 Fifth Avenue, New York, N.Y. 10022.

III. Time: 3 weeks. (The concepts will be developed throughout the school year. Many of the projects and activities are year-long. Being a good citizen will hopefully continue throughout life in and out of school.)

IV. Concepts:
   A. *Citizenship* is people working together toward a better society with an awareness of the rights and responsibilities of each individual.
   B. *Rules* are *unwritten laws*.
   C. Most *laws* help to meet human needs.
   D. People often disagree about what is a *fair rule* or *law*.

V. Objectives:
   A. The student will exhibit respect for others by demonstrating consideration of the rights of other individuals or groups.
   B. The student will voluntarily assist a person or persons in need of help as measured through observation.
   C. The student will understand the need for rules and laws as demonstrated through discussions and in his actions in and out of school.
   D. The student will be able to list two reasons why we need to cooperate.
   E. The student will be able to list two reasons why we have laws.

VI. Early Behavior Indicators:
   A. The student needs previous experience in group work.
   B. The student needs previous experience in pantomime.
   C. The student needs to have some previous skill in keeping a journal.

VII. Teaching Procedures:
   A. Introduce the students to the module by posing this question: What do you feel your rights are? Place all the responses on the board. Have the students categorize them, if appropriate. Discuss the responses and reactions.
   B. Have the children cut out magazine pictures of some of their rights. Put them on the bulletin board under the caption, "Your right to swing your arm ends where my nose begins." Discuss the results.
   C. Have students go back to their brainstorming list of rights and their bulletin board pictures. Identify and discuss the responsibilities that accompany each right. Discuss what happens when someone is irresponsible.
   D. Utilize the learning center material concerned with the Bill of Rights. Discuss the Bill of Rights and pose such questions as: "Of all the rights you have, which do you think is most important?" "Least important?" "Which right do you think will increase in importance as you grow older?" "Which do you use most?" "least?" In pairs, have children match the problem situation with the right that is being violated.
   (Have slow students make pictures of rights. Have gifted students find newspaper examples of rights being violated.)

How do these boys' values influence their perceptions of their responsibility for returning the money they found?

E. Have the students as a class (or in small groups) devise a Bill of Rights for Children (treating children as people). This effort might take several days, but it could be very rewarding as a social studies and language arts experience. Sample items we have seen included in Children's Bills of Rights are: "Don't keep us young forever." "Treat us as if we are normal even though we sometimes act peculiar." "Stand by us, not on us or over us." "Bring us up so we don't always have to depend on you." "Try to be consistent." Discuss the students' final product. They may want to share it with other teachers and administrators and/or with their families.

F. Have students make an individual or class coat of arms. Discuss likenesses and differences and why. How do your values influence what you think your responsibilities are?

G. Provide the students with one or more class periods during the module to have creative writing opportunities.

Sample Topics Include:
1. The people I like best . . .
2. I treat my friends . . .
3. When I'm with my friends, I feel . . .
4. I think most parents . . .
5. When we line up for recess, I . . .
6. On the playground I try . . .
7. We have rules because . . .
8. What do you think are the enemies of mankind?
   Do you think enemies can ever become friends?
9. What would you do if you found something valuable that belonged to someone else?
10. Pick out someone you know and describe him. Tell not only what he looks like but what he is like on the inside.
11. When someone feels bad I . . .
12. When I see a new student I . . .

(The slow learners might draw pictures instead of writing stories. If possible have them write brief sentences summarizing their pictures or let them tape the oral language aspect of the assignment.)

(Allow gifted students to select more than one of the topics or let them select one of their choice that is appropriate for the lesson and interview students/adults for their ideas.)

13. In school, I am helpful when . . .
14. When Mother is ill I . . .
15. When we have a substitute teacher I . . .
16. What do you think about jobs around the house?
    What do you want to do when you grow up? Why?
17. When I see someone littering, I am helpful by . . .
18. When I get into trouble, I . . .
19. I feel responsible when . . .
20. I disappoint people when . . .
21. The worst thing I ever did . . .
22. Which do's and don'ts do you hear most often?
    If you could choose two do's and don'ts, what would they be?

(Have slow learners cut out pictures to depict these topics. If possible have them write experience stories with teacher guidance to accompany each picture.)

(Gifted students might use these ideas and develop a survey to gather data from a variety of people. Have them tabulate and analyze their findings. Have them report those to the rest of the class.)

H. Encourage students to keep journals on how they have helped others and how others help them.

I. Introduce the students to the Cooperation Game. Play the game and discuss what happens when people fail to cooperate.

J. Discuss the reasons we need rules. For example, "Why do we need rules in the classroom?"

K. Have students survey the class to find out which rule they would most like to have changed in the classroom and why. Graph the results. If practical, allow the children to participate in some real-life problem solving, carry through the processes, and attempt to implement a rule change. (See Unified Science and Mathematics Unit entitled, *School Rules* published by Education Development Center, 55 Chapel Street, Newton, Mass.)

L. Students may want to determine what the rules of the school are and then plan a method for informing a new student or an upcoming class about these rules. If so, this project could take several weeks. A small group of students might assume this responsibility apart from the normal social studies period.

M. Have students explore written and unwritten laws that exist outside of school. Example: a stop sign (written), don't throw rocks at windows (unwritten).

(Have slow learners draw pictures of their findings.)

(Have gifted students survey members of the community for written/unwritten laws and tally/graph the results.)

N. Show the film, "Why We Have Laws" (Shiver, Gobble and Snore) by Learning Corporation of America, 711 Fifth Avenue, New York, N.Y. 10022.

Sample focus questions:

1. What happens when laws are disregarded or forgotten?
2. How do you feel when someone else breaks a law?
3. Can you think of a case when it might be necessary to break a law?

O. Provide the student with role-playing experiences.

Examples are:

1. A storekeeper turns his back and Betsy (second grader) takes two candy bars off the counter. She leaves the store and runs down the street to meet Toni. She shares a candy bar with her. Should Toni take it? What should Toni do?

Consider: What would happen if everybody took things?

Is stealing wrong?

What happens if you get caught?

2. Two children, Bill and Bob, are at a stop light. They walk against the red light; no cars go by. A third child (Henry) sees them do it. Should he warn them?

Consider: Why do we have traffic lights?

Even though no cars come, could the children be caught? Are they violating the law?

3. Barb and Bonnie go shopping with Barb's mother. Bonnie sees Barb pick up a child's card game and slip it into her purse. What should Bonnie do?

(Add puppets for slow learner motivation and as possible stimulation for verbalization.)

P. Summarize the module. Have each student write five "I learned" statements. Have each student share entries from his journal, provided he has been keeping one.

VIII. Evaluation:

    A. Student Checklist

	Always	Sometimes	Never
I try to follow the rules established in my classroom.			
I treat others in the classroom as I would like to be treated.			
I help people I see who need assistance.			
I try to cooperate with students in my class.			
I try to cooperate in out-of-school situations.			
I am aware that my actions affect others.			
I understand that my rights should not infringe upon others'.			
I accept the consequences for infringing on the rights of others.			
I understand that we need laws to protect people.			
I obey the laws because I understand we need them.			
I consider the rights of the minority.			

(Give slow learners an oral evaluation or conduct an interview with each child. Keep anecdotal records indicating their performance.)

    B. You could also use a checklist to gather, record, and analyze the contribution of each student. A sample is as follows:

Name	Asks Questions	Answers	Participated in Activity	Used Library To Gather More Information

The teacher, students, or both could develop the specific criteria to be used for the evaluation of any given module.

CLASSROOM RESULTS

Teachers found the time period acceptable. Several commented that many of the activities could be expanded beyond the time specified.

The concepts, teaching procedures, and evaluation techniques seemed to be appropriate. In many cases teachers extended them to meet the needs of individual students.

Comments about ways in which the module might be modified were offered by several teachers:

1. "I changed the teaching procedures so that we played the Cooperation Game as an introduction to the module. I felt we could draw on the experiences of the game during our later discussions."
2. "My pupils brought newspaper articles to class which showed how people's rights were being infringed upon."

One teacher said that the strongest point of the module was the idea that rules are made to *protect* individuals, not *restrict* them:

1. "The modules give ample opportunity to teach this."
2. "The major strength of this module is that it fits any existing social studies program."

Suggestions for future users were given by a number of teachers:

1. "I believe that a thorough discussion of rights is necessary before students can do a good job on Section B of Teaching Procedures."
2. "My students were not fully prepared to relate rights to pictures."
3. "More emphasis needs to be put on role-playing experiences. Students really enjoyed the situations that were included."

STUDENT BIBLIOGRAPHY

Addie, *Christopher for President*, New York: Golden Press, 1973.
Agle, Nan (Hayden), *Maple Street*, New York: Seabury, 1970.
Blue, Rose, *Nikki*, New York: F. Watts, 1973.
Cook, Fred J., *American Political Bosses and Machines*, New York: F. Watts, 1973.
Eichner, James A., *Local Government*, New York: F. Watts, 1976.
Katz, William Loren, *The Constitutional Amendments*, New York: F. Watts, 1974.
Levy, Elizabeth, *The People Lobby*, New York: Delacorte, 1973.
Lindop, Edmund, *The First Book of Elections*, New York: F. Watts, 1968.
Markun, Patricia Maloney, *The First Book of Politics*, New York: F. Watts, 1970.

Neufeld, John, *Edgar Allen*, New York: S.G. Phillips, 1968.

Wise, William, *American Freedom and the Bill of Rights*, New York: The Parents' Magazine Press, 1975.

TEACHER BIBLIOGRAPHY

Gibson, John S. "The Process Approach," in Donald H. Riddle and Robert S. Cleary (Eds.), *Political Science in the Social Studies*. Washington, D.C.: National Council for the Social Studies, 1966.

Hyneman, Charles S. *The Study of Politics: The Present State of American Political Science*. Urbana: University of Illinois Press, 1959.

Massialas, Byron G., "American Government: We Are the Greatest," in C. Benjamin Cox and Byron G. Massialas (Eds.), *Social Studies in the United States: A Critical Appraisal*. New York: Harcourt Brace Jovanovich, 1967.

"The Rights of Children," *Harvard Educational Review*, Part I, Vol. 43 (November 1973); Part I, Vol. 44 (February 1974).

Law in American Society Foundation: National Center for Law Focused Education. Chicago: Law in American Society Foundation, 1973.

UPPER

Personal Dimensions of Citizenship

This teaching module is designed for students in upper-elementary grades. Typically at this level students will study political science, usually referred to as local, state, or national government. Some textbooks refer to these topics as citizenship. The primary objective of this module is to help students realize that citizenship is willing and effective participation of the individual in society and that individuals have responsibilities to perform. The module provides opportunities for students to become personally involved with the topic by asking that students take a look at themselves, their families, school, and community and determine what responsibilities are a part of each role. Suggestions are made for a variety of activities such as interviewing, experimenting, role playing, simulation, and writing editorials. The local community as well as existing social studies texts that deal with rules, laws, government, and/or citizenship could provide excellent source material. By the end of the module the students will have encountered many experiences that hopefully will touch their personal lives and help them realize that consideration for others grows out of one's understanding that all individuals are worthwhile.

    I.   Grade Level: Upper Elementary

   II.   Special Materials:
      A.   Filmstrips

1. "Developing Basic Values" and "Consideration of Others"—Produced by Society for Visual Education
2. "What Liberty and Justice Mean"—Produced by Churchill Films (Optional)

B. Bicycle Safety Programs may be set up through local law enforcement agencies or through the State Police. For example, contact in the State of Michigan:

> Michigan State Police
> Community Services Section
> 714 South Harrison Road
> East Lansing, Michigan 48823
> Telephone: A.C.517 373-2839

C. Role Play/Moral Dilemma

CASE STUDY

Mother has been recently employed as a sales clerk at Wards. Father is employed as a bookkeeper for a small private firm, and earns about $11,000 per year. Bill, the oldest child, is in 8th grade, Kevin is in 4th grade, and Sheila is in 1st grade.

Because Bill expressed an interest in attending law school Mother has decided to work outside the home to earn money for current bills and for Bill's college expenses. She frequently works odd hours. Because Mother is working, the laundry is frequently left undone. Dinner is often thirty minutes late. Kevin is embarrassed when he brings his friends home after school and the beds are unmade and the dishes stacked in the sink. Mother frequently comes home after ten o'clock in the evening and doesn't have the energy to clean up the house. What should Kevin do? What can Bill do? What can Sheila do? What should Mother do? What can Father do?

Possible questions: Do you think a problem exists in this situation?

If so, what is it? If not, why not?

If you think there is a problem, what are some possible solutions?

What are the consequences of each solution?

Do you see similar situations in your own home? If so, how can you help out?

D. "Stranded"—Island Simulation Game

You and fifteen other people are stranded on an island located in the Pacific. The island is not on any navigation chart. It is about 5 miles long and 5 miles wide. The highest elevation is about 500 feet at one end. There are two caves on the island. About half of the island is covered with vegetation. You have also discovered an unmarked can filled with some corn. The only animal life on the island appears to be green worms and wild rabbits. Your physical condition at this time is good.

The object of this game is for you as a group to decide how you will organize yourselves on the island for survival. Think about such things as where you will live, how you will live, what you will eat, how you will have fun, and how you will be governed.

Sample Chance Cards:

Half of the group refuses to do its share of the work. What will the other half decide to do?

One man murdered another because he had stolen his food supply. How should the situation be handled?

Two of the stronger members of the group start annoying the rest. What will happen?

Three individuals refuse to carry water to their campsite. What should the others do?

Only one cave will provide shelter. It is large enough to house only 8 individuals. Which 8 will be selected? Where will the remainder find shelter?

Several people have contracted an undisclosed illness. There are no doctors available. What will happen?

III. Time: 2–3 weeks.

IV. Concepts:
A. *Citizenship* is viewed as the willing and effective *participation* of the individual in society.
B. *Consideration* for others grows out of one's understanding that all individuals are worthwhile.
C. Individuals have *responsibilities* to perform in society.
D. For society to function smoothly *concern for self* and *others* must exist.
E. *Rules* are *unwritten laws.*
F. *Rules* and *laws* are necessary to protect individuals.

V. Objectives:
A. The student will show concern and consideration for others as demonstrated in discussion, role playing, and real-life situations and measured through observations.
B. The student will support the rights of individuals in society as demonstrated in real-life situations and measured by observation.

    C.   By developing a school safety campaign, the students will guard the health and safety of others as measured by observation.

    D.   The student will help others in need as demonstrated in participatory activities and measured through observation.

    E.   The student will discuss and participate in role playing and simulations and as a result be able to demonstrate in real situations the value and need of rules and laws as measured by observation.

VI.   Entry Behavior Indicators:

    A.   The student needs previous experience in group work.

    B.   The student needs previous experience in interviewing and surveying.

    C.   The student needs previous experience in role playing, moral dilemmas, and simulation games.

VII.   Teaching Procedures:

    A.   Make sure that throughout the module you provide all children with many opportunities to read literary sources related to the topic. See section entitled Student Bibliography.

    B.   Begin with a role-playing situation performed by the teacher/school secretary. It could be done late the day before the module is to begin or early in the morning on the first day. At a prearranged time have the school secretary stomp angrily into the room, slam down a stack of papers on the desk and shout, "I don't care who you are or what you say, don't ever bring writing like this again to me and expect me to read it and type it. It looks like 'chicken scratch.' " She will then leave the room and slam the door. After the students have recovered from the shock, a class discussion should begin. Focus questions might include: What did she say? What are the facts? The inferences? Why is she angry? Should a person act like that? Why or why not?

    C.   Show the filmstrip, "Consideration for Others." Divide the class into 4 or 5 groups. Assign each group a topic such as: respect and consideration for peers, for elderly, for police, for parents, for the church, for the military.

    Focus questions such as the following could be posed: What is respect/consideration in relation to your topic? Why is respect important? What does respect/consideration mean to you? Can you give examples where respect/consideration was shown? Nonexamples? (Ability groups should not be used in this activity. Allow slow learners and gifted students to work together.)

    (Gifted students may wish to interview individuals in the community to assess their attitudes about respect/consideration. Allow them to summarize their findings and make a written report or verbally present the class with their information.)

    D.   From the ideas generated by all the discussion groups, the children could devise a list of behaviors showing respect. These should be discussed and a final draft made. Copies can be made for all students, and they can evaluate their own behavior for a specified period of time.

E. From a continuing class discussion of good citizen responsibilities, the idea of concern for others' safety can be defined through a survey of the principals, teachers, custodians, and other children. After tabulating the results, some students might want to plan a poster campaign to alert others to the hazards and need for safe conduct on school property. Students can be encouraged to plan ways of improving safety in and around school.

Focus questions: What are some things good citizens might be concerned about? Why might these be important? What do these ideas mean to you in terms of your school? What problems do we have? How might we find out more specifically what our problems are? How might they be solved?
[Have slow learners limit their experiences to the classroom. Have them draw pictures depicting hazards in the classroom or ways to alleviate the problems.]
(A gifted child might like to survey several schools in an attempt to find out if safety problems tend to be similar between and among schools. The child might like to compare rural and urban schools, for example.)

F. Depending on the school situation, an additional or alternative strategy could be employed. The idea for a bicycle safety inspection program could be determined as a need by the children. The inspection could be planned and operationalized by the entire class or by a committee of interested students.

G. Pose this question, "Is it important to help people in need?" An informal role-playing activity or a series of pictures could be used to generate further interest. Have students cite personal experiences. Have children suggest ways they could help people in their own community. (Some students, for example, might plan a visit to a convalescent home. The visit might include: a sing-along, choral readings, plays, group presentations, or a variety show. Upon return the group would discuss the trip.)

Focus questions: What did we see? How do you feel about what you saw? How do you think the residents might have felt? What are some other voluntary things we could do to help them? (Possible results: "Adopt-A-Grandparent Program"—a companion situation whereby the children could visit a resident regularly and do such things for him as reading, writing letters, running errands.)

H. Another suggestion that could be used to instill the need of helping others would be for the class/school to adopt a foreign child. A specified amount of money is paid each month to support the child, who in turn corresponds with the class. A suggested address:

Christian Children's Fund, Inc.
Box 26511
Richmond, Virginia 23261

Fund-raising activities could be planned incorporating interdisciplinary skills/content. (Suggested ideas: bake sales, making bread to sell, white elephant sales, car washes.)

I. Help students see that helping others applies not only to people outside our homes but also to our families. Have students role play a situation that involves helping and respecting families. Present the role-play situation with a dilemma. Provide a brief planning time for the actors/actresses. Discuss each reenactment. (See item II, C.)

J. Have the children design a questionnaire to see what roles children play in their homes. The questionnaire can be administered to their class and to other children in the school. The children in the class can then analyze the data and graph the results to see what tasks children do at home. A classroom presentation and discussion of the results might be beneficial as a summary exercise.

Focus questions for the discussion might include: Do you make your own bed at home? Do you help with the dishes at home? Do you empty trash? Do you do these things voluntarily or on request? What rules do you have in your home? How are they enforced? How are families alike? How are they different? Why?
(Slow learners will respond to the questionnaire and as a group you as the teacher will need to help them analyze it and depict the results graphically.)
(Gifted children can compare likenesses and differences among boys/girls, lower-elementary youngsters and upper-grade students.)

K. Challenge the children to a three-day experiment. In this experiment, the students would perform their specified tasks voluntarily at home. They would observe and record the changes in attitudes of parents, family members, and themselves. Following the experiment the children would discuss their feelings in small groups. Conclude with a discussion about the need for rules and concern for others at home, at school, and in the community.
(Slow learners will perform their tasks voluntarily at school with teacher guidance.)
(Gifted students can write editorials discussing the results of voluntary performance of home/school rules.)

L. Divide the students into groups of seven to ten each. Give them the Island Simulation Game handout sheet (item II, D.) and the instructions. After fifteen minutes, give chance cards to each group. The group may work on as many cards as it has time. Provide at least 30 minutes for small groupwork. Bring the class together to discuss the results. Help them formulate the conclusion that we need laws in society. Focus questions that could be used during the discussion: How did your group organize for survival? How did your group solve your chance card situations? What was one major problem all the groups had? Why did your group need to set up rules? Why do you think society needs laws? Explain. [Make sure gifted children and slow learners have an opportunity to work together.]

M. As a finale for this module, have the students gather data about the rules and laws of their community. Which ones are unwritten? Written? Students can interview individuals who are in law-related careers; they can acquire the local constitution and with proper guidance gain insights into how their community is run and the need for the laws that exist.

VIII. Evaluation: Teacher observation of students' participation in the activities and class discussion will be the basic method of evaluation. Expressed interest on the part of the students includes: bringing in articles and examples that relate to the material covered, asking questions, reading available books. The children's ability to demonstrate good citizenship qualities will also serve as evaluation of the success of the module. Two sample evaluation forms are included below.

TEACHER'S OBSERVATION FORM

Student's Name	Obj. A	Obj. B	Obj. C	Obj. D	Obj. E
	✔				
	○				
	✔				

(Make sure you conduct personal interviews with the slow learners to assess their progress. Make notes of the outcomes.)
(Use the personal interview technique for gifted students plus individual performance contracting to insure they are developing their potential.)

STUDENT PARTICIPATION CHECKLIST

1. No participation
2. Average Participation
3. Active Participation

Notes: Student's Name	Brought Articles	Asked Questions	Read Available Books	Did Research	Actively Participated in Simulation	Interviewed Individuals Connected with the Law

CLASSROOM RESULTS

Few special materials are required for the module and, in general, teachers found this to be a positive factor. They indicated that the module was easy to teach and that the suggested materials were interesting for the specified grade levels.

Three weeks seemed to be an appropriate amount of time for pupils to be able to achieve the objectives of this module.

The concepts were related to students' lives and therefore promoted ease of learning.

Most teachers considered the entry behavior indicators appropriate. Some indicated that role-playing experiences should be developed for those students who may have had little or no such experience previously before the module is introduced or else more attention should be given to it during the module.

Teachers felt the teaching procedures were quite appropriate. Students tended to get actively involved and enjoyed learning about citizenship.

Comments from classroom teachers included the following:

1. "Observation seems to be an appropriate form of evaluation since it shows effort and participation."
2. "The students could probe in greater detail the need for respecting opinions of their peers. This would be useful in a classroom situation where children have difficulty cooperating with each other and in getting along with others in school."
3. "My children wanted to go beyond the module. Thus children can develop rules and laws for their own classroom and possibly even for the entire school, such as behavior in hallways, lunchroom, and on the playground."

4. "Students who were extremely interested in a particular aspect of the module were able to do independent research on it. Their findings were presented to the rest of the class in an oral presentation, report, or other type of project."
5. "The module focuses on a topic which can and should be related to children's lives. The children are active participants in this learning situation and enjoy it. This was the strongest aspect of the module."

STUDENT BIBLIOGRAPHY

Bloomstein, Morris, *Verdict: The Jury System*, New York: Dodd, Mead, 1968.
Blue, Rose, *Grandma Didn't Wave Back*, New York: F. Watts, 1972.
Brindze, Ruth, *All about Courts and the Law*, New York: Random House, 1964.
Carlson, Natalie, *The Letter on the Tree*, New York: Harper & Row, 1964.
Fribourg, Marjorie, *The Bill of Rights*, Philadelphia: Macrae, 1967.
Gray, Genevieve, *Break In*, St. Paul: E. M. O. Corp., 1973.

TEACHER BIBLIOGRAPHY

Dove, Ann, Holly Churchill, and William B. Jarvis, *Micro-Community II for Elementary Grades, Grades 4–6*. Columbus, Ohio: Classroom Dynamics Publishing Co., 1973. (Kit)
Easton, David and Jack Dennis, *The Development of Basic Attitudes and Values Towards Government and Citizenship During the Elementary Years*; Final Report (ERIC ED016145). Washington, D.C.: Office of Education, Department of HEW, 1968.
Making Political Decisions: Citizenship in the American Democracy. Scottsdale, Ar.: Herald Press, 1978.
Mehlinger, Howard D. and John Patrick, *American Political Behavior*. H. S. Curr. Center in Government, Bloomington: Indiana University, 1968.
National Council for the Social Studies, *Social Education*. Washington, D.C.: National Council for the Social Studies, October 1976 and March 1977 issues.
Newman, Jason and Edward O'Brien, *Street Law: A Course in Practical Law*. New York: West, 1975.
The Rights and Responsibilities of Citizenship in a Free Society: A Law-Oriented Curriculum Guide for Grades K–12, The Missouri Bar Advisory Committee on Citizenship Education and The Missouri Department of Elementary and Secondary Education.

Family Membership

A family has been defined in various ways. Among the most common definitions are: All people living in the same house, a group consisting of parents and their children, a group of people related by blood or marriage, relatives, or all those descended from a common ancestor, tribe, clan, or race.

The content for the study of family is drawn from several disciplines such as anthropology, sociology, and political science. Key generalizations that provide a focus in planning and developing a module on the family include:

1. Families change in size and composition.
2. All human behavior is learned from other human beings through group interaction.
3. In every society and institution, regulations and laws emerge to govern behavior of individuals.
4. All members of a society are interdependent.
5. Every member of a society must function in different roles.
6. Norms and sanctions shape the behavior of group members.
7. Every individual faces a conflict between unlimited wants and limited resources.
8. Every individual needs love and someone to care.

A systematic and relevant program is necessary to insure that children have experiences related to their lives. To do this, the teacher and the school system must undertake a careful analysis of what would constitute the key components for the study of family. The following objectives may serve as a guide.

1. Given the need for individuality and the rights and responsibility of being an individual and a member of a family, a person demonstrates family membership by valuing and upholding the values of the family.
2. Given the need for individuality and the rights and responsibility of being an individual and member of a family, a person demonstrates family membership and the values of the family by demonstrating and resolving the problem of unlimited wants and limited resources.
3. Given the need for individuality and the rights and responsibility of being an individual and member of a family, a person demonstrates family membership and the values of the family by demonstrating the existence of interdependence.
4. Given the need for individuality and the rights and responsibility of being an individual and member of a family, a person demonstrates family membership and the values of the family by practicing the regulations that govern a family.
5. Given the need for individuality and the rights and responsibility of being an individual and member of a family, a person demonstrates family membership and the values of the family by interacting with other members of the family group.
6. Given the need for individuality and the rights and responsibility of being an individual and member of a family, a person demonstrates family membership and the values of the family by demonstrating understanding and practicing role shifts.
7. Given the need for individuality and the rights and responsibility of being an individual and member of a family, a person demonstrates family membership and the values of the family by abiding by norms and sanctions.
8. Given the need for individuality and the rights and responsibility of being an individual and member of a family, a person demonstrates family membership and the values of the family by sharing affection.
9. Given the need for individuality and the rights and responsibility of being an individual and member of a family, a person demonstrates family membership and the values of the family by accepting and adapting to change within the family.

The following sample teaching modules reflect one or more of the preceding objectives. We invite you to develop additional modules to provide students with real insights about family life and the multiplicity of reciprocal relationships that children are engaged in as family members.

LOWER

What Is a Family?

This teaching module is designed for children in the lower-elementary grades. Typically at these levels children will study the family. The primary objectives are to help children develop an awareness for what constitutes a family, how a family changes, how family members can cooperate in their work, and how family members can have fun together. The module provides opportunities for the children to become personally involved by asking that they look at their own families in terms of its members and how they can work and play together. Suggestions are made for a variety of hands-on activities such as making booklets and puppets, performing work at home, and learning games for family fun. Audiovisual materials which include children's library books, records, filmstrips and existing social studies textbooks could provide excellent source material. By the end of the module children will have opportunities to use the information that they have acquired in their own family setting and contribute to the learning of others.

I.   Grade Level: Lower Elementary

II. Special Materials:
   A.   Art materials
   B.   Cut out pictures illustrating families and nonfamilies
   C.   Record: SRA "Families and Our Working World" by Lawrence Senesh
   D.   Magazines
   E.   Filmstrip: "They Need Me—My Mother and Father" by Churchill Films
   F.   Forms for Work Done at Home (see item VII, K.)
   G.   Bulletin board depicting all types of families
   H.   Pictures depicting types of family work and types of family fun

III. Time: 2 weeks

IV. Concepts:
   A.   *Families* differ in *size* and *membership*.
   B.   *Families* are both *similar* and *dissimilar*.
   C.   Family members are labeled: *mother, father, sister, brother, aunt, uncle, etc.*
   D.   Families *change* in *size* and *composition*.

    E.   Family size may *change* due to such variables as *birth, death, graduation, marriage.*

    F.   Families have different kinds of *homes.*

    G.   Families have certain *needs* to be met.

    H.   Family members need each other and are said to be *interdependent.*

    I.   Family members provide *necessities* for each other.

    J.   *Work* is the physical or mental energy that is used to accomplish an objective.

    K.   *Work* is viewed differently by different people.

    L.   Family members do a variety of *types of work.*

    M.   *Fun* is viewed differently by different people.

V.   Objectives:

    A.   Students will be able to draw pictures of their families.

    B.   Students will be able to label all family members in their pictures.

    C.   Students will bring to class pictures depicting changes in their families.

    D.   Students will be able to verbally cite one way that they could be helpful at home. Students will implement their ideas at home during the week.

    E.   Students will be able to draw pictures depicting family fun.

    F.   Students will be able to teach their families at least one new game as demonstrated through observation.

VI.   Entry Behavior Indicators:

    A.   The students will be able to identify similarities and differences.

    B.   The student will be able to make comparisons.

    C.   The student will be able to use brainstorming techniques.

    D.   The student will be able to use role-playing skills.

    E.   The student will be able to use listening skills.

VII.   Teaching Procedures:

    A.   Ask these questions: Do you live by yourself? With whom do you live? (Help children conclude family.)

    B.   Have the children play the roles of family members: mother, father, grandfather, brother, sister, etc. Four to six children at a time will participate. Each group will select one situation. The situations will be: breakfast time, special holiday, Saturday morning, arriving home from school, working in the yard, getting into trouble, and eating dinner. The children in the audience are supposed to guess who the characters are and what they are doing.

        Discuss with the children their answers and opinions.

        Ask: How is it different at your house? How would you have played the roles?

    C.   Prepare a bulletin board with pictures of different families. Explain that each picture shows people living together as a family. Have the children bring in pictures for the bulletin board. Allow them to share what each picture illustrates.

D. Pose such questions as: Who is in this family? How many adults are there? How many children? How are these families alike? How are these families different? What are all the different names for family members? Write all these names on the blackboard. Examples: mother, father, brother, sister, grandmother, grandfather, stepfather, stepmother, etc. Who is in your family?

Pass out the white paper with *My Family* printed on the top. Then ask the children to draw a picture of their family. Remind the students to include themselves! Help the children print the "names" of the people in their families, such as mother, father, etc. When the children are finished with the drawings, display all the pictures and allow time for the children to look at them. Discuss the pictures with the children. Ask: How is your family like the families of other people in the class? How is your family different? Does everyone in this class have a family? How do you know? Stress that no two families are the same but they are all important.

(The teacher may want to have a small group session, for slow learners, centered on likenesses and differences. Many illustrations will be helpful.)

(Encourage gifted students to gather information about their family backgrounds, "Roots.")

E. Plan a discussion concerned with changes that take place in families. Do families always stay the same? How do they change? How has yours changed? (Bigger: new babies, grandparents come, remarrying of parents.) (Smaller: death, divorce, older siblings go to college, or get married.) Encourage the children to bring in pictures that illustrate changes in family size and composition.

F. Play SRA record—"Families and Our Working World."
Side 1, The New Baby. Discuss this situation. Has it happened to anyone in the class? Allow children who have had this experience to share it. You might invite a parent with a new baby to visit the class.

G. Assign the children to observe a family that they know, either their own, a relative's or a neighbor's, and tell how it has changed. Encourage them to bring pictures to class.

Discuss how sometimes changes in families make members sad or happy. Talk about feelings. Stress that changes make families different from each other.

H. Families also live in many different kinds of homes. Read a story about the various kinds of homes that families have. An example is *A World Full of Homes* by William Burns, published by McGraw-Hill. Relate the situation to the background experiences of the children. Discuss the fact that families have different types and sizes of homes. Ask the children to list some: house, apartment, trailer, etc. Instruct each child to cut out at least two magazine pictures of different sizes and kinds of homes. Make a bulletin board to depict the various types of dwellings or shelters that families occupy.

I.   Show the filmstrip entitled *They Need Me—My Mother and Father* by Churchill Films. Discuss the things that parents provide such as food, clothing, shelter, love, and friendship. Discuss how these needs can be met in a variety of ways.

J.   Have children brainstorm concerning all the ways they can help their families. Encourage children to implement one of their suggestions at home. On the following day discuss what each child did and how he felt before and after. Ask how he felt about what he did.

K.   Continue the discussion with the children focusing on the definition of work. Ask: What is work? What types of work are there? List their ideas on the board and then have the children play out some of these work roles. What type of work have you seen done at home? Who did it? List all of their ideas. Are there some types of work you have not done at home? Why? Could you do some of these things to help your family? Have the children fill in (with teacher's help) one new job they could do at home.

Example: I will _____
at home to help my family.   Student _____
                             Parent _____

The children should bring these back in two days signed by their parents. At this time discuss with the children whether they liked the

Utilizing all available school facilities can enhance children's learning opportunities. What key ideas about work as it relates to the family can be developed through this experience?

work they did and how they felt while doing it. Does work ever interfere with having fun? Discuss the idea that if everyone works hard and cooperates, often there is time for fun.

L. Show pictures and discuss:

What does your family do at home that you think is fun? Why don't we all do the same activities for fun? List family fun-type activities. Which ones are done by the whole family? Which ones are done by individuals within the family? Would you like to have your family do different things for fun than you do right now? What would they be? You might want to teach the children a series of games that they could play with their families at home.

(The teacher might want to conduct a small group session, for slow learners, to discuss various types of family fun. Each child could draw a picture to illustrate one type of fun the family enjoys or one type of fun the child would like the family to experience.)

(Gifted students could devise games and teach other students in class who in turn can teach their parents.)

M. Organize and have an indoor or outdoor picnic for the children and their families.

VIII. Evaluation:

There is one evaluation form for this module. Part of the evaluation is based on observation and the other is based on the assignments. The criteria for the module can be rated as follows:

√   Satisfactory
−   Did Not Complete
A   Absent
+   Extra Participation

Sample items to be included:

Name	Role Playing	Picture	Listening	Drawing	Participation	Discussion	Job Participation

CLASSROOM RESULTS

Teachers found the materials and concepts appropriate and adequate, although some felt that several of the concepts could be extended. For example, teachers said:

1. "I felt it necessary to deal in more depth with family changes in size and composition, incorporating differences in lifestyle, family needs, roles, and interdependence."
2. "I introduced the concepts of feelings of different people in the family concerning the problems of death or the absence of a parent."

The teaching procedures were considered to be specific and to offer many suggestions. Again, teachers adjusted the ideas presented to meet the needs of their children:

1. "I added the dimension of small groups through Magic Circle."
2. "The class observed families other than their own, and many of the students were truly amazed that other families did things so differently from theirs. They all shared stories and pictures of their observations."
3. "After discussing the various work roles of family members, the students selected a job to do with their family. I gave this assignment, as suggested in the module, and much to my surprise the students wanted to continue their jobs for the rest of the month. The parents were delighted at this sudden interest in schoolwork."

It was felt that more activities could be provided for those students who live in families with only one parent or guardian:

1. "I drew many resources from the library to help me with this problem and I used many of the activities centering on the idea that whoever takes care of these children is, in effect, taking their parents' place and therefore is just as important as their mother or father."
2. "Divorce, death, adoption, and desertion were topics I covered during 'Magic Circle.'"
3. "I used children's literature as a means of helping children relate to issues such as divorce, separation, desertion, and adoption."

Many teachers indicated that role playing was the strongest aspect of the module:

1. "I'm a firm believer that the only time to learn how to communicate your feelings is when you are young."
2. "The thing I liked the best was that the module stressed that there were no right and wrong families. All families were equally good."

There were many suggestions for future users of the module:

1. "Use as many visual experiences as possible."

2. "Children love to create things, so they should be encouraged to come up with ideas of their own."
3. "Be as flexible as possible to allow for the child's creativity."
4. "A section on family folklore or family heritage can prove very educational and rewarding to both students and teachers."
5. "If you cannot arrange a family picnic, suggest to the students that they organize a picnic for their family and relate their experiences to the class."

STUDENT BIBLIOGRAPHY

Arnstein, Helene S., *Billy and Our New Baby*, New York: Behavioral Publications, 1973.

Berger, Terry, *Big Sister, Little Brother*, Milwaukee: Advanced Learning Concepts, 1974.

Burns, William Aloysius, *A World Full of Homes*, Lexington, Mass.: McGraw-Hill, 1953.

Caines, Jeannette, *Daddy*, New York: Harper & Row, 1977.

Conta, Marcia, *Feelings between Brothers and Sisters*, Milwaukee: Advanced Learning Concepts, 1974.

Conta, Marcia, *Feelings between Kids and Parents*, Milwaukee: Advanced Learning Concepts, 1974.

Freeman, Lucy, *The Eleven Steps*, Garden City, N.Y.: Doubleday, 1975.

Greenfield, Eloise, *She Comes Bringing Me a Baby Girl*, Philadelphia: Lippincott, 1974.

Korpen, S. and Liesel Moak, *Mandy's Grandmother*, New York: Dial, 1975.

Miles, Miska, *Aaron's Door*, Boston: Little, Brown, 1977.

Zindel, Paul, *I Love My Mother*, New York: Harper & Row, 1975.

Zulotow, Charlotte, *A Father Like That*, illustrated by Ben Sheeter, New York: Harper & Row, 1971.

TEACHER BIBLIOGRAPHY

Green, Maureen, *Fathering*, New York: McGraw-Hill, 1976.

Scholastic Magazine, *Five Children* (1972); *Five Families* (1972); *Who Am I?* (1970); (three kits), New York: Scholastic Magazine Inc.

Shindelus, Mary J. and Mary Durkin, *People in Families* (first-grade level); *Taba Social Studies Curriculum*, Menlo Park, Calif.: Addison-Wesley, 1969.

Wernick, Robert, *The Family*, New York: Time–Life Books, 1974.

Wunderlick, N. A. and P. Pantalone, "Our Hearts Belong to Grandmas," *Instructor*, February 1977.

The American Family: Pioneer and Modern

This teaching module is designed for pupils in upper-elementary grades. Typically at these levels, students will study US history. The primary objective is to help students develop an awareness for the likenesses and differences in past and present family life. The module provides opportunities for students to become personally involved with the topic by asking that they take a look at their own family's contemporary lifestyle and then delve into family life of the past. Suggestions are made for a variety of data gathering techniques such as field trips, resource people, individual and group research, interviews, and questionnaires. Local, state, and US history books could provide excellent source materials. By the end of the module students will have opportunities to use the information they have gathered to assist them in clarifying their present attitudes and feelings about life today as compared to life yesterday.

I. Grade Level: Upper Elementary

II. Special Materials:
    A. Tape and slide series or pictures demonstrating the differences between family pioneer life and present-day family life
    B. *All Kinds of Families* by Norma Simon (book)
    C. You and Your Family—Survey (see item VII, B)
    D. Brown paper for Data Retrieval Chart
    E. Art supplies
    F. Library books (see Bibliography)
    G. Sears Roebuck catalogs, old and new

III. Time: 2 weeks

IV. Concepts:
    A. The *role* of *family members* in *pioneer life* was very different from the roles of *modern day* family members.
    B. Family life *changes* over time.
    C. A *pioneer* is one who goes before, preparing the way for others.
    D. *Roles* are sets of behaviors regularly expected of individuals.

V. Objectives:
    A. As a result of this module, the student will be able to write an essay comparing pioneer life in a given part of the United States with life in that area today.
        Ideas that might be included: Home maintenance, meeting daily needs, obtaining, preparing, and preserving food, obtaining, making, and caring for clothing.
    B. As a result of this module, students will decide whether they would have preferred pioneer life or present-day family life and list six reasons for their choice.

VI. Entry Behavior Indicators:
    A. The student should have previous experience in group work.
    B. The student should have previous experience in individual research.

VII. Teaching Procedures:
    A. Introduce the module by reading the charming book entitled, *All Kinds of Families* by Norma Simon.
    B. Provide the students with a Family Survey or have the class members devise their own. The survey or questionnaire is to be used to help students understand the role of their own families and the roles among family members.
    An example is as follows:

YOU AND YOUR FAMILY

1. Do you have a family?
2. Who is in your family?
3. Are you part of your family?
4. What is a family?

    _____ People who live in the same house.
    _____ People who live in the same house and do things together.
    _____ People who live in the same house and are related.
    _____ People who are related, but may not live together.
    _____ Don't know.
    _____ Other.

5. Does anyone in your family work away from home?
6. If so, who and what kind of work does he/she do?
7. Do you help with the inside or outside work?
8. What chores do you have to do at home?
9. Do you get an allowance?
10. Who cooks most of the meals in your family?
11. Do you have to do chores to earn your allowance?
12. Do any members of your family sew their own clothing or clothing for other members of the family?
13. Who does most of the grocery shopping in your family?
14. Who washes most of the clothes in your family?
15. Do you ever help cook, shop, sew, or wash the clothes for your family? Give specific examples.
16. What do you usually do when you get home from school?
17. How do you usually spend your school nights?
18. What do you enjoy doing most on weekends or holidays?
19. Look at the things you mentioned in questions 16, 17, and 18 and see how much time you usually spend doing things with your family. Do you wish you could:

    _____ Spend more time doing things with your family?
    _____ Spend less time doing things with your family?
    _____ Spend more time with only one person in your family?
    _____ Spend the same time you spend now with your family?
    _____ Don't know.

(The teacher may want to conduct a small group session, for the slow learners, during which time the students can complete the surveys.)

(Encourage gifted students to survey other individuals outside the classroom. Compare the results.)

C.   Administer the questionnaire. Analyze the results. The class could make a large graph-type bulletin board to reflect the findings. Have the class draw tentative conclusions.

D.   Have the students investigate their family backgrounds. Where did they come from? How did they live? What kinds of customs and traditions did they possess? How did they satisfy their basic needs? How did their families prepare meat, for example? Make bread? Prepare vegetables and fruits for winter? Encourage students to share pictures and objects that come from their backgrounds. Some children might have family members or relatives who could demonstrate one or more skills (such as bread making or making butter) that has been passed down from generation to generation.

(Have slow learners draw pictures and/or write short paragraphs that reflect data gathered about their backgrounds.)

(Some gifted students might like to study genealogy in depth. Family trees could be made.)

E.   Encourage students to write creative stories, poems, songs about their past. Compare their past with their present family situations. Discuss the advantages and disadvantages of each lifestyle.

(The teacher might work with the slow learners and create one song or poem that represents all children.)

(Encourage gifted children to interview elders and begin an oral history library for the classroom.)

F.   If your community or state has a pioneer cabin that is open to the public, we encourage students to visit it. Some of the experiences students might observe or actually be involved in might include:

Making bread and butter, smoking fish, making jam, drying fruits and vegetables, chopping wood, milking goats, making candles, natural dyeing, harvesting crops and storing them in a root cellar, spinning wood, trapping, and having a demonstration of pioneer tools.

If the opportunity is available, locate an appropriate film. Discuss the above activities in present-day terms. Which of these processes are carried out today? How do the processes differ? Encourage individual and/or group research.

G.   Invite a "History Buff" or antique dealer to the class to share ideas and information. Students should be involved in the planning of this activity.

H.   Visit a nearby museum to learn more about life of the pioneer families as compared to families today.

Encourage individual or group research for collecting data. Library time will be needed before and after the visit. A sample retrieval chart is included. The data gathered by your students might appear in this form:

COMPARING PIONEER FAMILY LIFE WITH MODERN FAMILY LIFE

Pioneer	Food	Modern
Pioneer	Shelter	Modern
Pioneer	Clothing	Modern
Pioneer	Energy sources and uses	Modern
Pioneer	Transportation	Modern
Pioneer	Communication	Modern
Pioneer	Leisure	Modern

Encourage students to add categories. Illustrations and pictures could also be added.

(Have slow learners work as a total group with the teacher to gather information.)
(Encourage gifted students to identify one or more activities in a specified category and do in-depth research. Some may wish to report their findings to the class.)

I.   Have each child complete this questionnaire and use it as a focus for class discussion and as a means of pulling the module together.

VALUES QUESTIONS

1. Being a pioneer full time was hard work. List the five modern conveniences you would miss the most if you would have lived during pioneer times.
2. If your family were going to move to a new planet and could not take everything it owned, what five things would you be sure to pack?
   What five things do you think your mother or father would want to pack?
3. If you had been a pioneer, what would have been your favorite chore?
4. What would have been your least favorite chore? Give two reasons for your response.
5. What do you most like doing with your whole family?
6. What do you most like doing with friends outside the family?
7. Would you rather be living in your area now or a hundred years ago? Why?

(The teacher may wish to hold a small group session with slow learners and have the students orally respond. The teacher could record their responses.)
(Have gifted students administer the questionnaire to a number of people and compare the results.)

VIII.   Evaluation:
     A.   The essay can serve as a vital evaluation measure.
     B.   Use a checklist for assessing and recording study habits and attitudes during time designated for research. The following will serve as an example:*

Behavior To Be Observed:	Names of Students
Locates sources of information	
Uses an index	
Uses a table of contents	
Uses a glossary	
Gathers data from charts, tables, maps	
Takes notes related to topic being investigated	
Gathers information from a variety of sources	
Organizes ideas in logical order	
Arranges information in logical order	
Draws "tentative" conclusions	
Is aware of author's bias	

     C.   A discussion graph would be a useful tool for assessment, especially if used with small groups. Chart who contributes, repeats questions, asks questions, and responds to questions.

---

*Adapted from Ellis, Arthur, and Janet Alleman-Brooks, "How To Evaluate Problem-Solving-Oriented Social Studies," *The Social Studies*, Washington, D.C.: Heldref Publications, Vol. 68, No. 3 (May/June, 1977) p. 101.

CLASSROOM RESULTS

Teachers found the materials and concepts appropriate, but some teachers felt that more time was needed to complete the activities in the module.

Students showed exceptional interest in family trees. One teacher added a four-generation chart to help meet student interest and needs: "My students really got turned on about the study of their own families."

The literary sources suggested in the module, as well as those provided by individual teachers, added a certain appeal. One teacher commented that the book *My Dad Lives in a Downtown Hotel* by Peggy Mann was a big hit: "About one-third of my class has experienced a divorce and never really had a chance to talk about it. The book provided a great entrée for such a discussion!"

Several suggestions were made for future users:

1. "Invite a visitor from another country to talk with your students about how their families are alike and different."
2. "Give yourself at least two extra weeks to complete the module. My students didn't want it to end."
3. "Encourage openness. Make the discussions lively."
4. "Locate information before you tackle the comparison section of the module."
5. "Use audiovisual aids and try to schedule a field trip to expand the experiences of the pupils."

STUDENT BIBLIOGRAPHY

Alleman, Janet and June Chapin, *Voice of a Nation*, Menlo Park, Calif.: Addison-Wesley, 1972.

Burns, Paul C. and Ruth Hines, *To Be a Pioneer*, illustrated by Frank Aloise, New York: Abingdon, 1962.

Madison, Winifred, *Call Me Danica*, Bristol, Fla: Four Winds, 1977.

Mason, Miriam E., *Caroline and Her Kettle Named Maude*, illustrated by Kathleen Voute, New York: Macmillan, 1951.

Mason, Miriam E., *Caroline and the Seven Little Words*, illustrated by Paul Frame, New York: Macmillan, 1967.

Perl, Lila, *Hunter's Stew and Hangtown Fry: What Pioneer America Ate and Why*, New York: Seabury, 1977.

Praeger, Ethel M., *Michigan—Land of the Big Water*, Chicago: Follett, 1965.

Sandler, Martin W., *The Way We Lived: A Photographic Record of Work in Vanished America*, Boston: Little, Brown, 1977.

Simon, Norma, *All Kinds of Families*, illustrated by Joe Lasker, Chicago: A. Whitman, 1976.

Tunis, Edwin, *Frontier Living*, New York: Crowell, 1961.

TEACHER BIBLIOGRAPHY

Banks, James A., Ed., *Teaching Ethnic Studies: Concepts and Strategies*, Forty-Third Yearbook of the National Council for the Social Studies. Washington, D.C.: National Council for Social Studies, 1973.

Cohen, L., "How To Teach Family History by Using an Historic House," *Social Education*, Vol. 39, (November 1975) pp. 466–469.

Gordon, Ira J. and William Breivogel (Eds.), *Building Effective Home–School Relationships*, Boston: Allyn and Bacon, 1976.

Hotkin, A. J. and H. C. Baker, "Family Folklore," *Childhood Education*, Vol. 53, (January 1977) pp. 137–142.

Scholastic Magazine, *Five Children* (1972); *Five Families* (1972); *Who Am I?* (1970); three kits. New York: Scholastic Magazine Inc. (filmstrips, records, etc. for early childhood—could be used for slow learners in this module).

Wernick, Robert, *The Family*, New York: Time–Life Books 1974.

Occupation

Occupation education, often referred to as career education, should not be defined too precisely. Rather it should be considered as a "means of helping youngsters to discover what their ultimate destiny in the world is."[3] Venn defined career education as "a concept, an approach to learning that represents expanded options for youth in school and renewal opportunities for those who have stopped school or are employed. It is a way to provide actual experience in real-life situations, relating education to our future careers and offering motivation for learning in school while developing skills which are salable."[4] Goldhammer and Taylor shed additional light on the issue by indicating that career education is a response to the pressing human issues of the day and provides a new paradigm for education. It is designed to capacitate all individuals for their multiple life roles. It is a systematic attempt to increase career options.[5]

The authors firmly believe that there is a vital element of compatibility between the social studies and career education or occupation education. In fact, career education might well be considered as a vital arm of social studies if career education emphasizes what I, as an individual, gain from the economy and what I must also contribute to the economy. Occupation education also, in most situations, emphasizes the structure of human relationships that are built around the provision for our economic and social needs.

The question that you as a social studies teacher must ask is, "What can I as a social studies teacher do to promote occupation education?" Perhaps the view you hold and express is a major contribution. Career education must be viewed in its total societal context rather than in the framework of just a narrow vocation or occupation. You, as a teacher, can help develop the kinds of materials that will help youngsters understand the reality of the world in which they live.

---

[3]Goldhammer, Keith, "Career Education and the Social Studies," *Social Education*, Vol. 37, No. 6 (October 1973), p. 484.

[4]Venn, Grant, "Career Education in Perspective," *Yesterday, Today, and Tomorrow* (Washington, D.C.: National Association of Secondary School Principals, 1973).

[5]Goldhammer, Keith and Robert Taylor, *Career Education Perspective and Promise* (Columbus, Ohio: Merrill, 1972).

The emphasis of career education or occupation education in the elementary grades is the broad exploration of occupations or career awareness. Smith suggests that the school is mandated to provide experiences whereby youngsters can:

1. expand their knowledge concerning the magnitude of the working world
2. appreciate the various broadly defined methods of work
3. systematically diminish the distortion among various occupations[6]

A systematic and relevant program is necessary to insure that children have experiences within the realm of this life role. The experiences must be seen by the child as an integral part of life—experiences that can be operationalized immediately. To accomplish this the teacher and school system must undertake a careful analysis of what would constitute a comprehensive occupational role and yet be cognizant of the developmental level of the students. The following objectives developed by the authors can serve as a guide:

1. Given the need for individuality and self-fulfillment, the person demonstrates responsibility in classroom work activities.
2. Given the need for individuality and self-fulfillment, a person demonstrates respect for others by participating and sharing in classroom and homework activities.
3. Given the need for individuality and self-fulfillment, the person demonstrates both in and out of school situations, understanding of the seven meanings of work by participating in real work situations according to his or her stage of development.

Below are activities reflecting seven different meanings of work:

1. Produce income and benefits
2. Occupy oneself in an interesting way
3. Maintain or increase social status
4. Have satisfactory social interaction
5. Give oneself a sense of identity
6. Supply goods/services
7. Be creative and self-fulfilling[7]

(According to Good and others, an alternative conception of work must also be considered. They suggest you see US Department of Labor, Bureau of Labor Statistics, "Work Attitudes of Disadvantaged Black Men: A Methodological Inquiry," by Philip B. Springer and Sidney C. Anderson, Report 401. Washington, D.C.: Government Printing Office, 1972.)

Most exemplary programs suggest that career education in elementary education should focus on overall types of jobs and broad interest areas instead of specific jobs.

[6]Smith, Edward, "Vocational Aspects of Elementary School Guidance: Objectives and Activities," *National Vocational Association* (June 1970), p. 279.

[7]Good, Patrick K., Michael G. MacDowell, Peter R. Senn, and John C. Saper, "Should We Teach about Work in the Social Studies," *Social Education*, Vol. 41, No. 2 (February 1977), p. 136.

The following is an example of highly recommended content from Gysbers and Moore's material, "Career Development in the Schools."[8] It is also reprinted in the October 1973 issue of *Social Education*.

SUGGESTED CONTENT AND ACTIVITY EMPHASES IN CAREER DEVELOPMENT PROGRAMS

Grades	Types of Learnings	ELEMENTARY GRADES	
		Selected Examples of Content	Selected Examples of Activities
K		Who am I?	Listening
1		How do I relate to my environment?	Observing
2	↑ ↑ ↑ Perceptual — Conceptual — Generalization ↓ ↓ ↓	Workers in the home and school	Contrasting
		Workers in the community	Differentiating
			Manipulating
			Field Trips
			Worker Role Models
3		Continuation of exploring self in regard to work and education world	Field Trips
			Demonstrations
4		Wider range of occupations examined	Work Simulation
5		Work takes on additional meanings	Role Playing
6	↑ ↑ ↑ Perceptual — Conceptual — Generalization ↓ ↓ ↓		
		MIDDLE SCHOOL GRADES	
7		Purposes of education	Simulation
8		Study of occupations	Tryout
9		Career decision-making processes	Work Simulation Exploring Work Experiences

Occupation or career education beyond the sixth grade should emphasize an investigation of the great variety of vocational choices that are open to individuals. Another way of expressing it is that career education beyond the sixth level emphasizes career exploration.

To achieve the goals of occupation education, there is absolutely no limit to the type and variety of teaching/learning strategies and class projects that you, the

[8]Gysbers, N. and E. J. Moore, "Career Development in the Schools," in G. Laws (Ed.), *Contemporary Concepts in Vocational Education*, First Yearbook (Washington D.C.: American Vocational Association, 1971).

teacher, can develop. The home, school, and community all provide a wealth of materials and thus are a bank of both primary and secondary sources.

It is not intended that occupation education be added to the curriculum. So often we want to "tack on" another piece of content, yet we are unwilling to remove anything! Occupation education thus should be integrated with those content areas already a part of the curriculum. In utilizing an integrated approach, it is hoped that career education will enable the child to relate occupational clusters to each other, to the economic growth, and to social interaction in general.

The market appears flooded with occupation or career education materials today. If you are planning a career education module with your students, we would suggest that you make use of one of the following exemplar programs. These will perhaps get you pointed in the right direction: US Office of Education Career Development Model; New Jersey Career Development Model; North Dakota Exemplary World of Work Project; Detroit's Developmental Career Guidance Project; Rochester's Project BEACON; or Texas' Career Development Curriculum Guide.

The following sample modules can serve as a springboard for developing occupational materials appropriate to your grade level.

LOWER

Initial Exposures to Careers

This teaching module is designed for children in lower elementary grades. Typically at this level children will study the family and the school and often some aspects of sociology will be emphasized. The primary objective of this module is to help children develop an awareness for the multiplicity of jobs that exist among family members, at school, and in the community and help them realize the interdependence of people in terms of work to be done. The module provides opportunities for children to become personally involved by beginning first with the likenesses and differences among children. Each child is able to identify his favorite activities and what activities he does at home, at school, or in the community that constitute work. During the module the child will have new job experiences. Suggestions for activities include making a bulletin board, puppetry, performing jobs at home, inviting parents to the classroom as resource people, planning and participating in a Career Day, and making a collage. The local community as well as existing textbooks that deal with family, school, or careers could provide excellent resource material. By the end of the module the child will have encountered many experiences that will touch his personal life and facilitate his present ability to provide help in family and school jobs to be done. In addition, the child will have an increased awareness of the multiplicity of jobs that exist in his community and the interdependence that exists among the individuals who perform them.

I. Grade Level: Lower Elementary

II. Special Materials:
   A. Pictures of children from various parts of the world
   B. Pictures of children engaged in a variety of activities
   C. Art materials
   D. "How I Can Help At Home" Checklist

HOW I CAN HELP AT HOME

Name _____

Job:	Sun.	Mon.	Tues.	Wed.	Thurs.	Fri.	Sat.
Make beds							
Pick up clothes							
Help with dishes							
Set table							
Take out garbage							
Feed pet							
Water plants							
Rake leaves							

   E. "How I Can Help At School" Checklist

HOW I CAN HELP AT SCHOOL

Name _____

Job:	Sun.	Mon.	Tues.	Wed.	Thurs.	Fri.	Sat.
Keep desk clean							
Water plants							
Pass out paper							
Hang coat up							
Take note to office							
Put litter in basket							
Put games away							

   F. "People I Know and the Jobs They Hold" Flow Chart

Interview people you know about the jobs they do. Complete the chart with the information you gather.

   G. *About Garbage and Stuff*, New York: Viking Press, 1973.

III. Time: About 3 weeks

IV. Concepts:
   A. *Individuals differ* in terms of *physical, intellectual,* and *emotional characteristics.*
   B. People are *interdependent* in terms of *work* done.

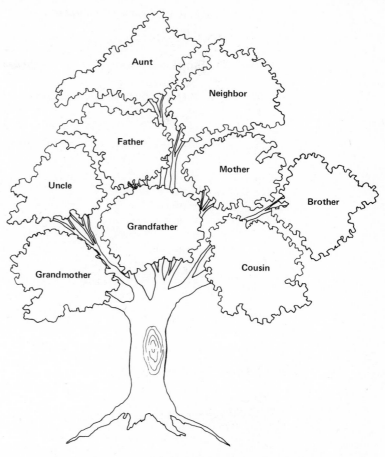

C. Members of individual *families* have *jobs* to do.
D. The *jobs* family members do satisfy needs.
E. Many *people work* to *meet* the *needs* of *children* at *school*.
F. There are many *jobs* to be performed in the *community*.

V. Objectives:
    A. The student will be able to orally list the occupation(s) of his family members.
    B. The student will be able to identify by drawing pictures, two jobs he helps with at home and two he helps with at school.
    C. Given pictures of school helpers, the student will be able to state orally the duties of each helper.
    D. The student will be able to identify six jobs or careers he has learned about and briefly describe each. This may be done and observed through role playing and pantomiming.

VI. Entry Behavior Indicators:

A.   The child should be able to participate in a class discussion.

B.   The child should be able to listen to others while they are speaking without interrupting.

VII.   Teaching Procedures:

A.   Show the students several pictures of children from various parts of the world. Pose such questions as, "What do you notice about each picture?" "Are there any similarities among these pictures?" "Differences?" The teacher should attempt to focus on the fact that individuals differ in physical, intellectual, and emotional characteristics. There are, however, many similarities that exist among most children.

B.   Show pictures of children engaged in various activities, eating various kinds of foods, and playing with various kinds of animals or toys. Discuss likenesses and differences.

C.   Have the students choose partners and discuss how they are alike and different from their partners. Use lists of characteristics to generate comparison, such as hair, eye color, height and weight, favorite colors, favorite foods, favorite books and records, etc.

D.   Make a bulletin board entitled "These Are a Few of My Favorite Things." After a brief discussion, ask students to draw pictures of their favorite things. They can be placed on the bulletin board.

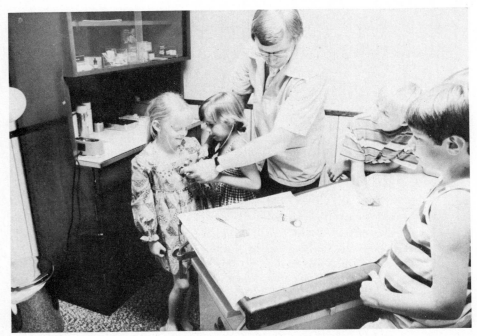

The community is an untapped resource for learning about occupations. With proper planning, coordination, and cooperation, both children and adults can be enlightened.

E.   Discuss the results of the bulletin board activity. Then pose this question, "Do any of the things you love to do represent work?" Why or why not? Brainstorm about the kinds of work children can do. Categorize the responses according to where it is done—at home, at school, in the neighborhood. Pose such questions as "How do you act when you are at your jobs?" "Are you careful?" "Why are these jobs important?" "How do you feel when someone says you did a good job?"

F.   Present the students with a series of situations that occur at home. (Examples: cooking, cleaning, setting the table, doing dishes.) Have students role play each. The audience must be prepared to describe what is happening. Questions focusing on the discussion might include: "What are some of the jobs a family must perform?" "What is your role in the family?"

G.   Discuss the "How I Can Help at Home" checklist. Have students record the appropriate data for one week and bring the results to class for analysis and discussion.
(The teacher may want to help slow learners fill in their charts each day at school.)
(Gifted students might interview their parents to find out what kinds of tasks they had to do when they were children.)

H.   Invite one or more families to class and have each person describe his or her role in the family and the jobs performed at home and any performed outside the home. Encourage them to bring pictures and manipulative materials for the students.

I.   Present the students with "People I Know and the Jobs They Hold" worksheet. Ask them to interview relatives and friends to learn more about the jobs they do.
Provide ample time for the completion of this activity.
(The teacher will want to go over the worksheet with slow learners as a group. Perhaps they could bring their information to school and the teacher could help them to complete it. They might also use pictures to represent the information.)
(Have gifted students seek in-depth information concerning the jobs of the individuals they interview.)

J.   Read the book *About Garbage and Stuff* by Ann Shanks. This book shows and tells about the importance of a job often considered undesirable in our society. Ask questions such as, "Why are these jobs necessary?" "What if no one would do them?"

K.   If possible plan a "Career Day" for children. Have each child visit a local establishment for a day. With proper planning, coordination, and cooperation this can be a fantastic experience for even the early elementary child! Discuss the results.

L.   In addition to jobs performed at home and in the community there are many jobs performed by people at school. Have children brainstorm about the possible ways they can help at school. Have them use the "How I Can Help at School" chart for a week and discuss the results. "What happens when someone doesn't do his job?" "Is it important to like what you do?" "How can you make your jobs more pleasant?" "Do boys and girls do the same jobs?"

M.   Invite various members of the school staff to the classroom to discuss their jobs. Prior to their visits have students generate lists of questions they would like to have answered.

(The teacher might want to meet with slow learners in a small group session to seek questions they'd like to have answered.)

(Have gifted students gather information about each of these individuals prior to the session and share unique information with the rest of the class. For example, for a hobby the superintendent might be a rose gardener.)

N.   Provide ample time for children to peruse the library to read books about careers.

O.   Have the students make a large collage to depict all the possible job opportunities (career opportunities that exist) in the community. As a total class or individually write a story (or stories) about "Occupations in Our Community Today."

VIII.   Evaluation:

A.   Personal interviews, though often very time consuming, can be extremely useful with students whose reading and writing skills are limited. This technique (tool) provides a teacher with a wealth of formative, diagnostic information as well as summative information. One interview per student during the module is desirable.

B.   Artifacts can be a very useful tool for the teacher. When the student's work is collected, analyzed, and displayed it has the potential of making assessment and diagnosis practical and meaningful.

CLASSROOM RESULTS

Teachers found the concepts and teaching procedures appropriate:

1.   "Examples were continually given both verbally and visually."
2.   The Career Day Visitations and 'acting-out situations' seemed to exhibit the most successful learning situations."
3.   "The teaching procedures were specific, yet left room to accommodate varying situations."
4.   "My particular group had never experienced any career orientation and they found the module stimulating."
5.   "The group I work with tends to be very theatrical and thoroughly enjoyed playing roles and being interviewers."

Several teachers shared their ideas for accommodating individual differences:

1. "A few children interviewed people about jobs while some brought their parents to class to discuss their jobs."
2. "Initially I had the children tell each other about the jobs they would like to hold when they are older; then I had them find pictures that depicted the occupation and write a brief paragraph telling why they wanted to pursue that career."
3. "Near the end of the module I had children make individual collages that depicted job opportunities."
4. "I had each child draw a picture using fabric crayons of what they wanted to be. I ironed them on one of my skirts, which I wore to class. The children loved the results.

According to teachers the strength of the module was interaction:

1. "It demanded interaction of students at all times."
2. "Expository teaching was limited and the availability of inquiry into personal households and community members in and out of school helped children gain a perspective of job duties and their importance."

STUDENT BIBLIOGRAPHY

Ancona, George, *And What Do You Do?* New York: Dutton, 1976.

Benson, Christopher, *Careers in Animal Care*, Minneapolis: Lerner Publications, 1974.

Benson, Christopher, *Careers in Education*, Minneapolis: Lerner Publications, 1974.

Berger, Melvin, *Jobs That Save Our Environment*, New York: Lothrop, 1973.

Cooke, David, *How Books Are Made*, New York: Dodd, Mead, 1966.

Davis, Mary, *Careers in a Bank*, Minneapolis: Lerner Publications, 1975.

Goldreich, Gloria and Esther Goldreich, *What Can She Be?* New York: Lothrop, 1973.

Greene, Carla, *I Want To Be a Fireman*, Chicago: Children's Press, 1959.

Greene, Carla, *I Want To Be a Mechanic*, Chicago: Children's Press, 1959.

Ray, Jo Anne, *Careers in Computers*, Minneapolis: Lerner Publications, 1973.

Rowe, Jeanne, *City Workers*, New York: F. Watts, 1969.

TEACHER BIBLIOGRAPHY

Goldhammer, Keith, "Career Education and the Social Studies," *Social Education*, Vol. 37, No. 6, (October 1973).

Goldhammer, Keith and Robert Taylor, *Career Education Perspective and Promise*, Columbus, Ohio: Merrill, 1972.

Good, Patrick K., Michael G. MacDowell, Peter R. Senn, and John C. Saper, "Should We Teach about Work in the Social Studies," *Social Education*, Vol. 41, No. 2, (February 1977).

Gysbers, N. and E. J. Moore, "Career Development in the Schools," in G. Laws (Ed.), *Contemporary Concepts in Vocational Education*, First Yearbook, Washington, D.C.: American Vocational Association, 1971.

Venn, Grant, "Career Education in Perspective," *Yesterday, Today and Tomorrow*, Washington, D.C.: National Association of Secondary School Principals, 1973.

Occupations and Human Equality

This teaching module is designed for students in the upper-elementary grades. Typically at this level pupils will study the United States, Western and Eastern Hemispheres, or they will have a course designed to teach about career education. In either situation this module could be useful. It begins with the existing careers in the students' immediate community. The primary objective of this module is to help students develop an awareness for the multiplicity of adult careers that exist in one's immediate community and then to assess what types of work upper-elementary students could do in the area. Finally students are given the opportunity to establish their own placement service for the community. Human equality will be practiced in their placement center. The module provides opportunities for students to become personally involved through completing an application, interviewing, and actually performing tasks in the community. Other activities include role playing, inviting individuals in nontraditional work roles to visit the classroom, preparing a bulletin board, and visiting a local business establishment. The local community as well as existing textbooks that deal with careers at local, state, national, or international levels could provide excellent resource material. By the end of the module students will have experienced many facets of career education. They will actually come to realize what it is like to be a part of the work force and will have acquired beginning skills that they can use now and forever in becoming contributing members of society in the world of work.

I. Grade Level: Upper Elementary

II. Special Materials:
   A. Bulletin board materials to depict "Careers and Human Equality"
   B. Record, "Free to Be" by Marlo Thomas, produced by *Ms. Magazine*
   C. Field trip preparations to visit a single business
   D. Resource books concerning Occupations/Minorities
   E. Magazines
   F. Job applications
   G. Placement center facility and materials

III. Time: 3 weeks (and longer for placement service)

IV. Concepts:
   A. We all have some things we like to do and some things we do not like to do.
   B. We are like other people in some ways and different in other ways.
   C. We all are good at doing certain things.
   D. Individuals play several roles in society.
   E. Careers formerly occupied by males are now being pursued by females, and males are beginning to pursue careers traditionally occupied by females.

    F. There are many careers represented in our school and community.

    G. Countless jobs must be performed by many different kinds of people everyday to insure that the community runs smoothly.

    H. It takes many kinds of people and many different jobs to run a single business.

    I. Every job/occupation has requirements that are specific to that career. Usually job applications are used in an attempt to match the individual to the job.

    J. Often interviews are conducted by placement services or employers in an attempt to match the potential employee with the job.

V. Objectives:

    A. At the end of this module, the student will be able to list 10 things he learned about Career Education and Human Equality as it applies to his community.

    B. By the end of this module the student will be able to identify specific skills needed for specific jobs, complete a job application, interview for a job, and through the Student Placement Center (established as a part of this module) acquire a job (weekend, after school, etc.) in the community.

VI. Entry Behavior Indicators:

    A. The student should have experienced an occupation or career awareness module in the early elementary grades.

    B. The student should have previous experience in small group work.

    C. The student should have previous experience in interviewing and using the telephone.

    D. The student should have previous experience in notetaking.

VII. Teaching Procedures:

    A. Begin the module with background music from "Free To Be" by Marlo Thomas.

    B. Focus the discussion on student reactions. How are we alike? How are we different? Is it OK to be different? Why? Why not?

    C. Have each student make a collage, a coat of arms, a picture, personal collage box, or other type of visual aid to depict himself (likes, dislikes, what he does, etc.). Share the results with the class. Focus on the point that even as one person we have many roles to play.
(The teacher might conduct a small group session with slow learners and suggest that each student identify 3 things that describe him or her. Perhaps all children should use similar media, such as a coat of arms or collage.)
(Gifted students might want to design 2 visuals—one that reflected them 2 or 5 years ago and one that reflects them today. Compare.)

    D. Begin the lesson by appearing in an outfit that depicts a role other than a teacher role that you play. (For example, a painter, cleaning lady, gardener, mechanic.) Discuss the fact that roles for women (or men) are no longer set and also the fact that we play many roles.

E. Have a blank bulletin board set up with the caption "Careers and Human Equality." Discuss its meaning. Have students find pictures that accurately represent the caption.

(Have a small group session for slow learners to discuss equal rights. Work on vocabulary building. Have students pantomime examples and nonexamples.)

(Have gifted students find examples of human equality in the community. Have them bring in pictures with captions to illustrate.)

F. Give students opportunities for individual or group research to learn more about careers now pursued by females, which formerly were pursued by males only and vice versa. Have them take notes and orally share their findings.

(The teacher will want to select high interest/low readability books for slow learners. They could share their stories in the small groups.)

(Have gifted students select one career and explore it in depth. They should be encouraged to write written reports.)

G. If possible, invite individuals from the community who fit in the above category to visit the class and discuss their chosen careers. Make sure students are involved in the initial planning. (For example, a male nurse, a female lineman, a female service station attendant.)

H. Introduce the students to the idea that there are many other jobs and careers represented in their community. Plan a walking trip to observe these. Have students keep a record of their observations. Discuss the results.

(The teacher will want to prepare a simple checklist to record observations for slow learners.)

(Gifted students might be encouraged to interview some of the individuals they observe during the field trip. They could do this during free time or after school.)

I. Use appropriate filmstrips, records, or books to help students realize that there is a multitude of careers in our world today. Have each student select one career he or she would like to learn more about and gather data accordingly. Whenever possible, utilize the human resources in the community. If students have not had a "Career Day" in school prior to this module, it could be a very worthwhile experience.

(The teacher might plan several small group sessions for slow learners during which time the students as a group would explore several careers, using high interest/low readability material.)

(Gifted students can continue their data gathering by interviewing individuals in the community.)

J. Plan and visit a local business in an attempt to help students see the variety of jobs that need to be done under a single management. Have each student interview a single employee. Record the data. When the class returns to school discuss the results.

(The teacher will want to accompany slow learners as a group to conduct an interview with an employee. The teacher will want to prepare a simple checklist that the students can use in gathering the data.)

(Gifted students could be encouraged to interview an employee in another business who has a similar job. Compare the results.)

K. Discuss with the students the fact that job applications/interviews are often used to screen individuals and match the job with the applicant. Have application forms available. Have students observe and react.

L. Help students see that many of the jobs they have observed are adult-oriented. Focus the discussion on, "What types of jobs could you hold?" "What types of requirements are there for those jobs?" "What types of experience have you had that make you a potential candidate for a specific job?" (Examples of jobs include washing cars, babysitting, gardening, raking leaves, shoveling snow, washing windows, etc.) With the cooperation of the principal, parents, community, other teachers, and students set up a Placement office that will take applications, conduct interviews, write ads for school newspapers, etc., in an attempt to employ students in their free time. Ideally, a school telephone could be "manned" for this purpose. (One hour, for example, each day) This project has been done and it works!

(The teacher will need to spend more preparation time with slow learners in small groups. Initially the employers could be individuals from the school.)

(Gifted students could be given leadership responsibilities in the Placement Office.)

M. Make sure that there are frequent sessions to assess problems, concerns, successes, etc., in the project. This project works very well when integrated with language arts.

VIII. Evaluation:

A. Use observations and anecdotal records to assess the behaviors of each child during the Placement Service preparation and implementation.

B. Checklists enable the teacher to identify basic skills and assess the extent of their use by the students. By keeping a daily or weekly checklist the teacher can diagnose both individual and group performance. An example follows on p. 286.

DATA GATHERING*

Behavior to be observed	John	Deb	Bob	Sue	Daisy	Mike	Tom	Jan
Locates sources of information								
Acquires appropriate materials								
Uses an index								
Uses a table of contents								
Uses a dictionary								
Uses several sources								
Takes notes								
Conducts interviews								
Arranges ideas in order								

CLASSROOM RESULTS

Teachers seemed to feel that the teaching procedures were appropriate. Making collages, interviewing, inviting speakers to the classroom, and having a placement service seemed to be the most popular activities. One teacher mentioned that her students really enjoyed filling out a MacDonald's application form and engaging in the role-playing activities.

Several teachers suggested additional activities to accommodate individual differences:

1. "Those who were more interested in learning only about one career were asked to try and locate someone in that field and get a personal interview with her/him."
2. "We spent several additional sessions on interviewing, since my students had limited skill at the outset."
3. "I encouraged my students to take the walking trips on their own. It was educational for them to visit certain local businesspeople."

For the most part, teachers felt career awareness was the strongest aspect of the module:

1. "I believe that encouraging the students to think about their abilities, interests, and values helps them to learn about career opportunities."
2. "Exposing students to the various careers through literature, talks, and role playing helps plant the seed toward forming a beginning concept of an area of work best suited to their interests."

A number of excellent suggestions were made for future users:

1. "I would recommend that a section be introduced on 'Documents I Will Need.' While

*Adapted from article by Arthur Ellis and Janet Alleman-Brooks entitled, "How To Evaluate Problem-Solving–Oriented Social Studies," published in *The Social Studies*, Washington, D.C.: Heldref Publications, Vol. 68, No. 3 (May/June 1977), p. 102.

(Encourage gifted students to write a biography about one of these individuals.)

F. Have parents bring examples of their leisure activities to school and share their skills with the students. Allow all children (with parental consent) to explore the possiblities of an activity that seems particularly appealing to them.

G. Have the class explore hobbies. Many of them do not cost much money. Read from the list in *Hobby Collections A–Z* in an attempt to find out which hobbies seem most appealing to your students.

H. With pictures or actual objects, help students categorize hobbies according to the following: doing things, collecting things, learning things, and making things. Point out to students that when they select a hobby they need to ask themselves the following questions: Will I be using muscles and positions that I have not used before? Will it be too expensive? Do I have the facilities for it? Do I have enough ability for it? Can the ability be developed? Is it safe? Will it cause friction in the family? Am I interested enough to keep at it? Is there anything else I might be more interested in? Will it take up too much time and require more strength and energy than I have? (Questions are abstracted from an article by Ruth Winter, "Learn To Love Leisure," *Detroit Free Press,* August 1976, 1-c.)

I. Discuss a variety of possibilities that the students might pursue. Invite individuals from your community to bring their hobbies to your classroom.

J. If you as the teacher have a hobby, bring it to school to share with the class.

K. Discuss with children leisure activities which are more easily done in groups and which ones can be done alone. Pictures for motivation would be useful. Focus questions might include:
    1. Which of these activities have you participated in?
    2. Do you like to do things in groups or individually? Advantages?   Disadvantages?

L. Provide children with some time every day during this module and time every week throughout the year to do some exploring with leisure-time activities. Books, films, and resource people from the community are needed to provide a wide range of learning experiences. Again encourage individuals from your community to provide assistance in this endeavor. Retired individuals are often an untapped resource.
    (The teacher or another adult might work with slow learners and provide instruction for a specific leisure activity for the entire group.)
    (Encourage gifted students to gather information about unusual or unique leisure activities.)

M. As a class develop at least one individual leisure activity. An example is skateboarding. Another example is soap carving. If, for example, you select skateboarding:

1. Show the film "The Magic Rolling Board." It points out leisure skateboarding versus professional skateboarding, individual versus group skateboarding and dangers and precautions of skateboarding.

2. Have students build skateboards. Write directions on the board. Read *What Did You Do When You Were A Kid?* by Fred Sturner with Adolph Seltzer, while they are working on their projects. Evaluate the products. Do individual skateboarding.

N. Discuss the various groups that are involved in leisure activities, such as families, Cub Scouts, Brownies, and 4–H. Focus questions might include: What do these groups do in terms of leisure? What can families do in their leisure time? What are some of the things your family does? What could our class do as a leisure activity? (Examples: Checkers, bowling, basketball, Monopoly.) Allow time as a class to explore group leisure activities. Evaluate the results.

O. Bring in pictures of leisure activities available in your community. Place on bulletin board. Encourage students to add to the collection. Discuss each one. It might be fun to identify each location on a large wall map.

P. Divide the class into seven groups. Each group should choose a topic from one of these seven categories—sports, nature, spectator activities, school and mental activities, creative activities, organizations, and collections. Locate the activities in the community that fit each. The research should include the answers to the following questions: Who can participate? When? Where? How much? Other questions can be added. The students could make a large display or plan and produce a community directory that includes all of the leisure activities that are available in a given community.

(The teacher might work with slow learners as a small interest group. The group could go with an adult to observe some of these activities in progress.)

(Have gifted students explore costs involved in the activities, numbers of various age groups that participate, and other interesting, meaningful statistics.)

Q. Invite representatives of these activities to visit the class. When this is not possible or efficient, perhaps students can make cassette tapes on site.

R. Plan an avocation fair for the school. Demonstrate what types of leisure activities are available in the community.

VIII. Evaluation:

Checklists enable the teacher to identify potential skills and the extent of their use by students in problem solving. By keeping a weekly class checklist the teacher is able to diagnose both individual and group progress. Two examples are provided. Anecdotal records could also be used.

A.   CHECKLIST*

Name	Took Part in Defining Leisure/ Avocation	Took Part in Classi-fying the Activities	Participated in Magazine and Bulletin Board Activity	Made Comments	Asked Related Questions

B.   EVALUATION CHART

Name	Listens to Others 1 2 3 4 5	Contributes to the Discussion 1 2 3 4 5	Sticks to Topic 1 2 3 4 5	Gives Others Turn To Speak 1 2 3 4 5	Asks Pertinent Questions 1 2 3 4 5

*Adapted from the article by Ellis, Arthur K. and Janet E. Alleman-Brooks entitled: "How to Evaluate Problem Solving-Oriented Social Studies" published in *The Social Studies*, Washington, D.C.: Heldref Publications, Vol. 68, No. 3 (May/June 1977), p. 102.

    C.   Assess each student's response to the idea that one person's leisure can become another individual's profession.

    D.   Keep anecdotal records that reflect each student's participation in leisure activities.

CLASSROOM RESULTS

Teachers were pleased with the concepts and teaching procedures. They seemed to like the built-in flexibility of the module. A music teacher indicated that she had great success when using this module as an integral part of her music curriculum: "By finding out that the children like to be involved with music in their spare time, I got to know the students better. Students who normally are not inclined to speak out did talk about music and the various ways it fits into their leisure time. Students began to share their ideas and interests with each other."

Suggestions for future users included:

1. "I would suggest that the module be taught on consecutive days if possible so there is carryover from one class session to another. Students will be more likely to remember their survey sheets, materials for the bulletin board, etc."

2. "Write a letter to parents explaining the module on leisure and your objectives for it. Encourage them to participate in the module."

3. "Plan to teach this module in the spring. Children have more leisure time in the summer and the module prepares them for it."

STUDENT BIBLIOGRAPHY

Cox, Jack, *The Boys' Book of Popular Hobbies*, New York: Roy, 1956.

Fleishman, Sid, *Mr. Mysterious's Secrets of Magic*, Boston: Little, Brown, 1975.

Jaber, William, *Wheels, Boxes, Skateboards*, New York: Drake, 1977.

Lamb, Geoffrey, *Mental Magic Tricks*, New York: J. Nelson, 1973.

Leaming, Joseph, *Fun for Young Collectors*, New York: Lippincott, 1953.

Salny, Roslyn W., *Hobby Collection, A–Z*, New York: Crowell, 1965.

Sarnoff, Jane and Reynold Ruffins, *The Chess Book*, New York: Scribner, 1973.

Severn, Bill, *Bill Severn's Magic Workshop*, New York: Henry Z. Walck, 1976.

Sturner, Fred with Adolph Seltzer, *What Did You Do When You Were a Kid?* New York: St. Martin's, 1973.

TEACHER BIBLIOGRAPHY

Brightball, Charles K., *Man and Leisure*, Englewood Cliffs, N.J.: Prentice-Hall, 1961.

Corbin, Dan H., and William J. Tait, *Education for Leisure*, Englewood Cliffs, N.J.: Prentice-Hall, 1975.

Dumazedier, Joffre, *Sociology of Leisure*, New York: Free Press, 1974.

Kraus, Richard G., *Recreation and the Schools*, New York: Macmillan, 1964.

Leisure Today, published as a special insert in the *Journal of Physical Education and Research* of the American Alliance for Health, Physical Education and Recreation, 1201 16th St. N.W., Washington, D.C. 29936.

UPPER

The Community as a Resource for Physical Fitness

This teaching module is designed for students in the upper-elementary grades. Typically at this level students will study the community, state, or nation and often some aspects of geography will be emphasized. At this level, frequently we find mini courses are added to give new spark and fresh dimensions to the existing program. We also find that in the upper-elementary grades physical education is often taught as a separate subject. This module could fit any of the three categories. If taught in physical education class, it could be team taught very successfully with the social studies teacher. The primary objective of the module is to help students come to understand what avocation or leisure really is, what avocation options are available in their community, and what it is like to participate in physical activities that are individual, dual, or group oriented. The module provides opportunities for students to become personally involved in field trips, interviewing, and actual participation. Suggestions for activities include surveying, mapping, individual and group research, and involving the local athletic department. The local community as well as existing textbooks that deal with geographic phenomena or physical fitness could provide excellent source material. By the end of the module students will have encountered many experiences that will touch their personal lives and facilitate their present and future selection of physical activities that can be done individually or with two or more fellow students. They will also experience physical fitness and recreation as they relate to the enjoyment of leisure time.

I. Grade Level: Upper Elementary

II. Special Materials:
   A. Magazines/Newspapers
   B. Student log books
   C. Resource books and persons
   D. Maps—school, community, state, and national
   E. Addresses for recreational resources in the community

III. Time: 4 to 5 weeks

IV. Concepts:
   A. *Leisure* activities should be *self-fulfilling, personally enjoyable,* and *nonobligatory*.

B.   *Leisure activities should not infringe* on the *rights* of *others* and there should be a reasonable probability that they will *not* be *harmful* to *self* or *others*.

C.   *Free time* or *spare time* is the period you spend away from the nitty-gritty obligations that maintain your existence.

D.   Leisure activity can involve *physical development*.

E.   Physical activities can be *individual, dual*, or *group oriented*.

V.   Entry Behavior Indicators:

A.   The student should have previous experience in group work.

B.   The student should have previous experience in discussions.

C.   The student should have previous experience in conducting surveys and interviews.

D.   The student should have previous experience in using the library.

E.   The student should have previous experience in writing letters for seeking information.

VI. Objectives:

A.   The student will be able to list ten activities that involve physical development.

Combining physical education and social studies affords students a unique opportunity for exploring the avocational life role.

B. The student will be able to describe in writing the various functions of the recreational resources available to him in the community.

C. The student will be able to describe three individual physical activities, three dual activities, and three group activities.

D. The student will be able to participate in at least one new individual physical activity, one new dual activity, and one new group activity.

E. The student will demonstrate through class discussion and actual participation his or her awareness of the value of physical fitness and recreation and their relationship to the enjoyment of leisure time.

VII. Teaching Procedures:

A. Prior to beginning the module ask students to keep a log for one week of the major activities that consume their time.
(The teacher will need to work with slow learners as a small group each day to assist them in recalling and recording their activities.)
(Gifted students can break down their information very specifically according to time, cost, etc.)

B. On the day the module is begun, have each student analyze the results. Have each student categorize the activities according to work, spare time, leisure, or other. Stress the fact that spare or free time is that period away from the nitty-gritty obligations that maintain your existence while avocation or leisure is self-fulfilling, personally enjoyable, and nonobligatory.

C. Discuss the amount of time logged for television. What does this suggest? What effects does it have on family life, etc.?
(The teacher will need to work with slow learners to discuss what programs they have observed on television, what they learned from viewing them, and explore what they might have done if television were not available.)
(Have gifted students gather in-depth information on children and adults concerning their viewing habits.)

D. Assess the amount of time logged for physical activity. What does this mean? Would the pattern be different during a different week? Would it be different with a given population?

E. Have students begin to explore (through surveys, maps, and telephone directories) the types of physical activities that are available in their community. For example, can they go bicycling, mountain climbing, jogging? Can they participate in rugby, archery, hockey?
(The teacher might want to work with slow learners as a small group, using lots of high interest/low readability materials and as a group explore the possibilities of a specific activity in their community.)
(Gifted students can attempt to determine the numbers who participate in each age group, sex, and other variables they wish to explore.)

F. Have students locate where these activities exist, or potentially could exist. Have them locate each on a community map that will be displayed as a source of information. (Make sure students do not overlook the more common or simple activities such as jumping rope, etc.)

(The teacher will want to work with slow learners as a small group and explore the activities that are available within the school setting. As a group have them identify these on a map of the school. Have them present their results to the rest of the class.)

(Have gifted students explore the availability of those activities within the state and nation. Report their findings to the class.)

   G. Based on the above data, have students form small groups and investigate each physical activity in depth. Include such information as the following in the investigation:

     1. Cost
- a. What equipment is needed and what will it cost?
- b. If a uniform or special clothing is needed what will they cost?
- c. Will the participant have to purchase any special equipment?
- d. Are there special fees, charges, or memberships to be paid?
- e. What transportation cost, if any, is necessary in getting to the playing area for practice and/or matches?

     2. Time
- a. How much time should one spend practicing in developing, maintaining, and improving skills?
- b. How long does it take to play a game/match?
- c. Is this a seasonal or year-long activity?
- d. Is this an activity for lifelong participation or only for youthful years?

     3. Location
- a. Is this an indoor/outdoor activity?
- b. How much space is required for this activity?
- c. Is space available? How often? Under what conditions?

     4. Single-dual-team
- a. Is this an activity one does alone for self-development?
- b. Is this an activity requiring another participant?
- c. Will this activity require team participation which would likely limit the frequency of play in later years?

     5. Enjoyment
- a. Do you enjoy participation in this activity?
- b. What do you enjoy about this activity?
- c. Does participation in this activity promote growth in concepts of fair-play and good sportsmanship?
- d. Is there an element of competition with yourself or with others which you find enjoyable?
- e. Is this activity enjoyable for you both as a participant and an observer?

By the end of the module, the students should make a decision as to how they want to inform others about their findings. For example, they could use the hallway display cases to share their information and perhaps generate further interest among their schoolmates, or they could have an assembly. Students should be given time to visit the various centers where physical activities are occurring to gather additional information.

H. Have students be given opportunities to read various books related to the physical activity they are exploring. Also find opportunities for them to experience the activity they are investigating.

(The teacher will need to provide small group sessions for slow learners at which time they can explore a given activity.)

(The teacher will need to make sure that challenging reading materials are available for gifted students. Consultation with the athletic department could yield a wealth of information.)

I. Discuss the physical fitness aspect as a part of leisure. Have the students survey members of the community to determine their interest in/or concern for fitness. Discuss the results. Does the sample seem to be sufficient? Would a survey 50 years ago have yielded similar results?

(Have slow learners work as a small group with the teacher and survey school personnel.)

(Have gifted students survey retired individuals and discuss their present views versus those of 50 years ago. Have them report to the class.)

J. Introduce students to the 8 areas of physical fitness. They are as follows:

1. Power—explosiveness, ability to push or pull
2. Strength—being strong enough to lift
3. Muscular endurance—going on in an activity without tiring
4. Cardiorespiratory efficiency—strong heart and good wind
5. Speed
6. Agility
7. Balance
8. Flexibility—to bend or move and stretch

K. Demonstrate each of these fitness areas:
   (The athletic department could be a great resource!)
1. Power—measure vertical jump
2. Strength—push-ups, pull-ups, climb rope
3. Muscular endurance—400-yard race, 100 sit-ups, folk dance
4. Cardiorespiratory efficiency—measure heart rate before and after a student climbs up and down one step for 3 to 5 minutes
5. Speed—25- or 50- or 100-yard dash
6. Agility—a shuttle relay
7. Balance—use balance beam, walk straight line with eyes closed
8. Flexibility—stand on chair and measure how far students can touch their toes and reach below their toes with knees straight.

L. Invite individuals from the school athletic department to discuss physical fitness. Provide time for students to ask questions.

M. As an optional activity encourage students to plan and implement their own personal physical fitness program. Acquire assistance from junior high and high school athletes.

N. Plan a field trip or series of field trips. Examples of places to visit include health spas, YMCA, YWCA, sporting goods stores, college or university athletic center. Make sure students have participated in the initial planning and have identified questions to be answered.

O. Encourage students to make a bulletin board highlighting the sports events both during and after school that exist in their community.

P. Allow students ample time to investigate new physical activities. Discuss them in terms of the following: seasonal versus nonseasonal, individual, dual, or group, timely or lifelong. Have students present mini reports to the class using various types of media.
(The teacher will need to form a small group with slow learners and explore one activity.)
(Gifted students can be encouraged to explore a given physical activity in another part of the world; for example, tennis in Australia.)

Q. As a class, allow time for physical activities. Allow students to participate in one or more familiar activities and at least one unfamiliar one. (The time allotted and the places where students can pursue the activities are examples of variables that the teacher will need to work out with parents and administration prior to beginning the module.) The teacher should guide students in being ingenious and resourceful.

R. Have the students decide on a way of informing their peers of the results of their investigation and involvement of physical development as one dimension of leisure. The most valuable outcome will occur when the student implements some of the ideas he has explored into his own life both in and out of school settings.

VIII. Evaluation:

A. The real evaluation concerning the success of the module is the student's out of school implementation of a physical activity into his own life.

B. An in-school evaluation that can be used is the "I learned" statements. They can be written. Each represents a student initiated response.

C. A checklist can be used to assist the teacher in identifying basic skills and the extent that each student is using them. An example is on the next page.

D. Keep anecdotal records. Include comments concerning each student's participation in discussions and in actual physical activities.

BASIC SKILLS CHECKLIST

Student Names	Asks Questions	Makes Accurate Observations	Locates Places on Maps	Applies Ideas	Sees Relationships	Records Data	Classifies Data	Analyzes Data	Draws Conclusions

CLASSROOM RESULTS

Teachers were satisfied with the teaching procedures. In several cases teachers modified them to meet the specific needs of their students:

1. "We kept records on how we spent our waking hours, and we used them as a basis for calculating the amount of leisure time we have and determining how we can spend it better."
2. "We explored types of physical activities that were available in our community."
3. "After our visit with the physical education teacher we put together an activity book. The book listed games and sports that were individual, dual, or group-oriented."

Teachers' views varied concerning the evaluation section:

1. "I liked the evaluation section."
2. "I liked the evaluation section because by using the 'I Learned' statements and the checklist method I could check the basic skills of the lesson without the pressure of grades."
3. "I did not use any of the three suggested means of evaluation. The students' eager attitudes and excited behavior was the best evidence that they were increasing their awareness of the topic of leisure."
4. "I did not use the evaluation procedures. Their enthusiasm showed me they were learning."

Teachers tended to use the activities provided for individual differences and in several cases included additional activities:

1. "I had my students do several assignments in teams, with the 'better' students helping the 'slower' ones. I find that the 'slower' students shape their ideas into workable projects when assigned in this way."
2. "Advanced students dealt with percentages while the average students worked with actual numbers taken from the survey. 'Slower' students merely copied the charts and graphs."
3. "Many of the more advanced students became interested in out-of-school projects such as shopping, pricing equipment, and going to the public library to gather more information."

Many fine suggestions for future users were included in the teachers' responses:

1. "Previous organization with the physical education department is a must before starting the module."
2. "Introduce the term 'leisure' to the class through discussions and conversations with the students before assigning the students to write a log about their leisure activities."
3. "Notify parents of the module and encourage feedback from them. You might write a letter explaining the objectives and activities, noting the depth at which the students will examine leisure activities. I feel this would ease the minds of some parents who think we are merely playing games."
4. "If elementary teachers do not teach physical education, they should participate in the activities of the class along with the students. Encourage students to keep records of these activities and to improve their time, score, and number accordingly."

STUDENT BIBLIOGRAPHY

Antonnacci, Robert J. and Jene Barr, *Football for Young Champions*, New York: McGraw-Hill, 1958.

Antonnacci, Robert J. and Jene Barr, *Physical Fitness for Young Champions*, 2d ed., New York: McGraw-Hill, 1975.

Archibald, Joe, *Baseball*, Chicago: Follett, 1972.

Bach, Alice, *The Meat of the Sandwich*, New York: Harper & Row, 1975.

Coombs, Charles, *Being a Winner in Track and Field*, New York: Morrow, 1975.

Monroe, Earl and Wes Unseld, *The Basketball Skill Book*, New York: Atheneum, 1974.

Radbauer, E. and R.S. Radbauer, *Gymnastics School*, New York: F. Watts, 1976.

Sueling, Barbara, *Sports*, New York: Lothrop, 1975.

Sturner, Fred with Adolph Seltzer, *What Did You Do When You Were A Kid?* New York: St. Martin's, 1973.

US Government Printing Office, Washington, D.C. 20402 (Series of booklets on sports, hobbies, etc.)

US News and World Report, May 23, 1977.

TEACHER BIBLIOGRAPHY

Cutton, George B., *The Threat of Leisure*, New Haven, Conn: Yale University Press, 1925.

Dumazedier, Joffre, *Sociology of Leisure*, New York: Free Press, 1974.

Luschen, Gunther, "Some Critical Remarks Concerning the Sociology of Leisure," *Society and Leisure*, Bulletin for Sociology of Leisure, Education and Culture, Vol. 5, 1973.

Morries, Michael (Ed.), *The Emergence of Leisure*, New York: Harper & Row (Harper Torchbooks), 1974.

Owen, John D., *The Price of Leisure: An Economic Analysis of the Demand for Leisure Time*, Montreal: McGill-Queen's University Press, 1970.

Smigel, Erwin O. (Ed.), *Work and Leisure: An Economic Analysis of the Demand for Leisure Time*, Montreal: McGill-Queen's University Press, 1970.

Leisure Education Advancement Project, National Recreation and Park Association, 1601 N. Kent Street, Arlington, Va. 22209.

Personal Efficacy

Personal efficacy can be defined as the process of seeking and obtaining control over one's own life, and in so doing, acquiring decision-making competencies that enable one to gain power over self. Fundamental to this role is the acquisition of a positive, yet realistic self-concept.

As a child moves through developmental stages acquiring knowledge and having a diversity of experiences he is forming the self. The self is something which has a development. George Mead believed that at birth the self-concept is not there, but it occurs in the process of social experience. He felt that it develops in the individual as a result of relations to that process as a whole and to the other individuals in that process. Mead indicated that the self is basically formulated during the preoperational and concrete operational stages of development. In the first stage we begin to organize our perceptions of how others react toward us in social situations. He stated, "We get then an 'other' which is an organization of the attitudes of those involved in the same process."[13] At the later stage we begin to structure not only individual attitudes but also those of the entire social group to which we belong. The individual generalizes from a sample of individual responses to that of a collective response from members of his social group. While each child's self-concept is a reflection, it also has a unique pattern of its own. As a child organizes himself, he does so through his own perceptual screen. This process establishes one's perceptions about self and is referred to as one's self-concept.

To develop personal efficacy, the teacher and school system must undertake a careful analysis of what would constitute a positive self-concept and control over one's life. The following objectives might serve as a guide:

1. Given the human need for individuality and a positive self-concept, a person demonstrates personal efficacy by upholding his own values and attitudes.
2. Given the human need for individuality and a positive self-concept, a person demonstrates personal efficacy by gathering all available information.

[13]Mead, George H., *Mind, Self, and Society* (Chicago: University of Chicago Press, 1962), pp. 135/154.

3. Given the human need for individuality and a positive self-concept, a person demonstrates personal efficacy by asking questions and clarifying his values and those of the community.
4. Given the human need for individuality and a positive self-concept, a person demonstrates personal efficacy by deliberating before drawing tentative conclusions and looking at alternatives and consequences.
5. Given the human need for individuality and a positive self-concept, a person demonstrates personal efficacy by taking action on his decision.
6. Given the human need for individuality and a positive self-concept, a person demonstrates personal efficacy by evaluating his action and using the evaluation as a referent for future learning.

The following sample modules reflect these goals. While personal efficacy may be the focus for one to two weeks of formalized instruction, the authors believe it will be experienced and nurtured throughout the child's life both in and out of school.

LOWER

All of Us Are Unique Individuals

This teaching module is designed for children in the lower-elementary grades. Typically at this level children will study "Me" followed by a study of the family and school. The primary objective of this module is to help children realize the likenesses and differences among themselves and that each individual is unique. The module provides a multiplicity of activities in which the child can become personally involved; for example, each child will make a drawing of himself, make a "Me" book, and have the opportunity to participate in "This Is My Week." Other activities include listening to records, viewing filmstrips, and making collages. The local community as well as existing social studies textbooks that deal with "Me," family, and school could provide excellent resource materials. By the end of the module the child will have encountered many experiences that will touch his personal self and facilitate his ability to accept the idea that each person is unique—and that it is OK to be different.

I. Grade Level: Lower Elementary

II. Special Materials:
   A. Butcher paper and other art supplies
   B. Chart for illustrating physical characteristics—differences
   C. Cartoons or puppets depicting similarities and differences in characteristics—likenesses
   D. Films entitled, "People Are Different, Aren't They?" and "Understanding Ourselves and Others," 5 film unit, Troll Associates, New Jersey, 1975.

E. Record entitled, "Free To Be . . . You and Me," by Marlo Thomas and others, Bell Records, New York.
F. Pictures depicting individuals engaged in a variety of activities
G. "What Can I Do by Myself"—Filmstrip, Troll Associates, New Jersey, 1975.
H. Record, "You Are Special" by Mr. Rogers, Small World Records.
I. Picture/symbol checklist, activities that you can/can't do
J. Magazines

III. Time: 1 to 2 weeks

IV. Concepts:
A. Each *person* is a *unique individual*.
B. Each *individual* is *similar* to others in some ways and *different in some ways*.
C. *Individuals differ* in the things they like to do.

V. Objectives:
A. Given a situation of identifying likenesses and differences of personal characteristics, the student will orally identify one likeness and one difference.
B. Given an opportunity to depict the concept "I am unique" the student will make a display that reflects his understanding of this and behave accordingly.

VI. Entry Behavior Indicators:
A. The student will need to have an understanding of the terms likeness and difference.
B. The student will need experience in large and small group activities.
C. The student should have had a previous introduction to the body parts.

VII. Teaching Procedures:
A. Using a cartoon display (puppets could be substituted) of likenesses and differences, explore the following ideas with the class:
1. What can you tell me about the picture(s)?
2. Do you find anything funny about the picture(s)? If so, what?
3. Is there anything different about the cartoon characters?
4. Are the cartoon characters similar in any way?
5. Which is more important, the way a person looks or the way a person acts? Why?
6. In what ways are we alike?
7. In what ways are we different?
(Plan one or more activities for slow learners that require them to observe likenesses of objects and one or more activities that require them to observe differences. Use as many concrete objects as possible.)

(Have gifted students draw their own cartoons to depict likenesses and differences.)

B.   Have the children make drawings of themselves using a piece of large butcher paper, 36″ × 48″ for each child. Have the students take turns tracing their bodies and cutting out the results. Have them draw in physical characteristics and clothes to make a life-sized person. Have a large mirror available for children to use. This can be most effectively accomplished in small groups. Ask the child to be looking at what is similar and what is different.
(Have upper-grade students available to assist slow learners in this project.)
(Have gifted students compose jingles or rhymes to accompany their drawings. Older students could be helpful in recording their ideas.)

C.   Show the film entitled, "People Are Different, Aren't They?" Introduce the film by asking the children what they think the title means. Accept all answers. List the ideas on the blackboard. Follow the film with a discussion focused on differences. Add to the original list.

D.   Begin a "This Is My Week" Bulletin Board and Display Table. Encourage the student selected (everyone gets a turn) to bring in pictures that illustrate unique features about himself. Suggest pictures of the child's home, family, favorite activities, hobbies, etc. A display table could be added for objects: favorite toy, book, school subject, etc. The child selected for the week could be involved in selecting a game for class to play, and/or with the help of teacher, make special food for the class. (Establish guidelines at the outset.) Examples of foods include popcorn, jello, and bakeless cookies. Set aside some time each week for this project and the related class discussion.
(The teacher will need to spend extra time with slow learners in preparing the bulletin board and display area. Make sure every child gets an opportunity to verbally tell about the objects and pictures.)
(Have gifted students write experience stories about the objects and pictures that they bring.)

E.   Play "Free To Be . . . You and Me." Discuss. For example, when listening to the children's recording, discuss its meaning and how it applies to the children's lives now.

F.   Using a series of pictures that reflects uniquenesses of human beings, pose the following questions:
   1.   Which of the activities depicted in the pictures are you able to do?
   2.   Which of the activities are you unable to do? Why?
   3.   Which of the activities depicted in the pictures would you like to learn to do? How would you go about learning the activity?

G.   Show the filmstrip, "What I Can Do by Myself?" Discuss:

     1.   Could you do any of the same things the person in the film could do? Which things can't you do?

     2.   How did the boy in the film feel when he couldn't do something?

     3.   How do you feel when you can't do something?

H.   Play parts of the record "You Are Special," by Mr. Rogers.

I.   Organize the students in two's.

Explain that they are going to try several activities and they will observe which activities each can do and which their partner can do. A simple checklist with picture symbols could be passed out for keeping a record. The following activities will be attempted:

1.   Whistle

2.   Wink

3.   Rub stomach and pat head simultaneously

4.   Stand on one foot for one minute

5.   Snap fingers

6.   Touch toes without bending knees

7.   Write name with the hand not normally used

Analyze and discuss the results. Focus questions might include: Is it necessary that all of you are good at the same thing? Why? Why not? Why do different people like different things?

J.   Have children draw pictures of something they are good at and something they'd like to become better at. Show and discuss the results.

K.   Have children make collages to depict their feelings and interests. Share and discuss.

(Have slow learners draw a picture or finger paint to depict how they feel at a specific time. Have each child draw a picture or bring in an object that reflects a specific interest).

(Have gifted students write experience stories to accompany their collages.)

L.   Make "Me" books. Share and discuss.

VIII.   Evaluation:

A.   Collect, analyze, and display what the students have made for the module; for example, the display for each student of the week, the collage, and "Me" books. These have the potential for making evaluation and diagnosis practical and meaningful. Be sure to keep a record for each child.

B.   Interviews are time consuming. However, for students whose writing and reading skills are limited they are especially useful. An interview can provide formative, diagnostic, and evaluative information.

C.   Checklists can be used to record behavior observed. Examples of criteria that might be appropriate for this module include:

1.   Demonstrates a positive attitude toward self.

2.   Respects the uniqueness of others.

3.   Helps others.

CLASSROOM RESULTS

Teachers using this module had many comments on evaluation:

1. "The observable behavior was quite evident, especially in certain students. Those who had previously been so concerned about doing things (work papers, art activities, free time activities) like their peers, began to demonstrate a certain independence in doing things their own way."
2. "In doing the 'Me' books I had the children draw three pictures: one of themselves, one of their family, and one of their home. I asked them questions about their family, their favorite pastime, favorite food, and something they disliked doing. This was very enlightening to me as well as to some parents."
3. "During the module I observed that many children became more concerned about the feelings of others and took it upon themselves to help others in a positive, responsible way."
4. "I kept a booklet and recorded each child's participation in the activities and discussions that we had."

Several teachers shared ideas and made suggestions for future users of the module:

1. "School bus safety could be added if you teach in a rural area."
2. "You might stress a 'no gum chewing rule' if you have a carpeted classroom, as we do."
3. "I had the children bring in baby pictures of themselves, and we tried to guess who each one was. We then used them to make a bulletin board. They loved this activity!"
4. "We went deeper into feelings and emotions. I made an emotion board that depicted sad, happy, angry, and frightened cartoon faces. During nonstructured activity times the children could place a circle with their name on it in one of the areas. I kept my eye on this board, and when a child put his/her circle in a particular area we would discuss his/her feelings. We tried to get at the source of his/her feelings, whether he/she was sad, angry, or frightened, and together tried to make it possible for him/her to move into the happy area."
5. "I would suggest that this module be taught at the beginning of the year. It is a great way to get to know your children and a super, positive way to start off the school year!"
6. "You might need more time than is specified for this module."

STUDENT BIBLIOGRAPHY

Berger, Terry, *I Have Feelings,* New York: Behavioral Publications, 1971.
Carrick, Malcolm, *Tramp,* New York: Harper & Row, 1977.
Fassler, Joan, *One Little Girl,* New York: Behavioral Publications, 1969.
Lessor, Richard, *Fuzzies,* Niles, Ill.: Argus Communications, 1971.
Turner, Helen, *I Am Big. You Are Little,* Menlo Park, Calif.: Addison-Wesley, 1975.
Viorst, Judith, *Alexander and the Terrible, Horrible, No Good, Very Bad Day,* New York: Atheneum, 1975.

TEACHER BIBLIOGRAPHY

Crowder, William W., "We're Alike, We're Different," *Teacher*, February 1975.
DeFranco, Ellen B., "For Parents Only," *PTA Magazine*, May 1974.
Gordon, Ira J., *Children's View of Themselves*, Association for Childhood International, 1972.
Hamachek, Don E., *Encounters with the Self*, New York: Holt, Rinehart, and Winston, 1971.

UPPER

Self-Identity and Personal Worth

This teaching module is designed for pupils in the upper-elementary grades. While most students at this level typically study the nation, Canada, and Latin America, Europe or Asia, frequently teachers attempt to sandwich in a short unit at the beginning of the year that takes a look at self. For those teachers we feel this module could be helpful. The primary objective of this module is to help students express their views about attitudes, values, and emotions. This facet of the individual often referred to as the affective domain is interrelated with the cognitive domain, and furthermore the effect has a direct bearing on what one does and how one interacts with others. The module provides opportunities for the student to become personally involved by beginning with a ranking game asking each pupil to respond with like, dislike, or no opinion or feeling. From there, the pupils begin exploring their attitudes and values and have opportunities to express them through a personal coat of arms. Suggestions for other activities include discussions, feeling boxes, collages, interviews, and a self-inventory. While most traditional textbooks will not prove too satisfactory, there are a few that deal with self-identity which will be very useful. Tap the library card catalog for a wealth of material. By the end of the module, the students will have experienced themselves in a variety of meaningful activities. It is hoped that these personal encounters and the interactions among peers will promote self-identity and a feeling of self-worth.

I.   Grade Level: Upper Elementary

II. Special Materials:
A. Art supplies including yarn, brown bags, small boxes, construction paper
B. Objects or pictures for Ranking Game
C. Pictures depicting feelings

III. Time: 2 weeks

IV. Concepts:
A. A person's *feelings* are unique.

      B. A person's *human emotions* influence what one does and how he or she interacts with others.

      C. An *attitude* is a single expression of liking or disliking.

      D. A *value* is an expression of what is desirable for an individual and society.

      E. A *trait* is a distinguishing feature or characteristic.

      F. An *emotion* is a feeling.

V.   Objectives:

      A. Upon completion of this module, the student will be able to write an essay about feelings and how they affect his or her behavior at school.

      B. Upon completion of this module, the student will write up a personal profile that reflects self.

VI. Entry Behavior Indicators:

      A. The student must have previous experience in discussion groups.

      B. The student must see a need for dealing with self in school.

VII. Teaching Procedures:

      A. Play Ranking Game—Have the students arrange desks in a circle. Hold up an item or picture of an object. Students are to respond as to whether they like, dislike, or have no opinion or feeling about the item held up. After showing the items, ask the students why they chose the responses they did. What things in their lives may have affected their choices? Allow plenty of time for discussion.

      B. Begin a discussion about values. Focus questions might include:

         1. What are they?

         2. Is it necessary for all of us to have the same values? Why? Why not?

         3. What are some attitudes you hold? How are attitudes and values similar? dissimilar? Provide many examples!

         4. What is one value you hold? Why?

      C. A coat of arms is a symbol of who you are. In medieval times this insignia was embroidered on the light garment worn over the armor and usually symbolized the name or status of the person wearing it. It usually included the person's achievements or aspirations. Have students design their own coat of arms. Include the following:

         1. Draw two pictures, one to show something you are very good at and one to show something you want to become better at. See Chapter 6 "Values and Value Processes."

         2. Make a picture to show one of your values. This is one value that you feel very strongly about and would never give up.

         3. Draw a picture to show a value by which your family lives. It should be one that everyone in your family believes.

         4. Imagine you could do anything you wanted to and you were successful at it. What would you want to do?

         5. Draw something in this box that you wished all people believed in.

6. In this last box you can use words. Write four words which you hope people would say about you. What does your coat of arms tell you about yourself? about your family?

Share and discuss similarities and differences.

(Show pictures and real examples of coats of arms to slow learners. The teacher will want to allow more time for completing the tasks and will probably need to provide the students with concrete examples).

(Have gifted children go to the library and find more information about the coat of arms. Let them share their findings with their classmates.)

D. Have students draw self-portraits to see how they view themselves physically. Discuss the pictures. Put the word "trait" on the board. The students will find out what it means through use of the dictionary. Have students put meaning into their own words. Ask what the word means to them. Discuss the various general traits reflected in the students' pictures.

Focus questions might include:
1. Does any one trait show through in your picture?
2. What traits do you see that you like? dislike?
3. What traits would you want to try to show?
4. What trait is most important to you?
5. What traits would you most like to develop yourself?
6. What traits would you least like to develop? Why?

(For slow learners the teacher will need to define trait and illustrate its meaning with lots of concrete examples. Use puppets, books, and pictures, for further examples.)

(Have gifted students plan, write, and produce a short puppet show or play to illustrate traits and how they affect us.)

E. Put the word "emotion" on the board. Have the students look up the word in the dictionary. Discuss the meaning. Have them write down on paper how they would feel if each of these things happened:

(The teacher will need to define the term for slow learners, and use lots of concrete examples for illustrative purposes.)
1. You have to stop playing to wash the dishes.
2. Someone reads a funny story to you.
3. You see someone hurt himself.
4. You win a prize.

(Have slow learners use masks or sack puppets or do pantomimes to illustrate their emotions.)

(Have gifted students write creative stories using specified situations and emotions.)

F. Have the students make collages or feeling boxes as a means of expressing how they feel about self. The finished collage is a synthesis of one's feelings, and visual perceptions of self. Discuss the results. Some students will want to display the finished product. Others may not.

Self-portraits can be an effective vehicle to learn about self and others. Can you think of provocative questions a teacher might ask to stimulate thinking?

G. Discuss feelings. (Pictures might be used to further stimulate discussion.) Focus questions might include:
1. How do feelings affect what you do? Give examples.
2. Do feelings ever affect your health?
3. Do you ever try to stop and understand your feelings? Why or why not?
4. Why do you feel happy? sad? guilty?
5. Can you cite situations where feelings really got in the way of what you were doing?
    (Use concrete situations for slow learners. Have students pantomime their feelings.)
    (Have gifted students bring in pictures that illustrate various feelings that they have. They might want to categorize their feelings and analyze the kind they have the most and the least. Some students might like to write poetry to represent one or more feeling.)
H. Have the students make a feeling collage on a paper bag or on a

cardboard box. Encourage them to find pictures that reflect the feelings they have from time to time. Share and discuss the end product.

I. If the teacher wishes, the collage could be extended to include and reflect the student's personality. If so, it could include likes and dislikes, reactions in specific situations, etc. Focus questions might include the following:
1. Why did you choose the things you did?
2. Why are they important to you?
3. What qualities represented on the bag did you feel were important? Would you say some of the things on the bag or box are materialistic?

J. Have the students do the following self-inventory:

Name _____

Hour _____

	GETTING TO KNOW YOURSELF		
	Yes	No	Sometimes
1) I study hard			
2) I lose my temper easily			
3) I like to be with people			
4) I can handle responsibility			
5) I have many friends			
6) I am good at sports			
7) I am generous			
8) I am a shy person			
9) I enjoy being with my family			
10) I take things seriously			
11) I make friends easily			
12) My grades at school are good to average			
13) I am adventurous			
14) I like to read			
15) My appearance satisfies me			
16) I like to talk			
17) I like school			
18) I am glad I am me			

Summarize

Share and discuss the result

(The teacher will want to decide which questions are appropriate for slow learners, and use them orally in an individual or group interview. Record the results.)

(The gifted students might want to make additions to the existing inventory or they might like to write autobiographies.)

K.　Have students interview each other as a means of gaining insight about others. The students could design a simple questionnaire to be used as a guide. The focus should be on feelings.

L.　Hold a discussion session as a means of focusing in on self and how one's feelings and actions affect the total class. Discuss ways of developing more cohesion and group unity. Some students might wish to formulate a class coat of arms. Focus questions might include:

    1.　Does everyone in class have to hold similar attitudes and feelings? Why? Why not?

    2.　How does your self-concept affect the class? Explain.

    3.　How does understanding one's traits affect one's interactions with others?

M.　Have students plan and present puppet shows or short plays to depict one or more of the topics covered in this module. These could be prepared in small groups.

VIII.　Evaluation:

A.　The essay and the student profile will serve as one source of evaluative data.

B.　A self-assessment instrument may be used. An example is as follows:*

Name:

	Always	Usually	Sometimes	Never	Not Sure
I take part in activities					
I respect other peoples' feelings					
I share my feelings					
I share my ideas					
I listen to other peoples' ideas					

C.　Anecdotal records would also be useful with this module.

*Adapted from Arthur Ellis and Janet Alleman-Brooks, "How To Evaluate Problem-Solving-Oriented Social Studies," *The Social Studies*, Washington D.C.: Heldref Publications, Vol. 68, No. 3 (May/June 1977), pp. 93–103.

CLASSROOM RESULTS

Teachers expressed a need for more time to develop the module adequately.

Several teachers modified the module to meet the needs of their specific classes:

1. "I found that my students had difficulty in expressing themselves on paper. We spent lots of extra time on individual writing projects."
2. "I used some dittoed stories from the Instructional Fair Company which presented emotions in story form."
3. "A section from the Follett book, *The World of Language*, which focused on pantomines, was used with this module."
4. "I used many stories which contained numerous examples of emotions. I tried to stress the importance of expressing our emotions and not being afraid of them. I cry sometimes too."

Several teachers offered suggestions for future users:

1. "Use the module as a basic guide, keeping in mind the students who will be using it."
2. "Try to develop and find other pertinent materials available in most classrooms. Often parents have resources to share, too."
3. "Have students keep a log of their own emotions for one day, and their causes and effects."
4. "Make use of bulletin boards in distinguishing emotions, traits, feelings, and values."

STUDENT BIBLIOGRAPHY

Brown, Roy, *The Cage*, New York: Seabury, 1977.

Clifford, Eth, *The Curse of the Moonraker*, Boston: Houghton Mifflin, 1977.

Hassler, Jon, *Four Miles to Pinecone*, New York: Warne, 1977.

Hoban, Lillian, *I Met a Traveler*, New York: Harper & Row, 1977.

Little, Jean, *Listen for the Singing*, New York: Dutton, 1977.

Nostlinger, Christine, *Konrad*, New York: F. Watts, 1977.

TEACHER BIBLIOGRAPHY

Brandwein, Paul F., and others, *Getting Together Problems You Face.* New York: Scholastic Book Services, 1971.

Channing L., *How To Understand Yourself and Others*, Greenfield, Mass.: Bete Company, Inc., 1975.

Fedder, Ruth, *You, The Person You Want To Be*, New York: McGraw-Hill, 1957.

Goodykoontz, Dr. William, *Growing Up Strong*, New York: Scholastic Scope, 1968.

Hamachek, Don E., *Motivation in Teaching and Learning, What Research Says to the Teacher*, Series No. 34, pp. 5–9, Washington, D.C.: National Education Association, 1968.

LeShan, Eda, *What Makes Me Feel This Way? Growing Up with Human Emotion*, New York: Macmillan, 1972.

Peters, Herman J., Bruce Shertzer, William VanHoose, *Guidance in Elementary Schools,* Skokie, Ill.: Rand McNally, 1965.

Phillips, Beeman N., and M. Vere DeVault, *Psychology—What Kind of Person Am I?* Austin, Texas: Steck-Vaughn, 1966.

Sources of Identity, The Social Sciences Concepts and Values, New York: Harcourt Brace Jovanovich, 1972.

Wrenn, C. Gilbert, Shirley Schwarzrock, *Parents Can Be a Problem,* Circle Pines, Minn.: American Guidance Services, 1970.

Wrenn, C. Gilbert, Shirley Schwarzrock, *To Like and Be Liked,* Circle Pines, Minn.: American Guidance Services, 1970.

SUMMARY

The preceding ten teaching modules serve to illustrate how the life roles can be used to organize instruction. Some teachers will want to elaborate on each of the life roles independently while others will want to identify the organizing concepts or themes and focus on one of the life roles. We have found some teachers using the modules to add life and relevancy to their dated texts, some using them as the social studies curricula, as "seeds" for developing their own materials, as a part of an interdisciplinary program, and still others using selected modules in part to meet state mandates. The "Classroom Results" serve to provide the potential user with helpful information from teachers who have tried the modules. We invite you to select at least one module that appeals to you, modify it to meet the specific needs of your students and give it a try.

Section C
THE ORGANIZING THEMES: EXEMPLARS FOR TEACHING

GOALS

1. Learn how to apply the authors' concept of organizing themes to selection, planning, instruction, and evaluation of instructional materials (prepared or teacher-made).
2. Gain greater insight into ways of involving parents and community in the planning, instruction, and evaluation of children.
3. Identify concepts and skills developed in school that affect the lives of children immediately as well as throughout life.
4. Gain new ideas for "hands-on" materials and strategies that cost little or no money yet allow children to be real problem solvers.
5. Learn how to interrelate the affective and cognitive domains that ultimately lead toward more intelligent decision making.
6. Formulate new ideas for helping children grapple with social studies problems within their lives and help them begin to see that what they do to solve these problems can make a difference.
7. Utilize the prototype modules or exemplars as "seeds" for developing plans for each individual classroom according to the needs and interests of the children in an attempt to improve the human condition.
8. Through the "Classroom Results," gain insights into problems, considerations, and suggestions for use of all or part of the modules in the individual classroom.

The ten organizing themes emerge out of the life roles. Each theme is illustrative of one of the basic problems affecting the lives of children and youth. We have indicated in preceding chapters that at various times in a child's formal and informal education, each of the supportive concepts will interface with each of the life roles. For illustrative purposes, we have included one prototype module for each theme; therefore, you will see how each organizing theme interfaces with one or more life roles. In the following diagram we will attempt to illustrate where the interfaces exist in each of the prototype modules. You will no doubt be able to find additional situations where interfacing exists. Keep in mind, also, that you will have opportunities in your classroom to develop many of the interfacing possibilities in greater depth depending, of course, on your pupils and the goals you establish.

It is not intended that you will use all of these teaching modules or that you should feel compelled to replicate them; rather it is intended that they will serve as an impetus to update your existing program or assist you in planning a new one. It is our hope that you will read them, react, reflect, and then use them with

LIFE ROLES AND ORGANIZING THEMES

| | INTERFACING* | | | | |
	Citizenship	Family	Avocation	Occupations	Personal Efficacy
Consumerism	- - - -	———	- - -	- - - -	- - -
Ecology	———	- - -	- - -	- - - -	- - -
Energy	———	———	- - -	———	- - -
Government and Politics	———	- - -	- - -	- - - -	- - -
Human Equality	- - - -	———	———	———	———
Human Life Cycle	———	———	———	———	- - -
Intercultural Relations	———	- - -	- - -	- - - -	———
Our Legal System	———	———	- - -	- - - -	- - -
Media	- - - -	———	———	- - - -	- - -
Morality	- - - -	- - -	———	- - - -	———

*Solid line indicates interfacing.

modifications or develop your own using the appropriate concepts, objectives, methodology, materials, and evaluative procedures.

This section is divided into ten segments: consumerism, ecology, energy, government and politics, human equality, the human life cycle, intercultural relations, our legal system, media, and morality. Each will be preceded by an introductory statement in an attempt to assist the reader in visualizing where each topic and illustrative module might fit into the existing curriculum. Following each module "Classroom Results" will be included in an attempt to provide information shared by teachers who have field tested the modules.

▶ Interface with
FAMILY

Consumerism ▶

MIDDLE

Children Become Advertising Executives

This teaching module is designed for students in middle-elementary grades. Typically at these levels children study communities and cities. In some states there is talk of mandates to teach consumerism in the elementary grades. In both instances, this module could be useful. The primary objective of the module is to help students develop a greater awareness of the influence of advertising on their lives. The module provides opportunities for students to become personally involved with the topic by asking that they begin with a series of jingles advertising products on today's market. Students are asked to complete the jingles. Other activities suggested in the module include a letter to parents, keeping advertising logs, consumer product testing, and a field trip to a nearby market. Textbooks dealing with communities and cities could provide resource material. By the end of the module, students will have opportunities to use the information they have gathered to begin making decisions about purchasing goods and services—decisions that they will continue to make throughout their lives.

I. Grade Level: Middle Elementary

II. Special Materials:
- A. Letter to parents describing the module and specific suggestions for helping their children.
- B. Advertising log

ADVERTISING LOG

Time	Advertisement	Medium	Target Audience

- C. Pictures of advertisements
- D. Notebooks for student materials
- E. Various types of packages for illustrative purposes

III. Time: 3 weeks

IV. Concepts:
- A. A *producer* is one who provides goods or services.
- B. A *consumer* is one who uses the goods or services.
- C. There are five basic *decisions* a consumer has to make: (a) whether to purchase the goods or services; (b) where to purchase the goods or services; (c) whether or not to finance the purchase; (d) whether or not to protect the good or service once it has been purchased, and if so, how; (e) what to do in the case of a faulty or especially outstanding product or service.
- D. *Advertising* is making a product/service known and appealing to the public in the hopes that they will want to purchase it.
- E. *Advertising appeals* to one or more of the following basic needs:

physiological, safety, love, esteem, self-actualization, aesthetic, and the need to know.

F.   The *cost of advertising* is passed on to the consumer.

G.   *Packaging* companies consider *appeal* of the box or wrapper, *protection* of contents, and *advertising techniques* most appropriate for the product.

V.   Objectives:

A.   The student will be able to produce a package and an advertisement for the product he will sell during "Market Day."

B.   Upon completion of this module the student will be able to write five "I Learned" statements about advertising/consumerism.

C.   The student will be able to depict in writing or visually what he thinks the world would be like without advertising.

VI.   Entry Behavior Indicators:

A.   The student will have previous experience in sampling, gathering, and analyzing data.

B.   The student will have previous experience in television viewing.

C.   The student will have previous experience in group work.

VII.   Teaching Procedures:

(Prior to beginning the module write a letter to parents describing the module. Include the objectives. Provide specific suggestions for parents in the event they want to share this experience with their children.)

A.   To introduce the topic and to illustrate the power of advertising design a questionnaire or show students a series of products with only a portion of the jingle visible. Have students fill in the missing words. (Examples: 1. Please don't _____ the Charmin. 2. You deserve a _____ today at MacDonald's. 3. Have it your way at _____.)
(Slow learners will probably need to have this administered orally. You might want to give them a shortened version.)
(Gifted students might like to administer the questionnaire or a similar one to neighbors, friends, and relatives to determine what variables might cause their level of consciousness about advertising to shift, for example, hours at work, age group, profession, etc. Make sure provision is made on the questionnaire to note crucial information.)

B.   Discuss the results of the questionnaire or visual quiz. Then ask students to list (in a specified time) as many things as they can think of that they would like to buy. When the time is up, ask students to try to determine where they heard about each of the products.

C.   Ask students to keep a log for one week of their personal exposure to ads. This should include all types of media: TV, radio, magazines, matchbooks, street signs, bumper stickers, etc. (see special materials).

(Take a walking trip to the nearest store with slow learners or provide students with opportunities to gather information from magazines, etc.)

(Ask gifted students to log the details connected with each ad.)

D.   Have students examine ads in various magazines such as *Road and Track, Cosmopolitan, Parents, Better Homes and Gardens, Weight Watchers Magazine, Jack and Jill, Sports Illustrated, Bicycling,* etc. Compare the ads. How do they differ? Have students construct a bulletin board to illustrate the meaning of *target audience*.

E.   Have students plan, construct, and administer a questionnaire to parents or other interested adults in an attempt to gather information about the types of advertising that influence them. Discuss/illustrate the findings.

(Have slow learners work as a small group gathering data. They might select teachers at school as their sample.)

(Have gifted students gather information about advertising in the past. Compare with the present.)

F.   Present the class with a mini lecture (accompanied by illustrations) to show the various techniques used in advertising. The ten most common techniques include: (a) Bandwagon (everyone's doing it!); (b) testimonial (when a famous person likes a product, this type of ad assumes other people will buy the product out of admiration); (c) transfer (this type of ad presents the product in a beautiful setting encouraging the buyer to associate the feeling evoked by the picture with the product); (d) scientific (this type of ad creates the impression of superiority by using scientific names or statistics); (e) plain folk (talking down to people or the humble approach is used); (f) more for your money (this type of ad claims you will save money or get more for your money by buying one brand instead of another); (g) symbols, logos, or slogans (this type of ad uses a symbol or catchy phrase to represent the product); (h) weasel claim (uses words like "virtually" or "helps," "looks like," "looks as if"); (i) compliment the consumer (ads using this approach frequently use the words, "You deserve the best" or "You've come a long way, baby"); (j) appeals (this type of ad is directed at the consumer's values or emotions).

(Design a word recognition–flash card game for slow learners.)

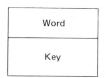

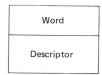

(Have gifted students design a game to be used with propaganda techniques.)

G.   Have students clip examples of each advertising technique from the media. Paste the ads in their notebooks. Label each.

H. Remind students to bring their completed logs to class. Have them share their results. Use the following questions as a springboard for discussion: What was the target audience for the majority of your ads? What types of advertising did you observe? What are your favorite ads? Why? Least favorite? Why? How do advertisers get your attention? How are women depicted in ads? Give examples. How are men depicted in ads? Give examples. Children? Boys? Girls? Give examples. (Some classes might want to consider racial groups as they relate to advertising.)

I. Pose this question—Do commercials need color? sound? Discuss student reactions. Then design a control and experimental group to test these phenomena. Discuss the results.

J. Bring to class a series of commercials that you have prerecorded on the videotape machine. Play back one or more of the commercials. Explain Federal regulations. Then discuss possible ways of testing several of the specified products to see whether the commercials are accurate. Have the students make plans to test the selected products. Discuss problems with a single test, etc. Allow ample time for testing. (Some students might like to do some product testing at home.)

K. Have students report their findings to other members of their class. Students may wish to demonstrate one or more tests.

L. Prepare the students for a field trip to the supermarket. Encourage them to generate a list of questions they would like answered. Then provide students with information about packages: (a) best looking according to color, shape, texture, words, total design; (b) protection of the contents; (c) types of information given via print; (d) variety of packaging techniques. Provide visuals whenever possible.
    (Have slow learners examine one package carefully.)
    (Have gifted students gather information about Federal regulations connected with packaging.)

M. Take students to the supermarket. Assign small groups to different sections of the store. Have them look for examples of catchy phrases or other gimmicks on packages to promote sales. Have students compare packages, placement on shelves, and other agreed-upon considerations. Choose one child or adult to assist in recording the data.

N. Discuss observations from the field trip. Focus questions might include: What was the most unusual thing you learned? What package did you see that was most appealing? What gimmicks were used?

O. Plan for "Market Day." Have each child make a product or bring a white elephant to school. Design the package and prepare and present the commercial. Sell the items. (The rules such as type/amount of money that can be used will be determined according to each unique situation.)
    (In an attempt to help the slow learners in this project, students may wish to incorporate. Suggest a gifted child work with a slow learner.)

(Gifted students could interview store managers/company executives to gather data about faulty/exceptionally good products.)

P.   Finally discuss what a consumer should do in the case of a faulty or exceptionally good product. Provide role-play situations. Role play/ discuss each enactment.

Q.   Summarize the module through a discussion and then have each student write (story, essay, poem) or illustrate what it would be like not to have advertising. Share the results.

VIII.   Evaluation:

A.   Evaluate the "I Learned" statements.

B.   Assess the "What It Would Be Like without Advertising" projects according to thought, effort, and feasibility of ideas.

C.   Use the "Individual" package designs and commercials to assess each student's understanding of ideas developed in the module. Record each student's performance or lack of progress.

D.   Keep notes concerning the individual student's involvement in group discussions. Is each student contributing, asking new questions, and responding to new questions? Have a private conference with each child to discuss the results.

CLASSROOM RESULTS

While most teachers felt the concepts and procedures were appropriate, a few suggested that more time could be spent on aspects relevant to students' everyday lives as consumers. One teacher felt that more activities related to producers would enhance the module.

Several teachers made suggestions for future users:

1.   "Make sure you plan several class discussions. Our group discussions could have been never-ending."
2.   "Have the class members bring in their own examples of comparative shopping."
3.   "Use more concrete examples when teaching about comparative shopping."
4.   "You might think about redefining consumer needs. I use the term biological needs."
5.   "Where possible incorporate all subject areas such as reading, mathematics, science, and social skills as well as language arts. This module lends itself well to the integrated approach."
6.   "Spend more time in planning the Market Day so it would be advertised well in advance. The students need to address the issue of potential volume that they will have to sell."

STUDENT BIBLIOGRAPHY

Berger, Melvin, *Consumer Protection Labs*, New York: John Day, 1975.
Campbell, Hannah, *Why Did They Name It?* New York: J. P. Bell, 1964.

Cohen, Dorothy, *Introduction to Advertising*, New York: Wiley, 1972.
Council of Better Business Bureaus, *Consumer's Buying Guide*, New York: Benjamin Co./Rutledge Books, 1969.
DeBartol, Dick, *Madvertising*, New York: New American Library, 1972.
Faber, Doris, *Enough! The Revolt of the American Consumer*, New York: Farrar, Straus, 1972.
Gay, Kathlyn, *Caution: Advertising*, New York: Holt, Rinehart and Winston, 1972.
Mason, Mont, *Crazy Commercial*, New York: Scholastic Book Services, 1975.
Maynard, Richard (Ed.), *Messages and Meanings: Media Persuasion, Advertising and Propaganda*, New York: Scholastic Book Services, 1975.
Saunders, Rubie, *Smart Shopping and Consumerism*, New York: F. Watts, 1973.

TEACHER BIBLIOGRAPHY

Baker, Samm S., *Casebook of Successful Ideas for Advertising and Selling*, Garden City, N.Y.: Hanover House, 1959.
Consumer Reports, "Chocolate Drink Mixes," (August 1976), pp. 499–503.
Divorsky, Diane, "The Big Business in Toys: A Target for Consumer Education," *Learning*, (November 1977), pp. 28–32.
Foxsworth, Esther H., "How To Spend That Hard Earned Dime," *Teacher*, (January 1977), pp. 94–96.
Hapgood, David, *The Screwing of the Average Man*, Garden City, N.Y.: Doubleday, 1974.
Kleppner, Otto, *Advertising Procedure*, Englewood Cliffs, N.J.: Prentice-Hall, 1966.
Masters, Dexter, *The Intelligent Buyer and the Telltale Seller*, New York: Knopf, 1966.
Volstad, Natalie. "What Every Young Consumer Should Know," *Parents' Magazine* (February 1974), p. 58.

Other Useful Materials

Filmstrips and Cassettes: *Advertising Target You!* E.M.C. Corp., 1976.
Advertising and the Consumer, Current Affairs, 24 Dansbury Road, Wilton, Conn. 06897
Film: "Supergoop" produced by Churchill Films, 662 N. Robertson Blvd., Los Angeles, Calif. 90069

▶ Interface with
CITIZENSHIP

Ecology ▶

LOWER

Cleaning Up the Local Environment

This teaching module is designed for children in the lower elementary grades. Typically at this level they study home, school, and community. The primary objective of the module is to help pupils develop a greater awareness for ecology and the problems that are incurred when people are not concerned with their environment. This module provides opportunities for children to become personally involved with the topic by asking that they begin with a film or other visuals in an attempt to determine what litter is. We suggest that they then take a walking trip around the school to find existing litter. Later children are asked to categorize and graph the types of litter they find and try to determine who causes the litter problem. Other activities suggested in the teaching module include a letter to parents, a visit to a recycling center, "litter art," and a social action project. Textbooks dealing with schools and communities could be helpful.

Supplemental materials on the subject are becoming more readily available. Keep on the alert because often they are catalogued as science materials. This teaching module affords the perfect opportunity to interrelate science and social studies.

By the end of the module the children should be prepared to use the information that they have gathered to embark on their lifelong concern for ecology, which is so necessary to improve the human condition.

I. Grade Level: Lower Elementary

II. Special Materials:
    A. Litter posters
    B. Children's literature (see bibliography)
    C. Art supplies
    D. Polaroid camera (optional)
    E. "A Pollution Game," *Knock the Four Walls Down,* by Nick Rodes and B. J. Amundson, produced P. A. Schiller and Associates, 1973. (optional).
    F. Survey sheets—Who Litters?
    G. Teacher-made game similar to "Candyland"—object is not to litter. If you litter you are penalized.
    H. Letter to parents explaining the module, your objectives, and some of the procedures you have planned. Suggest ways the parents could help their children with the materials covered in the module. Include a children's bibliography in the event they would like to take their children to the library.

III. Time: 2 to 3 weeks

IV. Concepts:
    A. *Litter* is scattered rubbish or materials that are scattered around.
    B. *Pollution* is the presence of unclean material.
    C. *Litter* and *pollution* can affect our *health* and *happiness.*
    D. We need not pollute. There are other ways of *disposing of waste.*

V. Objectives:
    A. By the end of the module the student will be aware of the proper way to dispose of unwanted material and will pick up litter as evidenced through observation.

The real test of children's learning can be measured when what is learned in school is applied to the out-of-school environment.

B.   The student will be able to draw pictures to represent three rules concerning litter.

VI.   Entry Behavior Indicators:
A.   The student will have some previous knowledge about his immediate community.
B.   The student will be able to classify objects according to similarities.
C.   The student will have previous experience in observing as a means of gathering information.
D.   The student will have previous experience in seeking information from others through simple interviews.

VII.   Teaching Procedures:
A.   Begin the module by showing an available film about litter, showing a series of pictures or posters about litter or reading a children's book about litter. Have the students brainstorm as to what litter is. List *all* of their ideas on the blackboard.
B.   After the brainstorming session, have the students categorize the various types of litter.
C.   Take a walk around the schoolyard and the streets surrounding the school. Search for objects left by people who no longer needed them. Take a basket and collect as many of these discarded items as you can find.
D.   Empty your collection of litter onto the floor. Then sort the objects

into several piles, placing similar objects in the same pile. When you have completed that, count the number of objects in each pile. With the help of the students, lay out the materials in graph form. If you have access to a Polaroid camera take a picture of the materials. Discuss with the children the fact that you have made a picture graph.

E. Using a large sheet of paper make a bar graph of the types and amount of litter found. (Use the picture graph as the reference.)

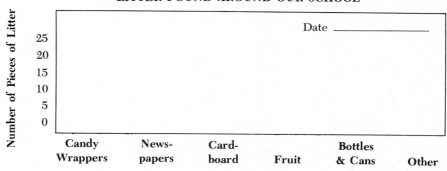

LITTER FOUND AROUND OUR SCHOOL

Using the graph, begin a discussion about the litter found around the school. Focus questions might include: What types of litter were found? What was the most common type of litter? Why do you think so? What types of litter are health hazards because they encourage disease or cause accidents? Introduce the term pollution. What types of litter reduce the beauty of an area? (Discuss how/why another individual's graph of this activity might be different from the one this class constructed.)

F. Children can "check out" who the litterbugs are. Discuss with the class who they think is littering and why. Decide when to observe for littering. Prepare a *simple* checklist that children can use in helping them make their observations. An example is on page 328.
(The teacher may need to have a session with the slow learners to make sure they can use the checklist. Perhaps each child would be asked to observe one person who littered.)
(The gifted students could be asked to help the teacher tally the information and picture the data that were acquired during the observations.)

G. Go over the results of the survey. Who are the most common litterbugs? What was the most common type of litter?

H. Select a children's book from the library that focuses on litter and the consequences. Read and discuss the story. A delightful example is: *Who Wants a Pop Can Park* by Renee Bartowski (see bibliography).

LITTER SURVEY

	Candy Wrapper	Newspapers	Cardboard	Fruit	Bottles	Cans	Other
Boy							
Girl							
Woman							
Man							

I. Discuss with the children how they feel about litter. Pictures could be drawn or a short puppet play could be devised.

J. Discuss with the children how they could find out how other people feel about litter. Introduce the idea of interviewing as a means of seeking information. People they could interview might include parents, older brothers and sisters, students in another class, neighbors, grandparents, teachers, local grocer. Sample questions might include: What is a litterbug? Why do people litter? What should be done with people who litter? Have the students pair off and practice interviewing using specified questions. Discuss the results.
(The slow learners could be asked to interview one person—parent or babysitter—to find out how people feel about littering.)
(The gifted students might be encouraged to use a tape recorder and interview younger/older groups to get their views on littering.)

K. Summarize the results of the interviews. Can tentative conclusions be drawn?

L. Revisit the areas around the school where you had found litter. Construct a very simple map of the litter areas and nonlitter areas around the school. Then with the class discuss where to locate trash cans or posters about littering. (If possible, work out with local community leaders a "Clean-up the Litter" program. Even early-elementary children can be involved and they will be very excited when they realize that their views and assistance can make a difference!)

M. Discuss the laws about littering, including the signs that are posted that impose fines for throwing trash on roads and streets. Discuss why people needed to make laws. How do you suppose they felt about littering?
(Have slow learners draw pictures that depict laws about littering.)

(Gifted students might be able to talk with law enforcers in an attempt to find out more about laws related to litter.)

N. Introduce the "Litterbug Game" (teacher-made). The game includes a game board and litter cards which the children pick when they land on a certain place. They will be penalized for littering and they will be able to move ahead spaces when littering does not occur. Six can play at a time or six games could be constructed out of paper.
(The teacher or a peer could have a mini session with slow learners to make sure they understand the strategy.)
(The teacher might ask gifted students to add more rules/strategies to existing game.)

O. Summarize with the students what they have learned to date about litter, then pose this question: What should we do with the litter we have collected? Burn it? (No, that pollutes the air.) Should we put it in the garbage bin for collection? Then where does it go? This leads to a study of solid waste disposal and possibly a field trip to a local site.
(Prepare simple card games for slow learners to develop word recognition and meaning.) Examples below:

Card game 1

Cut apart "Match"

Trash	Litter	Pollution	Recycle

Laminate for extended usage

(Extend to other concepts. Gifted children can make up additional rules.)

Card game 2

"4 of a kind"

Recycle	Recycle	Recycle	Recycle
		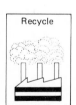	

Extend to other concepts. Gifted children can make up additional rules.

P. Introduce the term *recycling*. Read *Who Cares? I Do* by Munro Leaf and discuss the reason why recycling is so important. If possible plan a visit to a recycling center (scrap metal from old cars or recycled glass).

Q. Discuss what can be done in your classroom to solve the litter problem. Make a list of possibilities. For example, students could survey local schools, banks, and businesses to see if they use recycled paper. If not, perhaps the class will be able to use it or provide groups with suggestions. Other possibilities include making posters, giving speeches, developing an in-class recycling center, and planning, preparing, and presenting a program to other classes informing them what they can do to help solve the litter problem.

R. Have students use "appropriate" types of litter to make mobiles, pop art, or papier-mâché objects.

S. Plan to "pull the module together." With the help of the teacher the children could list all the things they learned about litter. They could then write an experience story or group poem about litter.

VIII. Evaluation:

A. By the end of the module, you hope that the children will be so highly motivated that they will automatically pick up litter around their community. This should be done voluntarily. They will, however, be encouraged to record where and when they picked it up on a large chart that will be available in the classroom.

SOCIAL ACTION EVALUATION

Name	LITTER WE COLLECTED			
	What Kind?	Where?	When?	How Used? (Recycled)

B. Study habits during the lessons

Name	Took Part in Discussion	Used the Library	Did Survey	Did Interview	Played Games

C. Evaluate the children's pictures that depict rules about litter in terms of: (1) accuracy, (2) appropriateness, and (3) acceptability.

CLASSROOM RESULTS

Teachers found the concepts, entry behavior indicators, and teaching procedures appropriate for their students. Several teachers did, however, have comments concerning the evaluation component:

1. "I used the objectives for evaluation. Our three rules were, 'Litter Is Ugly,' 'Litter Can Hurt,' and 'America Can Be Lovely.' "

2. "I employed parents in the evaluation process. At the end, parents were told of the concepts and my expectations. I then asked them to express their feelings about the degree of success of the module based on their child's interest and ability to relate what they had learned."

3. "Since this was an introduction to interviewing (as well as information-gathering from observations) for these youngsters, verbal responses worked best. I did record their responses but they became extremely restless during the process and seemed to lose interest. They really seemed to enjoy relating what their interview produced in the way of answers; however, when it was someone else's turn to respond, restlessness set in!"

4. "The picture match-up cards presented two problems: The youngsters are unable to read and thus associate the word with the picture. I hoped to avoid this by using only cut-up pictures, but this brought about a second problem—I had difficulty finding pictures."

5. "At this age I felt that the litter pick-up and emphasis on beautifying the area in front of the school were most important. The fact that the majority were concerned was evident: Each day when I walked into the room excited kindergartners would tell me about the 'ugly litter' they had seen while riding home on the school bus or how they had picked up trash around their road, yard, etc."

Teachers mentioned additional activities that were developed in conjunction with this module:

1. "We did a little of our own recycling. The glass bottles we found were washed, the labels removed, and decorated as vases for Mother's Day."

2. "We visited a recycling center."

3. "Students in my class created a song about litter. Each child was asked to contribute to the words, thoughts, or melody of the song."

4. "We got interested in the no-return–bottle ban in Michigan. I did a little research on it so I could relate information and answer the children's questions."

Several teachers offered suggestions for future users:

1. "When I started to get film request rejections and when certain books were unavailable, I panicked. Eventually I found all kinds of materials that were available. Involve the parents and community."

2. "Don't be afraid to try interviewing, surveying, and graphing with first graders. They can handle it!"
3. "Make sure children get to gather litter. They love it! Our pick-up covered both sides of the road in front of the school. We found twenty-three glass bottles, sixty-four cans, bags of paper, cellophane, etc!"

STUDENT BIBLIOGRAPHY

Avery, Bea, *Pollution a Big Problem*, California: Literary Press, 1970.
Bartowski, Renee, *Who Wants a Pop Can Park?*, Skokie, Ill.: Rand McNally, 1972.
Foreman, Michael, *Dinosaurs and All That Rubbish*, New York: Crowell, 1973.
Gutnik, Martin J., *Ecology and Pollution/Land*, Chicago: Children's Press, Inc. 1973.
Huff, Sidney, *Amy's Dinosaur*, New York: Dutton/Windmill Books, 1974.
Jennings, Gary, *The Earth Book*, Philadelphia: Lippincott, 1974.
Leaf, Munro, *Who Cares? I Do*, Philadelphia: Lippincott, 1971.
Miles, Betty, *Save the Earth, An Ecology Book for Kids*, New York: Knopf, 1974.
Podendorf, I., *Every Day Is Earth Day*, Chicago: Children's Press, 1971.
Shanks, Ann Zane, *About Garbage and Stuff*, New York: Viking, 1973.

TEACHER BIBLIOGRAPHY

Love, Sam (Ed.), *The Earth Tool Kit*, New York: Pocket Books, 1971.
Howell, Jerry F. and Jeanne S. Osborne, *A Selected and Annotated Environmental Education Bibliography for Elementary, Secondary, and Post Secondary Schools*, Morehead, Ky: Morehead State University, 1975.
Keach, Everett T., "Everywhere That Earthlings Go," *Early Years Magazine*, Vol. 8, No. 2 (October 1977), p. 34.
Needham, Dorothy, "Pollution—A Teaching and Action Program," *Grade Teacher* (October 1970) pp. 24–33.
Rodes, Nick, and B. J. Amundson, "What Is Trash?" *Knock the Four Walls Down*, Chicago: P. A. Schiller and Associates, 1973.
Roth, Robert E., *Environmental Education, A Bibliography of Abstracts from Research in Education*, Worthington, Ohio: Education Associates Inc., 1966–1972.
Wentworth, D. F., J. K. Couchman, J. C. MacBean, and A. Streecher, *Pollution: Examining Your Environment*, Montreal: Holt, Rinehart, and Winston, 1971.

▶Interface with
FAMILY,
OCCUPATION/
CAREERS

Energy ▶

MIDDLE

The Energy Problem Is Our Problem

This teaching module is designed for students in middle- and possibly upper-elementary grades. Typically at this level they study communities and cities.

Pupils at this level are also frequently exposed to current events programs. In some schools science and social studies are beginning to be taught as an interdisciplinary subject. In any of these three instances, this module could be helpful. The primary objective of the module is to help pupils acquire knowledge about what energy is, what it comes from, where the problems lie, methods of conserving energy, and with this information begin to make decisions about conservation. The module provides opportunities for students to become personally involved with the topic by asking that they take a look at their initial attitudes and feelings about energy. At the end of the module they will reassess their attitudes and feelings. Have the knowledge and experiences they have participated in modified their thinking? Other activities suggested in the module include brainstorming, viewing selected films, experiments, role playing and designing ways to conserve energy. Suggested strategies for individual and group contracting are also included. Social studies texts that include materials on communities and cities as well as current events publications could provide excellent source material. By the end of the module students will have opportunities to use the knowledge and ideas that they have acquired to clarify their present position on the topic and to begin acting more wisely concerning one of the most explosive social issues of our time.

I. Grade Level: Middle Elementary

II. Special Materials:
   A. Sheet of tagboard for posters
   B. Three candles and matches
   C. Test tube
   D. Plastic windmill (purchased in toy department of store)
   E. Experiment: Laminated water wheel and foil wheel.
      Construction for both:

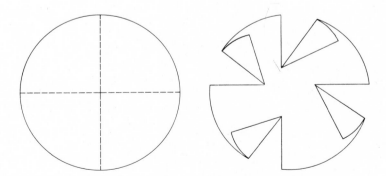

   Water Wheel: Use a plastic milk container or laminated tagboard. Make a hole in the middle large enough for a knitting needle to fit through.
   Foil Wheel: Use an aluminum foil pie plate. Make a hole in the center large enough for a test tube to pass through and turn easily.
   F. Saucepan and loose-fitting lid

G.   Hot plate
H.   Pictures of objects powered by wind and water
I.   Magnifying glass
J.   Two aluminum foil pie tins
K.   Glass dish
L.   Newspaper articles about energy collected as the module progresses
M.   Globe or world map
N.   Books, magazines, and pamphlets related to energy (see bibliography)
O.   Learning center (optional)
P.   Films: Examples of those we have used listed below. We are certain you could find many others to substitute!
     "Air Pollution," S.F. 10 min., color
     "Energy: A First Film," 8 min., color, BFA Educational Media
     "Pollution: It's Up To You," 10 min., color, NBC
     "Riches of the Earth" (revised), 17 min., color, S.F.

III.   Time: 3 to 4 weeks

IV.   Concepts:
   A.   While the *sun* is the *source* of *energy*, it is from *energy resources* (plants, moving water, wind, and fossil fuels such as oil) that we get most of the energy we need.
   B.   We use *technology* to get the energy we need.
   C.   Only within the past 100 years have the *forms* of *energy* which industrial nations rely on come into widespread use.
   D.   By burning various fuels, *pollutants* are produced.
   E.   *Alternative forms of energy* include nuclear energy, shale oil, solar energy, geothermal energy, and energy from wind, moving water.
   F.   There are many ways to *conserve* energy.

V.   Objectives:
   A.   Upon completion of this module students will be able to write an essay describing energy, its sources, and how it can be conserved.
   B.   Upon completion of this module students will realize that there is an energy problem, as evidenced by their conservation of energy which will be measured through observation in and out of school.

VI.   Entry Behavior Indicators:
   A.   The student will have previous experience in value clarifying.
   B.   The student will have previous skill in using library sources.
   C.   The student will possess skill in viewing media and be able to pick out key ideas.

VII.   Teaching Procedures:
   A.   Use a value continuum to assess the students' attitudes about the energy problem. "What is your attitude about the energy crisis?"

Record the attitudes and discuss the reasons behind each (Negative Ned, Neutral Nell, Positive Pete). Save for future reference.

B. "Brainstorm" by asking students to tell you what energy means to them. Write down their responses on the chalkboard. Then have children look up "energy" in dictionaries and text glossaries.

C. Provide students with books about the sun, the chief source of energy. Select one or more myths about the sun and read it to the students. Encourage students to share the myths about the sun that they've heard and/or read. Suggested sources include the *Children of Odin* by Padraic Colum, published by Macmillan and *Hawaiian Myths of Earth, Sea, and Sky* by Vivian Thompson, published by Holiday House.

D. Have children seated in a semicircle with a table located to the front and center. Darken the room as much as possible to prepare for the experiment. The teacher or students can demonstrate. On the table, place a candle. Explain that you are going to demonstrate three forms of energy and afterward you'll ask them to identify those forms. "Number One," light the candle. "Number Two," place your hand over the candle, draw it back quickly and say "ouch!" As you say "Number Three," light the three candles you have secured with clay in an aluminum pie tin. In the center of the tin you have placed a pencil and secured it with clay with a test tube inverted over the pencil. The test tube goes through the center of the inverted foil wheel. The foil wheel should begin to spin. Blow out the candles and help children conclude the three forms of energy are light, heat, and motion.

E. Show the film "Energy: A First Film" by BFA Educational Media.

F. After the film, on a large sheet of tagboard with the headings "Light, Heat, and Motion," write down sources of energy the children suggest to you. Encourage the class to add to the lists as the module progresses.

G. Discuss air and its properties, especially wind and what it can do. Use a plastic windmill to show the idea of motion, and discuss how human beings have used wind to do work for them.

H. Using a large tub, a pan of water, and the water wheel, illustrate how moving water can be a source of energy. Pour the water over the wheel which you have placed over the tub. Discuss why the wheel turned. Direct the children's attention to the lidded pan of water you have previously placed on a hot plate. As the water begins to boil, the loose-fitting lid begins to bounce. (Steam, a form of water, is moving the lid.) Have students collect pictures to illustrate how water helps us.

(The teacher will need to spend time with slow learners in a small group situation to review the experiments. If at all possible, perform the experiments again.)

(The gifted students might want to do added research work about how water helps us work. They might construct a bulletin board to depict their findings.)

I. Take the students outside. Using a magnifying glass, a wad of paper, and a pie tin, demonstrate how concentrated rays can ignite the paper. Discuss why this fire occurred and why this only happens when the light and heat are concentrated. (Discuss the hazards of looking directly at the sun.)

J. Discuss that paper comes from trees and that plants get energy from the sun to produce food. The plant store the energy and we use the energy when we burn them. Use posters or library books to add informational evidence.

K. Have students look around and name or bring things to you that would not exist if there were no sun. Some students might like to develop a bulletin board to illustrate their ideas.
(Have gifted students gather information about solar energy. Have them design, on paper, their own homes heated by solar energy.)

L. Show the film "Riches of the Earth" (revised). List all the examples of transportation the children give you and the types of energy used to power them. Using old magazines, have children cut out as many pictures as they can illustrating the forms of transportation listed, and make a chart. Have students gather information about transportation in their local area.

M. Show the film on electricity entitled, "To Be Continued." Invite a resource person from Consumers Power or other company in your area who will discuss electricity and its sources with the children. Make sure you involve students in the planning. (Consumers Power is an example of one company that provides pamphlets, coloring books, and comic books on a variety of subject matter related to energy and ecology.)

N. Briefly review the sources of energy and their uses. Discuss what the school day would be like if we had no energy. List the sources of energy found in the classroom. If possible, conduct class for one day with limited or no energy.

O. Divide the classroom into small groups. Explain that each group is a living unit. Present the following problem:
Your group lives in a city where coal is used to make electricity. Your house has an electric furnace and stove. One day your family wakes up to discover that there is no more gas, coal, or oil. What is it like? How would you proceed?
(Have gifted students do an in-depth study of how coal is made into electricity. Have them report their findings to the class.)

P. Using a burning candle and a glass dish held over it, show the lamp black collected on the dish. Discuss gases, smoke, and ash produced by burning various sources of fuel. Introduce the term pollution.

Q. View films about pollution, such as "Air Pollution" and "Pollution: It's Up To You."

R. Review the forms of energy with the students. List them under the headings "Pollutants" and "Nonpollutants." Discuss how these pollutants affect us now and how they will affect us in the future. If time permits, some of the children may want to make and illustrate these on a chart. Place the chart near the other two previously made.

(Work on vocabulary with slow learners and do some simple experiments, such as jelly in petri dish, to show dust particles in the air—a form of pollution.)

(Have gifted students construct a chart illustrating the population of the world and the energy consumed. Have them show the chart and discuss the findings with the rest of the class. They could also do some in-depth research in their community to determine to what degree the pollution exists.)

Some classes might want to look at the global aspects of the energy problem at this point.

S. Using the article in the November 1973 issue of *Better Homes and Gardens*, entitled "Forty-six Ways to Conserve Energy in Your Home," or the April 19, 1977 issue of *Newsweek*, and using any other

When assigning your students activities to be accomplished in small groups, insure that each student has a specific task to accomplish.

information you have gleaned from other readings on the subject, lead a discussion on the topic of using energy wisely.

T. Make a class book entitled *I Can Conserve Energy*; every child contributes one page to the book using the form "I _____, can conserve energy by . . . ." Have each child illustrate his page. (The pages can be bound together after they have been completed.) Place the book in your classroom library and allow the children to check the book out overnight.

U. Have the students form a list of all the possible ways of saving energy at home. Examples might include: turning off lights not being used, walking instead of riding in the car, using hand methods instead of electric for brushing teeth, opening cans, etc., turning down the heat and wearing a sweater. Encourage them to take action. They can either verbally report the results or have parents verify the results.

V. Show the film, "The Atom and the Kilowatt." Use library books for additional data gathering. Discuss the future and what sources of energy we will be using. Include atomic, wind, tidal, solar, geothermal, and coal gasification and liquidation.
(Have gifted students do further research concerning "Energy of the Future." Have them make a chart depicting their findings.)

W. Have the students redo the value continuum (see item A). Has anybody changed his or her position? If so, have him or her tell the class why. If some students feel even more strongly about their initial position, have them explain why.

X. Have students discuss and decide how they can help the energy situation. Let them spend time planning their strategies. (For example, the students may decide they want to inform the community of their findings. They might hold a series of meetings, complete with visual aids, to explain the energy situation to parents or other members of the community. They might decide to go on a family and/ or school campaign to save energy.)

Y. The following activities are geared to the individual or small group. The student might be given the entire list to select those he or she would like to do. A contract approach might be used, small groups might work together, or the activities could be developed and placed in a learning center on energy.

   1. Write a letter to your local power company thanking them for helping you learn about electricity. Tell them what you liked or disliked about their material.

       (The teacher may want to pick out one or two activities in the learning center and do these with the slow learner group as a whole.)

   2. Discuss with your father or mother the part energy plays in his

or her job. Bring in a list of problems they would have if there were no gas, coal, or oil left in the world.

3. Interview a gasoline station owner. Ask him the following questions:
    a. How has the gasoline shortage affected you?
    b. What recommendations would you make to your customers for conserving gasoline?
    c. What do you foresee in the future concerning gasoline and oil? Share your interview with your classmates.

4. How can we conserve energy in our school? List as many ways as you can think of. Discuss these ways with your classmates and other people in the building. You might like to make a mural or bulletin board depicting the results.

5. What sources of energy do factories in the area use? Write letters to these companies and ask them. Your teacher will help you with the names and addresses. Share the information you gathered with your class.

6. Make a collage out of magazine pictures showing machines which use electric motors to do work for us.

7. Electricity is used more during different times of the day and year than at other times. These times are called "peak" times. If too many people are using too much electricity during peak times there might not be enough energy to go around. List as many of the peak times as you can think of.

8. Make a list of ways that energy is wasted in your home. Discuss the list with your family.

9. List all the advantages and disadvantages you can think of for using candles, rather than electricity, as a light source.

10. Make a book entitled, *Machines of the Future*. On each page, draw and color a machine of the future. Under it, describe how it would work and what sources of energy it would use. (The machines should be your own inventions.)

11. Make a chart listing energy sources of the past and present under the headings "Caveman," "Pioneer," Man of Today." If you are unsure of your information, seek help from the library.

12. Look through the newspapers and cut out all articles you find concerning energy. Display them on a bulletin board, and discuss some of them with your classmates.

13. With the help of a friend, make up a song telling about ways of conserving energy. Teach it to others.

14. Almost two-thirds of all the oil in the world is found in what we call the "Middle East." The major producers of oil there are the countries of Kuwait, Saudi Arabia, Iran, Iraq, Libya and Algeria. Find these places on a globe or world map. Choose one

of these countries and discover a few things about it. Share these facts with the class.

15. Think of a day in your life. How do you use energy? Now think of the future. How might things be different? Write a story about the days in the life of a boy or girl in the future.

16. Find some friends to play the game: "Care and Conserve." This game consists of a playing board with 10 brown and 20 white squares, 6 markers, 30 white and 15 brown playing cards, and one die.

Playing Board: The white and brown squares should be placed on the board in the form of a path. A "Start" and "Finish" should be placed at the beginning and end of the trail respectively.

The Playing Cards: The white playing cards have writing on one side. Each card can be different or you can repeat some of them. Each card states one example for conserving energy with a positive numeral from 1 to 5 on it, depending on how important you feel that form of conserving energy would be. Example:

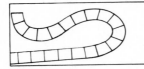

| You remembered to turn the lights off when you left the room. +2 | You turned down the thermostat when you went to bed. +2 |

Start
(The students can help design cards.)

| You open the refrigerator only when needed. +2 | You take the C Bus instead of asking mother to take you. +3 |

The brown playing cards also have writing on one side, stating examples of wasting energy and a negative numeral from 1 to 5. Sample cards:

| You leave the radio on all night. −3 | Last winter you turned your thermostat up to 80°. −4 | You run the dishwasher after each snack. −4 |

Object of Game: The first person to follow the trail from "Start" to "Finish" wins.

Procedure: The game may be played by 2 to 6 people. The players throw the die to see who goes first. The highest number begins. The play then proceeds clockwise. Cards are placed facedown in two piles according to colors. The first player begins by drawing a white card and reading it to the others. He then moves forward the amount of steps indicated by the numeral on the card. He returns the card to the bottom of the deck.

If he lands on a white square, he draws a white card when it is his turn again. If he lands on a brown square, he must draw a brown card on his next turn and, after reading the card aloud, must move backward the number of steps indicated on the card. Play continues in like manner around the board until one player crosses the finish line.

17. Have students devise their own board game, the object being to see how many ways energy is used in any given occupation. (First have students generate a list of occupations. Then have them make the rules. Teams for the game would be ideal.)

VIII. Evaluation:

A. Administer a short quiz on forms and sources of energy.

B. Develop a checklist concerning knowledge, ideas, and skills you expect students to either master or develop to a specified level or capacity. An example is below.[1]

C. Have students keep folders containing their group and/or individual projects. These might include answers to questions, essays, stories, maps, charts, diagrams, etc. Evaluate the results. Look for progress over time.

D. Each page of the book *I Can Conserve Energy* can be evaluated.

	Attacks Problem in Rational Manner			Gathers Data				Organizes Data			Summarizes Data			Draws Conclusions		
	Sets Hypotheses	Tests Hypotheses	Identifies Questions	Studies Prints	Uses Maps & Globes	Listens to Stories	Uses Books	Differentiates Data	Categorizes Data							
Bill D.																
Jim S.																
Bob V.																
Jim Z.																
Mary K.																
Janet A.																

[1]Adapted from Ellis, Art and Janet Elaine Alleman-Brooks, "How to Evaluate Problem-Solving-Oriented Social Studies," *The Social Studies*, Washington, D.C.: Heldref Publications, Vol. 68, No. 3 (May/June 1977), p. 101.

    E.   Evaluate the social action projects. For example, if students go on a campaign to inform the community of the energy crisis, the class should assess the results. What were the strong points? weak points? How could improvement be made next time?

    F.   Assess the verbal reports and/or parent verification concerning energy conservation out of school.

CLASSROOM RESULTS

Teachers felt that at least four weeks are needed to do an adequate job with the module. While most teachers felt the concepts were appropriate, one teacher indicated that some of the concepts needed clarification: "One example is the 'energy chain.' " "I felt that the kids had trouble in understanding how all energy can be traced back to the sun. We traced the process of coal formation and oil and gas production."

    Several teachers reported ways in which they modified the module to meet the needs of their students:

1. "Some kinds became excited about the use of steam to supply power. They experimented with a system of tubing, bottles, and teakettles to design a good source of power."
2. "Because third graders are still pretty young, I modified the module by making it shorter."

According to their teachers, many students went beyond the module:

1. "The more advanced students thought up questions that they wanted to be answered; for example, 'Can we study volcanoes to find out if that is energy?' and 'What different types of energy are used in transportation?' "
2. "One student made a model of an early American sawmill that used a waterwheel as its source of power. Another student made a model of a windmill and investigated the Dutch who used windmills as a source of energy."
3. "Several students brought in the article about a city in Ohio that is burning garbage and trash to assist in turning turbines that produce electricity."

Teachers indicated that several additional activities were included to accommodate individual differences:

1. "Designing hotdog cookers, counting revolutions of windmills in different locations, studying volcanoes, and growing plants are examples of activities I developed for individual differences."
2. "Individual students watched filmstrips to review the ideas discussed in class."
3. "Students added activities of their own. Some of them decided to keep a log of their daily energy use."

Suggestions for future users were provided by several teachers who taught the module:

1. "I think it would be a good idea to have the students put on a play about energy for the parents; perhaps then children would not return to school saying, 'My mom thinks it's too much trouble to turn off the lights or the television set.' "
2. "Encourage parents to get involved!"
3. "Allow more time for social action projects."
4. "Even if the experiment fails, the students get the idea and also the experience of something not working out. They then can speculate as to why it failed and test it again."
5. "I would suggest using the module at the beginning of the school year. It will really stimulate interest!"

STUDENT BIBLIOGRAPHY

Bindick, Jeanne, *Why Things Work; A Book about Energy*, New York: Parents' Magazine Press, 1972.

Federal Energy Administration, *"Energy Activities with 'Energy Ant,' "* Washington, D.C.: Federal Energy Administration, Office of Communications and Public Affairs.

Lefkowitz, R. J. and John E. Johnson, *Fuel for Today and for Tomorrow*, New York: Parents' Magazine Press, 1974.

Pondendorf, Illa, *Things Are Made To Move*, Chicago: Children's Press, 1971.

Pondendorf, Illa, *The True Book of Energy*, Chicago: Children's Press, 1971.

Pope, Billy N. and Ramone Ware Emmons, *Let's Visit an Electric Company* and *Let's Visit an Oil Company*, Dallas: Taylor Publishing Company, 1971.

TEACHER BIBLIOGRAPHY

Anderson, Calvin E., *A Teacher's Handbook on Energy*, Supporting Services Unit, 201 East Colfax Ave., Colorado Department on Education, Denver, Colorado, 1974. (One free copy)

Energy Conservation: Guidelines for Action, 1974 Region Nine Superintendent, Michigan Association of School Administrators, 421 W. Kalamazoo St., Lansing, Michigan 48933, 1974.

Fowler, John M., *Energy and the Environment*, New York: McGraw-Hill, 1975.

Fowler, John M., *Energy—Environment Source Book*, Washington, D.C.: National Science Teachers Association, 1975.

Fowler, John M., "Energy: Present Problems and Future Problems," *Science and Children*, Vol. 15, No. 6 (March 1978), pp. 13–14.

Hubbert, M. King, *Energy Resources*, Washington, D.C.: National Academy of Sciences —National Research Council, 1962.

Mervine, Kathryn E. and Rebecca E. Cawley, *Energy—Environment Materials Guide*, Washington, D.C.: National Science Teachers Association, 1975.

Smith, Stephen M., *Energy—Environment Miniunit Guide*, Washington, D.C.: National Science Teachers Association, 1975.

Government and Politics ▶

Participating in the Legislative Process

This teaching module is designed for pupils in upper-elementary grades. Typically at this level students will study aspects of state or national government. This module has been designed to consider one major facet of the legislative branch, namely how a bill becomes a law. The primary objective is to help students realize the multitude of regulations that govern our lives, and how these regulations are initiated from ideas to laws.

The module provides opportunities for students to become personally involved with the topic by asking that they begin by taking a careful look at their own lives and describing in writing everything they did from the time they awakened until the moment the module is initiated. The teacher is asked to plead for detail. The student is then asked to point out where rules or laws are evident. The purpose is to help students come to realize the impact of government regulations upon their lives. Other suggested activities include role playing, simulation, making a bulletin board, viewing films, and observing a legislative session. State or US social studies texts that deal with government could provide excellent source material. By the end of the module students will have opportunities to use the information they have gathered to assist them in participating in class government if it exists, and to begin building a participatory attitude toward government (once they have reached voting age).

I. Grade Level: Upper Elementary

II. Special Materials:
- A. Magazines with pictures depicting subtle ways the government regulates our lives
- B. *Who Really Runs America?* by Robert A. Lindstrom (see bibliography)
- C. Materials concerning your state government—legislative body
- D. Data retrieval chart
- E. Construction paper, lettering supplies, empty bulletin board to assist in simulating how a bill becomes a law
- F. *Democracy* (simulation) published by Webster
- G. "America Rock" a filmstrip and sound cassette by Xerox, which goes through the legislative process in cartoon form (optional)
- H. "How a Bill Becomes a Law" chart (see next page)

III. Time: 3 weeks

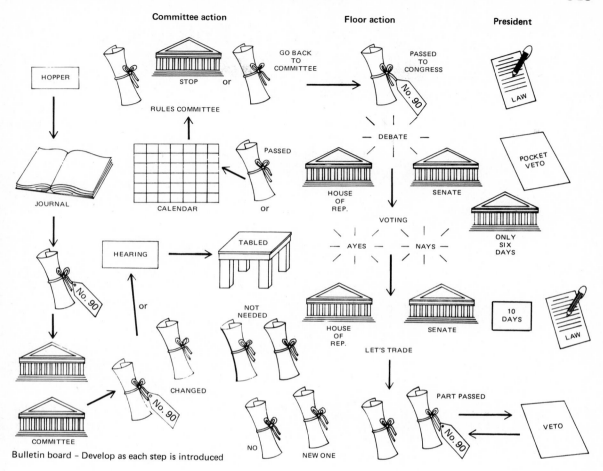

Committee action   Floor action   President

Bulletin board – Develop as each step is introduced

IV. Concepts:
    A.   A multitude of *government regulations* govern our lives.
    B.   The *legislative branch* of the government makes the laws.
    C.   The *legislative branch* is composed of two houses: *Senate* and *House of Representatives.*
    D.   A *bill* must go through a step-by-step process before it can become a law.

V. Objectives:
    A.   After completing the module, the student will be able to actively participate in actual or simulated experiences in passing rules/laws in the classroom.
    B.   Upon completion of the module the student will be able to list three ways that citizens can be more active in the legislative process.

VI. Entry Behavior Indicators:

    A.   The student will have previous experience in learning about rules/laws of the family, school, and community.

    B.   The student will have previous experience in simulation games.

VII.   Teaching Procedures:

    A.   Begin by asking students to describe in writing everything they did from the time they got up today to this very moment. Be specific! (For example, if they got up and immediately gargled with Listerine, please include the brand name.) As an option the teacher can write a very detailed vignette and ask students to list all of the places where government regulations entered into the picture. Discuss the results.

        (Have magazines available for slow learners so they can cut out pictures to depict their morning. They can make a poster to describe the events. They need not be concerned about accuracy of brand names.)

    B.   Pose this question: Who makes the laws? List student responses and then introduce students to *Who Really Runs America?* or another appropriate source. At this point students will be ready to investigate who makes the laws in their state and what are the qualifications. Library time will be needed. Develop a data retrieval chart for recording the information gleaned from the resources.

        (The teacher will need to provide very simple brochures for the slow learners and other easy reading material. Cassette tapes made by lawmakers would be very useful if presented in short segments.)

        (Gifted students could design and administer a survey to determine how many adults know who the present lawmakers are.)

    C.   Invite a state legislator to visit the class to explain in more detail what a legislator does and what his/her qualifications are. Focus questions might include: Why did you decide to become a legislator? What are the qualifications necessary? How did you go about getting elected? How do you see your role in helping members of this elementary class and their families? (Make sure students see the tie-in to their lives.)

Role playing can be a powerful tool in creating interest and involvement in government and politics.

D. As an option explore with students the possibility of pursuing politics as a career. As a class build a (political) career tree to illustrate the variety of options that are available in politics.

E. Pose this question: Why don't all good ideas become law? Have students list some ideas they think would make good laws. Select one and divide the class into the necessary sections (see chart) to illustrate what is needed for a bill to become a law. Add to the bulletin board display as you move through the simulation. We have tried this. We have seen it done several ways but this seems to be most effective.

F. Simulate "How a Bill Becomes a Law." Make sure you move slowly, systematically discussing each step.

G. After the class has completed the simulation of passing one law have them try another. Discuss the results. Focus questions might include: Was it a difficult process? Why or why not? How are citizens involved? Affected? Who can help legislators? Who does research on the bills? laws? What did you learn from this process? Do you think legislators are too powerful? Why or why not?

H. Have students play *Democracy*. This simulation illustrates the problems a legislator faces as he or she engages in the legislative process. Focus questions for debriefing might include: What strategies did you use to get your bills passed? What made you most frustrated? Did you feel committed to your constituency? Why or why not?
(The teacher or gifted peers will need to work very closely with slow learners if they are to be successful in the game.)
(Show gifted students how to play the game in advance so they can chair the small groups.)

I. If possible, arrange for a trip to the state capitol to observe the legislative process at work. Have students assist in planning for the experience. Encourage them to develop a list of questions they would like to have answered.

J. During the visit try to assist students in finding ways they and the adults they know can be more involved in the legislative process. Perhaps the lawmakers will be able to show letters from their constituency. Plan to visit with lobbyists, if at all possible.

K. Summarize the module. Have the class list the key ideas that were developed during the module. Categorize the responses. What generalizations can be formulated?

L. Have students write letters to their parents informing them what they learned and sharing with them ways in which they can be more influential/active in the legislative process.
(Assist slow learners in formulating their letters. The teacher might want to have students prepare a group experience story.)
(Gifted students might like to write letters to the editor explaining how citizens can be more involved.)

VIII. Evaluation:

A. During this module, the students will be doing individual and group research; therefore, an appraisal of study habits and attitudes would be appropriate. The following checklist is an example:

APPRAISAL OF STUDY HABITS

Behavior To Be Observed	NAMES OF CHILDREN					
	Maria	Sue	Jim	Craig	Ned	Pam
Locates sources of information						
Uses index						
Uses a table of contents						
Gathers data from charts, tables						

B. Another evaluation can be made during the simulations. The following is one example:

Student Participation Simulation	Juan	Joe	Iris	Bev	Jesus
Took part in simulation I					
Took part in simulation II					
Played according to the rules					
Showed interest					
Was able to pull out key ideas					

(Conduct private interviews to gather this data.)

C. Evaluate the letter to parents. Does it contain the key ideas developed during the module. Does it reflect understanding of the legislative branch and does it suggest ways citizens can be more active participants?

CLASSROOM RESULTS

Teachers found the concepts and teaching procedures useful. Some teachers liked the module very much because it fits well in the more traditional social studies curriculum. Others liked it because it used concerns of children in teaching how laws are made. Some teachers thought the concept of government was hard to grasp while others felt that organizing the class around government made the concept extremely meaningful.

The most appealing part of the module seemed to be the use of real concerns for bills, simulations, and field trips. One teacher mentioned the interviews with lobbyists as the highlight of the module.

Teachers shared comments for future users:

1. "If it's impossible to go to the state capitol, plan a trip to the mayor's office."
2. "If you play the *Democracy* game make sure you allow plenty of time. The rules are fairly complicated. I simplified them for my students."
3. "Involve parents in the teaching of this module. It's amazing how many of them are formally involved in government and politics on a regular basis."

STUDENT BIBLIOGRAPHY

Acheson, Patricia C., *Our Federal Government: How It Works*, New York: Dodd, Mead, 1969.

Kelly, Frank K., *Your Freedoms: The Bill of Rights*, New York: Putnam, 1964.

Lindstrom, Robert A., *Who Really Runs America?* Garden City, N.Y.: Doubleday, 1974.

Mazer, Norma, *A Figure of Speech*, New York: Delacorte, 1973.

Reuben, Gabriel H., *How Documents Preserve Freedom*, Chicago: Genetic Press, 1964.

Ross, George E., *Know Your Government*, Skokie, Ill.: Rand McNally, 1962.

Sagarin, Mary, *Equal Justice under Law*, New York: Lothrop, 1966.

Wise, William, *American Freedom and the Bill of Rights*, New York: Parents' Magazine Press, 1975.

TEACHER BIBLIOGRAPHY

Acheson, Patricia C., *Our Federal Government: How It Works*, New York: Dodd, Mead, 1969.

Crumeller, Roy E., "A Pet Project," *Teacher* (September 1977), p. 110.

Dvorin, Eugene P., and Arthur J. Misner, *Government in American Society*, Menlo Park, Calif.: Addison-Wesley, 1973.

Quigley, Charles N. and Richard P. Longaker, *Conflict, Politics, and Freedom*, Boston: Ginn, 1968.

Quigley, Charles N., *Your Rights and Responsibilities As an American Citizen*, Boston: Ginn, 1967, 1976 revision.

Quigley, Charles N. and Richard P. Longaker, *Voices for Justice: Role Playing in Democratic Procedure*, Boston: Ginn, 1970.

Radcliffe, Robert (Ed.), *Trailmarks in Liberty Series*, Boston: Houghton Mifflin, 1972.

▶ Interface with
PERSONAL
EFFICACY,
OCCUPATION/
CAREERS,
LEISURE, FAMILY

Human Equality ▶

Challenging Sex Role Stereotypes

This teaching module is designed for students in upper-elementary grades. Typically at this level they are exposed to US history. Usually at this level they also spend a part of social studies time on current events. In either of these instances, this module could be useful. The primary objective of the module is to raise the levels of consciousness among pupils concerning the changing roles of boys and girls, men and women in our society. The module provides opportunities for students to become personally involved with the issue by asking that they begin with their life lines—drawing or cutting pictures from magazines to depict their lives to date and then adding pictures to represent what they would like their future to be. They are then asked to look at the similarities and differences between sexes. Other activities in the module include: surveying older and younger individuals in the community to look at role changes that are occurring, inviting grandparents or older adults to discuss what it was like when they were growing up in terms of role expectations, and designing a stamp or banner as a symbol of people's rights in a nonsexist society. Social studies textbooks that include material on historical figures in society, current events publications, and literary works can all provide valuable resource material. By the end of the module it is hoped that students will have developed increasingly flexible ideas about sex roles that will continue to help them in their interactions with people and with decisions about their personal life.

I. Grade Level: Upper Elementary

II. Special Materials:
   A. Library books (see student bibliography)
   B. Art materials
   C. Magazines
   D. "About Me" survey

"ABOUT ME"*

My name is _____
I am a   female or male
Place an x beside each item that you would do.

*Each classroom teacher should modify or add to the survey to meet his or her specific needs.

_____ wash dishes	_____ sew
_____ make the bed	_____ sunbathe
_____ cook dinner	_____ call for a date with the opposite sex
_____ empty the garbage	_____ use hairspray
_____ mow the lawn	_____ take home economics in school
_____ wash the car	_____ take vocational agriculture in school
_____ purchase groceries	_____ wear beads or other jewelry
_____ babysit	_____ dance
_____ play volley ball	_____ shop for your own clothes
_____ play baseball	_____ smoke
_____ swim	_____ cry

E.   "My Opinion" survey

"MY OPINION"*

If you agree, circle Yes.   My sex is _____.
If you disagree, circle No.

1.	It is all right for boys to want to become nurses or secretaries.	Yes	No
2.	It is all right for girls to want to become cab drivers.	Yes	No
3.	It is all right for girls to want to become political leaders.	Yes	No
4.	It is all right for girls to want to become doctors.	Yes	No
5.	It is all right for boys to want to become librarians.	Yes	No
6.	It is all right for boys to want to become early elementary teachers.	Yes	No
7.	It is natural for boys to enjoy playing football.	Yes	No
8.	It is unnatural for girls to enjoy playing touch football.	Yes	No
9.	It is natural for girls to enjoy babysitting.	Yes	No
10.	It is unnatural for boys to enjoy babysitting.	Yes	No
11.	It is natural for girls to spend a lot of time making themselves look appealing.	Yes	No
12.	It is unnatural for boys to spend a lot of time making themselves look appealing.	Yes	No
13.	It is natural for women to want to stay home and raise children after marriage.	Yes	No
14.	It is unnatural for a man to want to stay home and take care of the children while his wife goes to school or works.	Yes	No

*Feel free to modify this survey according to the needs of your students.

F.   "Free To Be . . . You and Me" film or record

III.   Time: 3 weeks

IV.   Concepts:
   A.   _Individuals_ should be free to be themselves regardless of sex.
   B.   _Boys_ and _girls_ like to do many of the same things.
   C.   The _roles_ of _males_ and _females_ are _changing_.
   D.   The _freedom_ to _express_ the best _traits_ of both males and females (as a specific situation warrants) can be beneficial and helpful.

V.   Objectives:
   A.   The student will develop an advanced level of consciousness concerning the changing roles of boys and girls, men and women in our society as observed through role playing and class discussions. This will also be assessed during individual personal interviews.
   B.   The student will develop flexible ideas about sex roles as observed in essays and class discussions.

VI.   Entry Behavior Indicators:
   A.   The student will have previous experience in role playing.
   B.   The student will have previous experience in the use of reference materials.

VII.   Teaching Procedures:
   A.   Have students make their life lines. They can draw pictures or cut pictures out of magazines to depict their lives to date and then add pictures to represent what they would like their future to be. Attach each set on a separate long sheet of paper, making sure the pictures are in sequence. Share their life lines. Discuss likenesses and differences. Look for similarities. Discuss the results.
   B.   Ask students to complete the survey entitled "About Me." Tally, graph, and discuss the results. Have students survey older and younger students. Compare and discuss the results.
   C.   Show the film "Free To Be . . . You or Me." If film isn't available, use the record. Discuss the main theme of each song that is played. Does it reflect real life? Why or why not?
   D.   Have students complete "My Opinion" survey. Tally, graph, analyze, discuss. Focus questions might include: Why do you agree? disagree? Do you have any idea why you hold the attitude that you do? Discuss influences on our lives.
        (Have the slow learners work with the teacher in tallying the results of the survey. Prior to graphing the teacher will need to have a "skills session" with these students at which time they will learn what graphing is, how it can be used, and skills needed to graph results.)
        (Have gifted students make careful comparisons between the various groups surveyed. Then encourage the students to devise and administer a second questionnaire to determine why these differences exist.)
   E.   Have students survey other students, teachers, parents, grandparents, neighbors, community leaders, etc. Again, tally, graph, analyze, and discuss the results.
        (Limit the number to be surveyed for slow learners.)
        (Again, have gifted students make careful comparisons between/ among various groups surveyed. Speculate as to "why.")
   F.   Encourage students to use the library to gather information and ideas about the changing roles of females and males in society.

G. Invite grandparents or other older adults to class to discuss what it was like when they were growing up in terms of role expectations of females/males. Have students be involved in planning for the resource people. They can develop a list of questions they would like to have answered. Have students write letters inviting them.

H. Discuss with the students what their parents do—in and outside the home. Have students plan, prepare, and administer surveys in an attempt to gather information concerning their parents. They might plan, develop, and administer a similar survey to grandparents to determine changing roles of human beings.

I. Invite female factory workers, policewomen, lawyers, doctors, male nurses, secretaries, beauticians, early-elementary teachers, etc. to share their experiences. What obstacles including those related to sex did they have to overcome? Be sure to include students in the initial planning.

(The teacher will need to work with slow learners in an attempt to help them formulate the questions they would like to seek answers to.)

(Have gifted students interview several individuals from a selected profession in an attempt to make comparisons.)

J. Have students in small groups or as a total class design a stamp, a flag, or a banner as a symbol for people's rights in a nonsexist society.

K. As a means of "pulling the module together," have students write and present a play depicting a typical day in the life of a modern man and/or woman or the life of a man and/or woman thirty years from now. Present to another class. (Optional—Using a tune familiar to the students, write a new song for people in a nonsexist society.)

VIII. Evaluation:

A. Use a discussion checklist periodically throughout the module to assess each student's performance. An example is as follows:

Name	Asks Questions	Listens	Responds	Repeats

B. Use "I Learned" statements. Have the students write 5 of them. Encourage the students to pair off and share their statements.

C. Conduct personal interviews with the students in an attempt to find out what they have been learning through library sources and from large and small group activity. Keep a record summarizing each student interview.

D. Have each student write an essay describing the role of young men/women. Include at least 4 examples and give three reasons why they believe as they do.

CLASSROOM RESULTS

Teachers tended to feel that the time period is appropriate. A middle-school teacher indicated that his students were able to accomplish the objectives and complete the module in less time than he had anticipated.

The concepts seem appropriate, according to the teachers who field tested the module. One teacher added that if the concepts are not reinforced outside of school, they will probably not be as deeply embedded as the teacher would like them to be.

Several suggestions were made for future users:

1. "Make sure you invite grandparents to class to talk about their lives and roles. Kids love that aspect of the module."
2. "Older children could visit retirement centers, senior citizen centers, or nursing homes to meet with and talk to older citizens and get their views on role expectations of males and females."
3. "Field experiences could be arranged to see males and females in 'new' job situations. Women judges and lawyers could highlight the court/justice system and policewomen could do the same for the law enforcement system. This could be a double treat—'human equality' and rules and laws!"
4. "Have students follow news accounts of discrimination suits based on sex or race and keep scrapbooks of their findings."

STUDENT BIBLIOGRAPHY

Carol, B. J., *Single to Center*, Austin, Texas: Steck Vaughn, 1974.
Cleaver, Bill and Vera, *Lady Ellen Grae*, Philadelphia: Lippincott, 1968.
English, Betty Lou, *Women at Their Work*, New York: Dial, 1977.
Katz, Bobbi, *The Manifesto and Me*, New York: F. Watts, 1974.
Knudson, R. R. and R. R. Zanballer, New York: Dell, 1974.
Miles, Betty, *The Real Me*, New York: Knopf, 1974.
Morgan, Helen L., *First Lady of American Astronomy*, Philadelphia: Westminster, 1977.
O'Dell, Scott, *Carlotta*, Boston: Houghton Mifflin, 1977.
Smith, Doris, *Kick a Stone Home*, New York: Crowell, 1974.
Weiner, Sandra, *I Want To Be a Fisherman*, New York: Macmillan, 1977.

TEACHER BIBLIOGRAPHY

Blauforb, Marjorie, "Equal Opportunities for Girls in Athletics," *Today's Education* (November–December 1974), pp. 52–55.

Gornick, Vivian and Barbara E. Moran (eds.), *Women in Sexist Society*, New York: New American Library, 1972.

Greenfield, Jeff, "What It Will Take for a Woman To Be Elected President." *Glamour* (April 1976), p. 241.

Hahn, Carole L., "Eliminating Sexism from the Schools: An Application of Planned Change," *Social Education*, Vol. 39, No. 3 (March 1975), p. 133.

Holman, Dorothy Riggs, "Teaching about Women in Secondary Schools: Springboards for Inquiry," *Social Education*, Vol. 39, No. 3 (March 1975), p. 140.

Innocenti, Celeste, "You Raise Crops but You Rear Your Children," *Scholastic Voice*, Vol. 58, No. 9 (April 1975), p. 20.

Phillips, Mary Ann and Betty Pull, "Teaching Our Story in the Elementary Classroom, Fourteen Specific Suggestions for Teachers," *Social Education*, Vol. 39, No. 3 (March 1975), p. 138.

Scholastic Scope, "Being Male, Being Female, What Do You Think?" Vol. 24, No. 3, (February 1976), pp. 3, 14.

Sipilia, Helvi L., "Women and World Affairs," *Today's Education* (November–December 1974), pp. 66.

Tanner, Leslie B. (Ed.), *Voices from Women's Liberation*, New York: New American Library, 1971.

▶ Interface with
FAMILY,
CITIZENSHIP

The Human Life Cycle ▶

MIDDLE

New Insights into Aging

This teaching module is designed for students in middle-elementary grades. Typically at this level pupils study pioneers in the United States. This module, with a focus on aging, could be used to supplement that study. The primary objective is to sensitize students to this facet of life and to help them come to grips with the fact that things change over time and that aging is a natural process. The module provides opportunities for students to become personally involved with the topic by initially participating in a survey, then asking them to begin with the changes that have occurred in their own lives, and finally looking at others who have lived somewhat longer. Suggestions are made for a variety of activities which include brainstorming, making life lines, developing charts, surveying, and role playing. Social studies texts dealing with the US or other cultures could provide excellent source materials. Recently a variety of new children's literary sources dealing with this topic have become available and can enhance such a module immensely. By the end of the module students will have opportunities to use the information they have gathered to assist them in clarifying their present attitudes and feelings about aging and hopefully be able to relate to older people in a more positive and meaningful way.

    I.   Grade Level: Middle Elementary

   II. Special Materials:
       A. Letter to the parents explaining the key objectives in the module eliciting their reactions to the general topic, and asking for feedback prior to beginning the module.
       B. Sample Survey Instrument

SAMPLE SURVEY INSTRUMENT

1. How old is old? _____

2. How many old people do you know? _____

3. How many people do you know who are over 60? _____

4. How well do you know the people in question number 3? (Place a check on the appropriate line)
   a) very well   _____
   b) just a little   _____
   c) I just know the family of the older person   _____

5. Do you have any grandparents living? ____ How many? _____

6. If you have grandparents who are living, do they live with you? ____

7. If they are living and don't live with you, how often do you see them?
   a) about once a week?   _____
   b) about once a month?   _____
   c) about once a year?   _____
   d) other amount of time?   _____

8. What do you think older people talk about? _____
   _____

9. What do you think older people do for fun? _____

10. How are older people viewed in our media? (TV, movies, books, newspapers, etc. Give specific examples, if possible.) _____

11 Where do older people get their money once they retire? _____

12. Do they have enough money to spend it freely? (Explain your answer.) ____

13. Do you think that most older people are happy? (Explain your answer.) ____

14. When you see an older person walking slowly or with a cane, or appear to be confused, how do you feel? ____
   _____

15. Cite at least one experience you have had with an older person. ____
   _____
   _____
   _____
   _____

    C.   "Aging"—(30 min. color) Indiana University, A.V. Center, Bloomington, Indiana 47401.

    D.   Props—old clothes, make-up, canes, cotton balls, mittens, wool socks, wheelchair.

    E.   Visuals that depict older people in a variety of cultural settings.

III.   Time: 2 weeks

IV.   Concepts:
    A.   Things *change* over time.
    B.   *Aging* is a natural process.
    C.   *Cultures* vary as to how old people are treated.
    D.   Old people often suffer from *physical defects*.

V.   Objectives:
    A.   As a result of this module, the student will have contact with at least one elderly person as demonstrated in the student log and through observation.
    B.   By the end of this module the student will be able to write a paper describing how he or she wants to be when he or she is old.

VI.   Entry Behavior Indicators:
    A.   Students should have previous experience in working in small groups.
    B.   Students should have previous experience in hypothesis testing.
    C.   Students should have previous experience in developing and administering questionnaires.
    D.   Students should have previous experience in role playing.

VII.   Teaching Procedures:
    A.   Administer the Sample Survey Instrument. Discuss the results.
    B.   Have a brainstorming session. The task is to have the students generate as many ideas as they can about time, time flow, and changes with time. This will give students an opportunity to think through a very abstract concept.
    C.   Have the students draw a line on a long piece of paper which represents the development of their life period, including ups and downs and different phases, such as first birthday, first time at nursery school, beginning of public school, etc. The student can include anything that seems important and illustrate the events by drawing or writing at the appropriate place on the life line. Focus questions for the discussion might include: What was the turning point in your life? What was the highest point? lowest point? What do I remember most from my early childhood? As a total group, have students discuss and decide what their lives have in common and how they differ from one another.
    D.   Have the children interview at least one parent, close relative, or friend (grown-ups) and ask them to draw their life lines. This gives

them a chance to interact with an older person. Discuss what they learned about the life of an older person.

(Have the slow learners interview the teacher.)

(Gifted students might want to interview several people and compare their results.)

E. Lead a class discussion concerning the people the students know and the various age groups represented. Make a chart to depict the results. It will no doubt lead to the obvious conclusion that we know more people our own age or we know more younger people than older people. Discuss possible reasons for this fact.

F. Have each child or small group of children make a list of adjectives or descriptions that fit the individual or group's image of "what old people are like."

G. Using the adjectives identified by the students, it now becomes the task of the students to find out whether or not these ideas or perceptions are accurate. Examples: Are old people out-of-date? Are old people sick? Are old people usually crabby? Have the students design and administer a questionnaire to old people in an attempt to gather information. Discuss sampling techniques.

(The teacher might want to go with slow learners to gather the information. An alternative would be to provide these youngsters with multimedia as a means of gathering data.)

(Encourage gifted students to administer the questionnaire in a variety of settings where old people are found.)

H. The data can be tallied and placed on a large chart. The chart should include the hypothesized behavior of old people on the left (placed vertically) and the name of each child across the top (placed horizontally). They can check the results of the interviews by stating "yes" or "true," or "no" or "false." The students can thus analyze the results in an attempt to see whether their hypotheses were proven right or wrong according to the questionnaires. Keep in mind that the sample size will be very limited.

I. After the class has analyzed the chart and understood the stereotypes of the elderly in our society, show students a series of pictures depicting old people in various cultural settings. Focus questions for the discussion might include: Do they live with their families? Are they respected or ignored? What is their function in society as a whole? Have children use their texts and supplemental sources to gather information concerning old people in various parts of the world.

(Provide multimedia sources and books for slow learners that are high interest/low readability.)

(Encourage gifted students to do some in-depth research comparing old people from at least two different cultures.)

J. If possible, bring in an elderly person from another culture, for

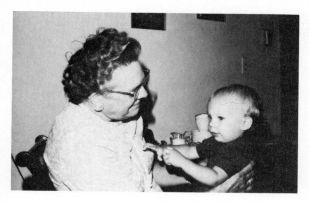

Grandparents as well as younger brothers and sisters can add an exciting dimension to the study of the human life cycle.

example, from Japan, to share his or her views with the class. Show a film illustrating aging in another culture. An example is entitled, "Aging," which shows two Jewish men discussing their views on growing old.

K. As a class discuss the question "How could we improve the way we treat old people, considering what we have learned from other cultures?"

L. For this lesson, the teacher will need to bring in old clothes and make-up to help transform students into old people. Each student will be asked to bring mittens, thick socks or boots, and perhaps a cane, cotton balls, or ear plugs. Half of the class will be old people and the other half will act as helpers. After a short period the roles will be reversed. Certain rules will be given to the old people. They have to wear mittens and socks (which will give them the idea of less mobility and pain such as arthritis). They can talk loud because they may have hearing problems. None of them can run or even walk fast. Perhaps one person could pretend that he or she was old and confined to a wheelchair. When all preparations have been made, subdivide the groups in fours. Directions should be given for each group to work out a role play with a beginning and a solution at the end. Sample situations are as follows:

1. At the cashier's desk two elderly women are confused about the change they got. They can't seem to count it.

2. In the train station an elderly man can't read the schedule for departures.

3. In the supermarket, the groceries are too heavy for an elderly woman to carry to the parking lot.

4. Two elderly people waiting at a bus stop, trying to get on the crowded bus and find a seat.

5. An elderly person tries to cross the street where there are no lights and a lot of traffic.

Discuss each enactment and at the end discuss what the students learned from this activity.

VIII. Evaluation:
    A. Have each student write a paper on the topic "When I am old I want to be like . . ." or "When I am old I want to be treated like . . . ." This will give students an opportunity to use the knowledge they have acquired and also clarify their own feelings about aging.
    B. Use open-ended statements. For example:
      1. My attitude toward old people is . . . . . .
      2. Difficulties in old age include . . . . . .
      3. A good way to react to someone who is confused is . . . . . .
      4. I am/am not afraid when I think of getting old because . . . . . .
      5. When I am old, I will . . . . . .
    C. Anecdotal records with teacher observations—Direct teacher observation of pupil behavior in problem solving is a valuable way to determine to what extent students are using certain skills to solve problems.

CLASSROOM RESULTS

Some teachers felt more time was needed for the module:

1. "I see upper-grade elementary kids possibly branching out into the heritage older people have given us. My children have visited the Eaton County Court House and saw older people spinning, weaving, quilting, lacing, churning butter, etc. They were fascinated and I feel they gained a new respect for the old, especially since I couldn't do any of those things."
2. "More time is needed for interviewing people and for hands-on demonstrations in class."

Favorable comments about the teaching procedures were expressed:

1. "I like activities that get the children out into the real world to experience things first-hand instead of sitting and being told."
2. "Seeing how much the children in the movie *Foxfire* learned by interviewing and visiting with older people in their community, I have come to appreciate these strategies as truly rewarding experiences."

Teachers offered several suggestions for modifying the module to meet the needs of their students:

1. "I used less textbook material and I suggest the use of more field trips."
2. "Have the students do more role playing."
3. "Have children learn how to spin, weave, knit, make soap, quilt, etc."
4. "Utilize small groups for discussing feelings and ideas."

Suggestions for future users included the use of field work:

1. "Make sure the students get out of the classroom and talk to older people. This lends itself to both the child learning more about the older person and gaining respect for the person's style of living."
2. "By experiencing the older person and his or her skills, customs, and traditions in a hands-on manner, the child is able to gain so much more than even a movie could provide."

STUDENT BIBLIOGRAPHY

Byars, Betsy, *After the Goatman*, New York: Viking, 1974.

Cleaver, Vera and Bill Cleaver, *The Whys and Wherefores of Little Belle Lee*, Philadelphia: Atheneum, 1974.

Donovan, John, *I'll Get There. It Better Be Worth The Trip*, New York: Harper & Row, 1969.

Goffstein, M. B., *Fish for Supper*, New York: Dial, 1976.

Laskey, Kathryn, *I Have Four Names for My Grandfather*, Boston: Little, Brown, 1976.

Le Shan, Eda, *What Makes Me Feel This Way*, New York: Macmillan, 1972.

Talbot, Toby, *Away Is So Far*, New York: Scholastic, 1974.

Tobia, Toby, *Jane Wishing*, New York: Viking, 1977.

Winthrop, Elizabeth, *Walking Away*, New York: Harper & Row, 1973.

TEACHER BIBLIOGRAPHY

Ansello, Edward F., "How Older People Are Stereotyped," *Interracial Books for Children Bulletin*, Vol. 7, No. 6 (1976), pp. 4–10.

Ansello, Edward F., "Old Age As a Concept," *Interracial Books for Children Bulletin*, Vol. 7, no. 8 (1976), pp. 6–8.

Bennett, Ruth, "Attitudes of the Young Toward the Old, A Review of Research," *Personnel and Guidance* (November 1976), pp. 136–139.

Joyce, William, (ed.), "Children's Images of Older People: Implications for Social Studies, *Social Education*, Vol. 41 (Oct. 1977), pp. 517–533.

National Clearinghouse on Aging, Administration on Aging, Department of Health, Education, and Welfare, Washington D.C. 20201.

Wood, Joyce, *Grandmother Lucy Goes on a Picnic*, New York: Collins, 1976.

FILMS

"Nell and Fred" (29 min., B/W) produced by McGraw-Hill Films, New York.
A true story of two old people faced with the decision of whether to move into senior citizens' housing or to live alone.

"The Rights of Age" (28 min., B/W) produced by International Film Bureau, 332 S. Michigan Ave., Chicago, Ill. 60604.

An examination of the kinds of social science experiences needed by the elderly, focusing on the case of a lonely widow.

"When Parents Grow Old" (95 min., color) available "Searching for Values," Series Learning Corp. of America, Film Rental Library, 50-30 Northern Blvd., Long Island City, N.Y. 11101.

This is an edited version of the movie "I Never Sang for My Father"; explores one's responsibility to aging parents.

▶ Interface with
PERSONAL
EFFICACY,
FAMILY

Intercultural Relations ▶

UPPER

Exploring Human Needs

This teaching module is designed for pupils in upper-elementary grades. Typically at this level students will study other cultures. While this module uses Balinese as the content vehicle or focus, any culture could be substituted. The primary objective of the module is to help students develop an awareness for the likenesses and differences that exist within a given culture and between cultures. The module provides opportunities for students to become personally involved with the topic by asking students to look at their own cultures in an attempt to determine whether or not what they observe and read about Balinese could exist where they live. The module relies heavily on inquiry and suggestions are made for hypothesizing, gathering data, and using a data retrieval chart for recording and analyzing the data. Specific social studies texts that focus on cultures as well as supplemental materials will be needed for this module. Keep in mind that the format of the module could be used with the study of any culture. By the end of the module students will have opportunities to use the information they have gathered to assist them in realizing likenesses and differences between and within cultures and begin sensitizing themselves to existing cultural diversity.

    I.   Grade Level: Upper Elementary

   II.   Special Materials:
       A.   Artifacts and pictures from the culture of your choice
       B.   Film of the selected culture
       C.   Blackboard
       D.   Resource books concerning the selected culture
       E.   Map depicting the place where the people live
       F.   Globe

  III.   Time: 2 weeks

  IV.   Concepts:

    A.   *Cultures* have both *similar* and *dissimilar characteristics.*

    B.   People of all cultures satisfy common *basic needs.*

    C.   People of various cultures satisfy certain common *basic needs* differently due to their level of *technology.*

    D.   People of various cultures satisfy certain common *needs* differently due to *geographic phenomena.*

    E.   *Needs* are often satisfied differently within the same culture.

V.   Objectives:

    A.   The student will be able to write a hypothesis from observations, test it through research and draw some conclusions regarding its validity.

    B.   The student will be able to list two reasons why basic needs are satisfied differently.

    C.   The student will be able to list three ways that the culture being studied is like his or her own and three ways the two cultures differ.

VI.   Entry Behavior Indicators:

    A.   The student will have previous experience in hypothesis testing.

    B.   The student will have previous experience in doing research in the library.

    C.   The student will have previous experience in group discussions.

VII.   Teaching Procedures: (*For illustrative purposes we will use the island of Bali; you can substitute the culture of your choice.*)

    A.   Show a film of Bali without the sound. It can be any film as long as it reflects their culture. The objective is for every student to carefully observe the pictures. Following the movie, students' observations will be listed on the blackboard with some discussion with the students as to whether their observations of these people could be observed where they live.

    B.   Locate the island of Bali in the Indonesian archipelago in relation to where the students in your class live. How far apart are these two places? How do their climates differ? Why? Ask the students if they can make a generalization at this point about how the people live.

    C.   Have students cut out pictures of things they consider similar to what they saw in the film and that would be similar in their own cultures. Have them make a bulletin board to depict their findings. (For example, a student might find a picture of a roulette wheel and relate it to the gambling done in connection with the cock fights.)

    D.   Return to the lists of observations made from the film and discuss how these could be grouped into categories. Have students label the categories. Identify those that the students feel to be the most basic needs of people. (Refer to the Taba strategy described in Chapter 3.)

    E.   Return to the categories. From these have the students generate hypotheses that can be tested. For example, some students might deduce that from the film the Balinese seem to be very religious.

Children throughout the world speak many languages. What nonverbal gestures do they have in common?

Even though there might be lots of religious activity in the film, it could be that this is unique to a specific village.

(The teacher can encourage slow learners to pose questions that they have as a result of observing the film.)

(Gifted students can be encouraged to do research concerning religions in general. Compare to those found in America.)

F.   As a total class, use one hypothesis as an example. Help students find a variety of sources that can be used to determine whether the hypothesis should be retained or rejected. Provide ample time for students to gather information. Try to have multimedia sources available so all students will meet some level of success.

(The teacher will need to work with slow learners as a small group using questions instead of the hypothesis and audiovisual materials with high interest/low readability.)

(Gifted students can generate a parallel hypothesis concerning their culture. Allow them time to gather data to support or reject it.)

G.   Allow students to work in groups once it has been determined which group will be responsible for which hypothesis or question. Encourage each group to use a variety of resources. At the end of each small group session have each group give a "mini" report. For example, one day each group might indicate to the class "the most unique thing they learned about the Balinese culture." Another day each might report on "the thing they learned about the Balinese that seems to be similar to their culture."

(If the slow learners are all working with the total class, make sure each has an opportunity to work with a gifted child. An option is to have all the slow learners work with the teacher on a specific hypothesis. Again, provide lots of media sources and high interest/low readability materials.)

(Gifted students can read in depth about the Balinese culture. Make sure ample library books are available.)

H. Have the students in each group make a data retrieval chart to include the key findings and citations or have them make a research booklet. The booklet should contain a minimum of two written pages stating the hypothesis, on what observations it was chosen, further evidence from observations, quotes from books, interviews, etc. and a conclusion as to why you do or do not feel the hypothesis should be retained. Allow a couple of weeks for the final product. Make sure that you have "mini" reports each day that there is group work.

I. Sprinkle large group instruction throughout this module. The teacher might utilize the time for discussion, for a resource person, to show another film, or for teaching map and globe skills.

J. Return to a discussion concerning common activities and how they vary from culture to culture and very often from one area of the country to another. Have the students find pictures to illustrate this. Introduce the term technology and illustrate how it affects the way people satisfy their basic needs.

(Have slow learners make two collages—one that represents high technology and one that represents low technology.)

(Have gifted students prepare, plan, and present a puppet show illustrating how technology affects the way people satisfy basic needs.)

K. Have the students use the text and supplemental sources and magazines to learn more about technology. Then have them construct a bulletin board comparing low level technology and high level technology. (They need not limit their work to Bali.)

L. Introduce the students to various forms of geographic phenomena. Allow the students time to identify the phenomena that exists in Bali. Provide them with examples from other parts of the world where similar conditions exist. Then provide examples where dissimilar conditions exist. After ample time for research and discussion help students formulate the idea that geographical phenomena does affect the way people satisfy their basic needs. Have students test it out using our culture.

(Present a "skills lesson" for slow learners, using lots of visual materials to illustrate common geographic features and identify the proper geographic terms. Discuss each.)

    (Gifted students can be encouraged to do in-depth research on one or more forms of geographic phenomena.)

M.   Return to small group work and elicit from each group examples they have found from research that illustrate the fact that people even within the same culture eat differently, live in different kinds of houses, and wear different kinds of clothes. List the responses. Encourage students to find pictures to illustrate these key ideas. Focus questions for the discussion might include: In what kind of culture (one with high level technology or low level technology) would you expect the people to satisfy their basic needs similarly? Why? Have you ever visited a place where the people satisfied their basic needs in similar ways? Encourage students to bring in/share examples they have observed as they have travelled to various parts of the world.

N.   Provide opportunities for students to share their data retrieval charts, research booklets, and any audiovisual materials they have acquired. (Conduct personal interviews for slow learners in an attempt to assess their performance and progress or lack of progress.)

    (Gifted students might plan and make a presentation to another group of students in another classroom.)

O.   Have the class list major understandings they have acquired concerning Balinese people and key understandings that seem to apply to other cultures which in turn is good preparation for the study of the next culture.

VIII.   Evaluation:

A.   Data retrieval charts and the research booklets can be collected, analyzed, and displayed. Student work has the potential to make evaluation and diagnosis practical and meaningful.

B.   Group evaluation checklist: This checklist could be designed for each child or for the total class.[2]

Behavior to be observed

                                                    Student Names

1.   Is sensitive to the needs of peers
2.   Is sensitive to the problems of peers
3.   Helps other students solve problems
4.   Willingly shares materials
5.   Willingly shares ideas
6.   Accepts suggestions
7.   Sticks to group decisions
8.   Is positive about group work

	Bill	Craig	Carlos	Iris

[2]See Ellis, Art and Janet Alleman-Brooks, "How to Evaluate Problem-Solving-Oriented Social Studies," *The Social Studies*, Washington, D.C.: Heldref Publications, Vol. 68, No. 3 (May/June 1977), p. 102.

    C. "I Learned" statements: The strength of "I Learned" statements is that they represent pupil-initiated responses and do not ask the learners to give the "right" answers.

    D. Essay test: Compare the Balinese culture with yours. Give three likenesses and three differences. Include at least one example to illustrate each likeness and difference.

CLASSROOM RESULTS

Teachers felt this module could be used with any level concerned with any culture. One teacher used Bali, one used Japan, another used Russia, and one used the Netsilik Eskimos. Obviously each teacher spent considerable time prior to the module gathering appropriate library sources and audiovisual aids. Teachers felt that in order to do justice to this module more than two weeks were needed:

1. "I spent an entire week focusing on the concept 'People of all cultures satisfy common basic needs.'"
2. "It took much more time using the inquiry method."
3. "Using resource people is a must but much more time is needed."

STUDENT BIBLIOGRAPHY

Covarrubias, Miguel, *Island of Bali*, New York: Knopf, 1936.

Hoefer, Hans, *Guide to Bali*, Singapore: Times Printers, 1970.

Holt, Claire, *Art in Indonesia*, New York: Cornell University Press, 1967.

Kinney, Jean and Cle Kinney, *Varieties of Ethnic Art and How To Make Each One*, Philadelphia: Atheneum, 1976.

McPhee, Colin, *A House in Bali*, New York: Asia Press, 1945.

Mead, Margaret, *People and Places*, New York: World Publishing, 1959.

Mershon, Katherine Edson, *Seven Plus Seven*, New York: Vantage Press, 1971.

Smith, Datus C., *The Land and the People of Indonesia*, Philadelphia: Lippincott, 1968.

Sprague, Sean, *Bali, Island of Light*, Tokyo: Kodansha International, 1976.

TEACHER BIBLIOGRAPHY

Banks, James A. (Ed.), *Teaching Ethnic Studies*, forty-second yearbook, Washington, D.C.: National Council for Social Studies, 1973.

Banks, James A., *Teaching Strategies for Ethnic Studies*, Boston: Allyn and Bacon, 1975.

Cortes, Carlos E., with Fay Metcalf and Sherry Hawke, *Understanding You and Them: Tips for Teaching about Ethnicity*, Boulder, Colo.: Social Science Education Consortium, 1976.

Ethnic Studies Teacher Resource Kit, Boulder, Colo.: Social Science Education Consortium, 1976.

Our Legal System ▶

Why We Need Rules

This teaching module is designed for children in lower-elementary grades. Typically at this level pupils will study the home, school, or neighborhood. This module with a focus on rules or laws could be used to supplement any one of those topics. The primary objective is to help children become aware that their actions are governed by commonly accepted rules and laws and that these are made to protect their health and safety as well as help them work and play more harmoniously. This module provides opportunities for children to become personally involved with the topic by asking them to help examine the rules that govern their family, school, and neighborhood. Suggestions are made for a variety of activities, such as inviting a panel of parents to discuss family rules and a walking tour of the neighborhood to observe unwritten and written rules and laws. Existing social studies texts dealing with family, school, and neighborhood can provide excellent resource materials. By the end of the module students should have a better grasp of the impact of rules and laws on their lives.

    I.   Grade Level: Lower Elementary

   II.   Special Materials:
- A. Bulletin board illustrating rules and laws in the child's world
- B. Puppets
- C. Letter to parents explaining the module—your objectives and some of the teaching procedures and evaluation techniques that will be used. Include specific suggestions for parents in the event they want to work with the child at home.
- D. Role-playing cards—situations that describe family rules used and abused
- E. Camera (optional)
- F. Art materials

  III. Time: 3 weeks

  IV. Concepts:
- A. *Rules* govern the *behavior* of people.
- B. Rules are *unwritten laws.*
- C. *Rules* help us in our work and in our play.
- D. *Rules* are designed to *promote* an *individual's health, safety* and *consideration* of others.
- E. Grown-ups as well as children follow *rules.*

   V. Objectives:

    A. The child will become aware that his or her actions are governed by commonly accepted rules and these are made to protect health and safety. This will be measured through observation.

    B. The child will learn that rules help us work and play together more harmoniously. This will be demonstrated through role playing, discussion, and the writing of experiences stories.

    C. The child will learn that people serve each other and resolve problems by having rules. This will be demonstrated through discussion and the drawing of pictures.

    D. The child will understand that those in authority will make and enforce rules. This will be demonstrated in role playing and class discussion.

VI. Entry Behavior Indicators:
    A. The child will be able to participate in a discussion.
    B. The child will show courtesy toward his or her classmates.
    C. The child will possess skills in observing.
    D. The child will possess skills in sequencing.

VII. Teaching Procedures:
    A. Introduce the module by showing pictures depicting rules within the home. Discuss each picture in terms of the rules illustrated. Who makes rules at home? What happens when someone doesn't follow the rules? Why are rules important?

    B. Have the children develop a group list of possible family rules. Discuss the reasons for the rules.

    C. Invite a panel of the children's parents to discuss family rules. Discuss the similarities and differences of family rules. Why are there some similarities? Why are there differences between and among families concerning family rules?

    D. Using role-playing cards, have children role play situations in which family rules are used and/or abused. Discuss each enactment. Example—role-playing card: In Judy's home, no one is to take food into the living room.. While the remainder of the family is outside, Judy goes into the room to watch TV. She's very thirsty so she decides to get a Coke. She spills it all over the sofa. What should Judy do?

    E. Discuss the fact that adults as well as children follow rules. Allow children to spend time observing adults and the kinds of rules they follow. As a class make a list of the results.

    F. Invite one or more adults to talk to the class about the kinds of rules they follow at work. Encourage the use of audio visual materials.

    G. Plan a walking tour of the neighborhood observing unwritten and written rules that are followed. Discuss who needs to follow them and why. The teacher should record the observations during the tour. If possible, take pictures of each of the observations. Upon returning to the classroom, discuss the results.

Most school regulations include behavior in the classroom. Will these children need any reminders?

(The teacher will need to spend time with the slow learners helping them learn what is meant by an unwritten rule or law. For example, no paper throwing might be an unwritten rule in the classroom. List with the children several examples before you take the field trip.)

(Gifted children may wish to interview a law enforcer to find out more about rules/laws.)

H. Upon returning from the field trip discuss the children's observations. Either in groups or individually, write experience stories about the rules they observed in operation. Have the children illustrate their stories. Share their stories. If possible, laminate the papers and bind the book for the school library.

I. Discuss the school safety patrol and the rules that need to be followed. If possible, bring in one or more students who are a part of the safety patrol to discuss and illustrate the rules through role playing, puppetry, or other media. These students make great resource people.

(The teacher might need to assist slow learners in formulating a list of questions that they would like to ask the safety patrol.)

(Gifted children might like to develop a booklet about safety patrol.)

J. Have children pictorially illustrate the safety patrol rules. Discuss why these rules are necessary and what happens when the rules are broken.

K. After the children have gathered information about these rules, they might wish to educate others. We saw a delightful film—made with much guidance by the teacher—by first graders for teaching preschoolers and kindergartners about the traffic rules they are expected to follow.

L. Have the children investigate the rules to be followed at school; for example, no running in the hall and no throwing snowballs. Have them survey others in an attempt to develop a complete list of these rules.

(The teacher might want to take the slow learners to another class or interview the principal to find out what some of the rules are.)

(Gifted children might want to investigate who makes school rules, and what happens when rules are broken.)

M. After children have gathered information about school rules, have them devise a way to inform others (for example, a new student at school) about these rules. Some group may decide to make a cassette tape, another might decide to make posters, and still another might decide to plan and present a puppet show to other classes.

N. As a culminating activity, have the children assess and possibly revise the rules in their classroom. Are there any rules they feel are unfair? Why? Why not? Who made the rules? Are more or less rules needed? Is there any rule they would like to have changed? If so, which one and why? In some cases, it might be acceptable to allow children to go through this open-ended inquiry process and attempt to get a rule in the classroom changed. Assess the results. Were their efforts effective? Why or why not?

O. "Pull the module together" by having the class list the things they learned about rules. Then have the children write letters to their parents informing them about their module on rules and what they learned.

VIII. Evaluation:

A. During the module, periodically use the flow of discussion chart to determine the number of children who have participated and also to assess the flow of conversation. The outcomes will also help you determine whether or not the class discussions were dominated by one person or if they were group sharing experiences.

C = Contributes
R R = Repeats what another said
Q = Asks question

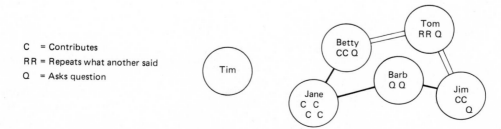

    B.   Have children draw pictures of the most important thing they learned. Share with the class. Compile. Assess the class learning.

    C.   Keep individual anecdotal records during the module in an attempt to assess the child's performance and progress or lack of progress.

CLASSROOM RESULTS

Teachers felt the materials were appropriate. Some suggested that more films and filmstrips be included, that traffic signals be used in role play or dramatic play, and that discussion pictures be added to enhance the module.

    Evaluation procedures were found to be useful:

1. "I have not used the flow of discussion chart very often before and I found it useful for me to check on my group."
2. "I was glad to see several different ways of evaluating children."
3. "I felt the evaluation techniques were more appropriate than questions having right and wrong answers."

Several teachers modified the module to meet the needs of their classes and community:

1. "I involved parents as resource people. We used questionnaires to find out how parents use rules and laws in their work and in their daily lives."
2. "I wrote a letter to parents suggesting they discuss their family rules with their children."
3. "I did not do the part on safety patrols, since we do not have them in our building. However, our children are all bused to school, so we discussed 'bus rules' instead."
4. "We dealt with bicycle rules, as many of my students are beginning to ride their bicycles on the roads."
5. "I made a tape of all the children talking at once. I played it back to them so they could hear what we sounded like. Then I discussed with them the importance of taking turns to speak and of waiting until the person who is speaking before them stops."

Teachers seemed to feel that student involvement was the strongest aspect of the module:

1. "Students were actively involved in discussions about rules, observing rules in their environment, evaluating these rules, working through the objectives, and reaching conclusions that led them to the concepts."
2. "Some of the poorer students presented excellent puppet shows and did a super job in role playing."

Suggestions for future users of the module included branching out and integrating the material with other content areas:

1. "I suggest you include swimming rules, bicycle rules, and rules about fire prevention."
2. "I used this module with my language arts class. It worked exceptionally well."

STUDENT BIBLIOGRAPHY

Bauer, William Waldo, *Going On Ten*, New York: W. R. Scott, 1962.

Coombs, Ira Charles, *Bicycling*, New York: Morrow, 1972.

Gray, Genevieve, *Keep an Eye on Kevin*, New York: Lothrop, 1973.

Hage, M. K., Jr., *How School Helps Us*, Chicago: Benefic, 1962.

Kessler, Leonard P., *Who Tossed That Bat?* New York: Lothrop, 1973.

Leaf, Munro, *Safety Can Be Fun*, Philadelphia: Lippincott, 1961.

Platt, Sylvia, *The Bed Book*, New York: Harper & Row, 1976.

Shapp, Martha and Charles Shapp, *Let's Find Out About Safety*, New York: F. Watts, 1964.

Sullivan, George, *Better Bicycling for Boys and Girls*, New York: Dodd, Mead, 1974.

Sylvester, Robert, *Manners Don't Come Naturally*, St. Louis, Mo.: Concordia, 1964.

TEACHER BIBLIOGRAPHY

Buggey, Jo Anne, "Citizenship and Community Involvement," *Social Education*, March, 1976, Vol. 4, No. 3, pp. 160–163.

Davison, Susan E. (Ed.), *Reflections on Law Related Education*, American Bar Association, Special Committee for Citizenship, 1973.

Davison, Susan E. (Ed.), *Bibliography of Law Related Materials: Annotated* (2d ed.), American Bar Association, Special Committee for Citizenship, 1976.

Davison, Susan E., "Curriculum Materials and Resources for Law-Related Education," *Social Education* March 1977, Vol. 41, No. 3, pp. 184–193.

Gerlach, Ronald A. and Lynn W. Lamprecht, *Teaching about the Law*, 1975.

Law in A Free Society, 606 Wilshire Blvd. Suite 600, Santa Monica, Calif. 90401.

►Interface with
FAMILY,
LEISURE

Media ►

UPPER

Children's TV Viewing Habits

This teaching module is designed for students in middle- or upper-elementary grades. Typically at these levels students study communities, cities, states, and nations. Inherent in one or more of these areas you typically find a topic called communication. At these levels you also frequently find a current events program. In either circumstance, a module on media could be "sandwiched in" to add a dimension that probably has more impact on the lives of children than any other source. The primary objective is to help students look at their viewing habits and to help them begin to realize the influence that television wields. The module provides opportunities for students to become personally involved with the topic by asking that they record what television programs they watch and why. This provides students with an assessment of their personal viewing habits. Other activities in the module include brainstorming, keeping a diary for a week of how students spend their time, analyzing specific television programs, and conducting experiments to determine the impact of the visual dimension in communication. Social studies textbooks that include materials on communication, current events publications, and literary sources can all serve as excellent supplementary material. By the end of the module, students will have opportunities to use the knowledge and ideas they have acquired to help them make more intelligent decisions concerning viewing habits.

I.   Grade Level: Upper Elementary

II.   Special Materials:
A.   Letters to parents describing the television module, the key objectives, and specific suggestions in the event they want to work with their children in the area of television.
B.   TV Survey:

TV SURVEY

1.   What types of television programs do you watch?
     ✔ Check each of the following that you watch
     ◯ Circle your favorite
     X   Mark an X by your least favorite

     _____ news
     _____ doctor
     _____ mystery or police
     _____ space shows
     _____ game shows
     _____ comedy
     _____ educational
     _____ other: Specify: _____

2.   About how many hours of TV do you watch on week days? _____
3.   About how many hours of TV do you watch on the weekends? _____
4.   Have you seen anything on television this week that you would like to read about? _____
5.   Does your family watch television together? _____
6.   Are there any shows your family does not allow you to watch? If so, specify: _____ _____
7.   Have you seen any programs recently that tie in to what we are studying at school? If so, specify: _____
8.   How often do you check a book out of the library? _____
9.   How would you summarize your television viewing habits? _____

C.   "Accounting for Myself"[3]

ACCOUNTING FOR MYSELF

	Sun.	Mon.	Tues.	Wed.	Thurs.	Fri.	Sat.
7–8 AM							
8–9 AM							
9–10 AM							
10–11 AM							
11–12 AM							
12–1 PM							
1–2 PM							
2–3 PM							
3–4 PM							
4–5 PM							
5–6 PM							
6–7 PM							
7–8 PM							
8–9 PM							
9–10 PM							
10–11 PM							

KEY: Read;   Watch TV;   Played Outside;   Ate;
Played Inside;   Baby Sat;   Z Zz Slept;   _____ Other

D.   Art Supplies/Magazines

III.   Time: 2–3 weeks

IV.   Concepts:
  A.   *Television* is a great medium for *communicating* with the masses.
  B.   Television is used in a variety of ways to *influence* its viewers.
  C.   There are numerous types of television *programs*.
  D.   There are basically five ways to *evaluate television content*. These
       include: (a) values expressed by programs and commercials; (b) prob-
       lems posed within the storylines themselves; (c) observed solutions

[3]Adapted from *Family's Guide to Children's Television.*

to problems; (d) alternative solutions; (e) distinctions between reality and fantasy.

V.   Objectives:

    A.   The student will be able to write an essay describing his/her TV viewing habits, give three examples, and state how the content of this module has affected those habits. If his or her habits have not been affected, state why not.

    B.   The student will be able to describe in written or visual form the most significant thing he or she learned from the television module.

VI.   Entry Behavior Indicators:

    A.   The student will have previous experience in television viewing.

    B.   The student will have experience in value clarifying exercises.

    C.   The student will have experience in using a survey to gather information.

VII. Teaching Procedures:

    A.   Begin by reading the book *Little House on the Prairie* by Laura Ingalls Wilder or *The Homecoming* by Earl Hamner. Discuss. Ask students if they see any tie-in to television. ("Little House on the Prairie" is based on the Wilder books and "The Waltons" is based on *The Homecoming* by Hamner.) Discuss the fact that books become television programs.

    B.   Conduct a student survey in an attempt to find out what children watch and why. Graph and discuss the results. It might be interesting to inform parents of the outcome. Discuss the amount of time spent in front of the television set.

         (The teacher might want to work with slow learners as a small group in the event they have trouble reading the questions.)

         (Suggest that gifted students survey older/younger students in addition to themselves. Compare the results.)

    C.   Conduct a brainstorming session in an attempt to find out other types of activities children engage in before/after school. Have students keep a diary, "Accounting for Myself" (see II–C) for one week. Analyze individual and group results.

    D.   Have the students list the values that they hold or they frequently see displayed. Pictures could be used to stimulate further discussion.

         (Make sure there are adequate visuals available for slow learners.)

         (Gifted students might want to do a quick survey of books in the library to add more variety to the list.)

    E.   Select a specific television program at school or at home. It might be possible to suggest this as a family activity. What values are espoused? What values are emphasized more than others through the behavior of characters within the plot? Discuss the results. (If this assignment is to be done at home make sure all students have access to a television set.)

F. Based on the initial survey, select another TV program for all students to view. This assignment might be best accomplished if done twice—first at school to demonstrate and then at home. The purpose is to evaluate the content of the program. Explain and discuss each of the criteria with the students. Then proceed with viewing, with discussion/analysis. The five criteria to be included are: (a) values espoused by programs; (b) problems posed within the storylines themselves; (c) observed solutions to problems; (d) alternative solutions; (e) distinctions between reality and fantasy.
(The teacher will need to provide lots of repetition in directions and examples for slow learners. It would also be best to have these students look for only one or two of the criteria.)
(Gifted students might compare between or among programs or they may begin looking for differences between books/television.)

G. Based on the results, invite a person who in real life (by nature of the position) compares to an individual on television. For example in real life the person might be a lawyer. How is the profession depicted on television? Elicit his or her reactions. (Make sure that the resource person has viewed the specified television program.)
(The teacher will need to assist the slow learners in preparing focus questions or else allow children of varying developmental levels to work together in formulating questions.)

H. Discuss with students the effects of taping television programs in terms of unreal circumstances or situations. To further illustrate this point, have each student write down a complete description of a recent day in his/her life. Then ask the students to draw a line through the parts they'd like to leave out and circle the parts they'd like to redo. Share the outcomes. Compare taped versus live shows.

I. Plan a visit to a nearby television studio and observe a show being taped. Compare to live show. (Make sure students have a part in preparing for this field trip.)
(Have students of differing developmental groups prepare questions they want to seek answers to while on the field trip.)

J. Discuss with students how eyes are used in the communication process. Then help them discover the visual dimension of television. Have students agree on a specific television program for home viewing. Involve the parents if possible. Identify two experimental groups and one control group. One group will watch the program with no sound; the other group will put on blindfolds and only listen to the sound track; the control group will watch and listen to the program normally. After the program encourage the students to describe in writing their description of the characters, the description of the story, the setting or scenes, the main event, and the ending. (Simplify the experiment for the slow learner in terms of the amount or kind of data to be gathered. Have each student draw a picture of one result.)

(If possible, have the gifted child play a different group role for each consecutive night. Compare the results.)

K. On the following day have each group pull its data together. Then have each group report its findings. How do the meanings and impressions differ between or among the groups? Why?

L. If students are still excited about the visual aspects, have them carry out a similar test for commercials.

M. After students have analyzed commercials according to sound, no sound, no picture, they will probably realize commercials are cleverly visual. Then design a simple experiment to test commercials presented on color television sets versus those presented on black and white sets. Do commercials depend on color? Why or why not? Have students provide examples as documented evidence.
(Have slow learners dramatize the results.)
(Have gifted students redo commercials that need color into no-color commercials. Dramatize the results.)

N. Conduct a discussion in which students attempt to pull together what they have learned about television viewing—most importantly, about their own viewing habits.

O. If possible, survey parents concerning their children's viewing habits. Invite parents to visit the classroom as resource people to discuss their opinions.

P. If parents and/or students feel a need to modify their habits or if they would like to see other possible uses of leisure time, a module on leisure would be very appropriate. Mini courses used to stimulate interest in other languages, crafts, hobbies, art, etc. could be pursued. Parents and other members of the community can be great resources.

VIII. Evaluation:

A. Have each student write an essay describing his or her viewing habits, giving three examples of how the content of this module has affected those habits. If his or her habits have not been affected, why not?

B. Problem-Solving Checklist (see page 379)[4]

C. Interviews: Conduct at least one interview with each child during the module to gather diagnostic and summative data.

CLASSROOM RESULTS

The entry behavior indicators, concepts, and teaching procedures drew little comment. Teachers indicated they were adequate. Some teachers had to modify the module to meet the needs of their students and/or comply with school rules:

[4]Adapted from Ellis, Art, and Janet Alleman-Brooks, "How to Evaluate Problem-Solving-Oriented Social Studies," *The Social Studies*, Washington, D.C.: Heldref Publications, Vol. 68, No. 3, (May/June 1977) p. 101.

Student's Name	Asks Questions	Makes Observations	Gathers Data	Records Data	Analyzes Data	Summarizes Data	Applies Ideas	Uses Many Sources

1. "Due to the fact that my students are in-patients at Pine Rest and some are on restricted programs, it was not possible for everyone to watch the same TV shows at once. Thus, kids watched different shows for their assignment, and we put more emphasis on comparing and contrasting the values, visual effects, etc."

2. "Our school does not allow students to watch television in school so I used the television viewing strategies as out-of school-activities or assignments. We discussed the results the following day."

3. "We do not have television sets at school, but I was able to bring my own."

4. "Due to our organizational scheme, the programs I wanted my students to view were not available, so I secured a willing high-school student to videotape them. That worked out fine!"

According to one teacher, the values component was the strongest aspect of the module:

1. "Since television is such a strong influence in kids' lives, it is crucial that they have the ability to critically evaluate what they are watching. They've got to be able to separate what's good from the trash!"

2. "Another strong aspect of the module is its unlimited potential to teach because of its appeal to human beings, especially children. As this module plants the seed to teach through media, the teaching will hopefully motivate children to be more introspective in assessing values. If the child doesn't change, maybe he or she will at least notice that there is an alternative."

Several teachers provided suggestions for future users:

1. "Plan well enough ahead so that you can make sure of getting into a television station at the appropriate time."
2. "Teachers should view as many television programs as possible before teaching the module."
3. "As a teacher, try to relate to shows the kids are crazy about, for example, *The Incredible Hulk*. Try to get back in touch with your feelings, wishes, and fantasies from your childhood."
4. "Kids look at TV as entertainment and are not used to looking at it with a critical eye. Be patient if they don't immediately show insight into the concepts."

STUDENT BIBLIOGRAPHY

Berger, Melvin, *Consumer Protection Labs*, New York: John Day, 1975.

Haeberle, Bill, *Radio and Television*, Minneapolis: Dillon Press, 1970.

Mason, Mont, *Crazy Commercial*, New York: Scholastic Book Service, 1975.

Maynard, Richard (Ed.), *Messages and Meanings: Media, Persuasion, Advertising, and Propaganda*, New York: Scholastic Book Service, 1975.

Pompian, Richard D., *Advertising*, New York: F. Watts, 1970.

Rayner, Ray, *The Story of Television*, Northbrook, Ill.: Hubbard Press, 1972.

Rosen, Winifred, *Ralph Proves the Pudding: The Proof of the Pudding Is in the Eating*, Garden City, N.Y.: Doubleday, 1972.

TEACHER BIBLIOGRAPHY

Cohen, Dorothy, "Television and the Perception of Reality," *National Elementary School Principal*, LVI (January/February 1977), pp. 22–29.

Johnson, Nicholas, *How To Talk Back to Your Television Set*, Boston: Little, Brown, 1967.

Koenipknecht, Bonita, "TV Trivia Analogies," *Learning* (December 1977), p. 22.

Mukerji, Rose, "TV's Impact on Children: A Checkerboard Scene," *Phi Delta Kappan* LVII, No. 5 (January 1975), p. 39.

Paine, Carolyn, "Unreal World of TV," *Learning*—Activity Poster (October 1977), p. 74.

Sarson, Evelyn, *Action for Children's Television*, New York: Avon, 1977.

Sarson, Evelyn, "Action for Children's Television/American Academy of Pediatrics, The Family Guide to Children's Television," *What To Watch, What To Miss, What To Change, How To Do It?* New York: Pantheon, 1974.

Williams, Sally and Judith Yardborough, "Children and TV," Office of Education (DHEW) (November 1972), (ERIC ED 070 287).

Morality ▶

Using Moral Dilemmas

This teaching is designed for students in upper-elementary grades. Typically at this level pupils study the nation as well as other nations throughout the world. At this level current events is also frequently a part of the social studies curriculum. This module could be used prior to exploring world dilemmas or it could be used as a part of the current events program. It focuses on moral issues. The primary objective is to help students realize that dilemmas are derived from history, literature, or problems of modern society. The module provides opportunities for students to become personally involved with the topic by asking them to examine a dilemma that involves a common problem at this level—namely shoplifting. The primary strategy used throughout the module is the moral discussion. No specific text is needed for this module; however, current social issues within your community or issues from the current events program could prove valuable as you develop other dilemmas. By the end of the module the students should have a better grasp of the diversity of opinions that persist within a given issue and hopefully, through moral discussions, the students' minds will be stretched as they are exposed to alternatives and consequences in their continuing quest for justice.

I. Grade Level: Upper Elementary

II. Special Materials:
   A. Props for role plays
   B. Bulletin board/materials for depicting "Dilemmas Found in Modern Society, Literature, and History."
   C. "Sharon's Dilemma"

SHARON'S DILEMMA[5]

Sharon and Jill were best friends. One day they went shopping together. Jill tried on a sweater and then to Sharon's surprise, walked out of the store wearing the sweater under her coat. A moment later, the store's security officer stopped Sharon and demanded that she tell him the name of the girl who walked out. He told the storeowner that he had seen the two girls together, and that the one who

[5]Alessi, Frank, "Sharon's Dilemma" abstracted from Barry Beyer's "Conducting Moral Discussions in the classroom," *Social Education*, Vol. 40, No. 8 (April 1976), pp. 194–202. This dilemma is based on a story by Dr. Frank Alessi of the Cortland (N.Y.) Public Schools. Reprinted by permission of the National Council for the Social Studies and Barry K. Beyer.

left had been shoplifting. The storeowner told Sharon that she could really get in trouble if she didn't give her friend's name.

III.   Time: 3 weeks

IV.   Concepts:
   A.   A *moral discussion* consists of a purposeful conversation about *moral issues.*
   B.   *Dilemmas* are derived from *history, literature,* or *problems of modern society.*
   C.   *Justice,* according to various stages:
       1.   Stage 1—Justice is getting rewarded for something I do.
       2.   Stage 2—Justice means that you will do something for me later if I help you now.
       3.   Stage 3—Justice means doing what all the people in the group approve of.
       4.   Stage 4—Justice comes about when everyone follows the rules on which we have agreed.
       5.   Stage 5—Justice means that people get their basic rights for which government was originally founded.[6]

V.   Objectives:
   A.   After completing the module the student will show indication of the following behaviors as measured through observation:
       1.   Improved listening skills
       2.   Improved self-esteem
       3.   Improved attitudes toward school
       4.   Added knowledge of key concepts
       5.   Growth toward stage change
   B.   As a result of this module, the student will be able to list/describe three dilemmas from real life, one from history, and one from literature.

VI.   Entry Behavior Indicators:
   A.   The student should have previous experience in both large and small group work.
   B.   The student should have familiarity with literary, historical, and real-life sources for information.

VII.   Teaching Procedures:*
   A.   Stage a dilemma using props and role playing. For purposes of

---

[6]Beyer, Barry, "Conducting Moral Dilemmas in the Classroom," *Social Education,* Vol. 40, No. 8 (April 1976), pp. 194–202. Reprinted by permission of the National Council for the Social Studies and Barry K. Beyer.

*Most of the activities should involve all students regardless of level of intellectual development in an attempt to expose all to several stages of moral development and to stretch the thinking of those at each level.

illustration we will use "Sharon's Dilemma."[7] The teacher can use his or her own creativity to establish the situation!

B. Begin by posing the question, "Are there any terms or phrases that need to be clarified?"

C. Ask students to clarify the existing facts in the situation. Then ask students to explain the nature of the dilemma that Sharon faces at this moment.

D. Have each student write his recommendation and reason for it on a sheet of paper. Then have students respond in some way such as raising hands to determine whether or not they think Sharon should give Jill's name to the security officer. If this fails to provoke a discussion and division of viewpoints, the teacher will need to introduce alternatives; for example the teacher could say that, "Suppose on a previous occasion Jill had told Sharon that two weeks ago she had taken a purse in another store because she couldn't get anyone to ring up the sale. What should Sharon do in that case?" (There are numerous other alternatives the teacher could create and introduce. Obvious preplanning is necessary.)

E. According to Beyer, when the class divides with no less than one quarter of the students on each side of the issue, the teacher can organize small group discussions in which students can share their reasons. Have students record these reasons on a piece of paper as preparation for the large group discussion.

F. Conduct a large group discussion. Two key points to remember: The teacher should be promoting student-to-student interaction and the teacher must insure that the discussion does deal with the moral issue.

Probe questions suggested by Beyer in dealing with Sharon's dilemma include the following:[8]

1. What is a "best friend"?

2. Does Sharon have an obligation to Jill? the storeowner? the law? herself? Why or why not?

3. Which set of obligations, to Jill, to the storeowner, or to the law, are most important? Why?

4. From the point of view of Jill (of the storeowner, of Sharon's parents), *should* Sharon tell? Why or why not?

5. Is it ever right to tell on a friend? Why or why not?

(The teacher might want to conduct an additional small group discussion for slow learners to insure that their views are recognized.)

(The teacher could encourage gifted students to acquire views of police officers, parents, etc.)

G. Complete the discussion by having the students who felt Sharon should tell summarize all the reasons given by those who said Sharon

[7]Beyer, pp. 194–202.
[8]Beyer, pp. 194–202.

should not tell. Have those who said she should not tell summarize the reasons given by those who held opposing views. Then give students time to reflect. Finally, have them choose once more what they think Sharon should do and respond on a piece of paper. The papers *are not to be collected and no grade* is to be assigned.

H.   Following are other examples of dilemmas that you as the teacher may choose to present.[9]

TO BE OR NOT TO BE AN INFORMER

The Davis Elementary School is having a serious problem with property damage. Since the opening of school in early September, it has been broken into on two occasions. Desks and chairs have been upturned, plants destroyed, windows broken, and walls defaced. This past week, playground equipment has been badly damaged. So serious are these crimes that the school officials are thinking of closing the school playground, the only space available for neighborhood children to play in after school hours. Fred is a student in the sixth grade. He is not one of the gang that has been doing the damage, but one of his best friends is. Fred doesn't want the school playground closed after school hours. At the same time he doesn't want to tell on his friend. In fact, he is scared to do it because the gang might mug him sometime to get even.

Should Fred tell on his friend so that the gang can be caught or should Fred remain quiet and protect himself?

TRICK OR TREAT—GIVE OR KEEP

Jan very much wanted to buy a tape recording of Bob Dylan's latest outstanding hit songs, but her mother said that she would have to pay for it with her own money. She had only $1.75 and needed $4.25 more. Halloween was not far off. Jan hit upon an idea of how to get the additional money. She asked her younger sister and brother if they wanted her to take them trick-or-treating. Of course they did. So, on Halloween night, Jan went out with her young charges. She took a UNICEF box with her. Neighbors and strangers willingly contributed dimes, nickels, and even quarters to such a cause. When she got home she found that she had collected $5.90, more than enough to buy the record. She knew the money collected for UNICEF went to make life better for children living in poor countries, but she really wanted that recording. Nobody knew how much she had collected. She could buy the tape recording and still have $1.65 to give to UNICEF.

Should Jan use the UNICEF money to buy the recording she wanted so much?

A BLACK FAMILY IN A WHITE SUBURB

Don's father is a black aerospace engineer. He works in a suburban plant, but lives in south central Los Angeles. By occupation and education he is a middle-class

[9]Kohn, Clyde, *Dilemmas for the Classroom*, unpublished material, 1976, used by permission of the author.

American, and could easily afford to live in an affluent suburb. He is active in civic affairs in central Los Angeles, and is an influential citizen in his community. Don doesn't mind going to school although the classrooms are crowded and the quality of instruction leaves much to be desired. Crime rates are high; insurance coverage is expensive; and food in local supermarkets is both of low quality and high cost. Don's father works with a white engineer who has a home in the suburbs, but who is being transferred to another city by the company. He, Jack, knows that Don's father would like to move to a suburban home. Should he sell his home directly to Don's father, or put it on the market through a real estate firm? Don's father could save money by buying directly from Jack, and if it is sold by a real estate firm he might not have an opportunity to buy it.

Should Jack sell his home in an all white suburb to Don's father? Why? There is another question: Should Don's father consider buying outside of the all black south central Los Angeles area?

The dilemmas may be presented in many ways, for example, in the form of a filmstrip, role play or simulation, film, orally, or through short readings.

I. You as the teacher, or even students, can write dilemmas to use in class discussions. If students develop them, you will need to spend time instructing them on how to write them. The following are key points to remember:
1. Build the dilemma so that a relevant moral or ethical predicament is presented.
2. Use real-life problems whenever possible so that individuals can identify with the setting and situation of the dilemma.
3. The story should be simple, interesting, and short.
4. The story should culminate in a decision.
5. Be sure that the situation you have selected is a genuine dilemma and not a story with a moral.
6. Ask questions about the choice, the reasons for the choice, and alternatives to the choice.
(The teacher needs to work with slow learners in an attempt to write one dilemma that has been a part or could be a part of their lives.)
(Allow gifted students to pick an incident from literature or history, write it, present it, and interview outside sources to compare responses.)

J. Have students explore history, literature, and the problems of modern society to find dilemmas. Discuss the ideas that they acquire. Have students make a bulletin board to depict their findings. (Make sure plenty of time is allowed for this activity!)
(The teacher will want to work with slow learners to explore one dilemma from modern society.)
(Allow gifted students to do research and explore one or more dilemmas in real depth.)

K. Make plans to incorporate the use of the moral dilemma in the classroom throughout the year, integrating it with social studies or one of the other content areas in an attempt to facilitate stage change among the students.

VIII. Evaluation:
    A. Probably the most effective evaluation for this module is observation. A checklist to record student performance can be used. An example is as follows:

Student	Improving Listening Skills	Improving Attitude toward School	Added Knowledge of Key Concepts	Facilitating Stage Change
Bob				
Pat				
Kay				
Steve				
Tom				
Bob				
Mike				

    B. Assess the descriptions of the dilemmas from real life, history, and literature that the student wrote about. Each teacher will need to establish key criteria (according to the students) prior to their describing the dilemmas. Graph individual stage changes.

CLASSROOM RESULTS

Teachers felt this module would take anywhere from two to five weeks, depending on the age level and sophistication of the children.

The favorite activity seemed to be staging a dilemma:

1. "My students really got into staging a dilemma. They brought numerous props from home."
2. "My students prefer learning by doing rather than learning exclusively through books."
3. "I didn't realize my students were so dramatic until we used this module."

Additional activities in some instances were provided to accommodate individual differences:

1. "The students in my class followed the news by reading newspapers or watching TV. We discussed some of the moral issues they found in their reading."
2. "Our class surveyed other classes and parents to see how they felt about specific moral issues."
3. "All sixth graders in our school take a nine-week course entitled 'Guidance'. The instructor is the elementary guidance counselor, who covers a unit concerning morals and values. We incorporated the module in her course and team-taught many of the sessions."

Suggestions for future users of the module were made:

1. "The teacher might try several small group discussions before tackling the group as a whole."
2. "It might be helpful to the entire group to ask other people from the community (for example, ministers, police, judges, lawyers, doctors) to come and voice their opinions about specific issues."
3. "Previous work in role playing would be beneficial to students' performance in this module."

STUDENT BIBLIOGRAPHY

Berger, Terry, *I Have Feelings,* New York: Behavioral Publications, 1971.
Cullum, Albert, *The Geranium on the Window Sill Just Died but Teacher Went Right On,* The Netherlands: Harlan Quist, 1973.
Fassler, Joan, *One Little Girl,* New York: Behavioral Publications, 1969.
Stone, Elberta H., *I'm Glad I'm Me,* New York: Putnam, 1971.

Special Note: If you were studying moral education through US history, you might select Martin Luther King as an example. The following sources would be helpful:
deKay, James T., *Meet Martin Luther King, Jr.,* New York: Random House, 1969.
Miller, William Robert, *Martin Luther King, Jr.: His Life, Martyrdom and Meaning for the World,* New York: Weybright and Talley, 1968.
Rowe, Jeanne A., *An Album of Martin Luther King, Jr.,* New York: Watts, 1970.

The following sources would be helpful if you were studying moral education through Native Americans:
Brown, Dee, *Bury My Heart at Wounded Knee,* New York: Holt, Rinehart and Winston, 1971.
Cooke, Alistair, *America,* New York: Knopf, 1973.

TEACHER BIBLIOGRAPHY

Beyer, Barry K., "Conducting Moral Discussions in the Classroom," *Social Education* (April 1976), pp. 194–202.
Blatt, Moshe, Ann Colby, and Betsy Speicher-Dubin, *Hypothetical Dilemmas for Use in Classroom Moral Discussion,* Cambridge: Harvard University Moral Education Research Foundation, 1974.

Fenton, Edwin, Ann Colby, and Betsy Speicher-Dubin, "Developing Moral Dilemmas for Social Studies Classes," Cambridge: Harvard University Moral Education Research Foundation, 1974.

Galbraith, Ronald E., and Thomas M. Jones, "Teaching Strategies for Moral Dilemmas," *Social Education*, Vol. 39 (January 1975), pp. 16–22.

Kohlberg, Lawrence, "Moralization: The Cognitive–Developmental Approach," in *Man, Morality, and Society*, Thomas Lickona (Ed.), New York: Holt, Rinehart, and Winston.

Moral Education and the Social Studies, Toronto, Ontario: The Ontario Institute for Studies in Education.

Stanford, Gene and Albert E. Roark, *Human Interaction in Education*, Boston: Allyn and Bacon, 1974.

SUMMARY

The preceding ten modules serve to illustrate how organizing themes can be used to organize instruction. Some teachers have used these themes to update their existing materials while others have used these as their social studies curriculum. Many teachers have used these modules as ideas or springboards and from them designed specific modules to meet the needs of their pupils. The learner verification reports serve to provide the potential user with pertinent information from teachers who have tried the modules. We invite you to select at least one module that appeals to you and to use it as you see fit.

INDEX